Christ and Theology

Christ and Theology

Toward Typological Realism,
a Synthetic Approach to Biblical Theology

SCOTT STINE

WIPF & STOCK · Eugene, Oregon

CHRIST AND THEOLOGY
Toward Typological Realism, a Synthetic Approach to Biblical Theology

Copyright © 2025 Scott Stine. All rights reserved. Except for brief quotations in critical publications or reviews, no part of this book may be reproduced in any manner without prior written permission from the publisher. Write: Permissions, Wipf and Stock Publishers, 199 W. 8th Ave., Suite 3, Eugene, OR 97401.

Wipf & Stock
An Imprint of Wipf and Stock Publishers
199 W. 8th Ave., Suite 3
Eugene, OR 97401

www.wipfandstock.com

PAPERBACK ISBN: 979-8-3852-3454-7
HARDCOVER ISBN: 979-8-3852-3455-4
EBOOK ISBN: 979-8-3852-3456-1

VERSION NUMBER 01/30/25

Unless otherwise indicated, all Scripture quotations are from the ESV® Bible (The Holy Bible, English Standard Version®), © 2001 by Crossway, a publishing ministry of Good News Publishers. Used by permission. All rights reserved. The ESV text may not be quoted in any publication made available to the public by a Creative Commons license. The ESV may not be translated in whole or in part into any other language.

To Kate and the kids:
May we all hear the Shepherd's Voice

Contents

Illustrations | ix
Preface | xi
Acknowledgments | xiii
Abbreviations | xv
Introduction | xvii

1. What Is the History of Biblical Theology? | 1
2. What Is Christ-Centered Biblical Theology Trying to Do? Goals and Context | 42
3. Seeking Out the Great Tradition: The *Sola*'s Context | 87
4. Biblical Theology and the Great Tradition: Toward Typological Realism | 127
5. Typological Realism as Approach | 167
6. Typological Realism Applied, Part 1: Historical and Theological Exegesis | 221
7. Typological Realism Applied, Part 2: Christophanies and the Spirit-Driven Life | 254

Conclusion | 287
Appendix: On the Practical Side of Typological Realism and Its Relationship to the Quadriga | 293
Bibliography | 299

Illustrations

Figure 1: Biblical Chiasm

Figure 2: Vos's Revelatory Triangle

Figure 3: Antitypical Adjustment to Vos's Triangle

Preface

What is written in the Law? How do you read it?

—Jesus, Luke 10:26

THE RESEARCH AND WRITING process for a doctoral dissertation is a strange one. The student sets out with an original research question. Once that question begins to be settled, the answers seem to take the researcher into logically prior fields as well as adjacent fields. Soon the research question changes because the research process has revealed that the student was actually asking a different question than what they originally thought.

In my case, I set out to research the relationship between the Christ-centered biblical theology of the late nineteenth to the early twenty-first centuries (Geerhardus Vos, Edmund Clowney, Charles Scobie, Graeme Goldsworthy, Greg Beale, and others) and the Protestant Reformation's formal principle, *sola scriptura*. My master's thesis centered around Christ-centered biblical theology and its relevance as an alternative hermeneutic to the covenant theology of my seminary brothers and the dispensationalism of many other Christian brothers and sisters. Goldsworthy's anchoring of Christ-centered biblical theology in Reformational hermeneutics piqued my interest as I considered pursuing postgraduate study. Off I went.

PREFACE

As I studied Reformational hermeneutics, I learned of the dependence of the Reformers on patristic and early-medieval hermeneutics. I realized, then, that tracing the relationship between Christ-centered biblical theology and the *sola* would not go far enough unless I properly define (and thus understand) the developments that led to the *sola*. Pretty soon I was inundated with patristic and medieval theology and bibliology. The question had seemed to morph more into something like, "What is the relationship between Christ-centered biblical theology and Augustine's hermeneutic?" Thus the first few chapters seek to answer that question, while the latter half of the project seeks to build on the answer, offering as a theological and biblical contribution a full hermeneutical method.

But as I am now a few months removed from defending and submitting my project, reflection shows me that the real question I was trying to answer is exactly what Jesus asked the testy lawyer in Luke 10: "What is written in the Law? How do you read it?" I've been obsessed with Jesus since my early twenties and have been pursuing how the Old Testament is the written form of his eternal Word-ness for the entirety of my adult life. At all points I've believed that the Scriptures are supposed to be read as a Christ-centered unity, but I've been unsure and unconfident about how this is the case. Thus my research was not only about continuing education but about settling my own faith.

It would be difficult to overstate just how profound of an impact my reading over this process has had on my personal faith. I plan to write at a later date on the most profound of all research episodes: my actualization of the Joseph/Judah/Jesus connection in Gen 37–50. That section of Genesis came alive in a way I never imagined. The church I pastor was, doubtless, annoyed with me by the end of the series I was then preaching through Genesis.

These chapters are my attempt at following the multitude that has gone before me in offering an answer to the question, "How should we read the Law?" I think that the law is to be read as Christ's voice witnessing to himself before his coming so that those later readers (including us) who are in pursuit of truth can have confidence that in their reading, they hear him speak. It is in this way that we the sheep "hear his voice" (John 10:27) and that what was written in former days was written for our encouragement (Rom 15:4). I hope that my work helps you hear the Shepherd.

Scott Stine
October 2024

Acknowledgments

COMPLETING THIS PROJECT WOULD not be possible without several people whom God has graciously given me for help, encouragement, and community. First, I must thank the First Baptist, Newton, New Jersey, church family. Without your support I could not have written this. Special thanks are due to Connie for her proofreading expertise. I'd love to list more of you by name, but here I cannot; my heart is wide open to you (2 Cor 6:11). Most importantly your names are written in a different Book.

I also want to thank my parents. The list of reasons would itself be dissertation-length, but most recently, thanks for letting Kate, the kids, and me come for a mini-sabbatical in July 2023 when I was at my wit's end with life, ministry, and writing.

I want to thank Rick Shenk who mentored me through the thick and thin of PhD work with supernatural patience and grace. I had significant personal challenges to work through over those years, and Dr. Shenk was the mentor and friend I needed.

Thanks also to Drs. John Harvey, David Croteau, and TK Dunn for their encouragements and suggestions both pre- and post-defense.

I also want to thank Dan Wicher, missionary in partnership with First Baptist (where he first became a Christian) for many decades. During a furlough visit in winter 2019, Dan responded to my disillusion with the DMin program I was in by encouraging me to pursue a PhD, saying my mind was more suited to it. I barely knew Dan and his beloved Sue at the time, but this encouragement proved prophetic.

I also want to thank Matt Keller, my best friend of over twenty years. There is not a paragraph on the following pages that does not have the imprint of our countless text messages, phone calls, emails, or podcast discussions. I still think you're smarter than me (actually now more so.)

Finally, I want to thank my wife, Kate. She is a living parable of the Trinity that only my eyes see: She loved me before I loved her, and has continued to love and serve me despite my continued unwitting (and sometimes witting) tests. My gracious state with the Lord is paralleled and typified by the gracious state I have with Kate. This project would not have happened unless she encouraged me, waited on me, and gave me the flexibility to spend countless hours reading, writing, editing, thinking, etc. I dedicate this book to her.

As the reader can see, my life has an embarrassment of riches. *Soli Deo Gloria.*

Abbreviations

BIER	*Biblical Interpretation in the Era of the Reformation* (Richard A. Muller, John L. Thompson)
CCBT	*Christ-Centered Biblical Theology* (Graeme Goldsworthy)
GCH	*Gospel-Centered Hermeneutics* (Graeme Goldsworthy)
GKGC	*God's Kingdom Through God's Covenant* (Peter J. Gentry, Stephen J. Wellum)
HS	*Holy Scripture* (John Webster)
HP	*Heavenly Participation* (Hans Boersma)
Inst.	*Institutes of the Christian Religion* (John Calvin)
ISGT	*Interpreting Scripture with the Great Tradition* (Craig A. Carter)
KTC	*Kingdom Through Covenant* (Peter J. Gentry, Stephen J. Wellum)
RHBI	*Redemptive History and Biblical Interpretation* (Geerhardus Vos)
RR	*Reformation as Renewal* (Matthew Barrett)
SG	*Seeing God* (Hans Boersma)
ST	*Summa Theologica* (Thomas Aquinas)

Introduction

THIS BOOK INTENDS TO examine the relationship of evangelical Christ-centered biblical theology of the late nineteenth to early twenty-first century with the hermeneutical foundations and assumptions of the so-called Great Tradition.[1] Historical study always runs the danger of revisionism slanted towards the historian's presuppositions.[2] Nevertheless it seems reasonably certain that the Protestant Reformation's formal principle (*sola scriptura*) is roughly equivalent with the scriptural

---

1. Chapter 1 will advance definitions, first, of *biblical theology* as a discipline that seeks to understand the Bible's organic unity, with particular emphasis on the way that both testaments relate to each other; and secondly, of *Christ-centered biblical theology* as a biblical-theological subgenre which reads the Bible with a Christian presupposition—that is, with faith—seeking the Bible's unity in the person and work of Jesus Christ.

As will be shown below, biblical theology precedes systematic theology in this way: If the latter logically organizes biblical doctrines in a systematic way, the former studies the way in which those doctrines are revealed across the biblical storyline. Biblical theology has to do with theology's biblical context; as such, it precedes systematic theology. Biblical theology assumes a discernible unity across the biblical narrative, not based so much on the individual perspectives of the biblical writers but on the wisdom of God who reveals his truth through them.

Finally, biblical theology, hermeneutically preceding systematic theology, precedes practical theology, which is the effect of the former two. It could be said that if biblical theology deals broadly with what the Bible is, systematic theology deals particularly with what the Bible teaches, and practical theology deals with what the Bible requires of those who read it.

2. As noted by Carl Trueman in *Histories and Fallacies*.

xvii

primacy of the Nicene hermeneutics of the patristic and early-medieval eras, referred to in recent historical theology as the Great Tradition. As such, Christ-centered biblical theology, built on the foundation of the *sola* as norming norm (that is, the sola as the authoritative standard by which the plausibility of both theology and exegesis are discerned), is both a hermeneutical development from within the Great Tradition and a hermeneutical check to it. The accuracy (or inaccuracy) of this claim is the topic of this project.

Echoing an emerging sentiment, Craig Carter in his *Interpreting Scripture with the Great Tradition* calls the church back to "the genius of pre-modern exegesis."[3] Posited is the conviction that hermeneutics controlled by Nicene orthodoxy is the Great Tradition. This tradition has in all ages held not only to the authority of Scripture but to the belief that Scripture has a discernible unity centered at its foundation on the person and work of Jesus Christ. Jesus taught that the Old Testament finds its ultimate meaning in him (Luke 24:25–27). So, Carter says, following the apostles, theologians within the Tradition have always held that the Bible holds together in Christ.[4] Carter quotes late theologian John Webster as having stated that "unity [to the Bible] is given by the fact that these texts, in all of their incontrovertible diversity of origin and composition and matter are gathered and formed into a unity *by Christ*. All things cohere in him, for he recapitulates all things."[5] Scripture thus reflects the creation as coming from Christ and reflecting him (cf. John 1:1–4). When Christ is Scripture's center, the church through faithful exegesis listens to him, walking the "narrow path" of discipleship (cf. Matt 7:13).

Webster has said elsewhere that Scripture is "the sanctified servant of God, in which the gospel is set before the attentive church."[6] Later a biblical definition of the gospel will be offered, but Webster's point is clear even if a gospel definition remains, for the moment, presupposed: It is through the medium of Scripture that God reveals to the world, and particularly to his church, the gospel of his Son, by which he saves (Rom 1:1, 17). The gospel, at the very least, concerns Jesus, and Scripture is its foundational written context.

Although Carter's work is critical of modern historical criticism— which, he claims, operates according to metaphysical presuppositions

---

3. Carter, *ISGT*.
4. Carter, *ISGT*, 148.
5. Webster, *Domain of the Word*, 18, in Carter, *ISGT*, 154; emphasis added.
6. Webster, *HS*, 70.

that cannot accept the Bible as the word of God—he does acknowledge that there are several strands of hope within modern theology.[7] At the top of his list is the recent interest in whole-Bible biblical theology. He cites the twentieth-century works of Brevard Childs, Charles Scobie, and Geerhardus Vos, as well as recent evangelical works by Greg Beale, James Hamilton, and Tom Schreiner.[8] The latter list of names contains redemptive historical methods employed with evangelical presuppositions in which the interpreter seeks Scripture's whole witness in its unity and diversity, reading each part in light of the whole through a "Christological-soteriological nexus."[9]

Carter cautions, however, that in order to move theology into closer alignment with the Great Tradition, evangelical biblical theologians will need to articulate a proper ontological basis. In other words, for biblical theology to get a strong start, it will need to be more purposeful in establishing Scripture's communicative activity on theological, not just redemptive-historical, grounds. Carter recommends John Webster's definition of Scripture as the "divinely instituted signs in the domain of the Word" through which God "accomplishes his act of self-utterance through human auxiliaries."[10] Beginning Webster's way, says Carter, would anchor biblical theology in the conviction that Scripture is God's way of revealing himself to the world to the end of redemption and fellowship with himself. Without such an articulated biblical ontology, recent redemptive-historical attempts at whole-Bible biblical theology might "present the message of the Bible as a unified, coherent, meaningful, relevant Word from God," but nevertheless fail to address the philosophical, dogmatic, and theoretical issues that make it problematic. If, therefore, biblical theology can use as its basis John Webster's theology of the Bible, biblical theology can be a tool for the church to return to and enjoy its Christ-centered roots and identity.[11]

In response to the aforementioned evangelical tendency to bristle at modern historical criticism, Kevin Vanhoozer has suggested that there is at least the possibility that these approaches, along with even

---

7. Carter, *ISGT*, 122.

8. See Childs, *Biblical Theology*; Scobie, *Ways of Our God*; Vos, *Biblical Theology*. As Carter, *ISGT*, 24, suggests, see Beale, *New Testament Biblical Theology*; Hamilton, *God's Glory in Salvation*; and Schreiner, *King in His Beauty*.

9. Quoting from Ramm, *Protestant Biblical Interpretation*, 166.

10. Webster, *Domain of the Word*, 8–9; quoted in Carter, *ISGT*, 25.

11. Carter, *ISGT*, 26–27.

postmodern, deconstructionist approaches, have something valuable to teach serious theologians.[12] Practitioners of new approaches often claim, for example, that since objectivity and therefore dogmatic conclusions are impossible, claims to such must be "power grabs";[13] thus, they say, it is therefore best to read all conclusions as suspect. Although this notion is self-defeating—being itself a conclusion—Vanhoozer suggests that it might present the theologian with a question worth considering personally: Is my interpretation an attempt at power or a pursuit of truth? Perhaps the interpreter should not be so quick to derive meaning from the biblical text unless he stops to examine himself. Vanhoozer concludes, therefore, that the interpreter should approach Scripture in a way that is both humble and confident, listening to Scripture on its terms while constantly examining himself against the supernatural claims of Scripture.[14]

Biblical Theology and the Demands of Theologians

To bring these strands of thought together, recent evangelical biblical theology appears, as this project will show, to be an attempt at biblical interpretation in light of what both Webster and Vanhoozer suggest: taking the Bible on its own terms and, with a commitment to historic Trinitarian orthodoxy, listening to Christ who leads his church by his word. Conservative whole-Bible biblical theology, in paying heavy attention to the Bible's unity-within-diversity, aims to provide a trustworthy inner-biblical context that will make exegesis, doctrine, and application clear and compelling. If the Bible's source is divine and its thematic unity is the gospel, every text shares a context with every other text. This fact makes listening, understanding, learning, and applying possible to a reasonable level of certitude, even if the reader's presuppositions and beliefs continue to be remolded and reshaped.

The suggested definition of the gospel is as follows: *The promise, confirmation, and fulfillment of God's plan to, through Jesus Christ, establish life-giving fellowship between himself and lost people for a promised eternity in new heavens and new earth that is nothing less than the eternal enjoyment of his presence, which is the beatific vision.*[15] This gospel is

---

12. Vanhoozer, *Is There a Meaning*, 178, 182.
13. See Goldsworthy, *GCH*, 130–38; Wright, *Scripture and the Authority of God*, 5.
14. Vanhoozer, *Is There A Meaning*, 462.
15. It might seem bold for an evangelical project to include the beatific vision in the

INTRODUCTION

indeed the Bible's unifying theme and thematic center. Below we'll consider whether pursuing a "center" or theme to Scripture is a worthwhile endeavor[16] or if it is better to pursue a *telos*, or goal.[17] For now it suffices to say, with Webster, that the Bible does have a unity within its diversity, and that the gospel of God's redemption is at least *a* central theme or belongs near the center. It would seem that this acknowledgment characterizes church history, giving the Great Tradition its formal contents.

Reformation-era hermeneutics were concerned, as it will be seen, with recapturing and advancing the Tradition. Although rightly influential voices have said that a gospel-centric approach to biblical theology is a development on the Reformational *sola*,[18] more likely is that it is consistent with the *sola*, though it might arrive there via modern sensibilities which are themselves influenced by the *sola*. Plainly, the Tradition was gospel-centric, as was the *sola*, and as are the newer evangelical approaches. Goldsworthy has stated that at the heart of the Reformation was the recovery of the historical Christ-event—the gospel—as the basis not only of Christian salvation, but also of the objective importance of the Old Testament.[19] If, therefore, the gospel message, defined by Goldsworthy in terms of the New Testament Christ-event and what it means for the trustworthiness of the promise-making God of the Old Testament, gives the Old Testament its ultimate meaning, then the consistency and propriety of a gospel-centered approach to biblical theology follows. A student of historical hermeneutics can, therefore, reasonably expect to find this gospel-centricity not only from the Reformation to the current day but pre-Reformation as well.

This project does not attempt to propose a gospel-centered biblical theological approach as an innovation. The biblical theology of

---

gospel. Later chapters will explain why doing so is appropriate. For now, mention might be made of John Piper's recent work *What Is Saving Faith?: Reflections on Receiving Christ as a Treasure* (105–7, 275) in which Piper defines saving faith in terms not only of "seeing Christ" (by faith), but of having God as treasure and hoping in future glory. The reader could also see Piper's *God Is the Gospel: Meditations on God's Love as the Gift of Himself* (65–69) in which the gospel is defined in terms of seeing the glory of God in the face of Jesus, who is himself the image of God (cf. 2 Cor 4:4–6); therefore, says Piper, the gospel is seeing God by faith now and by sight later. The gospel would seem, then, to be, by definition, bound to the vision.

16. See Scobie, "Structure of Biblical Theology," 6; Köstenberger, "Present and Future of Biblical Theology," 454–55; Hamilton, *God's Glory*, 38–40.

17. See Sacewater, "New Creation."

18. Goldsworthy, *Preaching the Whole Bible*, 25. See also Childs, *Biblical Theology*, 4.

19. Goldsworthy, *Gospel and Kingdom*, 18–21.

Goldsworthy and others already employs gospel-centeredness. Of note, although Goldsworthy stated in his earlier work that the kingdom of God—defined as "God's people in God's place under God's rule"[20]—is the Bible's unifying theme, careful examination of his whole body of work proves with plainness that he sees the gospel as the Bible's unifying theme. This fact explains the titles of both his first work, *Gospel and Kingdom*, and his more recent grammar, *Gospel-Centered Hermeneutics*.[21] Such a reconsideration of Goldsworthy's contribution is only worth mentioning to support the above suggestion that this project's goal is not to plow any new ground in suggesting a gospel-centric approach to biblical theology. Rather, the attempt here is to build upon ground already prepared, helping conversation partners toward a better clarity and practice of biblical theology.

A Second Question

Asking the earlier question regarding whether Christ-centered biblical theology is consistent with the Great Tradition has, during the course of research, led to another question: Do Carter and others alongside him who have worked for a resurgence of Trinitarian exegesis focus on the immanent Trinity (who God is in himself) to the detriment of the economic Trinity (what God does in time and space)? Carter and others argue compellingly that the church needs to return to a Trinitarian/Nicene exegesis. Some have been critical of Christ-centered biblical theology. Such biblical theologians, who argue compellingly that Christ-centeredness is firmly consistent with both Scripture and the Great Tradition, might respond that the Trinitarian thinkers are so immanent-minded that they are economically blind. This final consideration sets up well the project's structure.

Method

The first two parts, containing chapters 1 to 3, will address the first question: Is Christ-centered biblical theology doing what the Great Tradition does? Chapter 4 will assess the answers to this question. In the final section, three chapters will pursue a way forward for economic-oriented and

20. Goldsworthy, *Gospel and Kingdom*, 54.
21. Goldsworthy, *Gospel and Kingdom*, 54; Goldsworthy, *GCH*.

immanent-oriented exegesis to be mutually helpful and complementary. Since Scripture is a witness both to God's nature and works, both "sides" need each other in order to be consistently biblical and historically Christian. Calvin's famous "Scripture as spectacles" illustration will be engaged and developed as an analogy:[22] To understand Scripture rightly, hermeneutical "spectacles" need to have as their two lenses a theological lens that looks for God and an economic lens that looks for God's works in redemption.[23] Without such a set of lenses, imbalances will occur, and unavoidably so. Chapter 5 will seek, thus, to consider how a hermeneutical framework that employs both theological and Christ-centered orientations can be synthesized. Typology will be a means of synthesis under the name *typological realism*.[24] This term is a sort of appropriation of George Eldon Ladd's *biblical realism*. In contrast to C. H. Dodd's *realized eschatology*, in which the entirety of the Old Testament eschatological hope entered into time and space in Jesus's coming, Ladd famously argued that while the hope was inaugurated in Jesus's first coming, the hope will be consummated in his second coming.[25] Ladd was critical of what he saw as an overly platonic framework which drove a hard separation between what occurs in time and space and what constitutes God's eternity. Ladd does acknowledge, however, that God's revelatory structure has a threefold "tension" between what came first, what came in Christ, and what will come in the end.[26] God's revelatory structure, then, is escalating. It will be obvious as the current project progresses that typological realism holds much in common with Ladd's proposal, especially with its emphasis on revelation connecting hearers with what is real (i.e., *realism*). The current proposal differs, however, in centering

22. See Calvin, *Inst.*, 1.6.1.
23. At the risk of jumping ahead too quickly, let it be said that Augustine believed, based on texts like Isa 65:17–18, 66:22 (cf. 2:2–4); Eph 1:10; and 2 Cor 5:17 that both Testaments teach that creation occurred so that new creation could occur. The plan of creation is simultaneously a plan of salvation, and time is ordered to realize this larger plan. See Oort, "End Is Now"; Wilken, *Spirit of Early Christian Thought*, 136, 155–57.
24. *Typology* is best defined as the study of seemingly purposeful escalating parallels between persons, events, or institutions present in an earlier part of a narrative and those in later parts of the narrative. The *type* (what comes earlier) is usually so understood as a purposeful impression, image, example, or pattern prefiguring something greater later in the narrative (hence "escalating.")
25. See Ladd, *Theology of the New Testament*, 56; Dodd, *Founder of Christianity*, 115. Biblical realism as a title is included in the subtitle of Ladd's *The Presence of the Future: The Eschatology of Biblical Realism*.
26. See Ladd, *Theology of the New Testament*, 623.

typology as the way in which revelation occurs. Finally, chapters 6 and 7 will show typological realism in action: chapter 6 with an explanation of the method in exegesis and chapter 7 with an explanation of the method in theology.

Chapters 1 to 4 are historical and analytical, answering the original research question. Those chapters set up typological realism as the contribution of chapters 5 to 7. Readers who are more interested in typological realism are invited to skim ahead to the second half of chapter 4, which sets up the heart of the book, chapter 5. On the other hand, some readers might be more interested in the historical work since it seeks to compare disciplines that are often kept separate (i.e., Christ-centered biblical theology and Augustinian exegesis.) My hope is that this work can not only pique the interests of readers who have one of these sensibilities but can stir within them a new interest in the other. Let the reader decide!

This project will have been successful if it has attained two objectives: First, it has accurately determined the consistency of Christ-centered biblical theology with the hermeneutics of the Great Tradition; and second, it has convincingly (or at least clearly) provided a clear path for a hermeneutical method that synthesizes a Trinitarian orientation as both complementary to and helped by a Christ-centered redemptive-historical orientation. Christ-centered biblical theology, pursuing modern historiographical priorities alongside premodern Christological ones, is often unintentionally both atheological and impractical/pastoral, thus leaving it with an uneasy relationship with the Great Tradition. Synthesizing Christ-centered biblical theology with theological interpretation under the framing of typological realism, then, gives Christ-centered biblical theology all of the theological, redemptive-historical, and pastoral engagement needed to fit in with and advance the Great Tradition.[27]

The *quadriga*, the predominant hermeneutical method of the medieval era, championed and articulated most famously by Thomas Aquinas,[28] has discernible similarities to what is offered in typological realism. Similarities do not suggest redundancy as much as, at least, recovery, and at most advancement. Typological realism, with its synthesis of redemptive-historical and theological orientations, is a sort of synthesis of post-liberal priorities (because it reads Scripture historically) with

---

27. *Theological interpretation of Scripture*, which will be returned to later, can be defined as an approach to Bible reading that begins on theological, not grammatical-historical, grounds.

28. *ST*, 1.1.10

premodern priorities (because Scripture is God's redeeming and shepherding voice, instantiated from eternity.) Although the *quadriga* rightly handles texts both historically and anagogically (that is, looking forward, like in typology), typological realism orients hermeneutics historically because of theology and future-ward because of the beatific vision where discipleship and theology intersect. It seeks to consider history in light of theology because theology is needed to ascertain the meaning of history. On the other hand, Christology is needed to ascertain theology because Christ makes the Father known (cf. Matt 11:27; John 1:18). This project seeks, therefore, to offer a framework that is both upward- and forward-oriented.

1

What Is the History of Biblical Theology?

"We need to see not only where we are, but also how we came to be there."

—GRAEME GOLDSWORTHY

The Perils of Defining Biblical Theology

WHAT IS BIBLICAL THEOLOGY? This question seems about as hard to answer as Jesus's question to the disgruntled Pharisees of Capernaeum: "Which is easier, to say to the paralytic, 'Your sins are forgiven,' or to say, 'Rise, take up your bed and walk'?" (Mark 2:9).[1] Graeme Goldsworthy agrees, saying that biblical theology simply "means different things to different people."[2] Similarly, Peter Gentry has written that biblical theology, "whether used in academia or in the church, has a bewildering number

---

1. This comparison echoes Tim Keller, *King's Cross*, 34; quoting the Anchor Bible Commentary: "You know, after countless pages written on this, we still have a good question before us. Which *is* easier? It's hard to say." (Emphasis original)

2. Graeme Goldsworthy, interviewed by Nancy Guthrie, *Help Me Teach the Bible*, The Gospel Coalition, November 3, 2016.

of meanings today."[3] Gentry goes on to suggest that biblical theology seems to have a technical definition while also having a built-in range of meaning. Geerhardus Vos, whose works later chapters will consider, combined theological and historical considerations in his definition, writing that biblical theology "attempts to do justice to the unity and historical development of revelation, and to the theoretical and practical character of revelation. . . .Biblical Theology rightly defined is nothing else than the exhibition of the organic process of supernatural revelation in its historic continuity and multiformity."[4] Writing five decades after Vos, John McKenzie said, "Biblical Theology is the only discipline or subdiscipline in the field of theology that lacks generally accepted definitions of principles, methods, and structure. There is not even a generally accepted definition of its purpose and scope." Eckhard Schnabel recently wrote that little has changed between McKenzie's day and the current one.[5] Thus, Andreas Köstenberger has drawn attention to the need "for scholars to be precise in defining what they mean when they claim to engage in biblical-theological work and to carefully distinguish between biblical and systematic theology."[6] In order to trace the relationship of biblical theology to the hermeneutics of the Great Tradition accurately, this chapter attempts to clearly outline the history of the term's usage.[7]

Approaching the History of the Term

Johann Philipp Gabler's 1787 address entitled "Discourse on the Proper Distinction between Biblical and Dogmatic Theology, and the Right Determination of the Aims of Each" is generally accepted as the first use of the phrase "biblical theology." Defining dogmatic theology as the "theology of the church," Gabler posited the need for his colleagues to begin their theology on a "more scriptural foundation." As a representative

---

3. Gentry, "Significance of Covenants in Biblical Theology," 9.

4. Vos, "Doctrine of the Covenant," 79. Elsewhere Vos called biblical theology "that part of exegetical theology that deals with the revelation of God as an act of God, considering both its contents and form" ("Idea of Biblical Theology," in *RHBI*, 12).

5. McKenzie, *Theology of the Old Testament*, 15, quoted in Schnabel, "Biblical Theology," 244.

6. Köstenberger, *Present and Future*, 464.

7. Worth mentioning is James Barr's study of the difficulties in defining biblical theology in *The Concept of Biblical Theology: An Old Testament Perspective* (Minneapolis: Fortress, 1999.)

quote: "There is a truly biblical theology, of historical origin, conveying what the holy writers felt about divine matters."[8] Gabler's assertion appears aimed at calling theologians to remove their theological starting point from the church's traditional dogmas and place it into the unfolding (historic) revelation of Scripture.[9] Gabler's distinction is noteworthy, because most current biblical theology practitioners are not opposed to historic orthodoxy but are interested in approaching the organic, unfolding revelation of Scripture with orthodox presuppositions.

Further, according to Schnabel, although Gabler eventually abandoned the notion of there being a demonstrable unity between the Old and New Testaments, he does not seem to have abandoned the conviction that both testaments have divinely revealed truth that is universally significant. Otto Merk might be accurate, therefore, in attributing to Gabler a sort of "double biblical theology": biblical theology focused on the history of the text alongside biblical theology focused more on dogmatics.[10] Here the reader sees an example of the earlier assertion: Biblical theology has always been difficult to define.

Brevard Childs, the chronicler of the so-called "Biblical Theology Movement" of the early twentieth century, has made a helpful suggestion toward a definition: "The biblical theologian's reflection is directed to the connection between the Old and New Testaments in an effort to give an account of his understanding of the Bible as a whole, inquiring into its inner unity." Childs concludes, therefore, that "biblical theology has as its proper context the canonical scriptures of the Christian Church."[11] Therefore, although Gabler's caution against starting with established dogma might seem worth considering, for a biblical theologian to entirely throw off dogmatic convention is difficult when the whole context of biblical theology is the church's Scriptures. Whichever approach is taken, whether Gabler's or Childs's, the latter suggests something that D. A. Carson has elsewhere confirmed: The pressing issue within biblical theology is the examination of the unity and diversity found in the Old and New Testaments.[12]

---

8. Quoted in Köstenberger, "Present and Future," 445.
9. Bruno et al., *Biblical Theology According to the Apostles*, 1.
10. Schnabel, *Biblical Theology*, 227–28.
11. Childs, *Biblical Theology*, 8.
12. See Köstenberger, "Present and Future," 446.

As a final preliminary consideration, Anthony Thiselton has suggested three ways to logically understand the term biblical theology.[13] One way is to understand it as referring to the theology of the Bible, that is, theology proper within Scripture's pages. A second way is to understand biblical theology in context of the aforementioned Biblical Theology Movement, noting the hermeneutical methodology of those in the movement. Finally, a third way is to understand biblical theology as referring to the act of evaluating the major works of Old and New Testament theology. Neither the second nor third approaches seem to be particularly interested in engaging the text's unity and diversity. The first approach has promise because, as seen in the definitions offered by Gabler, Childs, and Carson, the goal of a significant number of biblical theologians is to understand the overall message of the Bible. It seems that biblical theology has become the pursuit of the Bible's overall message. To say as much might, however, jump ahead too quickly.

So, what about Thiselton's first definition? Is biblical theology simply or at least foundationally concerned with the study of the theology of the Bible? Schnabel engages the argument by suggesting that biblical theology has as its primary interest the very things which the term itself implies: the study of God (theology) found within the pages of the Bible (biblical).[14] Theology proper aims at understanding and examining the nature of God as revealed in theological sources, in particular the Bible.

Schnabel demonstrates that from the Middle Ages forward, theology proper began taking on a more robust definition which includes all teaching and doctrine from the Bible expounded by the church. In this light, biblical theology can be construed, according to Schnabel, in terms of "systemic presentation on the content and themes of the Old Testament and New Testament."[15] Webster, probably in agreement with Schnabel's broad way of approaching the issue, nevertheless suggests a more theological orientation: "Theology has a single but not a simple object: God and all things relative to God."[16]

These considerations are helpful in the way of learning to think about theology. If Webster is correct to define Scripture as the "sanctified servant of God in which the gospel is set before the attentive church," and both he and Schnabel are correct to suggest that theology has as its aim

13. See Thiselton, *Approaching the Study of Theology*, 35.
14. See Schnabel, "Biblical Theology," 225–26.
15. Schnabel, "Biblical Theology," 226.
16. Webster, "Place of Christology," 91.

understanding who God is and how all things relate to God, it follows, then, that biblical theology has as its goal understanding how the gospel is good news in relation to God and how all things relate to God. Since Scripture sets forth Christ as the one to whom redemptive history bears witness (John 5:40) and who comes to reconcile in his body all things (Col 1:27), it follows that biblical theology has as its goal observing, acknowledging, and appreciating how God evangelizes and redeems the world through the person and work of Jesus Christ.

The next chapter will argue that Scripture's contents requires the recognition that the gospel is its center. Goldsworthy has noted that since Christ's resurrection and exaltation meets the goal of the Old Testament, then the gospel (which concerns him, Rom 1:3) must control all exegesis and theologizing. Goldsworthy asks, in conclusion, "How can the gospel *not be* Scripture's center?"[17] As stated above, the next chapter will give more attention to the Bible's gospel-centeredness; what precedes is offered in anticipation of the development of this project's general direction and contribution. Biblical theology, though difficult to define, means something specific to evangelical thinkers who center hermeneutics on the gospel with good—even if not always well thought-out—presuppositions.

Before moving on, how others throughout history and recently have approached the study of biblical theology is worth further consideration.

The History of Biblical Theology, Revisited

There is no shortage of published histories of biblical theology, usually beginning with Gabler. Against the grain, Scobie and Schnabel both locate the advent of biblical theology pre-Gabler, arguing that from the time of the Reformation, biblical theology comprised a systematic approach whereby dogmas were contextualized and supported by biblical texts.[18] Schnabel calls this method the "traditional loci method,"

---

17. See Goldsworthy, *Interpreting God's Plan*, 38, 46; emphasis added. See also Hamilton, *What is Biblical Theology?* for a short treatment of the Old Testament as a gospel-shaped historical narrative. Also helpful is Dempster's *Dominion and Dynasty*, which is a longer treatment of the same topic.

18. Scobie, "Structure of Biblical Theology," 1. It is worth noting that Brevard Childs locates the start of biblical theology *as a principle* to the time of the church fathers. He examines how Irenaeus, Origen, and Augustine deal with the Bible's historic unity (Childs, *Biblical Theology*, 30–40) before examining Aquinas (Childs, *Biblical Theology*, 40–42) and then later, Martin Luther and John Calvin, both of whom held that Christ gives unity to Scripture (Childs, *Biblical Theology*, 43–50). Childs quotes David Lotz as

prevalent in medieval and contemporary systematic theology. According to Schnabel, a 1629 volume by Wolfgang Jacob Christmann entitled *Teutsche biblische Theologie* gave the world its earliest known use of the term "biblical theology."[19] Christmann's text is an example of the so-called "loci method." Schnabel continues, showing that the pietist Philipp Jakob Spener, along with others in the mid-eighteenth century, preferred a more historically oriented approach to the Bible's theology than previous generations' norms. If this is so, Gabler's aforementioned speech seems to have echoed a common sentiment of his day. A quote from W. F. Hufnagel, writing in *Handbuch de Biblische Theologie* (1785–89), both underscores and defines the preference for this historic approach to theology: "Proof-texts must be used to correct the theological system, not the system the proof-texts."[20] These thinkers were not necessarily trying to detach from historic orthodoxy but to examine it in light of Scripture.

Childs has argued that whereas Gabler clearly identified this new historic approach, his method gave way to some serious problems in the next generation of theology. After Gabler and others had argued for a reexamination of historic orthodoxy in light of Scripture, other thinkers followed who did not use any orthodox standard as an interpretive check. This fact led, according to Childs, to "philosophical applications of the text that produced symbolic application of ethical teachings from Scripture."[21] The effect was that the Bible's theology was all but marginalized, being replaced by an emphasis on ethics. In thinking influenced by the Enlightenment, which aimed at critiquing Christianity,[22] was a questioning of the historic relationship between the two Testaments. This question developed a chasm between Old Testament studies and New Testament studies. As theology moved closer to the nineteenth century,

---

saying that Luther was primarily a biblical theologian (Childs, *Biblical Theology*, 43). Finally, Childs posits in no uncertain terms that "for Luther, both in his earliest and later periods, the one centre of Scripture is Jesus Christ" (Childs, *Biblical Theology*, 44).

It is also worth noting that Irenaeus has been called "the first biblical theologian" for how diligent he was in showing the consistency and continuity of the Bible (Scobie, "History of Biblical Theology," 12.) More will be said in chapter 3 about the presence of biblical theology throughout pre-Reformation and Reformational hermeneutics.

19. Schnabel, "Biblical Theology," 226–27.
20. Quoted in Scobie, *The Ways of Our God*, 15.
21. See Childs, *Biblical Theology*, 5.
22. "Enlightenment critique is primarily directed against the religious tradition of Christianity—i.e., the Bible. . . [the Enlightenment] must assert itself against the Bible and dogmatic interpretations of it," said H. G. Gadamer in *Truth and Method*, 272.

one of Gabler's teaching colleagues, G. L. Bauer, released his *Theologie des Alten Testaments* (1796) followed by his *Biblische Theologie des Neuen Testaments* (1800–2).[23] These titles underscore that Old Testament studies were being distinguished from studies of the New. This division continued throughout the nineteenth century.

Examples of the motivation to break Old Testament studies from those of the New are seen in quotations from important nineteenth-century theologians, noted by Scobie. For example, Freiderich Schleiermacher said, "The Old Testament Scriptures do not . . . share the normative dignity or inspiration of the New."[24] Later, Adolph Harnack said, "To reject the Old Testament in the second century was a mistake which the church rightly rejected; to keep it in the sixteenth century was a fate which the Reformation could not yet avoid; but to retain it after the nineteenth century as a canonical document in Protestantism results from paralysis of religion and the church."[25] In other words, the modern mind no longer needs the Old Testament, and everyone knows it.

"History" According to Biblical Theology

The concept of the bifurcation of the Old Testament from the New is related to the notion of *history* in biblical theology. Early biblical theologians focused on reading the Bible as a historic narrative, with the goal of finding the biblical context necessary to effectively evaluate systematic theology. The metaphysics of the Enlightenment with its agnostic impulse, however, might have exerted some influence. The enlightened mind understood history primarily in terms of human progress instead of as a display of God's acts in history.[26] The effect is that these thinkers placed the emphasis on historical developments leading to their day instead of on what God has done in biblical history and what that might mean for their day. If earlier thinkers had said—rightly—that doctrine should be judged by Scripture, then by the nineteenth century their descendants, thinking they were simply going a step further, were actually going sideways, suggesting that history judges Scripture. In this misstep,

23. Schnabel, "Biblical Theology," 228.
24. Schleiermacher, *Christian Faith*, 132, quoted in Scobie, *Ways of Our God*, 19.
25. Schleiermacher, *Christian Faith*, 12, and Harnack, *Marcion*, 79, both quoted in Scobie, *Ways of Our God*, 19.
26. See Carter, *ISGT*, 93–94. This understanding of the effect of the Enlightenment on history will be returned to at several points throughout this project.

revelation is subjected to human opinion. Instead of Scripture in the normative position, prevailing opinion is the norm. If this were not the case, it seems safe to say that this misstep would have been avoided. Such a move was the opposite of the view of Scripture that dominates the Great Tradition, summarized by Calvin: Scripture is to be like spectacles for the aged.[27] Reality presented by Scripture is meant to become the plausibility structure for how the believer views reality. History, as such, cannot judge Scripture; to think so is to be exactly backwards, according to the Great Tradition. In the generations that followed Calvin and the Reformation, this backward-orientation came to dominate.

The Biblical Theology Movement

The so-called "Biblical Theology Movement" arose, therefore, as a response among scholars and theologians to the prevailing historical criticism which had gotten scholars "lost . . . in the minutiae of literary, philological, and historical problems."[28] Dating the rise of the Movement to just after World War I, Childs states that rising theological interests at the time, especially indebted to the work of Emil Brunner and Karl Barth, provided the ground for a rising interest in biblical theology.[29] Both Brunner and Barth, the former in America and the latter in Germany, were instrumental in placing the Bible at the center of systematic theology, as it was in earlier days.[30] As time had drawn on, Childs said, "The Bible had been hopelessly fragmented, and the essential unity of the gospel was distorted and forgotten. Biblical scholarship had deteriorated to an exercise in trivia, in which tragic process the profound theological dimensions were overlooked."[31] The loss was, according to Childs, twofold: first, the church's clear gospel-witness, which is meant to be a unified, consistent message from the Bible; second, theology, which, to echo Webster from earlier, the church receives from God as it listens to Scripture.

Anthony Thiselton identifies the leaders of the Movement as Childs, G. Ernest Wright, and John Bright. Wright defended a biblical view of history where theology examines history as the outworking of God's

---

27. Calvin, *Inst.*, 1.6.1.
28. Childs, *Biblical Theology in Crisis*, 15.
29. Childs, *Biblical Theology in Crisis*, 16.
30. Childs, *Biblical Theology in Crisis*, 17.
31. Childs, *Biblical Theology in Crisis*, 15.

WHAT IS THE HISTORY OF BIBLICAL THEOLOGY?

purposes. His books stressed God's revelation through history, the unity of the two Testaments, and the importance of the Old Testament for Christians.[32] Bright was one of Wright's contemporaries, and, like Wright and Barth, held a high view of the objectivity of God's activity in history, especially within biblical revelation. Finally, Childs was well known for, like Bright, defending the essential unity of the two Testaments and the importance of the Old Testament for Christians.[33] Childs also held that the Bible centers on the person and work of Jesus.[34] The upshot of their approach is that since the unified canon of Scripture provides each text's context, the church has enough foundation to exercise both the calling and ability of both proclaiming the gospel and arriving at trustworthy theological conclusions.[35] Some thinkers within the Movement regrettably had much in common with Enlightenment-influenced views of history and analysis. The shared view, nevertheless, that Scripture provides a unified and coherent message centering on Jesus places these biblical theologians at least near to the Great Tradition, if not in it.

Thiselton adds, importantly, that although the Movement made great strides for theology, it was not immune to criticism. Perhaps the most vocal critic was James Barr. Highlighting the gap created by linguistic difficulties for modern students of Scripture, he took issue with the Movement's thinkers' confidence in the Bible to proclaim, on its own, a clear and unified message to the world in the present.[36] To Barr, language and cultural gaps create a barrier too difficult for most Christians to span.[37] Barr concluded, therefore, that theology is best left to the experts who have the skills for historical investigation and can thus make creative contributions to the continuing theological conversation. This observation summarizes well Barr's approach: "Biblical Theology is done

---

32. Thiselton, *Approaching the Study of Theology*, 37.

33. Thiselton, *Approaching the Study of Theology*, 38.

34. See, for instance, Childs, *Biblical Theology in Crisis*, 103, and *Biblical Theology*, 8.

35. See, for instance, Childs, *Biblical Theology*, 8, and Klink and Lockett, *Understanding Biblical Theology*, 134–35.

36. See Thiselton, *Approaching the Study of Theology*, 39, as well as Barr, *Semantics of Biblical Language*.

37. Similar to Gotthold Lessing (1729–81) who argued convincingly to many of his day that the "ditch" between history and eternity is so great, revelation in history is impossible and therefore cannot be demonstrated. See Frame's description in *History of Western Philosophy and Theology*, 220–23, and McGrath's briefer treatment in *Christian Theology Reader*, 154–55.

by biblical scholars (as opposed to theologians or pastors), seeks something 'new' or innovative (rather than merely stating something handed down from the past—doctrinal theology), is essentially ecumenical, and is firmly set in a historical context."[38]

To identify the differences between Barr and the Movement is to highlight an essential difference in theological approach. Biblical theologians seem to want to listen to what they view as God's objective word for humanity given at particular times (Heb 1:1) which is binding for all time. In contrast, Barr and others of his ilk hold that since the Bible is a work of antiquity, fluency in historical study and scholarship is a requirement for understanding, and a student's conclusions must have as their end theological *progress* in the student's historical context. Put another way, the Movement pursued a reading that would lead to both hearing and doing, while Barr and others seem to have pursued a reading that would lead to the perception of relevance.

Although it might be the case that it had much in common with the Great Tradition, the Movement was probably not entirely consistent in its approach. Childs states that the Movement—again, of which he was a part—sought to pursue a theological system within a framework of Enlightenment assumptions.[39] These enlightened assumptions include a view of history where progress is the goal. One of the Enlightenment's leading thinkers, Immanuel Kant, states well another of the movement's goals: "Enlightenment is man's release from his self-incurred tutelage. Tutelage is man's ability to make use of his understanding without direction from another . . . 'Have courage to use your own reason!' That is the motto of enlightenment."[40]

Enlightenment assumptions, therefore, include not only a progressive view of history, but also a certain level of confidence in the individual's ability to think, reason, and conclude on their own. Parallels between Kant's viewpoint and Barr's method are not difficult to ascertain. The individual uses their own reasoning, objective ability to study history, and creativity to understand and apply the Bible. Perhaps it is fair to say that the enlightened theologian or scholar must study with *control* of the text.

Conversely, in biblical theology, although there might be, as Childs suggested, some level of this Enlightenment-influenced implicit control

---

38. Klink and Locket, *Understanding Biblical Theology*, 54.

39. Childs, *Biblical Theology*, 9.

40. Immanuel Kant, "What is Enlightenment?," 54, quoted in Barrett, *God's Word Alone*, 78.

in study, there at least seems to be an *attempt* to let the Bible speak on its own terms. Childs worked to establish a framework whereby the church could get back to listening to the Bible's own theology. That said, in light of Childs's own critique, this pursuit might have also been a pursuit for *progress* instead of a return to older principles and ideas, a type of twentieth-century *ad fontes*.

The Movement was probably a helpful development for theology, asking good questions and making good strides; but, in and of itself, Thiselton might be correct to conclude that it was incomplete.[41] Finally, because of conflicting ecumenical, historical, and scholarly interests, the Movement (according to those who accept that there was indeed a movement) was finished and fading into the background by 1960.[42]

In a similar fashion to earlier modern generations of biblical theologians, those in the Biblical Theology Movement were guilty of not letting Scripture's view of reality become their spectacles. They were concerned with reading the Bible as a Christ-centered unity, but they were less interested in letting that Christ-centered reality take precedence as the correct depiction of reality—to be their spectacles. Nevertheless, the Movement was an important development in the history of biblical theology as a discipline. If an Enlightenment-influenced approach to exegesis/theology can get close to premodern sensibilities, there is hope for even biblical scholarship to hear Scripture as Christ's voice.

A Lay of the Land: What Approaches Mark Biblical Theology Over the Last 100 Years?

Much more could be written on the historical development of the relationship between biblical studies and theology in the centuries since Gabler. Many historians of biblical theology include various approaches to the Bible's theology in their histories. Scobie, writing in *Tyndale Bulletin* in 1991, divides his history between systematic, historical, and thematic approaches, adopting the latter himself.[43] More recently, Schnabel asserts that biblical theology generally encompasses Old Testament theologies, New Testament theologies, and comprehensive (that is, whole Bible)

---

41. Thiselton, *Approaching the Study of Theology*, 40.

42. Scobie, "History of Biblical Theology," 18.

43. Scobie, "Structure of Biblical Theology," 1991; see also Scobie, *Ways of Our God*, 9–91; and Scobie, "History of Biblical Theology," 11–20.

approaches.⁴⁴ Given the fact that he then proceeds to examine no less than seven approaches in use in recent centuries, it is little wonder that he agrees with McKenzie in concluding that biblical theology is a nebulous discipline with no accepted definitions of its purpose and scope.⁴⁵ Schnabel offers helpful insights at the end of his article, which show that he thinks biblical theology has enough of an identity for a developmental way forward.

There have also been recent efforts at categorizing biblical theology approaches into taxonomies. The remainder of this chapter will consider two of them in pursuit of a clear definition with a brief historical interlude that is offered with the goal of narrowing.

The first taxonomy is that of Edward Klink and Darian Lockett. According to them, biblical theology has no less than five approaches in practice among theologians today. What follows is a summary of their paradigm, including brief definitions of the approaches and prominent practitioners.

Biblical Theology as Historical Discipline (BT1)

This approach engages a historical study of the Bible aimed primarily at identifying what the biblical text meant to the writers and receivers when particular books or sections were originally transmitted. This view is less interested in what the text means for the current day. The theologian's task is to find the original meaning (human authorial intent) and then to pursue creative conclusions for the present day. To identify the original meaning, the reader must, in light of the historical gap between the Scripture's time and the present, utilize historical tools. One example of this method is the aforementioned James Barr.⁴⁶

Biblical Theology as History of Redemption (BT2)

This view is an approach that relies on redemptive history to "discern the normative purposes of God as they unfold through the Scriptures."⁴⁷

---

44. Schnabel, "Biblical Theology," 225–26.
45. Schnabel, "Biblical Theology," 244.
46. See Klink and Lockett, *Understanding Biblical Theology*, 29–56.
47. This helpful summary statement comes from Peter Gentry, "Significance of Covenants in Biblical Theology," 11.

Practitioners of this model hold that there is a progressive unity to God's redemptive acts which come to a climax in the person and work of Jesus Christ. This historical narrative is meant to provide the widest context for every individual passage of Scripture.[48] Perhaps the most notable proponent of this approach is D. A. Carson.

Within BT2, Klink and Lockett identify three distinct "schools." The first is the so-called "Dallas school," so named because it generally relates to Dallas Theological Seminary. The Dallas school seeks to articulate a theology that runs through certain sections or groups of books within Scripture. The most well-known expression of this view is seen in various forms of dispensationalism, which will be considered below. The "Chicago school," so named because it has a scholarly relationship to Trinity Evangelical Divinity School, builds upon the Dallas approach by articulating locative themes and then connecting them beyond the various sections to the whole of Scripture. Finally, the "Philadelphia school" centers around Westminster Theological Seminary and includes contributions from the hermeneutical approach known as "Old Princeton." It builds upon both Dallas and Chicago, by (like Chicago) connecting themes from each section to the whole of Scripture and identifying how they ultimately find their meaning in Christ's redemptive work.[49]

Biblical Theology as Worldview-Story (BT3)

This view begins with the working assumption that the grand story of Scripture is the key to each text's meaning. Practitioners of this view do not necessarily seem to believe that Scripture must be without error because, since the Bible is centered around *story*, historical reliability is less important.[50] BT3 is therefore distinct from BT2 in that adherents of the latter are inerrantists while the adherents of the former might not be. Finally, more of an emphasis on historical investigation (in common with BT1) is present in BT3. Likely the most prominent current proponent of

---

48. Klink and Lockett, *Understanding Biblical Theology*, 74.

49. Klink and Lockett, *Understanding Biblical Theology*, 68–73. How neatly the Dallas school fits within BT2, if the focus there is only on particular sections of Scripture, is debatable.

50. See Wright, *Scripture and the Authority of God*, 20–39. Similarly, see Michael Bird and Peter Enns's chapters in Gundry, *Five Views on Biblical Inerrancy*, 83–116, 145–73.

this approach is N. T. Wright who uses historical considerations of Second Temple Judaism to set the table for the New Testament's context.[51]

Biblical Theology as Canonical Approach (BT4)

Brevard Childs, considered earlier, was a major proponent of this view. Klink and Lockett distinguish BT4 from BT1 by saying that whereas the latter (and even BT3) lets historical investigation influence conclusions read out of the text, the former sees the locus of meaning within the final form of the canon. The final form of the Bible gives each text its meaning because only a canonically ordered biblical theology can hold together both the descriptive (historical) and the prescriptive (theological) nature of Scripture.[52] If BT2 and BT3 find meaning for each text in the "big picture" of Scripture, BT4 finds meaning in the Bible's structure and organization. At the same time, dogmatic considerations (the church's theology passed down through the generations) should be kept in mind during textual study.[53]

BT4 as a distinct school illustrates an issue that is worth mentioning: Several of these approaches have commonalities. BT2 and 3 locate meaning in the overall story with obvious similarities to BT4. Further, no biblical-theological approach outright rejects historical study as unimportant when doing exegesis and theology since the Bible is the ancient book given by God to his people so they can hear and follow him throughout time. That said, the differences outlined here seem to warrant the Klink and Lockett paradigm as long as the reader bears in mind the similarities.

Biblical Theology as Theological Construction (BT5)

This final approach is almost the exact opposite of BT1 in that the reading of Scripture found here is concerned primarily with theology for the practitioners' present-day context. If BT1 is concerned with what the text meant *then*, BT5 is most concerned with what the text means *now* as a word from God to the world. The operating conviction is that the Bible has a theological nature. Similarly, practitioners employ the church's

---

51. Klink and Lockett, *Understanding Biblical Theology*, 93–122.

52. This helpful summary statement comes from Gentry, "Significance of Covenants in Biblical Theology," 12.

53. Klink and Lockett, *Understanding Biblical Theology*, 125–40.

WHAT IS THE HISTORY OF BIBLICAL THEOLOGY?

dogma to help the Bible make sense (similar to BT4). Another phrase for this approach is *theological interpretation of scripture*.[54] One example of this approach is seen in the work of Francis Watson, who argues that instead of sitting in judgment of the Bible, the Bible is dynamic, wherein Christ actively works to minister in the lives of believers and the collective life of the church.[55]

Klink and Lockett's paradigm illustrates the problem mentioned above: It is hard to define biblical theology in a consistent way. If biblical theology, as argued earlier, is concerned primarily with the unity of Scripture's overall form and message, then it is puzzling how BT1 can be considered an approach. BT1 is less interested in the unity of the message than it is in what light historical insight might shed on the pages of Scripture. On the other hand, if the inerrancy of Scripture is a criteria for the Great Tradition, perhaps neither BT3 nor BT4 fit either. BTs 1, 3, and 4 all have historical critical research as foundational in the work of exegesis.[56] That would leave only BT2 and BT5. Practitioners of BT2[57] and 5[58] have stated that critical tools have always been of help to the church in theological practice. The approach that this project will later advocate is somewhat of a synthesis of BT2 with 5. This study will take one more step toward that proposal after making two more examinations: the conservative turn in the history of biblical theology and what biblical theology looks like among conservative theologians today. Understanding Andreas Köstenberger's taxonomy requires consideration of the historical developments among evangelical biblical theologians from the Movement (and adjacent) to some of the emerging viewpoints of recent decades summarized by Klink and Lockett. Such developments represent a sort of "conservative turn, that importantly contributes to the current moment in biblical theology. The next two sections are an attempt at summarizing the conservative turn and beneficiaries of it.

---

54. Klink and Lockett, *Understanding Biblical Theology*, 157–68.

55. See Klink and Lockett, *Understanding Biblical Theology*, 171, and Watson, "Hermeneutics and the Doctrine of Scripture," 137 (Klink and Lockett, *Understanding Biblical Theology*, 171n6). It is probably the case that Carter, Boersma (who will be considered in detail in later chapters), and Webster would be categorized as BT5.

56. But it is worth noting that Graeme Goldsworthy, a BT2 practitioner, has written about the usefulness of historical critical tools in exegesis as long as their limitations are recognized. See Goldsworthy, *GCH*, 190–91.

57. Goldsworthy, *GCH*, 190–91.

58. See for example, Carter, *ISGT*, 126.

Conservative Turn: Fundamentalism, Philadelphia Biblical Theology, and Current Models

In the early twentieth century, a phenomenon with pertinence to biblical theology occurred: the rise of Christian Fundamentalism. Over the course of the prior century, academic theology had slowly adopted modernist ways of thinking influenced by Enlightenment presuppositions. Echoing aforementioned statements, Francis Schaeffer said that Enlightenment thinking "was an intellectual movement which emphasized the sufficiency of human reason and skepticism concerning the validity of the traditional authority of the past." Schaeffer also quotes the *Oxford Dictionary of the Christian Church*, which puts it this way:

> The Enlightenment combines the opposition to all supernatural religion and belief in the all-sufficiency of human reason with an ardent desire to promote the happiness of men in this life. . . . [Enlightenment thinkers'] fundamental belief in the goodness of human nature, which blinded them to the fact of sin, produced an easy optimism and absolute faith of human society once the principles of enlightened reason had been recognized.[59]

Another relevant definition of Enlightenment thinking comes from Matthew Barrett. Referring to Enlightenment-influenced thinkers as "modernists," Barrett states:

> The presupposition of the modernists was that our understanding of Christianity and biblical authority must be reconstructed and reconfigured due to the findings of modern thought and higher criticism. They insisted that we rid Christianity and the Bible of its many cultural and theological trappings that keep us from deciphering *those parts of Scripture that should be retained*.[60]

Around the turn of the twentieth century, many theologians and scholars held that such an Enlightenment-modernist thinking process all but strips Scripture of its authority over the church and the world. To claim that the modern world is so advanced that it can question certain parts

---

59. Schaeffer, *Great Evangelical Disaster*, 33.

60. Barrett, *God's Word Alone*, 110; emphasis added. Also helpful is Brian Daley's point that within historical criticism, the interpretation of historical reality is considered to be objective with no subjection to a scholar's own biases. Since a person's view of history is, thus, subjective, one comes to conclusions through "natural, inner-worldly explanations of why or how things happen." Thus, historical criticism is, by definition, "methodically atheistic." See Daley, "Is Patristic Exegesis Still Usable?," 185–216.

of Scripture while fully accepting other parts is to forsake the notion that Scripture is the word of God, error-free, because God's word is "like silver refined in a furnace . . . purified seven times" (Ps 12:6). Since this way of thinking was spreading in both the academy and the church, many feared that in losing Scripture's trustworthiness, the church loses its witness.[61]

One response to the rising influences of these views was fundamentalism. "Fundamentalism" as a term comes from a twelve-volume paperback series entitled *The Fundamentals*, released in the 1910s, outlining the traditional doctrines of conservative evangelicals, especially articulated by Princeton theologians Charles Hodge and Benjamin Warfield and other prominent theologians like G. Campbell Morgan.[62] The writings defended the Bible's infallibility, the virgin birth, and the deity of Christ and were hostile to a Darwinian evolutionary understanding of biological science. Fundamentalist thinkers could not all be said to think the same way. They had primary agreement, however, at least in the 1910s and following decades, on what could be considered foundational Christian beliefs—the "fundamentals." By the 1920s, "fundamentalist" became a type of general word to describe those who wished to designate themselves as "orthodox, Bible-believing Christians." It was also a term used by to describe anyone who identified as an evangelical, or a gospel-centered Protestant holding to historic orthodoxy in the Protestant tradition.[63]

According to Barrett, fundamentalism then evolved into two types. First was *populist fundamentalism*, with C. I. Scofield and Billy Sunday as figureheads. Due to the enormous influence of Scofield's dispensationalism, a dispensational reading of Scripture took prominence among adherents. Second was *intellectual fundamentalism*, whose most prominent figurehead was Princeton theologian J. Gresham Machen, representing a Calvinistic orientation, affirmative of and attentive to historic orthodoxy.[64] Interestingly, the enormously influential British preacher David Martyn Lloyd-Jones was called by many a "fundamentalist," though he never cared for the term.[65] The reason to mention Lloyd-Jones is that, although he was a preacher and not an academic, he would undoubtedly have more in common with the intellectual camp than with the populist camp.

61. See Ramm, *Protestant Biblical Interpretation*, 63–69.
62. See Thiselton, *Approaching the Study of Theology*, 182.
63. Murray, *Evangelicalism Divided*, 17.
64. Barrett, *God's Word Alone*, 110.
65. See *D. Martyn Lloyd-Jones*, 192.

Regarding the populist camp, the dispensational influence over Baptist theology in America became so widespread that fundamentalism and, by extension, dispensationalism has been labeled as a uniquely American phenomenon.[66] Regardless of a person's view, Scofield's dispensational reading of Scripture has pertinence to whole-Bible biblical theology in that it presented a way of understanding the whole of Scripture—the "big picture"—from Genesis to Revelation. This reading would over time lead to a newer development called progressive dispensationalism which has more in common with other redemptive-historical readings of Scripture than earlier dispensational readings did.

Regarding the intellectual camp, Machen is widely regarded as one of the most prominent theologians of the first half of the twentieth century. His *Christianity and Liberalism* made the famous claim that the modernist tendencies rising in influence within the church at the time of writing were more than a shifting attitude—they represented a religious viewpoint that is entirely antithetical to Christianity in the first place. In other words, as Machen famously put it, liberalism is its own religion.[67]

Due to the rise of widespread embrace of modernistic assumptions, Machen the fundamentalist was fired from Princeton in 1936. In a detail hardly imaginable today, Machen's defrocking was front-page news.[68] Nevertheless, Machen's release from Princeton was far from the end of his career in terms of theological contribution. He would go on to be the founder of Westminster Theological Seminary near Philadelphia. Westminster has been thought to have taken the Reformed mantel from Princeton.[69] When Machen left Princeton to found Westminster, several prominent scholars, such as Cornelius Van Til and John Murray, came with him.

---

66. See Marsden, "Fundamentalism as an American Phenomenon," 215–32. Also noteworthy is Nathan Hatch's *Democratization of American Christianity*, in which he shows that a tendency toward preoccupation both with the book of Revelation and America's prominence in the end times has been a feature of American evangelical theology since Revolutionary times.

67. Machen, *Christianity and Liberalism*, 67.

68. See Schaeffer, *Great Evangelical Disaster*, 34–35.

69. Machen said, "[Though] Princeton Seminary is dead, the noble tradition of Princeton is alive. Westminster will endeavor by God's grace to continue that tradition unimpaired." Quoted in Muether, "Remembering Old Princeton," 16. Muether says that Westminster was considered "the new Old Princeton."

One notable name for the history of biblical theology that did not follow the others was Van Til's earlier mentor Geerhardus Vos.[70] Vos, Princeton's first professor of biblical theology, was a Reformed theologian in the pre-modernistic Princeton mold. Because he was so close to retirement at Machen's release, Vos stayed at Princeton and retired three years later. A decade and a half later, Vos released his well-received *Biblical Theology: Old and New Testaments*.[71] As mentioned above, Klink and Lockett state three distinct forms of BT2, which, for reminder's sake, is "Biblical Theology as History of Redemption." Klink and Lockett give the name "Philadelphia school" to the form of BT2 which traces themes across all of Scripture and identifies their meaning in relation to the person and work of Christ. The reason Klink and Lockett refer to this school as the Philadelphia school is because the biblical theology which Vos articulated while at Princeton was then given continual expression and practice at Westminster Seminary. Vos began to articulate this viewpoint in his *Biblical Theology*.[72] He was not able to finish his *Biblical Theology* before he died; his New Testament section ends with his examination of the Gospels.

Nevertheless, his influence is unavoidable. Even though he did not teach at Westminster, his whole-Bible approach to biblical theology would prove influential there. Thirty years after Westminster began, it called its first president, Edmund Clowney. Prior to his appointment, Clowney taught at Westminster for fourteen years, putting forth the views which he would publish in his well-received *Preaching and Biblical Theology*.[73] In *Preaching*, Clowney follows Vos's approach in seeing the Bible structured according to an "epochal" schema; that is, the history of redemption unfolds progressively as God reveals himself in history over the course of several epochs, or distinct but related times in God's purposeful plan.[74] This process of revelation is unified and coherent, centering on and finding fulfillment in the person and work of Jesus, who is himself the Word of God (Rev 19:16), showing both what God is like and the way to him.[75] Therefore, Clowney says that biblical theology

---

70. See Olinger, *Geerhardus Vos*, 226.

71. Vos, *Biblical Theology*.

72. Klink and Lockett, *Understanding Biblical Theology*, 70. See also Bartholomew and Goheen, "Story and Biblical Theology," 148–50, for a discussion about the influence of Dutch theology in the Philadelphia school by way of Vos.

73. Clowney, *Preaching and Biblical Theology*.

74. Vos, *Biblical Theology*, 13–14; Clowney, *Preaching and Biblical Theology*, 89.

75. Clowney, *Preaching*, 50.

CHRIST AND THEOLOGY

follows the apostolic tradition of showing the fullness of the gospel from all of Scripture.[76] Finally, Clowney shows how important proper understandings of symbolism and typology are in order to practice a sound, appropriately Christ-centered biblical theology.[77]

Goldsworthy has drawn attention to Vos's influence first over those whom he taught at Princeton in the early twentieth century and then over the next generation of theologians who read and were taught from his *Biblical Theology*.[78] The Vos-Clowney approach, if they can be grouped together, seems to fit well with how Klink and Lockett define the Philadelphia school: an approach that seeks to trace themes throughout the whole of Scripture, finding their meaning in relationship to Jesus Christ. The presuppositions of such an approach must be understood, too. Two quotations provide the presuppositions of this approach. First, from Vos:

> If God be personally conscious, then the inference is inevitable that in every mode of self-disclosure He will make a faultless expression of His divine nature and purpose. He will communicate His thought to the world with the stamp of divinity on it. If this were otherwise, then the reason would have to be sought in His being in some way tied up in the limitations and relativities of the world, the medium of expression obstructing His intercourse with the world.[79]

Here Vos gives the first presupposition for the Philadelphia school: If God is absolutely powerful and free, then surely the clarity and coherence of his speech to humanity would be consistent with his nature and thus understandable. Since the Bible is, therefore, a covenantal book, written as God revealed himself to those whom he chose, the reader can trust not only that it is true, but that in it, they learn what God wants them to know.[80] The Bible is, thus, God's self-expression, to the end of

---

76. Clowney, *Preaching*, 68–73.

77. See Clowney, *Preaching*, 100–111. This point anticipates later sections of the current project.

78. Goldsworthy, *CCBT*, 81.

79. Vos, *Biblical Theology*, 20; quoted also in Clowney, *Preaching*, 14.

80. Here a Herman Bavinck quotation on the reasonableness of revelation is appropriate:

"To say that God is the Infinite, who, nevertheless, is able to reveal and actually has revealed Himself in finite creatures, is indeed to acknowledge the existence of an incomprehensible mystery, the miracle of creation, but does not amount to a palpable absurdity. We can maintain both God's infinitude and the existence of finite beings as long as we believe that God's is the ground of the existence of those beings." *Doctrine of God*, 34.

fellowship with people. Vos's reasoning, then, is consistent with Webster's aforementioned doctrine of God which undergirds biblical theology.[81]

Finally, of note is Clowney's contribution regarding the nature of biblical theology: "In tracing the progress of revelation, biblical theology rests upon the unity of the primary authorship of Scripture and the organic continuity of God's work in redemption and revelation."[82] If Vos establishes the reasonableness of God's ability to give a trustworthy revelation of himself to humanity, Clowney seeks to prove that the Bible is the product of God's so doing. An adherent can, therefore, be certain that the whole of Scripture is written by God through the agency of human authors. Further, it is certain that just as there is a unity to God's eternal Triune nature (John 14:11), so there is also a unity to the revelation which took 1500 years to complete.[83] As Bartholomew has said, listening to Scripture as the very words of God enables the hearer to hear his voice.[84]

Centering on the Gospel: From Vos and Clowney to Goldsworthy and Others

Understanding Vos and Clowney's presuppositions is necessary in order to understand their contributions to Christ-centered biblical theology in the later twentieth century and early twenty-first century. Likewise, discussion of such approaches seems impossible without mentioning Graeme Goldsworthy. Although Goldsworthy did not study *at* Philadelphia, his approach is discernibly *of* the Philadelphia school. Beginning with his first book, *Gospel and Kingdom*, Goldsworthy has written for over forty years to strengthen within biblical-theological studies a Christ-centered view of Scripture based firmly on Vos and Clowney's presuppositions. Belief both in the divine nature of Scripture and the

---

81. Worth mentioning is that this project will return substantially to Vos in later chapters.

82. Clowney, *Preaching*, 87.

83. Ridderbos hangs the possibilities of canonization and New Testament authority on Christology: "Jesus Christ is not only the canon Himself, in which God comes to the world, but He also lays down the canon and gives it a concrete, historical shape in the authority of the apostles, in their witness and tradition." *When the Time Had Fully Come*, 87, quoted in Bartholomew, *Introducing Biblical Hermeneutics*, 261.

84. Barholomew and Thomas, *Manifesto for theological interpretation*, 70. Also worth quoting is Packer from his masterful *Knowing God*: "Hearing God requires two beliefs: That He has good plans for the believer's life, and that He can effectively communicate to us in order to carry out his plans." *Knowing God*, 230–235.

essential Christocentric unity of its message undergirds Goldsworthy's approach to biblical theology.

In *CCBT*, Goldsworthy identifies what he sees as consistent evangelical presuppositions to undergird an evangelical biblical theology. These presuppositions are consistent with Vos and Clowney's offerings above. First is the *Doctrine of God*, in which the Bible is concerned with presenting God in his Triune nature, with Christ as mediator between God and men. Second is the *Doctrine of the Word of God*, in which God is known as the God who creates by speech and ultimately expresses himself in his Son, the Word. Third and fourth are canonical considerations, the first being that *the canon is the limit of inspired Scripture* and the second being that the *unity of the canon of Scripture* argues that Scripture is both unified and centered on Christ. Finally is *the human problem and God's response* where humanity is in rebellion against God and therefore subject to epistemological and moral misunderstanding, but God reveals his gospel to graciously help humanity into salvation and life.[85]

Goldsworthy has argued in virtually every one of his books that the salvation and life that comes through the gospel is none other than the kingdom of God promised in the Old Testament and inaugurated in the New with Jesus's coming (cf. Mark 1:15). Vos, Clowney, and Goldsworthy advocated this unity to the divine message, showing that they all operate according to the same evangelical presuppositions in their biblical-theological approach. Much of what follows in this chapter will engage with biblical theology from this same evangelical perspective.

Similarly, to Goldsworthy, humanity's primary problem is epistemological.[86] Humanity does not know how to think properly. So Scripture, in its account of Jesus as the one who brings humanity to God, redeems humanity's fallen epistemology so that he can think rightly and therefore know what is right and true.[87] This concept, which John Webster calls "hermeneutical conversion," is necessary to approach Scripture according to Webster's aforementioned definition of Scripture as the sanctified servant of God whereby he establishes fellowship with

---

85. See Goldsworthy, *CCBT*, 42–48.

86. This is similar to Calvin (*Inst.*, 1:1) who famously argued that humanity's main problem is that he does not *know* either himself or God rightly. So God, by the gospel, begins redemption through epistemology. Contrast this with the presupposition of modernism, following Descartes, where humanity not only can trust himself but can *only* trust himself (and thus, must do so.)

87. See Goldsworthy, *GCH*, 60–65.

lost people.⁸⁸ The fellowship thus established is, first, epistemological in nature: Humanity comes to know and rest in what the gospel promises them (cf. 1 John 5:13). The apostle wrote, therefore, "The Son of God has come and given us an understanding [*dianoian*: mind], that we may know him who is true" (1 John 5:20).

So, to return to Vos's and Clowney's contributions mentioned above, God knows himself perfectly, and therefore will reveal himself effectively and consistently. The Bible is his effective and consistent witness, the consistency of which is discernible in the person and work of Christ. Because of man's fallen nature which leads him to suppress the truth (Rom 1:18-23), Christ alone can give clarity and understanding to the seeking mind who listens to God's Word. This conviction shapes evangelical biblical theology in the current day and explains why such biblical theology is usually (always?) exercized with a pious, and not merely scholarly, attitude.⁸⁹

Biblical Theology in the 21st century

This brief identification of Goldsworthy with the Philadelphia school is meant to be a bridge to a further examination of evangelical biblical theology in the present day. Earlier pages discussed Klink and Lockett's paradigm to set forth the various *types* of biblical theology prevalent among theologians and scholars of the last fifty to a hundred years who take a generally conservative approach to the unity of Scripture. That said, the paradigm, although helpful, might not give a full picture of the field.

Peter Gentry, in offering a criticism, has suggested that for all of the help that *Understanding Biblical Theology* offers, yet "nowhere in the book do [Klink and Lockett] assess or critique the epistemological foundations of the different views."⁹⁰ Klink and Lockett treat each view

---

88. See Webster, *HS*, 6, 70.

89. Bartholomew, a respected chronicler of the history of biblical hermeneutics, has agreed with Scobie's claim that from 1870–1970, there was no "biblical theology," meaning individual scholarly works that organize the theology of the Old and New Testaments; cf. Scobie, *Ways of Our God*, 18, quoted in Bartholomew, *Introducing Biblical Hermeneutics*, 89. According to Bartholomew, however, the caveat is that such a claim might depend on how one defines biblical theology. It could be the case, as the current project argues, that Christ-centered biblical theology is present at all points of church history when Scripture is received as a Christ-centered unity, whether in writing, preaching, or teaching.

90. Gentry, "Significance of the Covenants," 12.

(BT1–5) as particular approaches in biblical theology that all depend on the same set of presuppositions. Gentry suggests that such a conclusion can hardly be defensible. He concludes, therefore, that since BTs 1, 4, and 5 operate (at least seemingly) on a foundation where human reason is set above the authority of Scripture, only BTs 2 and 3 can be called evangelical approaches to biblical theology.[91]

Holding to BT5 as a truly evangelical epistemological foundation seems unlikely. BT5 is essentially concerned with what Christ the Word might, through Scripture, be saying in the present, with heavy consideration given to Nicene orthodoxy, particularly to the reader and generally to the church.[92] Theological interpretation of Scripture is one movement that can be identified with BT5.[93] This interpretive movement seems to have had, at its inception, a clear mission of keeping in mind the history of orthodoxy when approaching the biblical hermeneutics, and thus listening to what ways Christ uses Scripture to shepherd, both practically and effectively, his church in the present. Craig Carter has suggested, however, that despite this early clarity, so many thinkers have "jumped on the theological interpretation bandwagon" that it now seems to mean to lack clear meaning.[94]

Carter and D. A. Carson have offered both criticism and commendation toward theological interpretation.[95] Carter and Carson suggest that although theological interpretation has some problems, such as the implied tendency to read into a particular text of Scripture a historic (and true) doctrine which might not be present in the plain reading of the text, theological interpretation is well within the Great Tradition if the reader approaches Scripture on its theological foundations to hear what God says.[96] Such a concession begins to anticipate the hermeneuti-

91. Gentry, "Significance of the Covenants," 13.

92. Klink and Lockett, *Understanding Biblical Theology*, 173.

93. For insight into the views contained in theological interpretation, see Billings, *Word of God*; and Treier, *Introducing theological interpretation of Scripture*.

94. See Carter, *Interpreting Scripture*, 19.

95. See Carson, "Theological Interpretation of Scripture," 187–207.

96. The exegetical potential of approaching the text on theological grounds but from different historical, ecclesial, and dogmatic perspectives was dealt with well in Kathryn Greene-McCreight, *Ad Litteram: How Augustine, Calvin, and Barth Read the 'Plain Sense' of Genesis 1–3*. McCreight shows that because of shared theological and epistemological foundations, the three titular exegetes arrive at distinct but discernibly similar conclusions in their "plain readings" of the text. As an example, Augustine allowed *polysemy* (different readings of the same texts) while Barth allowed for *polyvalence* (different themes and motifs of the same texts). Both, with Calvin, had a "ruled

cal remedy that the current project seeks to offer. If it is true, then it must be the case that a person can have an evangelical perspective in their practice of theological interpretation/BT5. One example worth mentioning is Kevin Vanhoozer, whom Carter concludes reads within the Great Tradition[97] and who has himself written the *Dictionary for theological interpretation of the Bible*.[98]

As long as the twin evangelical presuppositions mentioned above—belief in the divine authorship of Scripture and the Christocentric unity of the message therein—are kept together, a BT5 proponent can be consistently evangelical. If so, Peter Gentry might need to reexamine his position about excluding BT5's place in evangelical biblical theology.

The question remains, however, whether BT1 and BT4 are forms of biblical theology in the strict sense. Again, following Goldsworthy, biblical theology is here defined as the discipline of biblical study that is concerned with how every text relates to every other text, taking as a presupposition that the Bible has a divine author and a unified message centering, in some way, on Christ. Both Carter and Gentry might be correct to caution against the presuppositions of historical criticism, which are prevalent in BT1, BT4, and, to some degree, in BT3. If Klink and Lockett's description is correct, then BT1 uses historical critical tools to only find the text's meaning in its historical context.[99] If, per BT5, the Jesus of history is the Jesus of the present (Heb 13:7), then the meaning of the text is the same in the present as it was when originally written, though the application of the text might change.[100] Thus Vanhoozer has said that although the meaning of the text never changes, the Holy Spirit applies it to the believer in fresh ways that are consistent with Scripture itself.[101] BT1 sounds more like it is interested in historical study than it is in what that historical study might have to offer toward fellowship with God. If so, Carter's dismissiveness of the historical critical method is

---

reading" of Scripture in which the rule of faith (the gospel) was the fence of interpretive freedom. See McCreight, *Ad Litteram*, 80, 228, 249.

97. See Carter, *Interpreting Scripture*, 251.

98. Vanhoozer, *Dictionary for theological interpretation*. A later chapter will return to theological interpretation as its essential presuppositions and goals will be considered as a potential partner to be paired with redemptive-historical biblical theology to reach the goal of a biblically sound and historically consistent hermeneutic.

99. See Klink and Lockett, *Understanding Biblical Theology*, 33.

100. Klink and Lockett, *Understanding Biblical Theology*, 173.

101. See Vanhoozer, *Is There a Meaning*, 407–16. This quasi-allegorical approach will be considered in the next chapter.

understandable.¹⁰² At the very least, suggesting that the historical method is a form of biblical theology sounds forced.

Second, that the historical method is important to BT3 is also true. Can proponents of BT3 generally do biblical theology within the Great Tradition, particularly from evangelical presuppositions? BT3 is concerned with reading each text in light of the overarching narrative or story, employing both historical tools and theological meaning when necessary to understand the text.¹⁰³ It is possible that a person using the BT3 approach could do so from an evangelical perspective. The emphasis on the "big picture" that is in common with BT2 suggests that some within BT3 might actually just as comfortably fit the BT2 label as long as the historical tools are used to understand the Bible *as* God's word.

Finally, the historical method is also important within BT4. What distinguishes BT4 is that it is somewhat of a hybrid school. Like BT1, it employs the historical critical method in exegesis, but, like BT5, it holds that the Bible is the church's book and that the church's doctrine should have a say in ascertaining meaning.¹⁰⁴ Even further, like the Philadelphia school within BT2 (and some of those within BT3¹⁰⁵), BT4 has its proponents that consider the Bible's center to be Jesus Christ.¹⁰⁶ Uniquely, though, BT4 makes the structure of the biblical canon—how it is ordered, how the story flows, etc.—every passage's ultimate context.¹⁰⁷ For example, the meaning of the Gospel accounts is closely related to their ordering in the New Testament canon. An imagined position might argue that since Matthew focuses on the Jewishness of Jesus, he is therefore, before anything else, Israel's messiah. Then, only after the messages of his being a man of action (Mark) and a man of compassion (Luke) are established is the reader ready to understand Jesus's divinity, which John highlights.

To see the place of historical methods within BT4 is not difficult. The historical process must be pertinent in two ways: first, to examine the piecing together of the canon in its present form; and second, to

---

102. See Carter, *Interpreting Scripture*, 250. Commenting on Carson's "Theological Interpretation: Yes, But. . .", Carter says, "Carson wonders if anyone has a kind word for the poor maligned Enlightenment. I am afraid I do not." All throughout *Interpreting Scripture*, Carter equates the historical critical method with Enlightenment methodologies, persuasively so.

103. See Klink and Lockett, *Understanding Biblical Theology*, 100.

104. Klink and Lockett, *Understanding Biblical Theology*, 135.

105. See, for example, Wright, *Simply Christian*, 89–104.

106. Klink and Lockett, *Understanding Biblical Theology*, 135.

107. Klink and Lockett, *Understanding Biblical Theology*, 143.

respond to the historical method. In other words, it is probably the case that BT4 is post-historical critical and, therefore, a development.

A canonical approach is compatible with evangelical presuppositions if proponents of the approach presupposed that the canon is divinely authored and ordered. It seems that, therefore, BT4 can be practiced using evangelical presuppositions, as Stephen Dempster and John Sailhamer have done.[108]

Therefore, discernible today among proponents of BT2, some proponents of BT3, some of BT4, and many of BT5 is biblical theology as a discipline geared toward seeking the unity of the whole of Scripture. Because of this project's goal of examining whether evangelical Christ-centered biblical theology recaptures or advances Great Tradition hermeneutics, the following pages will mostly consider approaches among those within BT2 and 3. BT5 is roughly equivalent to theological interpretation, which later chapters will consider relative to biblical theology. Theological interpretation has much in common with biblical theology such that both disciplines complement each other. The disciplines, however, are distinct lenses in the hermeneutical spectacles.

Current Trends in Biblical Theology

Evangelical Biblical Theology (BT2, BT3, and BT5)

The goal of this project is to determine the nature of the relationship between evangelical Christ-centered biblical theology and the hermeneutics of the Great Tradition. Two early twentieth-century developments with relevance to current Christ-centered biblical theology include the rise of Fundamentalism and the defrocking of J. Gresham Machen from Princeton, which led to the founding of Westminster Theological Seminary. The aforementioned Biblical Theology Movement also had relevance. It is now time to consider these developments' long-term impact. The purpose is to demonstrate the evangelical presuppositions that undergird the current approaches to Christ-centered biblical theology among evangelicals.

---

108. See for instance, Dempster, *Dominion and Dynasty*; and Sailhamer, *Meaning of the Pentateuch*.

The Impacts of the Biblical Theology Movement and Philadelphia (BT2)

First will be an examination of the impact of the aforementioned Biblical Theology Movement. Although the Movement was not necessarily conservative, Childs seems to have clearly held some affinity with traditional Nicene orthodoxy.[109] The late Donald Robinson, the Anglican archbishop of Sydney from 1982 until 1992, taught theology at Moore College in Australia with young Goldsworthy as his student. Goldsworthy has written extensively on Robinson's influence over his thinking.[110] Robinson, says Goldsworthy, was the first to posit to him a threefold structure to divine revelation that has itself governed how Goldsworthy has both taught and preached biblical theology ever since: During the first stage (Old Testament history), God establishes by revelation the pattern of the way into his kingdom; during the second stage, prophetic eschatology (that is, Old Testament writings and prophets), God confirms the earlier pattern through the prophetic use of the pattern's imagery in looking forward to the messianic last days; and finally, in the third stage (New Testament), Jesus the Messiah comes to inaugurate the promised kingdom and begin the last days.[111] Goldsworthy calls this biblical-theological paradigm the Robinson-Hebert schema since it is a sort of hybrid of ideas from A. G. Hebert (1886–1963) and Robinson. Of interest is that Robinson lists as some of his influences: Old Testament scholar Norman Snaith, New Testament scholar C. H. Dodd, and Biblical-Theology-Movement proponent G. Ernest Wright.[112] Robinson was a lifelong friend of Brevard

---

109. See especially Childs, *Biblical Theology*, 8–10 and later sections of the book which outline historically orthodox themes as they arise within biblical theology. Still, Bartholomew has noted that Childs would at times let his historical-critical commitments outweigh his orthodox commitments; cf. Bartholomew, *Introducing Biblical Hermeneutics*, 101–3.

To Childs, biblical theology was primarily a theological endeavor, concerning "theological reflection on both the Old and New Testament" (Childs, *Biblical Theology*, 55), pursuing, as Daniel Driver has shown, how both Testaments can be read with integrity as witness to Christ. See Driver, *Brevard Childs, Biblical Theologian*, 100. Nevertheless, to Bartholomew's point, one can see in Childs's "Critique of Recent Intertextual Canonical Interpretation" his apologetic impulse toward historical-critical interlocutors and their presuppositions.

110. See, for example, Goldsworthy, *CCBT*, 24–26, 170–213.

111. Goldsworthy, *CCBT*, 24–26.

112. Robinson, "Origins and Unresolved Tensions," 2–3.

Childs.[113] Though the Movement had some influence over Robinson, he held unswervingly to evangelical presuppositions of the authority, integrity, and unity of Scripture.[114] It follows, then, that the Movement had at least a positive *intersecting* effect with Moore College's biblical theology, which Robinson taught and Goldsworthy popularized.

Goldsworthy has worked to show that the Robinson-Hebert schema is an improvement on the Vos-Clowney approach. If Robinson and Hebert place the organizational onus more on revelation in history, Vos and Clowney place it more on epochs of time.[115] In particular, the Robinson-Hebert approach focuses on the sameness of God's message throughout time, while the Vos-Clowney approach construes redemptive history as a set of distinct but unified—indeed, interlocking—eras of redemption.[116] There are clear parallels between the approaches in that they both seek to listen to Scripture as God's voice, and both understand the person and work of Christ to be the ground of Scripture's unity. Both camps fit together within the so-called Philadelphia school of BT2, per Klink and Lockett.

This point leads to the impact of Machen and Westminster. If in some way Vos led to Clowney, then Clowney led to the late Tim Keller, whose influence over reformed evangelical preaching is difficult to overstate. Keller went to lengths over the course of his preaching and writing ministry to state his indebtedness to Clowney.[117] Carter has also tied the celebrated work of G. K. Beale to the influence of Vos over biblical

---

113. See Shiner, "Servant of the Church of God."

114. Robinson, "Origins and Unresolved Tensions," 2.

115. See Goldsworthy, *CCBT*, 149, 171.

116. Worth mentioning is a point that will return later: Both Vos and Clowney held a biblical theology where revelation *expanded from the center*, not changing what came earlier but giving greater clarity. See Vos, "Idea of Biblical Theology," 11. This speech was Vos's inaugural address upon taking the Princeton Biblical Theology chair, given on May 8, 1894.

117. See for example Keller's dedication to Clowney in *Prodigal God*. Keller disseminates a Christ-centered approach to Scripture and preaching that has much in common with both Vos-Clowney and Robinson-Goldsworthy in *Preaching*. See especially 70–90.

Similarly, Bryan Chappell centralizes a Christ-centered approach to preaching in *Christ-Centered Preaching*, 249–82. Chappell urges the preacher to adopt a *Fallen Condition Focus* in which Jesus, in his person and work, is the hero to all of the listeners' primary problems. As such, says Chappell, the Bible's message is that "God must make provision for fallen creatures who cannot provide for themselves." (Chappell, *Christ-Centered Preaching*, 261.) In other words, the gospel concerns what God does to save his people, and Scripture's narrative bears that out.

theology through Westminster.[118] To all of these writers and pastors, Christ is himself the Word and unifying theme to Scripture. The gospel of God's Son is the plausibility structure for their frameworks, the gospel controlling exegesis, exegesis controlling doctrine, and doctrine, though imperfectly, controlling all of life.

Fundamentalism and Dispensationalism

Perhaps more significant is the impact of so-called fundamentalism over whole-Bible biblical theology. Dispensationalism became a default theological way of approaching Scripture among so-called fundamentalists, and in particular those who were not of a Calvinistic persuasion. The dispensational system divides the biblical narrative into seven distinct historic ages "which condition human life on the earth."[119] These historic ages—dispensations—each constitute "a stage in the progressive revelation of God constituting a distinctive stewardship or rule of life."[120] Therefore, "man's relationship to God is not the same in every age," as man is tested in different ways depending on the stage of revelation in which man finds himself.[121]

Another distinctive teaching of dispensationalism is that there is a major discontinuity between the nature of Israel during the Old Testament age and that of the church during the New, and that God has a future for national Israel in a still-future dispensation. Scofield's system has had an influence over Baptist theology (and theology among the "Bible Churches") in America that is difficult to overstate.

Dispensationalism has developed somewhat over the years leading to new forms, some of which are moderate. One influential school is what Craig Blaising and Daryl Bock, as representatives, have labeled *Progressive Dispensationalism*.[122] Blaising and Bock have summarized the difference between older forms of dispensationalism and progressive dispensationalism, saying that "the latter offers a more unified view of the biblical covenants than earlier forms of dispensationalism," stating further that the Abrahamic covenant, whereby God promises Abraham

---

118. Carter, *ISGT*, 24. Of relevance, Beale taught at Westminster from 2010 to 2021.
119. Scofield, *Scofield Reference Bible*, Eph 1:10 note, 1250.
120. Chafer, *Major Bible Themes*, 126.
121. Chafer, *Major Bible Themes*, 127.
122. See Blaising and Bock, *Progressive Dispensationalism*.

a seed through which he will bless the nations, is the foundational covenant for all other covenants.[123] Clearly this dispensational approach differs from earlier approaches, having more in common with other forms of whole-Bible biblical theology.

Although there are certainly still many "old-school" dispensationalists, progressive dispensationalism has gained some traction through the efforts of the teaching at Dallas Theological Seminary, which is itself usually associated with dispensationalism.[124] Goldsworthy seems to be correct in saying that dispensationalism, in its various forms, is a type of biblical theology because it is concerned with how the whole of Scripture holds together.[125] Klink and Lockett locate dispensationalism within BT2 under the Dallas School subcategory. Nevertheless, of the various dispensational approaches, the progressive approach seems to have more in common with other versions of biblical theology because it treats Scripture more as a unified narrative than do its dispensational hermeneutical ancestors.

Finally, in his summary of encouraging signs for a return to the Great Tradition, Carter mentions the biblical theology found in the works of Southern Baptist Theological Seminary professors James Hamilton, Peter Gentry, Stephen Wellum, and Thomas Schreiner.[126] These men, being Calvinistic Baptist professors, seem to at the very least have a sensitivity toward the tension between the biblical theology of Reformed thinkers like Vos, Clowney, and Goldsworthy on one hand, and on the other, the biblical theology of non-Reformed thinkers, many of whom espouse dispensational views. This conflict seems to be the reason for Gentry and Wellum's popular academic work *Kingdom Through Covenant*, which espouses a biblical theology using an "alternative reading which seeks to rethink and mediate between [dispensationalism and covenant theology]."[127]

Progressive Covenantalism as a Middle Way

In *KTC* (2012), Gentry and Wellum argue for a view called *progressive covenantalism* which states that the biblical covenants, starting with the creation covenant of Gen 1–3, form the backbone for and, as such,

123. Blaising and Bock, *Progressive Dispensationalism*, 53.
124. Thiselton, *Approaching the Study of Theology*, 178.
125. Goldsworthy, *CCBT*, 126.
126. Carter, *ISGT*, 24. Worth noting is that at the time of this writing, Gentry has accepted a new appointment at Phoenix Seminary.
127. Gentry and Wellum, *KTC*, 23.

require pedagogical fluency in order to understand the whole biblical narrative. Gentry and Wellum are clear that they do not think that covenant is biblical theology's "center" (as it is in covenant theology) but that correctly grasping the centrality of covenant to the narrative plot structure of the Bible is necessary for one to understand "the whole counsel of God" (Acts 20:27).[128] The book is called *Kingdom Through Covenant* because it is "*through* the biblical covenants viewed diachronically that one learns how the saving reign (i.e. Kingdom) of God comes into the world."[129] The covenants between God and man unfold and lead to the new covenant, promised through the Old Testament prophets, even if not always using explicit language. In the new covenant, the promises made under previous covenants find their fulfillments.[130]

It is worth offering few brief reflections on *KTC*. First, Gentry and Wellum are fair and balanced toward other approaches, and their fairness is seen in Gentry's comment in a later article that they never meant for their progressive covenantalism to have the final word in biblical theology.[131] Second, in contrast with the first point, Gentry and Wellum are clear that they do not think one can truly understand the biblical narrative without adopting their view on the importance of the covenants.[132] Most biblical-theological thinkers would agree that the covenants are an important biblical-theological element. To say that the theologian must centralize the covenants in order to understand the Bible appears, however, to be an overstatement. Neither the Acts sermons nor the theologically systematic arguments of the Epistles require such a high place for the covenants if one will understand redemptive history.[133]

Finally, progressive covenantalism is a subset of what has been called *new covenant theology*, a theological movement among Calvinistic baptists who do not hold as tightly to the normative need for historic baptist confessions and who think that the new covenant is intended to be the operating vantage point from which students of Scripture understand the Old Testament.[134] Although new covenant theology is somewhat nebu-

---

128. Gentry and Wellum, *KTC*, 21.
129. Gentry and Wellum, *KTC*, 601; emphasis added.
130. Gentry and Wellum, *KTC*, 548.
131. Gentry, "Significance of Covenants in Biblical Theology," 32.
132. See Gentry, "Significance of Covenants in Biblical Theology," 22–23, 26–27, 30–31; Gentry and Wellum, *GKGC*, , 52, 133, 251.
133. On this point, see Boersma, *Violence, Hospitality, and the Cross*, 165–68.
134. Parker and Wellum, *progressive covenantalism*, 2–3, 73.

lous in its approach to biblical theology, it seems, as will be seen below, to have in common with Goldsworthy and Beale that the Christian reader of Scripture should view the whole Bible from the perspective of the New Testament's Christocentric presuppositions. Pertinent works within new covenant theology state that one of its goals is to provide a middle way between covenant theology and dispensationalism. It might be true, then, that progressive covenantalism is more than simply a subset of new covenant theology, and is instead its clearest articulation.[135]

Some further thoughts in the way of assessment will emerge alongside other analysis after the next section, which provides a summary examination of the various approaches to biblical theology among conservative scholars. Köstenberger's paradigm, summarizing biblical theology among evangelicals, will be examined as the final piece in the biblical theology "puzzle." The previous few sections have concluded that those who practice biblical theology assume that Scripture is both inerrant and unified, and that there is, in good faith, some degree of variety among approaches. Köstenberger's article demonstrates that those who do such biblical theology hold in common Christ's centrality to the biblical narrative.

Köstenberger's Paradigm

Andreas Köstenberger has summarized the various evangelical approaches to biblical theology in a 2012 article entitled "The Present and Future of Biblical Theology." He draws attention throughout the article to the advancements that have characterized the previous decade and a half of evangelical biblical theology.[136] He begins the examination by considering Gabler's definition of biblical theology as a more historic discipline than dogmatic theology whereby the reader follows the biblical storyline as it unfolds and therefore begins theological study on a more "scriptural foundation." Köstenerger then cites Carson as saying that biblical theology is primarily concerned with the unity and diversity of the Old and New Testaments.[137] He then divides the various approaches into what he sees as four distinct approaches:

---

135. But see Reisinger, *Abraham's Four Seeds*; White, *What Is new covenant theology?*
136. Köstenberger, "Present and Future of Biblical Theology," 464.
137. Köstenberger, "Present and Future of Biblical Theology," 445–46.

Classic Approaches

Here the theologian or scholar studies the Bible book by book and then synthesizes his findings. Köstenberger sees examples of this approach in the *New Dictionary of Biblical Theology*[138] and in Scott Hafeman's *Biblical Theology: Retrospect and Prospect*.[139] In the *New Dictionary,* Brian Rosner states that "biblical theology is primarily concerned with the overall message of the whole Bible. It seeks to understand the parts in relation to the whole."[140] Therefore, biblical theology must work with the literary, historical, and theological dimensions of Scripture. Hafeman outlines a five-step process in hermeneutics.[141] One strength of this approach is that it seeks to allow the reader to practice what biblical theology was concerned with from the time of Gabler: to listen to Scripture on its terms so that the hearer understands the overall message.

Central-Themes Approach

This approach builds upon the classic approach but identifies particular themes that arise from Scripture. Köstenberger cites Charles Scobie[142] who said that biblical theology has to do first with the Bible's theology, and thus, a thematic approach will have a theological construal. To Scobie, biblical theology is a "bridge discipline," working between the historical study of the Bible and the use of the Bible as authoritative Scripture by the church.[143] As mentioned above, Scobie identifies several programmatic themes throughout Scripture. Köstenberger also cites Roy Ciampa as an example of a central-themes approach. One strength of this approach is that, like the classic approaches, it listens to the overall message of Scripture but is more accommodating of various particular ideas or themes that might arise from within Scripture.

---

138. Alexander and Rosner, *New Dictionary of Biblical Theology.*
139. Hafeman, *Biblical Theology.*
140. See Köstenberger, "Present and Future of Biblical Theology," 447.
141. Köstenberger, "Present and Future of Biblical Theology," 449.
142. Scobie, *Ways of Our God.*
143. See Köstenberger, "Present and Future of Biblical Theology," 450.

Single-Center Approach

This approach sees one theme as the "sole center" of biblical theology. Köstenberger is critical of this approach from the outset of his examination on the grounds that Scripture is so diverse and vast and that its theology is so interwoven.[144] Nevertheless, the question is worth asking: What if Scripture itself points to one overarching unifying theme?

The weight of this question seems to be the reason that James Hamilton has argued that God's glory in salvation through judgment is the center of biblical theology.[145] His *God's Glory In Salvation Through Judgment* is a whole-Bible biblical-theological study that seeks to uncover God's saving and judging glory as the unifying theme of all of redemptive history. Nevertheless, Köstenberger, along with Stephen Dempster and Garhard Hasel, sees the notion of a single center as difficult to establish, if not monochromatic and reductionistic.[146]

Story or Metanarrative Approaches

To quote Köstenberger, "This approach does not identify one theme as the central idea but argues that there is an overarching metanarrative—the story—that unifies the Scriptures."[147] Köstenberger examines T. Desmond Alexander's *From Eden to the New Jerusalem*, which argues that the goal of the biblical narrative is the new heavens and new earth image in Rev 21–22. The reader who grasps this is able to understand the context of every passage. Köstenberger then mentions Goldsworthy and his redemptive-historical, Christ-centered approach, adapted from Donald Robinson.[148] Finally, Köstenberger considers G. K. Beale, whose *New Testament Biblical Theology* focuses on how the biblical storyline moves from Old Testament to New and how the narrative of the New is framed by that of the Old. To Beale, the New Testament retells the

---

144. Köstenberger, "Present and Future of Biblical Theology," 452.

145. Hamilton, *God's Glory in Salvation*.

146. Köstenberger, "Present and Future of Biblical Theology," 454–55. Worth noting is Carter's endorsement of Hamilton's approach and conclusions, in Carter, *ISGT*, 24. See also Dempster, *Dominion and Dynasty*, 20–43. Dempster argues that what makes single-center approaches problematic are that they are unnecessary, given that reading and rereading the text clearly reveals the patterns that God intends to be seen.

147. Köstenberger, "Present and Future of Biblical Theology," 455.

148. Köstenberger, "Present and Future of Biblical Theology," 456.

story of the Old in the life of Jesus, thus transforming the Old Testament storyline and launching "the fulfillment of the eschatological already-not yet new-creational reign" of God's people in Jesus.[149]

Köstenberger concludes his assessment of the various schools by pointing out some similarities and some differences. The primary similarity is that they all have Christ as the center or "pivot-point of redemptive history."[150] God's unified message to the world is that Jesus is his Son and the world's Redeemer and that the whole of the Scripture bears witness to him. Even if an approach is not concerned with a "center," it still sees Christ as the one who encompasses in himself the primary witness of Scripture.

One important distinction that Köstenberger sees between the approaches is that some approaches take a more inductive approach while others take a systematic approach. How this conclusion can be deduced is unclear because, based on Köstenberger's paradigm, each approach seems to be trying to listen to Scripture on its own terms (inductive), while the practitioner seeks to subject his presuppositions to scriptural analysis.

Perhaps Goldsworthy is right in concluding that no one approach has the right to say it has the final word.[151] Each approach has a legitimate claim to consistency with how the Bible unfolds and comes into its final form. A later section will return to this conclusion because of its importance to the relationship between biblical theology and the Great Tradition.

Evaluation of Köstenberger's Paradigm

Köstenberger has done a good service to students of biblical theology who would like to understand better the various conservative approaches. Köstenberger's four categories generally group together conservative approaches into particular camps so that, added to Klink and Lockett's

---

149. Beale, *New Testament Biblical Theology*, 35, quoted in Köstenberger, "Present and Future of Biblical Theology," 458. See also Beale, *New Testament Biblical Theology*, 951–57, where he argues that the fulfillment of the Old Testament promises in the life and glorifying of Jesus might appear at first to be a surprising fulfillment but should not be considered impossible, especially considering that Paul says the gospel fulfills the "mystery kept secret for long ages, but now revealed" (Rom 16:25). The apostles taught—and the church has historically believed—that Christ is himself the mystery kept secret for so long, coming at the right time.

150. Köstenberger, "Present and Future of Biblical Theology," 459.

151. See Goldsworthy, *CCBT*, 98.

paradigm, the biblical theology student can evaluate and make an informed decision about what is most consistent.

One critique worth offering concerns particular categorizations. As mentioned earlier, Goldsworthy takes a single center in his approach to biblical theology which some have said is the kingdom of God, which he calls the Robinson-Hebert schema, explained in his *CCBT*.[152] But the three-step paradigm simply explains the big picture of Scripture's redemptive-historical storyline through the person and work of Christ. The center of biblical theology to Goldsworthy is the gospel, thus his bold claim: "The name 'evangelical' properly belongs to those who see the *evangel*, the gospel of Jesus Christ, as the governing principle for the understanding and interpretation of all Scripture."[153] That is, the gospel is the key or *center* of biblical interpretation. Clearly Goldsworthy, with the gospel as his center, belongs under the "single-center approaches" heading. As such, Goldsworthy's gospel-centered approach is consistent with the Tradition *if* his theological presuppositions are clearly defined.

Toward the end of his article, Köstenberger acknowledges theological interpretation, though negatively. He suggests that theological interpretation blurs the line between biblical theology and systematics/dogmatics by seeking to "read the Bible creedally for the twenty-first century."[154] The way, however, in which the line is blurred remains unclear. It might have something to do with the aforementioned lack of definition in theological interpretation. A later chapter will consider the benefits that theological interpretation offers to biblical theology.[155]

Finally, Köstenberger, seemingly in agreement with Gabler, states that, "The goal of biblical theology . . . must continue to be accurately perceiving the convictions of the Old Testament and New Testament writers."[156] An examination of the literature available on biblical theology suggests that many thinkers from Gabler's day to the present make the mindset, convictions, and feelings of the biblical writers paramount in pursuing clarity of meaning in exegesis. Considered below will be whether such a biblical-theological pursuit is necessary.

---

152. Goldsworthy, *CCBT*, 24–27.
153. Goldsworthy, *CCBT*, 77. Emphasis original.
154. See Köstenberger, "Present and Future of Biblical Theology," 462n93.
155. In fact, this consideration is central to this project's thesis.
156. Köstenberger, "Present and Future of Biblical Theology," 462.

A Broader Evaluation of the Various Evangelical (BT2, BT3, BT5) Approaches

As mentioned, all of the approaches in Köstenberger's evaluation seem to have evangelical legitimacy. Each approach represents an attempt to listen to Scripture on its own terms, trying to make sense of the Bible's content in all of its unity and diversity. These various approaches are trying to exegete within the Great Tradition because they are first trying to *listen* to Scripture as the unified witness of the triune God before analyzing what it says.

Each aforementioned organizing paradigm, whether from Klink and Lockett, Gentry and Wellum, or Köstenberger, is helpful in understanding the field of evangelical biblical theology. Indebted is every biblical-theological student to those who have done the hard work of sifting through, organizing, and analyzing the seemingly endless approaches throughout history. A couple of rebuttals might, however, be worth proposing.

First, to Gentry and Wellum, to say that a correct grasp of the covenants is *necessary* in order to understand Scripture is probably an overstatement.[157] Because the Bible is the means through which God draws people to himself and reorients their reality, covenants are a biblical category that belong in systematics but are not necessarily foundational. Further, a covenantal structure like the one Gentry and Wellum offer can help towards understanding the God who creates relationship. Still, the writers of the New Testament show that the priority is knowing Jesus as the one to whom redemptive history has led and found fulfillment. In fact, the mention of covenants from the mouth of Jesus in the Gospels is minimal although he was insistent that the disciples understand that the Scriptures witness of him (Luke 24:44–46; John 5:39). The believer can only fully appreciate Christ if he or she understands who Christ is and what he came to do. Clarity about Christ's identity and redeeming work for and in believers is the central topic for the rest of the New Testament.[158]

---

157. See Gentry, "Importance of Covenants for Biblical Theology," 22–23, 26–27, 30–31; Gentry and Wellum, *GKGC*, , 52, 133, 251.

158. To be fair, Gentry and Wellum explicitly say that the covenants are not "central" to biblical theology, but they do form the "backbone" to the biblical metanarrative (Gentry and Wellum, *KTC*, 21–22). It seems that they are aware of the dangers of over-centering covenant. Nevertheless, sample quotes like the ones quoted and footnoted throughout this chapter seem to make the centrality of covenant in progressive covenantalism difficult to avoid.

Conversely, the presence of covenantal terminology from Acts to Revelation is less than ubiquitous, and this fact seems undeniable. A covenantal focus seems, at the most atomistic level, to have as its goal understanding the nature of the relationship between God and his people. Calvin is worth remembering for saying that the goal of biblical study is right knowledge of God and of self. God uses Scripture to reconcile lost people to himself, thus bringing them into reality. To argue (even if Calvin would) that covenantal fluency is necessary for biblical clarity seems to be a stretch.[159]

Second, to Köstenberger, his conclusion that biblical theology has to do with discovering the feelings of the writers of Scripture is questionable. If Scripture primarily has a divine author through human agency, is not the goal of identifying the human author's feelings and thoughts at most a means to the end of understanding God's? Köstenberger would likely agree with such an assertion, but whether his appropriation of Gabler's idea is misleading for the new student of biblical theology is worth consideration. A shared interpretive mindset among the human authors is at most a means to the end of understanding the unified message present in the eternal mind of the divine Author.[160]

Third, the notion that there cannot be a single center to Scripture might need reconsideration. The best response to this assertion is a question: Why can there not be a center if Scripture itself bears one out? If listening to Scripture on its own terms leads to a demonstrable unifying theme or center, why should it be dismissed, unless by proof? Most who dismiss single-center approaches seem to be dismissing the idea more than the actual attempts. Scobie, for instance, takes a multi-theme approach, arguing that there are a few themes that clearly are meant to take precedence within biblical theology.[161] Curiously, he criticizes what he calls an "obsession with finding *one single theme or center*" for biblical theology, on the grounds that there is no agreed-upon consensus.[162] But in offering what he thinks are the four unifying themes of Scripture, he

---

159. Again worth mentioning is Boersma's challenge to the tendency in Reformed biblical theology to over-centralize covenant. See Boersma, *Violence, Hospitality, and the Cross*, 165–68.

160. Divine authorial intent and its relationship to human authorial intent will be a topic in the next chapter.

161. See Part II in Scobie, *Ways of Our God*. Scobie makes as central themes God's Order, God's People, God's Servant, and God's Way.

162. Scobie, *Ways of Our God*; emphasis added.

is himself participating in the so-called "obsession." Surely he does not assume that everyone will accept his paradigm, as helpful as it is.

Finally, there will be a few less substantial reflections. Most evangelical biblical theologians seem to acknowledge that in some way, true biblical hermeneutics are by definition Christ-centered. Carter says that the Great Tradition takes Christ as Scripture's unifying theme and center. As the church listens to Scripture, the church hears Christ. Although there is a variety of themes among evangelical approaches to biblical theology, each approach is trying to help readers read Scripture *as Christians*, as those called to keep their eyes on Jesus (Heb 12:1–2). Evangelical interest in whole-Bible, Christ-centered biblical theology is an attempt by conservative theologians to bring their understanding of Scripture into greater alignment with the Christ-centered view of reality that is not only evident in Scripture but which the Great Tradition has maintained throughout church history.

Today's Christ-centered conservative evangelicals might not be working with the same metaphysical presuppositions as their ancient forerunners, or at least they might be assuming the presuppositions without understanding them.[163] Therefore, this project's goal is to discover the nature of the relationship between Christ-centered biblical theology and the hermeneutics practiced by those with premodern metaphysics. That question will require two more chapters in order to glean some conclusions. Before moving to such a comparison, the assumptions/presuppositions and goals of biblical theology need consideration, which the next chapter will pursue.

Biblical theology is a discipline that seeks to understand the Bible's organic unity with particular emphasis on the way that both Testaments relate to each other. As a biblical-theological subgenre, Christ-centered biblical theology reads the Bible with a Christian presupposition—that is, by faith—seeking the Bible's unity in the person and work of Jesus Christ.

Conclusion

The history of biblical theology has advanced by a winding road. Among early biblical-theological thinkers, it was a way of scrutinizing doctrine by Scripture. As the Enlightenment began to take heavy influence, scrutiny was aimed at Scripture itself. Although the faithful church's message

---

163. See Carter, *ISGT*, 154.

was the gospel, popular theology wound through historical-critical methods, eventually through the Biblical Theology Movement, and finally met with the generally Christ-centered thinking of those earlier labeled as "fundamentalist." The effect has been a more Christ-centered reading of the Bible that both listens for God like premoderns and reads historically like moderns. These thinkers, representing many "camps," are Christ-centered still, utilizing the historical tools at their disposal, trying to exegete in a way that is faithful to Scripture's presentation of Christ as the source, power, and goal of all of reality (Eph 1:10; Heb 1:3). There are various approaches to biblical theology among well-meaning scholars and theologians, but the gospel is the centering theme and telos wherever Christ is known. Wherever this gospel centrality is present, the faithful tradition is intact. Nevertheless, there are issues which the next chapter will address.

This chapter has tried to show that Christ-centered biblical theology operates simultaneously with both a post-liberal priority (to read the Bible historically) and a premodern one (to hear the God who speaks.) Conservative Christ-centered biblical theology operates with this dual impulse. Put succinctly, Christ-centered biblical theology is trying to hear God speak across Scripture's storyline. The next chapter will develop more fully what Christ-centered biblical theology hears as it listens to God speak.

2

What Is Christ-Centered Biblical Theology Trying To Do?
Goals and Context

"In focusing on the redemptive storyline, [the redemptive-historical method of interpretation] has also tended to prioritize the narrative economy of God's actions over the eternal ontology of his being and has thereby collapsed the transcendent into the immanent."

—CARL TRUEMAN

"When Christ said, 'Before Abraham was, I Am,' (John 8:56), he was saying not just that he is Abraham's and David's seed, but that he is Abraham's and David's Lord."

—EDMUND CLOWNEY

WHAT IS CHRIST-CENTERED BIBLICAL theology trying to do? The previous chapter pursued a history of biblical theology in order to accurately define Christ-centered biblical-theological approaches in recent years. In general terms, Christ-centered biblical theology is a post-Enlightenment hermeneutical approach that operates on a primary pre-Enlightenment presupposition. A historical preoccupation identifies these redemptive-historical approaches as post-Enlightenment.¹ Nevertheless, these redemptive historicist biblical theologians, despite their late modern historical position, do not neglect the Christocentricity that also characterized their premodern ancestors. They read Scripture historically *to* hear and enjoy Christ piously. As such, a comparison between the subjects of Köstenberger's organizing paradigm² and the more theologically attuned approach of Vos and Clowney shows that both sides centralize Christ in the creational and redemptive purposes of God, and therefore, in interpretation.³ Hence the assertion that if biblical theology is Christ-centered, it is *both* pre- *and* post-Enlightenment. The current chapter asks several questions that emerge both from Scripture's own pages and from Christian orthodoxy, seeking to clarify the Christ-centered goals of this evangelical biblical-theological approach and considering both grammatical-historical (that is, scholarly) and evangelical (believing) impulses. Below, those questions will follow.

First, there are important cautions to bear in mind: Historical endeavor, though central, can, if carelessly handled, take on such a progressive definition that meaning is lost.⁴ Acknowledging the Christocentric impulse of the biblical theologians in which Christ as Word gives meaning to all of life (and thus to hermeneutics) is important. The historical endeavor insulates itself from being, as Boersma rightly cautions, subject to the dangers of progressivist narration by seeking a constant orientation (and reorientation) to Christ the Word, who "upholds all things" (Heb 1:3) and "for whom all things exist" (Col 1:16). In other words, history progresses insofar as Christ's purposes unfold. Perhaps redemptive-historical approaches to biblical theology assume this without saying so explicitly.

As an example, Goldsworthy has said that Christ-centered biblical-theological exegesis is, at best, the endeavor to ascertain the "word of the one God" and "the one word of God," which is, in the end, the "word about salvation" that is "about Christ."⁵ Similar to premodern

1. Interesting is Michael Cameron's assertion that beginning interpreters have a historical, "bottom-up" approach to biblical interpretation, which often, as it did for Augustine, shifts to a spiritual, "top-down" approach as the believer matures. Cameron, *Christ Meets Me Everywhere*, 10.

2. See Köstenberger, "Present and Future of Biblical Theology," 454–64.

3. See chapter 1 above for Vos and Clowney's importance in the development of broadly Reformed biblical theology in the twentieth century.

4. See Hans Boersma's caution in *Scripture as Real Presence*, xiv, 24–25.

5. See Goldsworthy, *Preaching the Whole Bible*, 11–20.

interpretation (which was, as the next chapter will address, concerned with coming to Scripture to hear God's voice), Goldsworthy's Christ-centered, redemptive-historical method does not seem far off *if* the "ascertaining" is equivalent to listening.

Although this project is not yet prepared to fully consider the parallels between Christ-centered biblical theology and the premodern hermeneutics of the Tradition, at least some metaphysical similarities should be obvious: Scripture is the voice of God to put Christ the Word before the reader/listener. Christ-centered biblical theology seems to at least be trying, from within a post-Enlightenment, historically-oriented framework, to hear Christ the Word as the voice of the one true God.

Chapter 1 considered Klink and Lockett's organizing paradigm of the biblical-theological field.[6] Whereas their approaches labeled BT2 (redemptive-historical approaches), BT3 (metanarrative approaches), and BT5 (theological construct approaches) seem to be operating under evangelical presuppositions, BT1 (historical-critical approaches) and BT4 (canonical approaches) could, indeed, operate under truly evangelical presuppositions as long as the approaches seek Scripture as God's word. Although not every reader may agree that such an inclusive analysis is accurate or helpful, there are definitely thinkers from every approach that have one thing in common, which might be more easily discernible among some schools than others: a Christocentric hermeneutical impulse from a position of faith, whereby Scripture is hermeneutically contextualized by the believing church.

Klink and Lockett, as chapter 1 sought to show, rightly delineate the deficiencies in the BT1 and BT4 approaches. Craig Carter has argued, however, that these deficiencies might also be present in BT2 and BT3.[7] "Deficient" does not necessarily equate to "useless" any more than "strength" equals "perfection." Hence Christ-centered biblical theology, if practiced from within an ecclesial, faith-filled context, can be of great value to the church in gaining clarity about God's nature and voice.[8]

---

6. See Klink and Lockett, *Understanding Biblical Theology.*

7. See Carter, *ISGT*, 24–25, 100–120.

8. As in Carter, *ISGT*, 24, where Carter shows the strengths of the biblical theology of particular redemptive-historical thinkers. As this chapter will seek to show, some of these thinkers do not exegete consistently with the metaphysics that Carter says are necessary for hermeneutics to be truly Christian. Nevertheless, as Carter says, there is value in their suggestions.

This is because the gospel concerns the Son of God and how Jesus must be, based on the revelatory content of redemptive history as recorded by inspiration in Scripture, the Son of God (Rom 1:4). Defined in terms of the fulfillment of God's earlier salvific and eschatological promises (1 Cor 15:3–8), there is both a definite historical orientation because Christ fulfills promises in history (Rom 15:8–9) and a theological orientation because the ultimate goal of his work is to bring people to God for fellowship (John 17:3; 1 Pet 3:18). So, as Goldsworthy says, evangelical hermeneutics must be gospel-centric, because this is what it means to be evangelical: to let "the gospel of Jesus Christ [be] the governing principle for the understanding and interpretation of all Scripture."[9]

Carter asserts, however, that if biblical theology wants to be consistent with the hermeneutics of the Great Tradition, it will need to operate under the tradition's metaphysical presuppositions.[10] In particular, it will need to presuppose the metaphysical belief that God speaks *from* eternity *into* time and space (neither to which he is subject) so that what occurs in history is an extension, in some way, of what is in eternity. Christ-centered (redemptive-historical) biblical theology goes partway toward this by construing the unfolding of redemptive history in a Christ-centered way, implying the existence of absolute truth/reality that can be known. To answer Carter's insistence, however, steps can be made toward advancement if the metaphysical presuppositions of so-called Christian Platonism are explicitly pursued.[11] In short, if redemptive history is merely a sequential unfolding of events and unrelated moments across time, Boersma is probably correct to infer that history necessarily becomes its own meaning. On the other hand, if history is the unfolding of God's eternal purposes across time, meaning is neither relative nor changing. It is as eternal as God is, coming into greater clarity as time elapses across God's redemptive project.

Given that there is shared agreement among biblical theologians that Christ is central in the hermeneutical endeavor, this chapter's "big" question (What is biblical theology trying to do?) must be answered by answering several smaller ones. The first will be: Who, according to Scripture, is

---

9. Goldsworthy, *CCBT*, 77; see also Bebbington, "Nature of Evangelical Religion," 36, 51–55.

10. Carter, *ISGT*, 22–24.

11. See Carter, "Response" to Jason Derouchie's "Redemptive-Historical, Christocentric Approach" in *Christ in the Old Testament*, 228–30. See also Carter's fuller explanation in "How Then Shall We Theologize?"

Jesus? That is, who must he be if he is to be central to the hermeneutical endeavor? Second, how, in terms of theme, history, and grammar, does the Bible present him? This question is not redundant with the previous one because it moves beyond the identity of Christ to consider the various ways that Christ is presented. Christ-centered biblical theologians believe that there is power in seeing Jesus as central to the biblical record; further, they believe that this is the Bible's revelatory purpose.

If Jesus is who Scripture says he is, as Scripture presents him to be, then he must be, in some ways, *active* in the hermeneutical act. Doubtless such an assertion is not without controversy as it challenges postmodern notions of objectivity and presupposition-less thought. However, in a similar way that a woman speaks of a written novel as having "changed her life" to the point that she would not be ashamed to tell the author "*you* changed my life," so it is not inappropriate to consider what ways Christ might be active in the hermeneutical endeavor approaching Scripture. The third question will, therefore, engage so-called Speech-Act Theory, asking, "What act does he—that is, God/Christ—perform on the reader?"

Finally, we will ask the question: How can one be sure that what the Bible says is the truth? This question will engage another late modern assumption that there is no such thing as truth but only opinions. To argue, as this chapter will, that truth exists is not to suggest that any one individual knows it perfectly (because the best that a human can hope for in the current sphere of knowledge is to "know in part," 1 Cor 13:12), but that one can come to a lesser degree of certainty which, though not exhaustive, is decisive. Such a claim is no more brazen than to claim that truth cannot be known. To suggest as much is the definition of self-defeating.

Once these questions are answered, some considerations will follow of recent and semi-recent discussions between biblical theologians and those who are friendly and/or critical. All of this will serve to find a clear answer to the question, "What is biblical theology trying to do?"

Who Is Jesus?

Although engaging the field of Christology might seem bold based on the field's massive breadth, two recent interlocutors are worth considering when discussing hermeneutics. First is Stephen Dempster. Dempster has stated, "Too often Christians have let the New Testament dominate

WHAT IS CHRIST-CENTERED BIBLICAL THEOLOGY TRYING TO DO?

interpretation of the Old without first trying to engage the latter in any meaningful way."[12] Dempster's point is not to suggest that the New Testament fails to point backwards to the Old, but that Old Testament studies make it seem as if Christians do not feel equipped to understand it unless they approach it through Jesus. Relevant is Goldsworthy's argument that biblical theology's goal is to interpret the Old Testament by establishing its relationship to the (New Testament) revelation of God in Christ.[13] To be clear, after the resurrection, Jesus taught his disciples how to read the Old Testament (Luke 24:27) to the point that it opened their minds to a deeper level of understanding than perhaps they thought possible (Luke 24:45).[14]

But Dempster is drawing attention to an important aspect of biblical theology: The New Testament everywhere presupposes that the revelation of God in Christ has a context that is driven by the Tanach (TNK). The historical writings (Gospels, Acts) especially make clear everywhere that Jesus's coming fulfills promises, types, symbols, etc. Without having some degree of understanding of these from the Old Testament record, one is limited in how much one is able to even understand Jesus.[15] Even the first chapter of Matthew, the first book of the New Testament, presents Jesus both as the *Immanuel* promised in Isa 7:14 and as he who saves people from their sins (Matt 1:21–23) in context of an Old-Testament-sweeping genealogy through David back to Abraham (1:1–17).

But based on the New Testament itself, that clarity about the content of the Old Testament will be limited without Christ's illumination: He is the one who makes God known (John 1:18); he makes clear that which was mysterious before (Rom 16:25); and reflection upon the faith of the Old Testament saints is supposed to lead the reader to look not to

---

12. Dempster, *Dominion and Dynasty*, 36.

13. Goldsworthy, *Gospel and Kingdom*, 123–27.

14. One example of the transformation is that the apostles began to retrospectively understand what they saw Jesus do before the cross *in light of* Old Testament revelation, concluding that he gave the revelation its ultimate meaning (John 2:22).

Another effect is that the they were able to boldly proclaim how Jesus's work and subsequent giving of the Holy Spirit make sense of and confirm the promises of the Old Testament. The three thousand who came to faith at Pentecost (Acts 2:41) believed that Jesus is the Lord and Christ promised by David and the prophets; conversely, Stephen's executioners were moved to rage by being told that they were just like all of those throughout redemptive history who rebelled against the Holy Spirit's ministry in their midst (Acts 7:51–53). It is worth pondering whether such boldness by the once-timid disciples would be possible had Jesus not effectively transformed them post-resurrection.

15. Dempster, *Dominion and Dynasty*, 36.

them, but to *him* (Heb 11:1—12:2). Hence the encouragement to faithful discipleship among believers in him, because he is "the same yesterday, today, and forever" (Heb 13:8). Because he is the I Am, "who was and is and is to come" (Rev 1:4, 9), the Old Testament is a sort of manual for the discipleship of those who know God through him, who "through him, are believers in God" (1 Pet 1:21).[16]

This seems to be in view when Paul tells Timothy that the Old Testament is to be read and heard as the means through which God equips godly people to fulfill their calling as fruitful and set-apart Christians (2 Tim 3:15-16). Reading must occur, thus, as Dempster shows, *forward* (that is, reading the New as fulfillment of the Old) while also *backward* (reading the Old as preparatory for the New).

This is why (moving now to the second interlocutor) Richard Hays, in his appropriately titled *Reading Backwards*, has stated that one purpose of the New Testament is to help people to understand how to read the Old. Responding to charges that Christian teaching often "twists" and "misreads" the Old Testament Scriptures, Hays says that at the center of the New Testament's message is the belief that Jesus's redemptive work had been accomplished "according to the Scriptures" (1 Cor 15:3-4; cf. Luke 24:47).[17] Hays shows, echoing Hans Frei, that the canon has a "unity ... [a] single cumulative and complex pattern of meaning," and this unity is found in seeing Jesus as the one who holds both Testaments together.[18]

These points do not ignore the clear contrast between the Old Testament and the New. As Michael Cameron has shown, what drove ancient groups such as the agnostics, the Marcionites, and the Manicheans to reject the Old Testament was what they perceived to be a radical discontinuity between it and the New.[19] But thinkers such as Justin Martyr (c. 100-165) and Augustine (354-430) worked to show how a Christ-centered framework makes sense not only of all of reality but especially of the Old Testament.[20] Irenaeus's (c. 130-202) *On the Apostolic Preaching* is

---

16. See Augustine's interesting explanation of the New Testament's treatment of Jesus's eternality in terms of the tetragrammaton in *Treatise on Faith and the Creed*, 7.

17. Hays, *Reading Backwards*, 14. See also his more voluminous *Echoes of Scripture in the Gospels*.

18. Frei, *Eclipse of the Biblical Narrative*, 33; in Hays, *Reading Backwards*, 3.

19. See Cameron, *Christ Meets Me Everywhere*, 6-7.

20. For Martyr's contribution, in particular his battle with Marcionite and Jewish biblicism, see Bennett, *Scripture Wars*; for Augustine, see Cameron, *Christ Meets Me Everywhere*.

Finally, O'Keefe and Reno have shown in *Sanctified Vision* that early thinkers were

WHAT IS CHRIST-CENTERED BIBLICAL THEOLOGY TRYING TO DO?

perhaps the clearest example of how Christ's being the Word compellingly paints how Old Testament hermeneutics are supposed to operate.

The point is this: From the earliest days of Christian thinking, there has been a clear struggle to understand the relationship between the Testaments. There was always, however, a clear witness that Christ the Word possesses the Old Testament eternally. So the Old Testament, like the New, witnesses to him. The only difference is the chronological relationship of the revelation to the saving Christ-event.

The goal of offering these considerations is to explain who the Bible says Jesus is. Woven into the fabric of the two-testament structure is the person of Jesus as the fullness of revelatory truth. At least, such is implied by the aforementioned content of the transition between the Testaments, the first chapter of Matthew's Gospel: First, being the descendent of Abraham and David (1:1), Jesus is himself the true Israel (that is, faithful covenant partner) and Davidic king (who will reign eternally); second, being the one in whom consists the perfection of the God-with-us promise (Isa 7:14, 8:8), he must himself be the divine presence within humanity (Matt 1:23); finally, being named *Jesus*, the Greek version of Hebrew *Joshua*, meaning "the Lord saves," he is himself the salvation of the Lord in its fullness.[21] This seems to be why Simeon, after setting eyes on the newborn Jesus, could say in prayer to God, "My eyes have seen your salvation" (Luke 2:30).[22]

Matthew's early description provides this section a good framework to answer the question: Who is Jesus?

---

not interested in answering every possible hermeneutical and exegetical question, but in showing how Christ compellingly repaints reality into a glorious tapestry of divine life to be shared by the faithful. Although it is true, as Augustine was fond of saying, that patristic preachers and writers wanted to be persuasive, a lack of conversions was not going to crush their faith. Christ as the Word made flesh was their whole reality, and their teaching and preaching is the best evidence of this fact.

21. See Stern, *Complete Jewish New Testament Commentary*, Matt 1:1, for an explanation of the importance of his name being the same as Joshua; for a patristic explanation, Irenaeus's *On the Apostolic Preaching*, 50, has the bishop explaining that, like Joshua took leadership after the Law and carried Israel into the land, so the New Testament "Joshua," Jesus, enters after the Law and saves the people.

22. See Reeves, *Rejoicing in Christ*, 33–35. Reeves argues that Simeon's being a God-seeker and finding God's salvation in Jesus in the temple fulfills the Mal 3 promise that "the Lord you seek will come to the Temple."

True Israel and Son of David (Matt 1:1)

By locating Jesus in the line of Abraham and David (Matt 1:1), Matthew identifies Jesus with the history of Israel. By also implying, however, that Israel never truly returned from exile (1:12, 17)—which he seems to do by ending the genealogy at the deportation to Babylon—he goes even further, presenting Jesus as the one who can save Israel from its exile. The fact that the prophets said that Israel would itself journey back to the land from their exile (e.g., Isa 10:20–22; 14:1–2; Jer 29:14; 30:1–22) shows Matthew's boldness to begin his account by implying that Israel's exile continues (even after some did return: Ezra 1; Neh 1) and that Jesus completes the story of how they will return.[23]

This is why Matthew, in a text that has puzzled many grammatical-historicists and historical critics, quotes Hosea's telling of Israel's flight from Egypt (Hos 11:1), saying that it finds its fulfillment in Jesus's parents bringing him to Egypt only to bring him back out later (2:15). Matthew's point seems to be that Jesus is the true, antitypical Son of God and thus true Israel, who himself brings the people back from exile to God.[24]

This answers why Matthew starts by showing Jesus's descent from Abraham and David: He is both the promised seed to Abraham who will overcome the enemy's advances (Gen 12:1–3, with literary parallels with Gen 3:16) and the son of David who will rule eternally in a kingdom of holiness and purity (2 Sam 7:11).[25] Matthew is not shy about the frequency of times Jesus was called "Son of David" (no less than nine times), echoing the introduction of Jesus as such (1:1). The reason seems simple: Jesus is indeed the promised son of David who fulfills the promise of

---

23. For a good case for Israel's continuing exile after their return, see Boersma, *Violence, Hospitality, and the Cross*, 160–75.

See also Beale, *Union with the Resurrected Christ*, 239–68. There, Beale makes a compelling case that the New Testament presents Jesus as the "way" so that the Jewish people will see that they, who are still in exile, can come back into fellowship with God through him. Hence the emphasis on the "way" in Isaiah and in Acts: Israel's not returned yet, and they do not return until Jesus brings them to God.

24. Also worth mentioning is N. T. Wright's interesting construal of Matthew's early chapters. To Wright, Matthew begins with a Genesis-like genealogy (Matt 1), then has Jesus surviving an Exodus-like escape from slaughter (Matt 1); then after baptism, a parallel to the exodus (Matt 3), Jesus withstands a time of testing in the wilderness (Matt 4), paralleling both Leviticus and Numbers only to then stand up and speak the Word to his hearers (Matt 5–7), like Moses in Deuteronomy. See Wright, *New Testament*, 402.

25. For an equation of the promise to Abraham with the promise to David, see Goldsworthy, *CCBT*, 111–32.

WHAT IS CHRIST-CENTERED BIBLICAL THEOLOGY TRYING TO DO?

a godly seed to Abraham, and he not only rules eternally but "makes many to be accounted righteous" (Isa 53:11) by his work at the cross. As the faithful covenant partner, he becomes qualified to save the people from their sins (1:21) by paying their ransom (20:29), establishing a new covenant in his blood (26:28).[26]

One major contribution of Dempster's *Dominion and Dynasty* is his capable demonstration of the kingly structure of the TNK. Concluding with Chronicles's restatement of dynastic history, the Tanach "awaits a Davidic king who will (like David and Solomon, only in a greater and eternal way) build the temple."[27] This is because, Dempster says, echoing Irenaeus, Jesus's life recapitulates the lives of both Adam and Israel:[28] He accomplishes in his perfect work as the Son of Man that which the people of God had failed to accomplish in every opportunity prior. This point sets up the next identifier of Jesus.

Adam, the One in Whom Is the New Creation Full of God's Presence (Matt 1:23; 18:20; 28:20)

Luke spends the first two chapters of his Gospel anchoring Jesus's identity in Old Testament history, similar to Matthew. In chapter 3, Luke gives Jesus's genealogy, differing from Matthew's in that Jesus is traced all the way back to Adam (3:38), who is the "son of God." Identifying Jesus as the son of Adam identifies Jesus with humanity so that he can recapitulate the life of Adam in his failure and thus save people who descend from him.[29] Hence Irenaeus, seeking to vivify the connection, draws two clear parallels between Adam and Jesus: Whereas Adam was born of virgin ground, Jesus was born of a virgin woman; whereas the

---

26. Worth mentioning is Wellum's *Person of Christ*, 51–64, in which he shows the importance of Jesus as the faithful and obedient "people of God" in himself. Jesus is the only way, Wellum shows (echoing Anselm from a thousand years earlier in *Cur Deus Homo*), that sinful people can be saved: God somehow identifies with them and pays their ransom on their behalf.

27. Dempster, *Dominion and Dynasty*, 231–32. It might be argued that the Christian way of organizing the Old Testament, placing the "minor prophets" at the end, concluding with Malachi, anticipates that the next thing that will occur in revelatory history will be God's appearing in his temple (Mal 4:1). Dempster's point is well made: The anticipation of a Davidic king is a clarifying necessity that is often missed by ignoring the Tanach structure.

28. Dempster, *Dominion and Dynasty*, 231–32.

29. Reeves, *Rejoicing in Christ*, 48–53. Echoing Anselm, Reeves, in a sample quote, says, "Only because he is human can he redeem our humanity."

tree of the knowledge of good and evil in the garden became the tree of disobedience, the cross became Jesus's tree of obedience.[30]

But this point does not make a distinct contribution from the previous one unless one aspect is added: Jesus, in obeying his Father, does so on humanity's behalf to the end that humanity can enter back into God's presence in the saving way that was lost in the fall. So Paul says that it is by Christ's obedience that many are made righteous and that believers, through him, even reign in the very royalty that he possesses (Rom 5:17, 19). In this way, "Christ died, the righteous for the unrighteous, that he might *bring us to God*" (1 Pet 3:18; emphasis added).

The emphasis of Beale's *New Testament Biblical Theology* is on Jesus's recapitulation that establishes humanity's entrance into new creation in which they live godly lives (cf. Titus 2:11–14). Because of Jesus's perfect life, substitutionary death, and exaltation, the new covenant people that he creates, comprised of believing Jew and Gentile, are "the end-time Israel" who come "into existence as an eschatological new creation in fulfillment of OT prophecy."[31] That is, following prophetic promises of a new covenant people who love and serve the Lord (e.g., Jer 31:31–34), they thus are characterized by living like Jesus in fellowship with the Father, experiencing, by the Holy Spirit dwelling within, the beginning of the eschatological new creation.[32] This is only because Jesus, as Oscar Cullmann has shown, is the last Adam who succeeds and can thus, on this basis alone, "remake men."[33] Christ the Word had earlier created good—yet fallible—people by breathing into the dust of the ground (Gen 2:7); in the last days he was remaking people "from above" (John 3:3). As the obedient God-man, only he could do this. This point explains why emphasis throughout Matthew's Gospel is placed on his presence with his followers (1:23; 18:20; 28:20): He is himself their very life as they journey by faith (Col 3:4).

Thus far, Jesus is the kingly Son of David who recapitulates both Adam (as man) and Israel (as the people of God). By his perfect life, substitutionary death, and resurrection, he and he alone is able to remake God's creation, filling it with his presence. Truly, as both Testaments aim to show (Old: Prov 8:12–31; New: John 1:3–4; Col 1:16; Heb 1:3–4), it is *his own* creation that he intends to make new and stay present with it forever.[34]

30. See Irenaeus, *On the Apostolic Preaching*, 53.
31. See Beale, *New Testament Biblical Theology*, 835.
32. Beale, *New Testament Biblical Theology*, 961.
33. See Cullmann, *Christology of the New Testament*, 104–6.
34. Worth mentioning is Beale's argument throughout many of his works (*Union*

The Word Who Is God (Matt 1:21; 11:27)

Hays's aforementioned *Reading Backwards* is an attempt to prove, contrary to works from such names as Bart Ehrman,[35] that each Gospel—not just John, supposedly written much later than the rest—aims to present Jesus as no less than the full presence of divinity in a human life. Hays aims in response to show that each Gospel has its own distinct witness to Jesus's divinity. For example, Hays highlights Jesus's ability to calm storms (4:38–41), which only God can do (Ps 107:23); Matthew's conclusion that Jesus will be with his disciples in fulfillment of the God-with-us promise (28:20; cf. 1:23); and Luke's easy-to-miss equation of Jesus with the God of Israel (8:39). The point is clear: The Gospel writers want to convey that Jesus is no less than the incarnate Son of God who is worthy of faith and praise.[36]

Similarly, in a series of well-received essays, Richard Bauckham considered the question of why the earliest Christians, many Jewish, were willing to worship Jesus with such language of divinity that he was identified with the God of Jewish monotheism. In his celebrated essay "God Crucified," Bauckham argues that the reason these early believers exalted Jesus is because, to them, Jesus "belonged inherently to who God is."[37] Whereas Jewish believers would have daily recited the *shema* (remembering God's uniqueness), yet these believers saw in the person and work of Jesus the fullness of saving divinity, appropriate to his name as Yeshua, "God who saves." That is why, as Bauckham shows, the uniqueness of God in the *shema* is restated repeatedly throughout the New Testament (e.g., Mark 12:29; John 10:30; Rom 3:26; 1 Cor 8:6; Jas 2:19): He remains unique as the one true God. Since Jesus is also worshiped, the conclusion must be that Jesus is identifiable with the one God of Israel (Matt 14:33; 28:17; John 9:38; 20:28)."[38] Thus, Paul's treatment of Jesus

---

with the Resurrected Christ, New Testament Biblical Theology, and Temple and the Church's Mission) that the presence of God in the New Testament is meant to be understood in the context of his filling presence in the tabernacle and temple in the Old Testament. God's filling glory blesses Israel's tabernacle/temple obedience (Exod 40; Lev 9; 2 Chron 5, 7; etc.), so because of Christ's obedience, those who believe in him are "filled" (Col 2:10) and are the "Temple of the Holy Spirit" (1 Cor 6:19).

35. See Ehrman, *How Jesus Became God*.
36. Hays, *Reading Backwards*.
37. Bauckham, *Jesus and the God of Israel*, 30–32.
38. Bauckham, *Jesus and the God of Israel*, 94–100.

as divine was not an innovation but a response to what he saw happen.[39] In short, the messianic Jewish believers could not avoid Jesus's divinity, and neither would they want to. He was not merely given divine characteristics in some writings or sermons, but he was everywhere worthy of being called "Lord" or something equivalent (Acts 2:36; 3:15; 5:31; 7:52, 8:24; 9:5; 10:36).

If, then, his divinity as the saving God-man is so clearly a shared conviction, Wellum asks, why is Jesus not everywhere in the New Testament referred to as the Word, the God-man, etc.? In other words, engaging Ehrman and similar thinkers, why is Jesus's divinity made so explicit in John but not so much in the other Gospels or on every page of the New Testament? Wellum says that the resolution is not nearly as difficult as it seems: Virtually every writer of the New Testament *does* refer to Jesus in terms of divinity, in one way or another. If the terms are more explicit in some areas than others, the reason is that his uniqueness as the God-man, which is the very fountainhead of the Christian message, needs to be explicated.[40]

But one might take the response a step further, as Wellum does (echoing Anselm): The Old Testament everywhere demonstrates man's value in the eyes of God (Gen 2:18–20; Ps 8:3–4; Ezek 18:32; Hos 2:23), but it also highlights that man's sinful state is such that he cannot atone for, and thus save, himself (e.g., Job 15:14, 25:4; Ps 130:4). Nevertheless, since man owes the debt, he alone is responsible to pay it.[41] So how else could Jesus be worthy of making the payment if he did not fully identify with humanity? And still further, how could Jesus, as Wellum posits, bear the just punishment for man's sin were he not able, himself constituting divine justice, to do so?[42] The point here is not to labor details. It is to suggest that textual preoccupation can lead one to, as it were, "miss the forest for the trees," the trees representing proofs of Jesus's divinity or lack thereof in isolated texts and the forest representing that the only way he could possibly have done what he did is if he is indeed the Son of God. Thus the orthodox in the early church took it as self-evident that Jesus must be eternally God the Son: There is no salvation otherwise, and no other explanation of the facts can be true.

---

39. Bauckham, *Jesus and the God of Israel*, 200–230.
40. Wellum, *Person of Christ*, 65–67.
41. See Anselm, *Cur Deus Homo* 2.2–3.
42. Wellum, *Person of Christ*, 45–49.

Thus, the emphasis in the early church is on Christ's being the Word made flesh. That Jesus was called the Word does not imply that John's Gospel was everyone's favorite. The believers' whole understanding of reality had been changed by learning that the Word who made all things and in whom all things subsist had stepped into his creation to identify with and save humanity. Worth mentioning here is Augustine's treatment of the Nicene Creed's teaching. Commenting on the creed's stating that the eternally begotten Word "came down from heaven, and became incarnate," Augustine states, rather boldly, "The Word condescended to also *be created among men*," asserting that this—the incarnation—is in view when he speaks as the wisdom of God being "created" in Prov 8:22.[43] Christ is not "created" in the sense that, as Arius would have said, there was a period in eternity when Christ was not; but he, according to the eternal economy of God, took to himself a human nature and perfected it so that he could perfect human nature. All that Christ assumes, concluded Gregory of Nazianzus, Christ heals and perfects.[44]

As earlier mentioned, Irenaeus's *On the Apostolic Preaching* deserves to be read alongside all of the best of Christ-centered biblical theology today. In fact, if Carl Trueman's charge is correct that biblical theology in showing Jesus as the Christ is sometimes guilty of inadequately considering the metaphysical implications of the Son as the eternal Word,[45] Irenaeus's work is unique. Irenaeus, like Paul in Athens, begins with ontology, showing that Christ is not only the promised messiah but the eternal Word who said to Moses, "I am who I am" (Exod 3:6). The Son, as the Word who orders all things, is the Christ insofar as his work indeed redeems that which was already his.[46] Irenaeus then proceeds to focus the rest of the work on showing that the apostles' message was that Christ the Word recapitulated virtually every aspect of Old Testament history. The effect of Christ's work is that as believers trust in him, they learn to

---

43. See Augustine, *On Faith and the Creed*, 3.

44. Gregory of Nazianzus, *Letter to Cledonius 101*, in *On God and Christ*, 161.

45. See Trueman, "Preface" in Carter, *Contemplating God*, xi. Trueman argues that whereas biblical theology rightly engages economy, by ignoring eternal ontology, it collapses the transcendent into the immanent. See also his article "Revolutionary Balancing Act," 1–4. For a sample quote, "One of the problems I have with a relentless diet of biblical-theological sermons from less talented (i.e., most of us) preachers is their boring mediocrity . . . contrived contortions of passages which are engaged in to produce the answer, 'Jesus' every week. It doesn't matter what the text is; the sermon is always the same."

46. See Irenaeus, *On Apostolic Preaching*, 28.

carry out the ultimate telos of the law, love for God and love for others (Matt 22:31), fulfilling its righteous requirement in him.[47]

To summarize, the New Testament in broad strokes paints Jesus (as does the history of Christian teaching) as the true Israel, the Davidic king, the last Adam who brings a new creation, and the Word for whom and by whom all things exist. Such a Christ-centered orientation to the biblical narrative seems hardly deficient as a representative of truly Christian preaching of the spirit of Acts. To begin on this presupposition is to let the Living Word lead the way into and through his written word.

How Does the Bible Present Him?

Following the previous question focused on *who* the Bible presents Jesus to be, the next question concerns *how* the Bible does so. As a guide, Carter shows that there are primarily five ways that Jesus is presented in Scripture.[48] Each of these ways, or interpretive senses, will be considered below, with a Gospel explanation preceding the final sense.

Typology

In typology, a person, event, or institution present in an earlier part of a narrative is a purposeful impression, image, example, or pattern prefiguring something greater later in the narrative. Types, as Barrett has noted, point forward not only to greater but to climactic realizations.[49]

The ultimate example of typology is in the typological orientation of the Old Testament prophets' usage of earlier Old Testament history to describe the perfect and saving experience of the messianic day. Observing this, Donald Robinson summarizes, "Israel's imperfect past will be experienced perfectly in the last day, in the new creation."[50] Perhaps the best way to understand this is to have a look at Goldsworthy's paradigm for biblical unity, which he calls the "Robinson-Hebert Schema" (named after his mentor Donald Robinson and Hebert.) In Goldsworthy's paradigm, the Bible outlines redemptive history in three stages: Old Testament history (type), prophetic eschatology (confirmation of the type),

---

47. Irenaeus, *On Apostolic Preaching*, 83.
48. See Carter, "Premodern Approach," 118–19.
49. See Barrett, *Canon, Covenant, and Christology*, 29–38.
50. See Goldsworthy, *CCBT*, 172–73.

and messianic fulfillment/day of the Lord (antitype). At each step the themes are the same, though the first stage shows actual occurrences of the themes in history, the second uses those occurrences to prefigure the messianic day, and then the day of the Lord brings the fulfillment.

First is Old Testament history (type):

Old Testament History
Creation (Gen 1–2)
Covenant (Gen 9; 12; 15; etc.)
Exodus (Exod 12–14)
Entry into and Possession of Land (Josh 3–5; 10–11)
Jerusalem (2 Sam 5; 1 Chron 11) and Temple (1 Kgs 5–8; 2 Chron 2–4)
Davidic King (2 Sam 7; 1 Kgs 8)

Most biblical theologians and scholars would agree that these themes represent the most important aspects of the Old Testament narrative. Evangelical Christianity treats these events as revelatory ends to themselves. They constitute revelatory truth meant to be seen and heard as God's word.

But Goldsworthy, commenting on the New Testament's reading of the Old, says that these events are, in the final analysis, preparatory for the messianic day. Hence, the Old Testament prophets show that the announcement of the "day of the Lord" brings these same themes in newness (thus confirming the types):[51]

Old Testament History	OT Eschatological Promise
Creation (Gen 1–2)	New Creation (Isa 11:1–9; 65:17–18)
Covenant (Gen 9; 12; 15; etc.)	New Covenant (Jer 31:31–34)
Exodus (Exod 12–14)	New Exodus (Isa 40:1–5)
Entry into and Possession of Land (Josh 3–5; 10–11)	New Entry into and Possession of Land (Ezek 34:11–16; 36:24–28)
Jerusalem (2 Sam 5; 1 Chron 11) and Temple (1 Kgs 5–8; 2 Chron 2–4)	New Jerusalem (Isa 44:24–28) and Temple (Hag 1–2; Zech 4:6–9)
Davidic King (2 Sam 7; 1 Kgs 8)	New Davidic King (Jer 23:1–6; Ezek 34; Amos 9:11)

One should not be surprised to find that the New Testament's structure follows this same thematic framework. In the person and work of Jesus

---

51. Goldsworthy, *CCBT*, 148.

the Son of God, what was revelatory and preparatory about the themes becomes redemptive, and eternally and gloriously so. The effect is that although redemptive perfection is not yet fully present, it is, nevertheless, present and decisive.[52] Thus Goldsworthy proposes that the New Testament is written to present the fullness of redemption (the antitype) as:[53]

Old Testament History	OT Eschatological Promise	New Testament Fulfillment
Creation (Gen 1–2)	New Creation (Isa 11:1–9; 65:17–18)	Jesus Establishes New Creation (John 1; 20:22; 2 Cor 5:17; Gal 6:15)
Covenant (Gen 9; 12; 15; etc.)	New Covenant (Jer 31:31–34)	Jesus Establishes New Covenant (Matt 26:28; 2 Cor 3:6; Heb 8)
Exodus (Exod 12–14)	New Exodus (Isa 40:1–5)	Jesus Leads Believers in a New Exodus (Luke 9:31; Matt 6:13; 1 Cor 10:6–11)
Entry into and Possession of Land (Josh 3–5; 10–11)	New Entry into and Possession of Land (Ezek 34:11–16; 36:24–28)	Jesus Is the "Land" in which God Is Met (Heb 12:22–24; Rev 14:1)
Jerusalem (2 Sam 5; 1 Chron 11) and Temple (1 Kgs 5–8; 2 Chron 2–4)	New Jerusalem (Isa 44:24–28) and Temple (Hag 1–2; Zech 4:6–9)	Jesus's New Jerusalem (Gal 4:26; Rev 21:21) and Temple (1 Cor 3:17; 2 Cor 6:16; 1 Pet 2:6)
Davidic King (2 Sam 7; 1 Kgs 8)	*New* Davidic King (Jer 23:1 6; Ezek 34; Amos 9:11).	Jesus as Davidic King of Kings (Matt 9:27; 12:23; 15:22; 21:9; Rom 1:1–4)

Goldsworthy's paradigm does not exhaust typology's fullness. The paradigm shows the structural integrity and unity of the biblical narrative in terms of typology. Scripture does, indeed, have a typological structure, which would explain why Goppelt argued that the primary revelatory purpose of the Old Testament is to communicate the gospel in typical form to both the church and the world.[54] Thus Leonhard Goppelt devotes the entirety of his *Typos* to showing how the New Testament cannot be understood apart from understanding how Christ and his work is the

---

52. Beale's comment is appropriate, building on Ladd's "already and not yet" explanation, that believers experience the beginning of the eschatological new creation so that it changes how they live. Beale, *New Testament Biblical Theology*, 961. See also Ladd, *Presence of the Future*, 327–28.

53. Goldsworthy, *CCBT*, 150–69.

54. Goppelt, *Typos*, 204–5.

antitype of what came before. New creation is the antitype of creation, the new covenant is the antitype of the old, and so on.

If this construal is difficult to accept, one has only to remember Matt 12, where Jesus says repeatedly that his coming is *greater* than what occurred in earlier redemptive history, including what those occurrences represent in Jesus's usual method of synecdoche: the temple (old covenant worship; 12:6); Jonah (and the prophetic ministry; 12:41); and Solomon (and the kingship; 12:42).[55] That the Christ-event is greater than all that came before is not an insight; that that is the point might be.

Prophecies

Interestingly, Carter argues that prophecies are the least-frequent Christological tool present in the Old Testament.[56] Carter does not seem to intend to suggest that prophecies are sparse, only that in keeping with God's usual method of employing figures, parables, and riddles to reveal his redemptive truth,[57] a study of Christ's presence in the Old Testament that leans *exclusively* (or even primarily) on direct prophecies will find itself limited in comparison to what is available.

These observations explain two New Testament phenomena: first, Paul's continual insistence on Christ's revelation of mysteries (*mysterion*) once hidden (Rom 16:25; Eph 1:9; 3:3; 3:9; Col 1:27); that is, as Dempster has said, there would be a messiah, he would come from David, and he would reign. Which person is the messiah, the exact branch from David's lineage, and the type of reign he would have were not entirely clear. When Jesus came, however, clarity is available when reflecting on the details of his life: His name is Yeshua ("God saves"), he is from David's lineage, and he rose from death to send out God's Spirit so that his followers could live in his presence and power until he returns.

The above is a small example of the nature of Old Testament messianic prophecy and the dangers of leaning too heavily on it. On the other hand, once the Christ-event occurred, those who knew him could not avoid the conclusion that he was the one promised. Too much "lined up" for another explanation to be legitimate. The Old Testament was a

---

55. Goppelt, *Typos*, 228.
56. Carter, "Premodern View," in *Five Views*, 239.
57. A central argument to Grier's *Momentous Event*, citing Num 12:8; Hos 12:10; Mark 4:34; John 16:25–29.

witness to him who had, for his followers, reoriented reality.[58] Indeed, Augustine taught that Christianity *is* Christology: the pursuit of "knowing Christ" in all things (1 Cor 2:2; Phil 3:8).[59] The Scripture's mission and the church's job is, as he said, to "tell of Christ and call to love."[60] So *all* of the promises of God—whether explicit or not—find their "amen" in him (2 Cor 1:20). Believers may not think otherwise.

Prosopology

Prosopology depends on an advanced Christology. It applies to hermeneutics the observation that the New Testament identifies particular prayerful Old Testament voices as the voice of the Son speaking to the Father, as when Heb 10:4–5 has Jesus speaking the very words of Ps 40 to the Father. Via prosopology, the reader, on Christological grounds, hears the voice of Christ the Word throughout Old Testament in prayerful, sometimes inner-Trinitarian texts.

Matthew Bates defines prosopological exegesis somewhat more broadly:

> A reading technique whereby an interpreter seeks to overcome a real or perceived ambiguity regarding the identity of the speakers or addressees (or both) in the divinely inspired source text by assigning nontrivial *prosopa* (i.e. nontrivial vis-a-vis the plain sense of the text) to the speakers or addressees (or both) in order to make sense of the text.[61]

In other words, as Michael Cameron has said, prosopology is "impersonation," whereby a person—in the case of the Old Testament, by speaking—prefigures someone else, in this case Christ.[62] Carter summarizes prosopology in terms of Christ's presence via the Father's speech to the Son (see how Old Testament texts are interpreted in Heb 1), the Son's replies, or the messiah's prophetic proclamation. Carter says, thus,

---

58. See O'Keefe and Reno, *Sanctified Vision*, 114–40. Also worth mentioning is Brian Daley's work in *God Visible*, showing that the fathers believed that one could not understand reality apart from Christ the Word, hence their repeated emphasis on the fullness of his identity.

59. Daley, *God Visible*, 173.

60. See Augustine, *Instructing Beginners in the Faith*, 4.8.

61. Bates, *Hermeneutics of the Apostolic Proclamation*, 218, quoted in Carter, *ISGT*, 192.

62. Cameron, *Christ Meets Me Everywhere*, 20.

"The Old Testament is not just about Jesus, but *by* Jesus, the Son and Messiah."[63] Via prosopology, every passage is, in some way, the voice of Christ himself.

Such an understanding of the Old Testament enables Carter to relabel prosopological exegesis as *Christological Literalism*: By prefigurement, those who predated Christ typified his submission to and trust in the Father. If this is true, then every text has some Christological connection.[64] Since Jesus said himself that only he makes the Father known (Matt 11:27), any telling forth of fellowship between man and God, as in the Psalms or any other Old Testament text, must at some level find its source in Christ the Son of God. As Boersma has said, whereas Jesus is the antitype to earlier types, he is, as the Word, first the *arche*typal source of the earlier types.[65] Thus, in *Christological literalism*, the historical context does not drop out in connecting the text to Christ; instead, it finds both its source and ultimate fulfillment—and thus its literal understanding—in its relationship to Christ.

Recapitulation[66]

In recapitulation, the "characters" of the Old Testament, regardless who, personally experience aspects of what Jesus would need to experience in order to bring redemption to humanity and, in his body, reconcile man to God.

Based on Eph 1:10, where Christ "sums up all things" in himself, Christ-centered biblical theologians since Irenaeus have drawn attention to Jesus's living the life that humanity should live but has not. John Behr, commenting on Irenaeus's *Heresies* (1.9.2), concludes of his recapitulation view that, to Irenaeus, "The gospel of the crucified one is . . .

---

63. Carter, "Premodern View," in *Five Views*, 240; emphasis added.

64. See Carter, *ISGT*, 195–99.

65. See Boersma, *Five Things*, 34–35; Boersma, *Scripture as Real Presence*, 24–25. Boersma and typology will be returned to in detail in a later chapter.

66. Worth mentioning at the beginning of this section is that the forward-looking historical element in Christological literalism is essentially equivalent to recapitulation. What separates recapitulation as a distinct heading is its ability, as historically oriented, to stand alone as a redemptive-historical approach. Christological literalism is a multidirectional approach that partners recapitulation with a Christological/theological ontology. This fact is probably why Carter categorizes recapitulation alone in his "premodern" contribution to *Five Views*, while containing it within Christological literalism in *ISGT*.

CHRIST AND THEOLOGY

the prism by which Scripture is seen as speaking of Christ, recapitulating what had previously been written in the proclamation of the earthly sojourn of the Word of God."[67] As a sort of response to (and affirmation of) Dempster's assertion that one cannot understand the New Testament without understanding the Old, Irenaeus and biblical theologians since him have taught that one cannot understand the Old without seeing Jesus as the perfect version of all that came before. The Testaments thus mirror each other: The Old shows the need for salvation, full of God's promises that he will bring it; the New shows how God brought it, and how it affects the world (i.e., in the new lives of Christians), hence Augustine's famous maxim: "In the Old Testament the New is concealed; in the New the Old revealed."[68] In this same vein, Beale's *New Testament Biblical Theology* shows that not only does Christ recapitulate Adam, Israel, and all of the godly, but that Christians then, by Christ's own Spirit within (Rom 8:9–11), recapitulate the same.

What distinguishes aforementioned prosopology from recapitulation is that whereas the former sees *Christ as eternal Word* speaking via real human, preincarnate voices, the latter sees *Christ as the obedient man* prefigured in the real lives of those who predated the incarnation. Carter's Christological literalism can be summarized as an approach that partners historically oriented recapitulation with prosopology, which is based on a Christological-theological ontology, into a multidirectional approach to Scripture as Christ's voice. Prosopology, though not confined to emphasis on Christ's divinity, rests on an advanced Christology; recapitulation also considers anthropology, focusing on Christ's life for man's sake. As Wellum (and Anselm before him) have made clear, only via the God-man can man the sinner be reconciled to God the holy.[69]

The Gospel

In summary, the gospel is the preaching of Christ from the Scriptures as the true Israel, the Davidic king, the last Adam who brings salvation, and the eternal Word by means of prophecy, typology, prosopology, and recapitulation. According to Paul, the gospel concerns God's Son *as*

---

67. See the discussion in Behr, *Formation of Christian Theology*, 123.

68. Augustine, *Quaestiones in Heptateuchum VII*. See also Augustine, *On the Spirit and the Letter* 27.

69. See Wellum, *Person of Christ*, 45–50; echoing Anselm *Cur Deus Homo* 2.2.

descended from David according to the flesh (Rom 1:1–3); thus Jesus preaches that the gospel is his own establishment of the kingdom of God (Mark 1:15; Matt 12:28). By his death, burial, and resurrection (1 Cor 15:1–8), he brings righteousness, peace, and joy via the indwelling of the Holy Spirit which is the content of the kingdom (Rom 14:17). For this reason, Vos has drawn attention to the difference between how saving faith is presented in the Synoptic Gospels versus John's Gospel: In the former, people are called to believe in and be changed by the gospel (Mark 1:15; 10:29; 16:15); in the latter, they are called to believe in Jesus as the God-man who saves (1:12–13; 3:16; 5:24; 7:38; 14:1). The objects of faith are one and the same: Jesus, the God-man who saves, because he *is* the gospel.[70]

Thus many key New Testament texts explain the gospel (some form of *evangelion*) in terms of Old Testament realities. As a brief sampling:

- In Gal 3:8, the scriptural promise to Abraham of a blessed seed (Gen 12:1–3) is called the gospel.
- In 1 Pet 1:22–25, the eternal Word of God that never changes or fades (Isa 40:6–8) is called the gospel by which believers are saved.
- In 1 Cor 15:1–8, the gospel which saves is defined in terms of Jesus's death according to the Scriptures, his burial, his resurrection according to the Scriptures, and subsequent appearances.

A multitude of texts define the gospel in terms of Jesus's fulfillment of promises and patterns so that humanity will be restored to God, hence Goldsworthy's definition of the gospel as "man restored to right relationships in Christ . . . restoration of relationships between God, man, and the world."[71] Similarly, Calvin said that the gospel "includes all of the promises by which God reconciles men to himself," through which "sinners, without any merit of their own, are justified by the paternal indulgence of God."[72]

If the above were said to exhaust the matter completely, one might think that Christ only relates to the Old Testament via prophetic promise. It seems clear, however, that to say as much would not go far enough.

---

70. See Vos, *Teaching of Jesus*, 88–90.

71. In Goldsworthy, *Gospel and Kingdom*, 122.

72. See Calvin, *Inst.*, 2.9.2, 2.10.4. Note Calvin's highlighting of the *paternal indulgence* of God. It is when one hears God's voice in his Son, *as Father*, that they run home to him. The gospel has a Trinitarian shape.

CHRIST AND THEOLOGY

If Christ is (a) the Word, (b) the antitypical figure of all prefigurements, and (c) the archetype of all previous types, then his relationship to the Old Testament extends beyond history. He is himself the source, means, and goal of all of redemptive history. In other words, if, as Paul says, "all things exist . . . through him and for him" (Col 1:16), it is especially true of the history of revelation, what Augustine called *sacred history*.[73] After all, God is only known because the Word who is the Son makes him known (Matt 11:27; John 1:18; 14:6–8).

This project's introduction defined the gospel, therefore, as this: *The promise, confirmation, and fulfillment of God's plan to, through Jesus Christ, establish life-giving fellowship between himself and lost people for a promised eternity in new heavens and new earth that is nothing less than the eternal enjoyment of his presence, which is the beatific vision.* Notice that central to the gospel is fulfillment of promises for restoration, particularly of fellowship between God and people. The gospel, then, is the proclamation of the Old Testament as a Christ-centered unity on both theological and historical grounds. Carter, therefore, echoing Augustine and Irenaeus, strikingly defines the gospel in terms of Christology and its presence in the Old Testament:

> The Christological interpretation of the Old Testament is a matter of Christ's personal authority. It is something very close to what Paul calls 'the gospel' in Galatians, and therefore not something made up by human beings. *It is the gospel of God.* That Jesus has in his death and resurrection fulfilled the Old Testament messianic hope is definitely good news.[74]

The conflation of the gospel with Christ's having fulfilled the Old Testament messianic promise anticipates one more way that Christ is present in the Old Testament, purposely separated from the rest of the list by this brief "gospel" interlude. The reason for separation is this: The following sense, not without controversy among evangelicals,[75] can only legitimately be based on strong Christology and bibliology. The gospel, by which God's redemption establishes peoples' fellowship with him, becomes, as will be seen later, the way in which believers' understanding of reality is reoriented around Christ the Word. The gospel, which concerns both the

---

73. See Augustine, *De Doctrina Christ* II, 28, 42–44; see also Oort's comments in "End Is Now," 2.

74. Carter, *ISGT*, 141; emphasis added.

75. See, for instance, Goldsworthy's considerable criticisms of allegorical sense in *GCH*, 101–108.

(divine and human) person and work of Christ, becomes new spectacles, making visible new things which were not visible before. If Christ is the Word, sacred texts can be heard practically via what Peter Stuhlmaker has called a "Christological clamp": The Old and New Testaments cannot be bifurcated from each other. The Old Testament's Christological *res*, all through this chapter considered in depth,[76] is not a theoretical parallel to New Testament faith. Rather, it tells of the working of God with his people in earlier days so that his people in the current day can be sure they are in the truth.[77]

Spiritual Sense

This sense depends like prosopology upon both an advanced Christology and bibliology. Old Testament texts, regardless of genre, have not only a Christological meaning via their ontological or historical relationship to Christ the Word, but they might have some type of application to the believing hearer that is not immediately obvious in the very words themselves. In other words, there might be a deeper meaning than what meets the eye. The believer hears the application based on their soteriological/ spiritual relationship with Christ who is both the text's source and goal.

This is on display in both Paul's allegorizing of Hagar and Sarah to make a gospel point (Gal 4:21–31; cf. Gen 21:10; Isa 54:1) and in Paul's implying a deeper application of the ox-muzzling text (Deut 25:4) to the financial support of pastors (1 Cor 9:10–12).[78] Note should be made that, based on the consistent yet analogical relationship of the temporal world to that which is eternal, there are legitimate parallels that can be identified in these perhaps seemingly unrelated texts. Christ the Word holds all things together (Col 1:17; Heb 1:3), so texts can, to borrow from one critic, be "decontextualized" to make a gospel point, whether a Christological teaching or an application to those who are united by faith to Christ.[79]

---

76. Stuhlmacher, *How to Do Biblical Theology*, 9, quoted in Barrett, *Canon, Covenant, and Christology*, 21.

77. This point depends on Packer's chapter on God's unchangeability in *Knowing God*, 75–81. Packer ends any speculation about a "ditch" between Scripture's historical context and the reader's context by saying that the God who inhabits eternity (Isa 57:15), and thus does not change and is not subject to time, is himself the connection.

78. It is also likely that Hos 11:1, mentioned earlier as applied to Jesus in Matt 2:14, illustrates the "deeper meaning" point as well.

79. Vlach, *How Does the New Testament*, 22. By "context," Vlach means grammatical-historical context.

Rather, to do so is to follow the apostles in their newly bespectacled view that because of the Christ-event, the Old Testament can only be (and is intended to be) understood as a witness to him. Actually, to read texts this way is not to "decontextualize" them at all but to apply their true Christological sense to the hearer's own context.

Since all texts are signs of eternal realities, texts can have (a) a historical, plain sense, (b) an allegorical/spiritual sense, (c) a moral sense, and (d) an eschatological (heavenly) sense. All of these senses must be both canonically consistent (and only can be if the gospel is clear and controlling) and noncontradictory to the historical sense of the text.[80] As Peter Masters, pastor of Spurgeon's Metropolitan Tabernacle since 1970, has pointed out, the very practice of the apostles themselves (in the aforementioned examples) shows that the gospel of the Son of God opens up the entirety of Holy Scripture for discipleship and instruction in this "spiritualizing" way. The Bible is a book, yes; but when read according to its divine purpose, it is not like any other book and thus should not be treated as such.[81] Although the historical sense of a passage is the historical basis of interpretation, the eternal basis is Christ as eternal Word who gives meaning to all things. To read his word in any other way is to, at worst, ignore his preeminence in all things, hence Carter's summary of

---

80. See Aquinas, *ST*, 1.1.10; see also Kreeft's helpful commentary notes in *Summa of the Summa*, 48–50.

For the sake of clarity, allegorical interpretation can be defined as spiritual interpretation of the meaning of a passage of Scripture considering the context of the reader as sheep listening for the voice of the Shepherd who speaks to them by Scripture. The grammatical-historical meaning of a text does not exhaust the ways in which the reader can appropriately receive and apply the passage. As chapter 3 will note, Origen operated with a threefold hermeneutical paradigm that included allegory while Augustine and his contemporary John Cassian expanded the threefold paradigm to include a fourth sense. In Augustine's paradigm, the *quadriga*, which dominated the hermeneutics of the Great Tradition through the medieval era, allegory is a secondary sense subject to both the rule of faith (that is, the biblical gospel articulated in different ways but consistently across different generations) and the literal/plain sense apprehended by grammatical-historical methodology.

81. See Masters, *Not Like Any Other Book*; Masters, in a way that would probably be striking to many evangelicals (were they more familiar with him), decimates a premodern methodology of interpretation that keeps the gospel central while keeping every page of Scripture the voice of Christ the Word to his sheep at all times. Masters's book, not even 150 pages, deserves wide readership, and is an example of a continuing presence of premodern exegetical methodology within evangelicalism even in a time when most say that it is only recently that evangelicals have begun to recover these methods. Masters shows the presence of the method in the likes of Calvin, Henry, and Spurgeon, among others.

the baseline presupposition of truly Christian interpretation (and what should be the baseline of Christ-centered, biblical-theological interpretation): "God speaks, and God speaks to us." "God speaks," in the historical sense of the passage, and "God speaks to us" in senses which stem from the first sense, bring the Christological truth of the eternal Word into the day of the hearer for their upbuilding and fellowship with him.[82] When the Bible is opened and met with eyes coming to behold God's glory in his Son, God acts on the individual in an effective way. The next section turns to the nature of that act.

What Act Does God Perform On the Reader?

Carter, as seen earlier, asserted that for biblical theology to be consistent with the Great Tradition, it will need to adopt John Webster's ontology of Scripture. To be clear, this project seeks to respond under the belief that Carter's proposed Christological literalism, though helpful, gives an insufficient place to redemptive history. The differences are hinted at in the aforementioned differences between recapitulation and prosopology. The current project seeks to follow Carter, building a Christocentric hermeneutic on the foundation of Webster's biblical ontology.

Webster's ontology can be articulated as such: God utilizes creaturely writing to serve his purposes, the most important of which is his self-presence. In short, "The biblical texts are creaturely realities set apart by the triune God to serve his self-presence."[83] The ultimate usage of Scripture is according to its purpose as God's "communicative presence,"[84] whereby it comprises, says Webster, "divinely instituted signs in the domain of the word," through which "[God] accomplishes his act of self-utterance through human auxiliaries."[85] Into his creation which he upholds and sustains, God speaks via the human auxiliaries of Scripture to make himself known.

The act is more than mere speech. As Timothy Ward has shown, citing texts such as Ps 29:5–8 ("the voice of the Lord breaks the cedars") and Isa 55:10–11 ("my Word . . . shall prosper in the thing for which I

---

82. Carter, *ISGT*, 187. What precedes is an introduction to the so-called *quadriga*, the fourfold interpretive framework of both the late patristic and medieval era. The *quadriga* will return to focus in the next chapter.

83. See Webster, *HS*, 17–27.

84. Webster, *HS*, 2.

85. Webster, *Domain of the Word*, 8–9.

sent it"), whenever the God of the Bible speaks, the effect is palpable. His speech is his act, and his act is effective in time and space.[86] As he speaks, those who hear him have direct contact with his presence, even if it is a condescended presence to human capacities (and by human capacities).[87]

What is the effect? Again, as Webster states, Scripture, as God's self-communication, "is, the act of the Father, Son and Spirit which establishes and maintains that saving fellowship with humankind in which God makes himself known to us and by us."[88] He speaks both his eternal nature and temporal acts in peoples' hearing, and his speech is able to effectively draw into and maintain fellowship with himself who is the Trinity. Hence, Jesus called Peter "blessed" for having been taught by the Father that Jesus is the Christ (Matt 16:17), and hence Jesus, in explaining why some come to him and some do not (John 6:45), cites Isa 54:13 which shows that God himself actively teaches people. God speaks by his Word, which is able to create, stir, and grow faith and obedience (Rom 10:10). God spoke in a sanctified way via the human writing of the text across many centuries until its final form; he further continues to utilize these writings to the same ends: conveying his presence to his hearers, redeeming and sustaining the fellowship that they share with him.

Such an understanding of God's continued usage of Scripture is a Christian appropriation of so-called "speech-act theory."[89] Ward summarizes speech-act theory in terms of language as "a means through which one person performs actions in relation to another."[90] When one speaks, one acts in reference to the one spoken to. Since God is eternal, sovereign, and in a covenantal relationship with those who are eternally chosen in his Son (Eph 1:3), a word spoken by him in an earlier time has the same nature as the word repeated at a later time. In other words, God's commands given in the Old Testament day have a revelatory relationship to the person reading thousands of years later.

Ward states that God's speech-action "is not an event that occurs only at the high points of God's linguistic action, such as his creating, cursing, and covenant-making. Instead it is characteristic of God's action

---

86. See Ward, *Words of Life*, 23.
87. Ward, *Words of Life*, 30, 36.
88. Webster, *HS*, 8.
89. See for instance, Searle, *Speech Acts*; for a reflection on speech-act that is more influenced by Christian metaphysics, see Wolterstorff's *Divine Discourse*. For additional analysis, see also Goldsworthy, *GCH*, 208–10.
90. Ward, *Words of Life*, 57.

that runs throughout the Old Testament."[91] The entirety of Scripture—not just the "high points"—are the exposition of God's action as Creator, Provider, and Redeemer. If that is the case, whenever Scripture is read and heard, it remains the set-apart voice of God unto the end of establishing and maintaining fellowship with his people through his Son. "*Communication from* God is therefore *communion with* God, when met with a response of trust from us."[92]

Church's Identity and Call

This communion is what constitutes the church's identity. It is the community of people throughout time who hear the Word of God as the Trinitarian voice to establish and maintain fellowship. Calvin, famously saying that the distinguishing marks of the true church are the right preaching of the gospel and right administration of the sacraments, thus elevated the primacy of the Word over all else: "If the church is founded on the doctrine of the apostles and prophets by which believers are enjoined to place their salvation in Christ, then if that doctrine is destroyed, how can the church continue to stand?"[93] In other words, the presence of the Word is what makes the church the church.

Webster adds that the church's primary act is a passive one, that is, the act of listening: "The definitive act of the church is faithful hearing of the gospel of salvation announced by the risen Christ in the Spirit's power through the service of Holy Scripture. As the *creatura verbi divini*, the creature of the divine Word, the church is the hearing church."[94] At first glance, the suggestion that the church's first task is listening might seem strange. Is not the church's job to "go" and "make disciples," and "baptize them?" Of course. Before a person can exercise that call, they must know how to direct people to hear; they need to have heard the call, which is why both Jesus's early followers (Matt 3:16) and his apostles (Matt 17:5) were told to *listen to him*: They will fail to call others to listen to Christ if they cannot hear him.

---

91. Ward, *Words of Life*, 23.
92. Ward, *Words of Life*, 31–32. Emphasis original. See also *Words of Life*, 65, for an interesting study of the times through Scripture that God is even equated with Scripture (e.g., Matt 19:4–5; Rom 9:17; 1 Thess 2:13).
93. Calvin, *Inst.*, 4.2.1.
94. Webster, *HS*, 44.

That is the way that the gospel is not only the message spoken in the Scripture, but the very means through which God calls and leads his people. Again, this makes the church the church: They hear, respond, obey, and participate in God's kingdom endeavor. The need for all three of (a) Christocentricity in the church's approach to Scripture (as in Christ-centered biblical theology), (b) healthy theocentricity (as in the Great Tradition), and (c) theocentric/Christocentric bibliology is obvious: Jesus is himself the eternal spoken Word who fulfills the promises of God and uses his sanctified means of speech, the Scripture, to shepherd his people in the truth. That last word—truth—leads to the final consideration worth examining. First, to summarize, what is the church? The body of people who listen to the Shepherd's presentation of himself via the Scriptures. As they hear, they feed.

How Can One Be Sure that What the Bible Presents Is God's Truth?

Christian Platonism

This section will consider the late modern tendency to relativize truth[95] and how biblical theology can respond effectively via a mature appropriation of the Christian Platonic framework (which it already implicitly holds). Proposed here is that for the listening church, the gospel performs the act of "hermeneutical conversion" such that believers can know what is true (after, of course, becoming convinced that they can know what is true) and find freedom in this knowledge (John 8:34; 1 John 5:20).

A major movement has arisen among evangelicals of recent years to return to what has been called Christian Platonism. Some well-known critics of Christian Platonism seem to confuse Christian Platonism with gnosticism, the latter of which teaches that the material world is evil and the nonmaterial world is good.[96] On the contrary, Christian Platonism is simply another way of labeling the framework of reality that renders Christian teaching intelligible. Many thinkers have thus ably shown that all Christians think within a Christian Platonic framework whether they

---

95. See Goldsworthy, *GCH*, 130–38; see also Wright, *Scripture and the Authority of God*, 5.

96. See, for instance, Wright, *History and Eschatology*.

realize it or not.[97] To help understand this, what Hans Boersma has called the "Five Points of Christian Platonism" is worth considering:

1. Anti-materialism—The physical realm is not all that exists. There is more than bodies.
2. Anti-mechanism—There is more than just mechanical cause and effect. Empirical observation does not answer every question. An impersonal view of reality is impossible.
3. Anti-nominalism—Two individual objects can share the same essence while maintaining distinctness and uniqueness.
4. Anti-relativism—Goodness exists as a property of being; humanity does not have the final word about whether something is "good."
5. Anti-skepticism—Humanity has the ability to know that which is real or true, even if it is an imperfect knowledge.[98]

Carter has shown elsewhere that Christian Platonism is distinct from pure Platonism in that the latter sees humanity as continuous with divine nature and thus capable of ascending by human effort to the realm of the divine. Conversely, the former maintains the distinction between humanity and divinity while also maintaining the possibility of engagement and interaction—in Christian terms, fellowship—between the two.[99]

The last point in Boersma's paradigm, when placed alongside of Carter's main point, is what serves this chapter's purpose best: Can truth be known? Can the church be sure that she is hearing Christ's voice? As Boersma implies, knowledge in a postlapsarian world is always going to be limited. "We know in part" (1 Cor 13:9, 12); "we don't know what we shall be . . ." (1 John 3:2). That unclarity does not mean that knowledge is *utterly* impossible. To suggest as much is self-defeating: A person would be saying that they *know* that nothing can be known. On the contrary, John essentially concludes his letter full of tests and proofs of God's presence in believers by saying, "I write these things to you who believe so that *you will know* that you have eternal life" (1 John 5:13; emphasis added). Knowledge might be imperfect, but at least knowledge exists. In fact, he who speaks to the church by his word has perfect knowledge (Ps 139:4; Isa 46:10; Rom 11:33), and his act of knowing is identical with

---

97. See, for instance, Gerson, *Platonism and Naturalism*.
98. Boersma, *Five Things*, 43.
99. See Carter, *ISGT*, 66; *Contemplating God*, 79–81.

his essence.[100] As the church listens to the voice of God by his Son the Word, they, though incapable of knowing all things, nevertheless hear him speak, who does. Augustine, in his comments on the Nicene Creed, stated that God the Father possesses "both the will and the power to declare himself with utmost clarity to minds designed to obtain the knowledge of Him;" this is quite the contrast to man, who struggles to put right words to thoughts that he wants to convey.[101] God is able, as seen in Bavinck's aforementioned quote, to perfectly convey what he intends, so that the human mind is able to receive it; "my word" says the prophet, "shall accomplish that which I purpose" (Isa 55:10).

Hermeneutical Conversion

But in order to hear God speak by his Son, an epistemological transformation must first occur. Webster calls this transformation *hermeneutical conversion*.[102] In it, the individual believer or group of believers learns how to hear God's voice, the gospel, as the unchanging Word given to them in their particular context. For example, this "conversion" for a twenty-first-century hearer would move them from a sort of individualized (and thus, relativized) way of approaching truth to a framework that begins by assuming the existence of knowable absolutes that are meant for good.[103] Many proposals for how to frame this transformation have been offered, such as Boersma's *Heavenly Participation*,[104] which will be engaged in later chapters. For now, Goldsworthy's description of the conversion will be engaged.

All through his career as a biblical theologian, Goldsworthy has sought to propagate a hermeneutical method that brings the thinker to see that the gospel—earlier described as the saving acts of God in the Son—is the only epistemological lens worth discerning reality. Goldsworthy's *GCH* shows a robust attempt to reconstruct a truly evangelical (that is, gospel-centered) approach to Scripture that assumes one can utilize critical tools in a precritical way.[105] As such, the Bible is a book, but,

---

100. See Aquinas, *ST*, 1.14.1 for an exhilarating study of God's perfect knowledge.
101. See Augustine, *On Faith and the Creed*, III.
102. See Webster, *HS*, 6, 70, 88.
103. Two good recent studies on how late modernism has arrived at subjectivity are Trueman, *Rise and Triumph*; Wilson, *Remaking the World*.
104. Boersma, *HP*,.
105. See Goldsworthy, *GCH*, 183–98.

echoing Masters, it is also much more. Goldsworthy engages somewhat with Kevin Vanhoozer to argue that a Trinitarian set of presuppositions helps one to read the Bible as inspired literature.[106] Then follows historical, then theological, then ministry considerations.[107] If truth is thought impossible to grasp because of the multitude of dangers present even from the beginning of any and every approach, a Trinitarian start holds immense promise.

Goldsworthy has himself been critical, along with other biblical theologians of his generation, of the use of so-called Greek categories to describe God's nature.[108] This does not seem to suggest any apprehension toward Nicene Trinitarianism, but it does seem to challenge some of the logical (and even biblical) implications of God being an eternal Trinity. In particular, as Steven Duby has said, God's perfections include his *aseity, immutability, impassibility, eternity,* and *simplicity*.[109] While König challenges the notions of aseity, immutability, impassibility, and simplicity, Cullmann challenges the notion of eternity. These thoughts are explained as Greek-inspired impositions on the God of the Bible who works in and saves in time. Similarly, Goldsworthy challenges the notion of spiritualizing/allegorizing in hermeneutics, construing such a practice as an imposition that hides the gospel; if this were true, it would be ironic given that the practice of allegorizing seems to have always been aimed at elucidating the gospel.[110]

Works like Duby's, as well as others like Matthew Barrett's *None Greater* and *Simply Trinity,* have attempted to show that any supposed difficulty in engaging divine metaphysics using so-called Greek categories is misplaced for one simple reason: Scripture itself marshals such categories to describe God. Every chapter of Barrett's *None Greater* begins with exposition of a scriptural text that illuminates the perfection studied. Duby draws attention to the fact that the New Testament itself incorporates terms such as "divinity," "deity," and "divine nature" to speak of what it means for God to be God. Further, Duby concludes that N.

---

106. Goldsworthy, *GCH*, 199–216.

107. Goldsworthy, *GCH*, 217–72.

108. See Goldsworthy, *GCH*, 91–108, 130–38. For the same argument by other writers who have influenced Goldsworthy, see Adrio König, *Here Am I!*; Cullmann, *Christ and Time*; *Christology of the New Testament*.

109. See Duby, *Jesus and the God*, 23–32. Also helpful is Dolezal's *God Without Parts*.

110. In a puzzling irony, Goldsworthy does not in his criticism engage any primary sources but only secondary sources, a point which he admits in *GCH*, 107–8.

T. Wright's call to return to biblical, Jewish categories (because, Wright supposes, Jesus himself would have been "puzzled" by the concept of a hypostatic union) drips with irony given that Paul, Jewish man that he was, used terms like "divinity" and "divine nature," in his own writing![111] That metaphysical concepts have no place in biblical theology will not stand, simply being ways of describing who and what God is, this God who has revealed himself as an eternal Trinity to temporal, time-and-space-bound humans.

So whereas Goldsworthy and other biblical theologians do well to locate the center of Christ-centered biblical theology in the person and work of Jesus, there might even need to be a further "conversion" of thought so that Scripture's metaphysical theological categories have room to work in the mind of the thinker. "Trinitarian" should not only mean "Nicene,"[112] but "biblical." Nevertheless, there appears to be a persisting friction between Trinitarian approaches and redemptive-historical approaches.

Goldsworthy demonstrates an example of hermeneutical conversion in his *According to Plan*. So explained, Goldsworthy says, naturalistic thought has to "convert" to allow God not only involvement but his due dominance in defining categories and terms. The gospel shows how sin and confusion have polluted humanity's thinking to the point that theistic considerations are at best marginalized, and how Jesus is the Son of God who enters creation to deal with sin and overcome this materialistic bias.[113] As regards approaching the nature of reality, people begin as *secular humanists*, where reality consists of "here and now," empirically defined. They are then presented with the gospel which, by showing Christ's identity, opens their thinking to the possibility of theism, though maintaining a commitment to anthropocentric reality. This step Goldsworthy calls *theistic humanism*. As the gospel continues to do its work, the next step is into *Christian theism*, where the God of the Bible becomes the unifying center of reality, even if Jesus as redeeming God-man has not yet, as it were, joined the Father on the hermeneutical throne.[114] Thus, the final hermeneutical step is *redeemed Christian theism*, where not only is

---

111. See Duby, *Jesus and the God*, 40–41. Duby is addressing N. T. Wright's comments in various works critical of "metaphysical" categories in favor of more "biblical ones" (see *How God Became King*, 11–13; *Incarnation*, 52–59; *Biblical Theology*, 157–58).

112. See Carter, *ISGT*, 111, 223.

113. See especially Goldsworthy, *According to Plan*, 29–70.

114. Cf. Rev 3:21; 7:17; 22:5.

reality theocentric or Yahweh-centric but Christocentric (since, based on their conversion, they now know Jesus as YHWH).[115]

This is the way that Christ leads people to learn to think like him. They have received "the mind of Christ" (1 Cor 2:14). For gospel-centric hermeneutical conversion to be truly anchored in the gospel by which Christ the Son, by his suffering, brings people to God (1 Pet 3:18), God's nature has to be a priority so that he can be truly known and enjoyed. Otherwise the gospel may not even be understood, let alone explained, if the gospel involves the suffering of God's Son and how this suffering brings people to God.[116] How the supposed absence of the language of metaphysical categories in the Bible could render them so off-limits in biblical theology is puzzling. "Trinity" is also absent from the Bible, though biblical theologians do not usually bristle at it. Biblical theologians know not only that the concept is everywhere in Scripture but that nothing is more central to the Christian faith (and to the nature of reality) than a right understanding of God, regardless of the grammatical latitude necessary.

Economy vs. Immanent

This friction is seen with little ambiguity in a series of periodicals from around 2000 by Graeme Goldsworthy and Carl Trueman. They traded respectful challenges regarding the relationship of Christ-centered biblical theology and theology proper. As aforementioned, Trueman argued that the Christ-centered approach has dangers because of (he fears) its purely historical, economic orientation. The net effect, according to Trueman, is that "divine economy without divine ontology is unstable and will collapse."[117] The church's creeds and confessions keep God's nature clear in the mind of the church.[118] So, says Trueman, ignoring them to give preeminence to the Christ-centered redemptive-historical approach will so emphasize God's saving acts that neither theology nor hermeneutics will ever ascend to what the saving acts say about God.

---

115. Goldsworthy, *According to Plan*, 48–58.

116. This is Fred Sanders's argument in *Deep Things of God*. To Sanders, the nature of the gospel has such a Trinitarian shape that one need not choose between being "gospel-centered" or "Trinity-centered."

117. Trueman, "Revolutionary Balancing Act," 1–4.

118. See Trueman's *Creedal Imperative* and its sequel *Crisis of Confidence*.

In response, Goldsworthy said that biblical theology merely tries to follow the biblical authors in letting the saving acts of God reveal his nature. Since the ultimate *res*[119] of the saving acts is Christ himself, without whom no Christian has any immediate access to any text's meaning, biblical theology seeks to see Christ so that he will lead everywhere else. Goldsworthy notes that the Apostles' Creed, Nicene Creed, and the Anglican Catechism all couch God's nature and person in economic terms.[120]

Goldsworthy might oversimplify the supposed economic priority in the aforementioned creeds. Each of them begins with God as he is (*in se*) before proceeding to God's works, especially in the Son. Although the economy is present in the creeds, their structure is not obviously or overwhelmingly economic but theological, explaining the economy in terms of the Trinitarian nature.

Perhaps Trueman oversimplifies in suggesting that economy-oriented approaches ignore theology. A look at the early chapters of Goldsworthy's *Preaching the Whole Bible as Christian Scripture* or Scobie's *The Ways of Our God* would surely convince anyone that a theological instinct is present. Although Goldsworthy and Scobie both put the emphasis in economy, neither ignores or marginalizes theology.

Nevertheless, based on aforementioned frequent comments of celebrated biblical theologians like Wright, Goldsworthy, König, and Cullmann, there is an uneasiness about so-called classical theism and the place that these categories should hold in biblical theology. These theologians seem to be good examples of the definition of Christ-centered biblical theology as defined in the previous chapter: They have a premodern understanding of God—that is, they believe in, worship, and see Scripture as the means to hear him. They also have a modern epistemology: they struggle to get beyond time and space to explain the nature of reality, even if, like Goldsworthy, they admit that God is beyond it. He is, somehow, so committed to his economy that what is beyond it (if anything is) cannot be known.

---

119. For any reader unfamiliar, *res* is simply Latin for "thing" or "object," though it has been used in various disciplines dating to classical times to refer to "purpose" or, in Platonic-influenced paradigms, the "real" to which the symbols point. Here, Christ is referred to as the purpose and reality from which the saving acts flow and to which they point.

120. Goldsworthy, "Ontology and Theology," 37–45. Worth noting is that as of 2021, Trueman has still not moved off of his conviction. His forward to Carter's *Contemplating God with the Great Tradition* demonstrates that he still holds that redemptive-historical biblical theology has serious limitations which theology alone can correct.

WHAT IS CHRIST-CENTERED BIBLICAL THEOLOGY TRYING TO DO?

Into this conversation, Craig Carter recently wrote a review of Zondervan's rerelease of Wayne Grudem's celebrated *Systematic Theology: An Introduction to Biblical Doctrine*. Carter's comments seem to finger the very nerve of the issue that seems to exist between theology-focused approaches and redemptive-historical approaches. To Carter, theology has a God-centric dual focus: first, God's inner being, and second, God in his outer working.[121] Theology uses the economy to move toward theology. Contemplation deduces what the acts of God must reveal about the being of God, asking the question: What must be true about God for God to have done what he has done?[122]

If this is the case, Carter says, then despite the name, Grudem's work is less a systematic theology and more of a biblical theology. Whereas systematics seek as their ultimate end the contemplation of God as he is and how that knowledge reshapes the thinker's continuous approach to Scripture, biblical theology's ultimate end is to find human authorial intent in light of the whole of Scripture (merely) as a part of systematics. As such, biblical theology is an important part of systematics but only a *part of it*.[123]

Thus, Grudem is probably guilty of something that he does not intend: Like Gabler and the earliest practitioners of biblical theology,[124] he refuses to begin the theological process with theology proper, creedally defined, on the grounds that to do so would be to impose a presupposition on the text. In so doing, he (unintentionally?) follows a biblicism that has more in common with the aforementioned anti-classical theistic biblical theology than it does with Nicene Orthodoxy. If so, Carter concludes, Grudem's embrace of eternal functional subordinationism should not be surprising:[125] the creeds help guard against using insufficient language to describe God. If in theology one only allows "biblical" language, one will likely fall prey to error at some point, whether heterodoxy or anthropocentric biblical delineation.

The fairness of Carter's critique is left to the reader. The point is that the criticism is weighty and is coming from several directions:[126] If bibli-

---

121. See also Turretin, *Institutes of Elenctic Theology* 1.5.1–1.8.13.
122. Carter, "How Then Shall We Theologize?," 1–2.
123. Carter, "How Then Shall We Theologize?," 3–4.
124. See chapter 1 above.
125. Carter, "How Then Shall We Theologize?," 4.
126. Attention could also be drawn to Bates's critique of typology-centered approaches to biblical theology, since typology is significant for redemptive history. To

cal theology argues that Scripture itself sets the table for theology so that it should be followed how it is written, theology-oriented approaches argue that it is *the Trinity* who *uses* Scripture to set the table for theology so that *God* must lead. Neither side fully rejects the other, but both sides are critical of the other's starting point on the basis of the nature of their ontological foundations (or so it seems).[127]

The difference can seemingly be reduced to one admittedly loaded question: What is the source, focus, and goal of biblical theology? If the goal in redemptive-historical biblical theology is finding Christ as the Bible presents him, the source, focus, and goal in theology-centric approaches is rightly understanding how God has revealed saving truth in time and space so that the church can know and contemplate him, who to know is eternal life (John 17:3). This difference, which anticipates later chapters in the current project, deserves one more preliminary consideration: the question of authorial intent.[128]

Divine Authorial Intent and Human Authorial Intent

Carter states in his critique of Grudem's *Systematic* that the goal of biblical theology is to locate the biblical human author's intent in his writing of particular texts and how the text contributes to the larger canon. So understood, the emphasis in biblical theology is primarily economic, focusing on what the human authors understood about divine matters, especially divine actions. As such, Carter says, "Biblical theology is an integral part of systematic theology and absolutely necessary as both a basis for, and a limit on, theological speculation."[129] This is an important

---

be clear, Bates's critique was of Hays's approach, but it included criticism of typology in general with Bates calling typology a "fairly recent" concept in theology. See Bates, *Birth of the Trinity*, 72. This approach will be returned to in later chapters, as it seems that Bates overstates the case.

127. See, for instance, Carter's response to Jason Derouchie's Christ-centered redemptive-historical approach in *Five Views of Christ*, 228–33; it would appear difficult to not conclude that the redemptive-historical approach and the premodern approach are very close and have the most in common of any pairing in the *Five Views* book.

128. Worth mentioning here is that a later chapter will consider a Peter Gentry article criticizing Bates and Carters's prosopological approaches. Gentry says that these approaches are not necessary for how the New Testament sees Christ in the Old; indeed, Gentry says, these approaches undercut the canonical consistency of Scripture. See Gentry, "Preliminary Evaluation and Critique." More will be considered in chapter 4.

129. Carter, "How Then Shall We Theologize?," 2.

point: theocentrical exegesis is not opposed to biblical theology; it uses biblical theology as an important step on its journey to know God.

Elsewhere, Carter restates the importance of biblical theology focused on human authorial intent, endorsing the biblical-theological works of Southern Seminary professors Thomas Schreiner, Peter Gentry, and Stephen Wellum, and on more than one occasion James Hamilton.[130] Hamilton's works, coming in longer (*God's Glory in Salvation Through Judgment*), shorter (*Typology*), and much shorter forms (*What is Biblical Theology?*), provide a good cross section of the sort of thematic biblical theology that seeks to focus on what the human authors knew as they wrote and how they sought to contribute to a thematic canonical "center." To Hamilton, Scripture's center is God's glory via acts of judgment. The human authors had to have some degree of clarity about this theme, concluding (based on oft-cited texts like 1 Pet 1:13 and John 8:56) that "God made clear to human authors what he wanted them to know and what he wanted them to say."[131] Thus, since biblical theology pursues the clarity of the human authors, the importance of the grammatical-historical method is obvious: It is used to gain clarity on the personality, time, and setting of the writer so that the text is not the only link between reader and writer.

What follows is not an attempt to minimize the pursuit of human authorial intent. It does, however, seem worthwhile to examine the tonnage this pursuit should hold if attempting to construct a biblical-theological method using Webster's biblical ontology. Matthew Barrett has written on the concept of *sensus plenior*, which states that the receiver of revelation does not necessarily need to grasp the fullness of the revelatory purpose in order for his writing to be carried along by the Spirit (2 Pet 1:20–21) and thus fulfill the divine purpose (cf. Isa 55:10–11). Rather, as redemptive history continues, that which was earlier unclear later becomes clear. Hence Paul's statement that Christ's person and work fully reveals that which was earlier mysterious (Rom 16:25): Since the Word, earlier revealed, was incarnate, went to the cross, rose from the dead, and ascended back to heaven, sending forth his truth-witnessing

---

130. See Schreiner, *King in His Beauty*; Gentry and Wellum, *KTC*; Hamilton, *God's Glory in Salvation Through Judgment*. Carter shows support for these works in *ISGT*, 24.

131. See Hamilton, *God's Glory*, 555. To be fair, this quote does not say that God gave utter clarity about what the writers were saying. A careful study of *Typology* and *What is Biblical Theology?* will show the reader, however, that Hamilton prioritizes the clarity of the human writers of Scripture (unless his position has changed before the time of this writing).

Spirit (John 14, 16), revelatory fullness can be ascertained according to God's ultimate purposes.[132]

The fact that Abraham *did* see Christ's day and rejoice (John 8:56) does not mean that he had such a perfect clarity about it that if exegesis can somehow identify what all he knew, the gospel will have a stronger and more sure foundation.[133] Paul, based on texts earlier cited, did not seem to think that that was necessary. He seemed to be at peace with the notion that the manner of Christ's fulfilling earlier promises and recapitulating all things in himself—and the resulting glorious salvation—was made clearest post-incarnation. This point does not imply that the earlier (foretelling) revelation, at the time of revealing, has *no* meaning: It was enough to stir the hope of believers and carry them by faith (Heb 11.) But as time progressed, God's revelation progressed to greater clarity.

Beale might be correct, then, to suggest that as this progress occurs, later revelation clarifies what came earlier such that what was revealed in earlier texts has "grown in meaning." Again, the earlier is not reduced to insignificance or fiction, but it is filled out, fully bodied, and clarified so that those with ears to hear can hear, confident that they hear the voice of God.[134] These are the means whereby New Testament believers have access to the Old Testament as that which "belongs to" them (Deut 29:29). God has spoken in the last days by his Son via his saving work in incarnation. What was written earlier might remain veiled to those hardened in heart, but when they turn to Christ, the veil falls off (2 Cor 3:16). The most important aspect of exegesis, thus, is the Word himself giving illuminating clarity by his Spirit to the one who hears with faith.

That any biblical theologian would disagree outright with what has been said is doubtful. What precedes highlights that of which orthodoxy-driven exegetes have criticized biblical theologians: locating the starting point of exegesis in the wrong place, namely in the mind of the human authors. If the starting point can be relocated theologically/Christologically (perhaps a big "if"), the sides can move closer.

---

132. See Barrett, *Canon, Covenant, and Christology*, 21, 26. Further help on *sensus plenior* can be found in Longenecker, *Biblical Exegesis in the Apostolic Period*, xxxiii; Brown, *Sensus Plenior of Sacred Scripture*.

133. In any event, the discussion of human authorial intent would not apply to Abraham, because he, as far as is known, was not a biblical author.

134. This point is latent in Beale's body of work. For an accessible summary, see Beale, *Temple and Church's Mission*, 377–81.

WHAT IS CHRIST-CENTERED BIBLICAL THEOLOGY TRYING TO DO?

Theology, Biblical Theology, and Practical Theology

As Christ-centered biblical theology has normalized the pursuit of human authorial intent via pre-Enlightenment and post-Enlightenment-influenced grammatical-historical method, the effect has been twofold: First, the grammatical-historical method is treated as *the* method of exegesis (to find the human authors' clarity), and second, exegesis stops short both of theological conclusions and practical application unto fellowship with and participation with God.[135] Theological metaphysics become, at best, a sidebar in biblical theology, and at worst, an object of scorn. The same could be said of practical theology, as well: Goldsworthy has said that the duty of the preacher of biblical theology is not to apply practically.[136]

Thankfully, there are plenty of biblical theologians who have avoided the (seeming) impulse to neglect practical application. Beale's *New Testament Biblical Theology* has an excellent practical chapter on applying the redemptive storyline to life. As Beale shows, the New Testament is a recapitulation of the Old Testament, first by Christ, then *by Christians*. The practical implications of this are obvious, considering obedience, journeying through the wilderness, living by faith in the promise, living as light in darkness, etc.[137] This is part of the reason that Köstenberger, in the taxonomy examined in the previous chapter, was so affirmative of Beale's approach. Similarly, Gentry and Wellum's work has a short section for practical application that is also helpful, as does Hamilton.[138] More could be offered as exemplary, though these examples seem, based both on lack of volume and frequency, to be more the exception than the rule. Schreiner's work includes practical "interludes" throughout that read as though they were added later, though such an assertion is not easy to prove. For practical Christian living to have a place in Christ-centered biblical theology seems to be a struggle. Trueman might have a point in saying that "the answer is always 'Jesus.'"[139]

Even more dire is considering theological metaphysics in Christ-centered biblical theology. Even Hamilton's work, which is entirely

---

135. Carter, "How Then Should We Theologize?," 7–8.
136. Goldsworthy stated this in his *Help Me Teach the Bible* podcast interview. See Goldsworthy and Guthrie, "Graeme Goldsworthy on Biblical Theology," at 15:50.
137. See Beale, *New Testament Biblical Theology*, 835.
138. See Gentry and Wellum, *KTC*, 565–86; Hamilton, *God's Glory*, 565.
139. See Trueman, "Revolutionary Balancing Act."

focused on God's glory (Hamilton writes, "This book is written that God would be glorified"[140]), takes the economic conclusions of exegesis into "living boldly" and "knowing God *in all of his judging and saving glory*."[141] Gentry and Wellum include a chapter entitled "Theological Implications" which begins with theology proper, then Christology, then other theological categories. This inclusion is commendable, but everywhere, their commitment to contextualizing theology economically (usually in terms of "covenant") will not let them advance to theological contemplation. Their section on Christology deals with Christ in terms of a covenantal understanding of his identity and work. The section on his identity, however, collapses into his works before the section on his works even begins.[142] There is an aversion to the type of metaphysical contemplation that Carter describes, which seems to be what makes practical Christian living possible. Perhaps that is why Christ-centered biblical theology struggles with both theology and practice: It is, as Carter says (and Trueman implies), only focused on one aspect of the exegetical and theological process. Carter cannot, therefore, reject redemptive-historical biblical theology, but suggests *adding* to it because of its incompleteness.[143]

Signs of Hope in Philadelphia BT2 (Biblical Theology as Redemptive History)

Because of the supposed compatibility between the premodern, theological/Christological approach to Scripture and the approach that Klink and Lockett label "BT2" (biblical theology as redemptive history), especially the "Philadelphia school,"[144] there seems to be hope. Greg Beale, whose redemptive-historical approach plants him squarely in this school, is centered on the repetition of patterns throughout the biblical narrative so that believers will have confidence in the faithfulness of God and live out the pattern themselves. As aforementioned, in Beale's approach, there are all three of (a) redemptive history as the context of revelation, (b) doxology (which is theological in orientation) as the end of revelation,

---

140. Hamilton, *God's Glory*, 565.
141. Hamilton, *God's Glory*, 567; emphasis added.
142. Gentry and Wellum, *KTC*, 657.
143. See, for example, Carter, "Response" to Jason Derouchie, "Grammatical-Historical Christ-Centered Approach," in *Five Views*, 232–33.
144. See chapter 1 above.

WHAT IS CHRIST-CENTERED BIBLICAL THEOLOGY TRYING TO DO?

and (c) discipleship as the application. Also in that school is Goldsworthy who, as his catalogue grew, seemed to be more sentient to the theological endeavor.[145] He seems to be clear that modern grammatical-historical tools can be marshaled by the biblical theologian as long as the ultimate endeavor is to *"listen to God."*[146]

One wonders if there could be a return to the theological orientation of the "fathers" of Philadelphia BT2, namely Geerhardus Vos and Ed Clowney. Time spent in Vos's work leaves the impression that biblical theology is more than a historical study.[147] It is, as Vos said, "the history of revelation in the context of the covenant."[148] Or to the point, if theology proper concerns "God alone," biblical theology concerns his revelation as an act of divine perfection. In revelation, Vos said, "the triune God reveals Himself as the everlasting reality, from whom all truth proceeds, and whom all truth reflects, be it the little streamlet of Paradise or the broad river of the New Testament losing itself again in the ocean of eternity."[149] Note that to Vos, biblical theology as history of revelation is primarily concerned with *theology*, namely, what the history of revelation reflects about God. All of Vos's works demonstrate this theological construal of the history of revelation, even if Vos, to return to the three-part ideal of the previous paragraph, was not himself known for practical application.[150] A later chapter will demonstrate that redemptive history understood as unfolding of revelation does not imply that what came earlier was somehow lesser than what came later. What comes later is *fuller*, which is the purpose of the God who reveals; as Vos says, "Revelation is perfect from the beginning. At all points that revelation occurs, it comes from the God who is perfect, and is perfect for the moment as he has seen fit." Vos adds that there is in the later fullness never a loss of

---

145. See Goldsworthy, *Preaching the Whole Bible*, 13–18; GCH, 234–72.
146. Goldsworthy, GCH, 183–98.
147. As subsequent chapters of the present project will aim to show.
148. Vos, "Doctrine of the Covenant," 76.
149. See Vos, RHRI, 13.
150. See Jay Adams's critique of Vosian preaching, saying it tends to "avoid application" which, Adams says, should be the goal of preaching; *Truth Applied: Application in Preaching*, 20–21, 33. See also Dennison's response to Adams that the reason for Vos's aversion to direct applications is that he sought, by setting peoples' minds forward, to give them the mind of Christ, focusing them on the heavenly, on self-denial, and suffering well. Olinger, *Geerhardus Vos*, 210–12.

what came before but an expansion from the center, "an organic unfolding from within."[151]

Similar to how Goldsworthy saw himself as the mantel-bearer of Donald Robinson's approach, so Clowney saw himself as the mantel-bearer of Vos's. Clowney was critical of other biblical-theological approaches that kept the focus on the human speakers or hearers, instead arguing for a truly Christocentric approach that sees him as not only the recapitulatory human savior but as the eternal Word and Lord of all.[152] Christ is himself the eternal Lord who steps into his creation, whether through Old Testament theophany (which would then, in a sense, make them Christophanies[153]) or in incarnation as the final Word of God to humanity in the last days.[154] Clowney seems to have understood, with Vos, that the task of biblical theology was the setting forth of the eternal truth unto the faith—understood as apprehending the unseen—of the hearer. This point makes sense of why Clowney recommended that all preachers regularly return in their studies to Vos's *Biblical Theology* with a copy of his sermons collected under the title of *Grace and Glory* right alongside of it.[155] In those sermons, Vos sets out the connection between seen revelation and what these revelatory events and their content say about the unseen realities that are true in the eternal Word.[156]

Vos was not only a biblical theologian but a systematician in his earlier professorship. The literary fruit of his systematics appointment is available in his 1200-plus page *Reformed Dogmatics*, with the first volume concerning theology proper at some 200-plus pages, and Christology, the third volume, spanning around 250. The Trinity comprises, therefore, over a third of his dogmatic work.[157] The point of mentioning this is to show that Vos's approach to biblical theology was not first as a historicist or biblical scholar but as a theologian. The relationship between

---

151. Vos, *RHBI*, 10.

152. See Clowney, *Preaching and Biblical Theology*, 50–54.

153. See Clowney, *Preaching Christ in All of Scripture*, 16–17. This topic will be returned to in chapter 7.

154. Clowney, *Preaching and Biblical Theology*, 67, 71.

155. Clowney, *Preaching and Biblical Theology*, 19–20.

156. Vos, *Grace and Glory*. See especially "Heavenly Mindedness," an exposition of Heb 11:9–10 (Vos, *Grace and Glory*, 121–43). Here is Vos's genius marriage between revelatory history and the eternal.

157. See Vos, *Reformed Dogmatics*.

revelation and the Revealer rarely needs to be reiterated in Vos's works: The perfection of the Triune Revealer permeated his work.

This centralizing of theology/Christology in Vos's approach is distilled well in a summary quote from Clowney: "When Christ says, 'Before Abraham was, I am,' (John 8:58), he is saying not just that he is Abraham's and David's seed, but *Abraham's and David's Lord*."[158] Again, as in Vos, this conclusion comes from more than an examination of the redemptive-historical content and context—it comes from seeing revelation as the outgoing of the Triune goodness, that he would be known, treasured, and followed. Theology, redemptive history, and, thus, practicality are all present.

Conclusion

The reason for this extended look at the Vosian-Clowney approach is simple: The approach confirms an earlier-mentioned criticism while also suggesting a way forward. That is, as the previous chapter demonstrated, evangelical Christ-centered biblical theology has both Enlightenment-influenced predecessors (with their presuppositions) and premodern theological-Christological goals (with those presuppositions). If this assessment is accurate, Carter and Trueman might have a point in critiquing biblical theology for not having the theological/Christological nexus that was present in their predecessors, namely Vos and Clowney.[159]

All Christ-centered biblical-theological paradigms share a few assumptions: one divine plan (usually from eternity[160]), Christ as center, the Bible as accurate and inerrant, and redemptive history as the context of revelation. Biblical theology often does not construe revelation in theological terms because of what appears to be an aversion to explicitly centering the theological metaphysics of the Great Tradition. In light of the earlier note about Barrett's and Duby's works, it is hoped that this aversion can lose some of its power or ubiquity: One need not

---

158. Clowney, *Preaching Christ in All of Scripture*, 42; emphasis added.

159. To be fair, Carter was also critical of Vos's supposed aversion to critiquing post-Enlightenment metaphysics; see Carter, *ISGT*, 28–29. It is likely the case, however, that the reason Vos did not spend so much time critiquing Enlightenment thinking is that he was more focused on getting to the theological-Christological heart of revelation than he was on scholarly conversation.

160. Though both Cullmann and König critiqued the notion of a timeless eternity; see Cullmann, *Christ and Time*, 51–68, and König, *Christ Above All*, 16.

start exegesis on a confessional/credal ground; the Scripture itself reveals God's nature as consistent with the theology of classical theism.

Nevertheless, Boersma might have a point in asserting that the credal tradition, though not sharing the authority of revelation, is a sort of sacramental reality through which Christ makes himself known as he unfolds the meaning of his revelatory truth throughout history. The Bible *is* the revelation of truth, and the creeds are the result of the pursuit of clarity by the faithful.[161] As such, there does not need to be a choice between (for example) the Nicene Creed and the Bible. As Carter has said, what the Bible reveals, Nicea articulated, hence its ecumenical acceptance.

If biblical theology is biblicist and historicist, it runs the danger of collapsing, first, the immanent into the economic; second, fellowship with God into mere historical scholarship; and third, perhaps worst, orthodoxy into heresy.[162] But when biblical theology uses the tools at its disposal to hear God, it is firmly at home in the Tradition. Further, it will have greater commonality if, in seeking to hear God, it aims to *behold* him. Whether the Great Tradition can be so construed needs to be considered now. It is that topic that the next chapter takes up, once a final answer is offered to this chapter's question: What is Christ-centered biblical theology trying to do? *It is trying to hear Scripture as a Christ-centered testimony in the context of redemptive history, though it has weaknesses in both theology and practical living.* In short, although the approach is rightly Christ-centered, it is too often theology-averse, and perhaps more often application-averse. Now, to understanding the Great Tradition.

---

161. See Boersma, *HP*, 137–69.

162. Carter shows in his critique of Grudem that heretics throughout ecclesial history have always argued on biblicist grounds, rejecting the credal tradition. "How Then Shall We Theologize?," 9. Also worth mentioning are both Barrett's recent work *RR*, and Nick Needham's *2000 Years of Christ's Power* series on church history, both of which show the latency of biblicism among heretics through the ages.

3

Seeking Out the Great Tradition
The *Sola's* Context

> "The plentitude and end of the Law and of all the sacred
> Scriptures is the love of a Being which is to be enjoyed and
> of a being that can share that enjoyment with us."
>
> —St. Augustine

THE PREVIOUS CHAPTERS CONSIDERED biblical theology in terms of both its historical development since its origin (chapter 1) and its goals according to its current usage (chapter 2). In the narrowest terms, evangelical (Christ-centered) biblical theology happens within the context of the listening church hearing Scripture as God's voice via a unified message in the gospel of his Son, Jesus Christ. Evangelical biblical theology is neither as theologically oriented or as practically concerned as it could or should be. Put another way, Christ-centered biblical theology is always Christ-centered in the context of redemptive history but infrequently oriented toward theology proper or practical living.

Given this project's interest in the nature of the relationship between biblical theology and premodern hermeneutics (that is, Great Tradition), it is now time to respond to this conclusion with an inquiry into premodern hermeneutics and the Reformation-era conviction known as *sola scriptura*. Biblical theology, generally speaking, is a Protestant exegetical discipline rooted in the *sola*.[1] It follow, then, that a pursuit of the presuppositions of Christ-centered biblical theologians is, therefore, a pursuit of those of the sixteenth-century Protestant Reformers. This question—alongside others like it—has generated no shortage of thought and writing over the course of recent centuries. It might seem, therefore, to be a bold endeavor to add any fresh insights to the conversation. Nevertheless, the scope of this project insists that this question be considered in historical context. As a reminder, the original research question governing this project is, "What is the nature of the relationship of evangelical Christ-centered biblical theology to the hermeneutics of the so-called Great Tradition, which the Protestant Reformers claimed, via *sola scriptura*, to be continuing?"[2] This chapter seeks the goals and assumptions of Reformed hermeneutics so that the question can be answered.

The thesis of this chapter can be stated in a few sentences: As Renaissance thinkers sought to go *ad fontes*, that is, "back to the (classical) sources,"[3] the Reformers were convinced that biblical exegesis, the driver of both theology and preaching,[4] needed to also return to its primary source: Scripture alone, in context of the listening church. This was the point of *sola scriptura*. *Ad fontes* led the Reformers to return to Scripture under the conviction that out of all of the classical sources, the Bible alone is divinely inspired.[5] The working assumption was that if the Scripture can be understood in its gospel-centered unity, the church enjoys fellowship with Jesus who, as Craig Carter has stated, "is present in the text."[6] As exegesis took this trajectory, the Reformers were recapturing Augustine's own exegetical practice as Augustine's exegesis was *both* "close" (focused on the immediate context of particular passages) and Christ-centered (with the gospel as each text's broad context). It can be said, therefore, that the Reformation was more than the triumph of Augustine's soteriology over his ecclesiology.[7] The Reformation was

---

1. See Goldsworthy, *Gospel and Kingdom*, 16–18.

2. A supporting question that will be of interest in this chapter is, "Did the *sola* anchor the Reformers' approach to premodern interpreters, or was it revolutionary?"

3. See George, *Reading Scripture With the Reformers*, 56.

4. As seen in Bray, *Biblical Interpretation*, 201.

5. Chester and Reeves, *Why the Reformation Still Matters*, 44. This point will be important throughout this chapter.

6. Carter, *ISGT*, 36–37.

7. As famously stated in Warfield, *Calvin and Augustine*, 321–22.

the triumph of Augustine's exegesis over his exegetical legacy, his actual exegetical practice over stereotypes of it.

First will be a consideration of Augustine's hermeneutic, highlighting that his understanding of the literal and spiritual senses is somewhat different than what is typically thought of him. The authoritative "sense" for any text is the literal/historical meaning which is contextualized by the Christocentricity of the canon as a whole; the spiritual sense is the prayerful, pastoral application of the literal/plain sense, so that believers can hear God in the their day. As the previous chapter saw, Great Tradition hermeneutics operate on two beliefs: "God speaks" and "God speaks to us" (borrowing, again, from Carter). In short, Augustine knew that if the Spirit guides exegesis by the centering of the gospel/rule of faith, various senses can be used appropriately so that believers are built up.

Following this study of Augustine will be a consideration of some of the hermeneutical developments of the medieval period. As it will be seen, the literal sense began to fade because of an increasing dominance of the allegorical sense, especially abuses of it. Against this backdrop, it will be seen that several prominent names, Thomas Aquinas the most prominent of all, began to call again on the importance of the literal sense to guide pious interpretation. There arose a desire to return to Augustine's pastorally sensitive hermeneutic that reads Scripture theologically and christologically, that is, according to the rule of faith. As such the Reformation was inevitable. It was, as Phillip Schaff said, a "historical necessity."[8]

After this will follow an examination of the hermeneutics of the sixteenth century Protestant Reformers. Attention will be given to the Reformation emphasis on close exegesis, subjecting the text to the Bible's contextual rule, the rule of faith, understood as being synonymous with the gospel of God's Son (Rom 1:2, 9.). Calvin, it will be seen, especially made major developments in this Augustinian exegesis that reads the text closely as a witness to Christ.

Finally, the chapter will conclude by examining some potential counterarguments against the proposed narrative of historical development. Considerations will be made for those who say that the Reformation was about recapturing the textual single meaning, as well as whether the Reformation's hermeneutics led to the grammatical-historical method,

---

8. Schaff, "Principle of Protestantism," 73.

which, isolated from the rule of faith, might open the door to the abandoning of Scripture's supernatural character.[9]

This chapter aims to show that the Great Tradition generally, and Reformational hermeneutics specifically (via the *sola*), exhibit so many similarities to current evangelical (Christ-centered) biblical theology that a discernible relationship is unavoidable. Great Tradition exegesis is exegesis in the context of the listening church, as disciples hear God's voice via Scripture bidding them to behold the glory of Christ to the end of Christlike transformation over time. It seems that this gospel-centric exegesis is the type of exegesis to which evangelical biblical theology aims. If this is the case, Christ-centered biblical theology might be the continuation of the Great Tradition. One of the previous chapter's central conclusions—that biblical theology is too often atheological and impractical—will need, however, to be considered before establishing too close of a relationship between Christ-centered biblical theology and the Tradition.

Augustine in Context

Heiko Oberman has shown that one of the central factors in the need for the Reformation was the rise of nominalism. People, by and large, had grown weary of merely hearing about proposed truths; they wanted to experience truth.[10] In other words, they wanted to not just hear arguments that these things are true (as could be the case in a nominal universe), but they wanted to know personally how these things truly change lives (or, how they are *real*). As it will be seen below, Reformers worked so that their parishioners knew how to experience *assurance*. They wanted believers to hear in the gospel promise a certitude that would motivate rest in Christ and the love for him that would follow.[11] More will be said about this certitude below, but it is important at the outset of this section to mention the desire for experiential certitude as driving Reformational motivation.

What does this have to do with Augustine? Augustine's hermeneutic was permeated by a concern for edifying pastoral application. This

---

9. See Boersma, *Scripture as Real Presence*, 271–75. See also Masters, *Not Like Any Other Book* for an accessible, pastoral guide for spiritual interpretation from an evangelical perspective. Masters's book predates much of the recent literature on the subject.

10. Oberman, *Dawn of the Reformation*, 25–27.

11. See Schreiner, "Calvin and the Exegetical Debates," 207–15.

concern was driven, as Hans Boersma has shown, by the church fathers' sacramental worldview that demands a sacramental view of hermeneutics. To be clear, their so-called "sacramental worldview" consisted of the belief that all that exists participates in some manner in the life of God and points to him as Creator, Sustainer, and Redeemer.[12] Since Christ fills all things (Eph 4:10), any individual is never *absolutely* isolated from his presence but is either under his judgment or his grace (John 9:22) in the context of receiving life from him and either pleasing him or not. In one sense, to even exist in the first place is to partake in grace because God does not have to create and sustain, and sin, one would think, disqualifies someone from having the right to exist. God as eternal giver (Acts 17:25-26) makes the sun rise and the rain fall on the just and unjust, the good and the bad (Matt 5:45). So, the God who is the eternal fountain of life (Jer 2:13) and being (Rom 11:36) constructs his creation in such a way that it contains sacramental means through which people know the nature of how God gives life and redemption. His people—the church— are not only under his grace in creation (receiving life and being from him) but in redemption (receiving the grace of the son of God through the gospel). So the church has a natural impulse to find the presence of God and his word in all things. Their evaluation of all that they experience, then, undergoes transformation as they walk with Jesus (2 Cor 5:16) and he changes how they think.[13]

As regards hermeneutics, their interpretative framework is not only influenced by this sacramental worldview but is controlled by it. They read all texts of Scripture as witnesses to Christ who fills all things, and their search for meaning is found in relationship to that conviction. A text's ultimate context is not its historical setting (its *sitz im leben*) but its relationship to Christ, and through him, to the believer.[14]

This point means, in practical terms, that biblical interpretation is *a Christian practice*, exercised in relationship with Christ who is himself the living Word to whom the written word points (and who is himself, as eternal Word, the source of the written word).[15] "The Scriptures testify to me" (John 5:39). Whereas the historical context of a particular text

---

12. See Boersma, *Scripture as Real Presence*, 1, 25.

13. For a penetrating look at this phenomenon, as described in the text cited, see Beale, *Biblical Theology of the New Testament*, 303-4.

14. Boersma, *Scripture as Real Presence*, xii-xv.

15. As in Webster, *Domain of the Word*, 115-20. His term for Christian interpretation is "regenerate reasoning."

is important insofar as it helps the interpreter to understand the setting of the original writing, the ultimate context is the mind of the God who knows all things and graciously extends his word to the listener to establish and maintain fellowship with them.[16] Thus, the ultimate context of a text is pastoral, not historical.

Some might object that such a pastoral hermeneutical framework is a breeding ground for ontological, postmodernist relativity. An undisciplined grammatical-historical hermeneutical framework can lead to such relativity. Boersma has shown that if history is separated from a Christian providential framework (that is, history as God's project to unfold his will), then the question of what is true is in danger of being jettisoned in favor of mere historical comparisons.[17] History, if not understood in reference to its relationship with Christ, is just a study in progress, with the current moment being the *summum bonum* of progress. The rightness or wrongness of a moment or event is irrelevant because it cannot be right or wrong—it is only a part of an unfolding narrative of which the current day is the highest point.[18]

Thus, says Boersma, the fathers held that history is a participation in the life of God such that a historical moment's meaning and health depends on the strength of its relationship to Christ. History is, therefore, to be interpreted in light of reality, which is contained in the person of Jesus Christ the *real*.[19] Practically, this means that whereas a text might propose a difficult imperative which can be ignored by an in-depth proposal of its historical setting, the more important question than the text's *sitz im leben* is this: How can that historical setting be understood rightly in the first place if not in terms of its relationship to the God who rules over history and also speaks via the text?

This analysis is preparatory for understanding Augustine's hermeneutic. It is not that a text's *sitz im leben* has no meaning but that history can only be understood in light of Christ as the face of God's reality (2 Cor 4:6). History is no less subject to speculation than the present moment, for, as Luther said, the Word is more sure than life itself.[20] The Word itself *is* reality as it comes to the reader from the God who is

---

16. See Webster, *HS*, 17–30.
17. See Boersma, *Scripture as Real Presence*, 275.
18. See also George, *Reading Scripture with the Reformers*, 45.
19. For an interesting example of seeing this in cooperation with exegesis, see Carter's examination of Augustine's treatment of Ps 3, in *ISGT*, 206–9.
20. Quoted in Oberman, *Dawn of the Reformation*, 93.

himself ultimate reality. Because of this, historical considerations are to be understood as a *part* of the hermeneutical process, not the whole or even the goal of the process.

Luther's aforementioned quote demonstrates what distinguishes truly Christian exegesis: Since Christ is the logic behind all order (John 1:1–4), then without acknowledging and attaching all things to him, even the most neutral and fact-concerned study will yield unclear, biased, and uncertain results (i.e., no certitude.) Only if exegesis starts with Jesus can it show truth unto certitude, for "the truth is in Jesus" (Eph 4:18). The Christian who starts with and ends with Jesus is the "spiritual person" who "judges all things" (1 Cor 2:15). To them, Scripture is a divine witness about both the divine and all things in context of divinity.

Augustine's Hermeneutic: Interpretation by the Rule of Faith

Now it can be understood why Augustine employed his pastoral/allegorical hermeneutic. In practicing allegory, he did not teach that Scripture can say whatever one fancies it to say (a common objection to allegorical exegesis.)[21] Rather, it is that Scripture's plain sense says what God intended in its writing, but the scope of application is included in (or effectively attached to and therefore read from) the plain reading because of how God, shepherding his people, intends to use it across time. As he shepherds his listening/reading people, working in their lives in similar ways that he did when he first inspired the written text (for Jesus is "the same yesterday, today, and forever," Heb 13:6), there might be varying pastoral applications of the text to their situation, and those applications can be called "the word" if it is understood that the literal sense is the inspired sense. Carter showed that patristic exegesis holds, first, that "God speaks," and second, "God speaks *to us*."[22] Augustine held that the goal of exegesis was not merely unfolding the historical sense of a text but applying the text pastorally to the people of God in the current day.[23]

21. See, for instance, Goldsworthy, *GCH*, 94–106.

22. See Carter, *ISGT*, 187.

23. Helpful is a summary of DeLubac's explanation of allegorical exegesis: The nature of Scripture demands that a text must contain different levels of meaning such that narrowing exegesis to a study of the literal sense might minimize the Divine Author's intention for the text's use in the current day based on the fact that the text is now a part of a completed canon. In other words, since the original text is now a part of a larger body of work, the complete canon of Scripture, one should expect a growth of "meaning." See DeLubac's four-part *Medieval Exegesis*. This "growth of meaning" is also

This conviction explains why Augustine was so insistent that for sound hermeneutics to be practiced, one must wrestle with the text, following it into clarity. Book 2 of *De Doctrina Christiana* is given to helping the exegete advance through the basics of doctrine so that they can learn to then be able to handle the more "ambiguous" things of Scripture after having been humbled by the text.[24] A person could not be humbled by the text unless the person be subject to the text in the first place. To Augustine, the aforementioned "basics of doctrine" consist in what is found in "the more open places of the Scriptures and in the authority of the church,"[25] namely what is comprised in the rule of faith. The Apostle's Creed is likely the best brief summary of the rule of faith, but Reformed theologian Johann Alsted would summarize the basics many centuries later in terms of the Trinity, the fall of the human race, Christ as redeemer, the existence of true blessedness, and there being a single way into it.[26] To synthesize with what was argued in the previous chapter, this short list of Bible "basics," often called the rule of faith, could be called a summary of the Christian gospel. The rule of faith, says Oberman, *is* the gospel,[27] controlling hermeneutics by contextualizing every particular text in light of Christ and his redeeming work. When the rule controls exegesis, the Scripture is clear, or "perspicuous," as it would be called in the sixteenth century.[28] Such clarity as articulated in the term "perspicuity" does not imply errors in the text of Scripture; rather, in time, apparent difficulties become clear as the word is understood more and more by the faithful. It interprets itself, as Cranmer would articulate, in agreement with Augustine.[29]

This conviction was the foundation of *sola scriptura*: Since Scripture is clear in itself when read as a gospel witness spoken by Christ the eternal Word, tradition only need serve a *ministerial* role in helping to interpret. Scripture alone is *magisterial*.[30] Tradition can err, as can any man or

---

picked up in Beale's various works, which will be returned to later.

24. Augustine, *On Christian Doctrine*, 78.

25. Augustine, *On Christian Doctrine*, 79. Cameron contends that the "basics" of which Augustine spoke, he explicated in *Instructing Beginners in the Faith*, on which *Doctrine* was written to build. See Cameron, *Christ Meets Me Everywhere*, 19–22.

26. Quoted in Heppe, *Reformed Dogmatics*, 11. It should also be mentioned that to others, Carter included, the theology and Christology of the Nicene Creed is the test of orthodoxy.

27. See Oberman, *Dawn of the Reformation*, 270–73.

28. Oberman, *Dawn of the Reformation*, 270–73.

29. Thompson, "Sola Scriptura," 181–84.

30. See Barrett, *God's Word Alone*, 45. Worth mentioning is Wilken's discussion of

woman. Scripture, on the other hand, cannot, and it is thus set apart in its perfection. Luther's stance was, therefore, that not only is Scripture the only inerrant authority but that the church fathers believed this, too.[31]

Augustine at the very least *implied* the perspicuity of Scripture when he gave instructions for handling less clear texts. He said that if a text's meaning is unclear, the exegete might be helped by a "recourse to reason." But since "reason" has the danger of subjective bias, it is much safer, says Augustine, to follow Scripture's own lead.[32] Scripture is clear in itself, at least when exegesis is controlled by the rule of faith. Similar to practitioners of Christ-centered biblical theology, Augustine placed a premium on following Scripture as it comes. To Augustine, truly Christian exegesis lets Scripture lead. Augustine's polemical works were, therefore, never shy to use "proof texts." He was not a "biblicist" but a holder to Scripture's authority on the ground of God's Trinitarian and speaking nature.[33]

Further, Augustine would famously say that unless the text teaches behavior or belief, it is to be understood figuratively. A critic of relativism might seize upon this point as an example of loose hermeneutics. Augustine immediately after states that any figurative interpretation must be consistent with the Bible's behavior ethic (that is, love for God and neighbor) and system of belief (that is, right knowledge of God and of neighbor).[34] In other words, a figurative interpretation must never contradict what is elsewhere clear in the more open places of Scripture. Again, to Augustine, Scripture is clear—perspicuous—in light of itself, understood ontologically relative to God and ethically relative to love.

This point might explain why Augustine famously (infamously?) drew such heavy parallels between the six-day creation of Gen 1 and both the Christian's discipleship experience and the various eras of world

---

this ancient interpretation: "The unique vocation of early Christian thought was to provide a unified interpretation of the Scriptures, one that was comprehensive, centered on the triune God, and definitive." "Definitive," says Wilken, not because of a method, but because of Scripture's own content as the vessel of the gospel. See Wilken, *Spirit of Early Christian Thought*, 314–15.

31. See Vanhoozer, *Biblical Authority After Babel*, 134–39, and Barrett, *God's Word Alone*, 33–45.

32. Augustine, *On Christian Doctrine*, 102.

33. See Barrett's explanation of biblicism in *RR*, 21. Biblicism, says Barrett, is an idolatry of word over against meaning. Augustine used proof texts to prove what is true without being guilty to any degree of bibliolatry. He pursued biblical fidelity as a means to the end of God's truth.

34. Barrett, *RR*, 88.

history.³⁵ It is not that the entire point of the creation account is only apprehended in terms of Christian discipleship and a parallel to the stages of world history. The creation account has several clear parallels to both. So Augustine, assuming the truth of the account (and being, perhaps surprisingly, respectful to those who disagreed that the text of Gen 1 was to be taken literally³⁶), was interested in "using allegory to communicate the truths of the faith in a vivid way to his readers."³⁷ He believed that the text of Scripture always had a historical/literal meaning *and* a spiritual meaning.³⁸ The spiritual meaning is contained in what is prophesied in the telling of the history;³⁹ in the case of Gen 1, the future stages of world history and the Christian's discipleship experience are included in the spiritual meaning. The important point to note is that the figurative sense is not *added to* the historical or literal sense and neither can it contradict it.

So, then, what is the figurative sense? Mitchell Chase has argued that the allegorical sense is the application of the literal sense to the edification of the church. Controlled by the rule of faith—the gospel—allegory's goal was not to add something to Scripture that is not there but to show the final horizon of a text's purpose as pastoral application to the people of God in every age. As Chase shows, "The words of the human author did not exhaust the meaning of the passage."⁴⁰ Chase notes that, whereas allegory was indeed considered to be an "add-on" to the literal sense, Aquinas understood that any spiritual sense is "embedded in" the literal sense⁴¹ such that the God who inspired the text means for it to be applied spiritually. Aquinas is consistent with Augustine here, teaching that the figurative sense is the pastoral application of the literal sense.

One helpful example of Augustine's concern for a close reading of the text can be found in his *De Trinitate*. The care with which Augustine engages the biblical text to prove the divinity of both Christ and the Spirit is no product of someone who disregards the literal sense.⁴² Rather,

---

35. See Augustine, *Instructing Beginners in the Faith*, 69–70, and *On Genesis*, 48–54.

36. See *On Genesis*, 173. There, Augustine has a surprisingly accommodating tone toward those who might disagree with him.

37. Augustine, *On Genesis*, 9.

38. Augustine, *On Genesis*, 173.

39. Augustine, *On Genesis*, 60.

40. Chase, *40 Questions*, 208.

41. Chase, *40 Questions*, 217. See also Carter, *ISGT*, 99, and Aquinas, *ST*, 1.1.10, where Thomas says, "The spiritual sense is based on the literal, and presupposes it."

42. For example, see footnote 42 under 1.6.11 of Augustine, *De Trinitate*, where he

Augustine's questions throughout *De Trinitate* demand a belief in the clarity, inspiration, and edification of the scriptural text. A study of Augustine's major works shows clearly that he is concerned with the plain meaning of the biblical text. He spoke, therefore, of the need to "master" the interpretation of the Scriptures' teaching on the person of the Son, such "mastery" meaning to have a commanding "handle" on all of the various and complex texts describing the Son's nature.[43] But he also understood that he, as a spiritual under-shepherd, had a pastoral responsibility to his people.

Finally, Augustine's *Instructing Beginners in the Faith* provides an interesting example of his view of Scripture's unity in the context of what would later be called redemptive history. Alongside of Irenaeus's recapitulation theory, one might find here the ancestral foundation of modern evangelicalism's love of Christ-centered, redemptive-historical approaches to the text.[44] Vos, Clowney, Goldsworthy, and others would doubtless find this work of Augustine's to be helpful in strengthening the case for the discipleship benefits of redemptive history throughout time. Augustine believed that redemptive history continued past Scripture and into the present (as seen in *City of God*), and thus, believers listening to the text in the present day are spiritually connected to believers who are present in the text.[45] Therefore, pastoral application was far from a jump from the literal sense: It rests *upon* the literal sense, and can never live by itself apart from it.

Quadriga

It was this concern for both the literal sense and the pastoral sense that gave rise to the fourfold *quadriga,* usually attributed to Augustine. What follows is Richard Muller's summary of the method:

---

deals with a question about texts' using the word "God" and how one can tell if such texts refer to the Trinity or a person of the Trinity: "The context *always shows* which it is" (emphasis added; note Augustine's confidence in Scripture.)

43. Augustine, *De Trinitate*, 89.

44. Worth noting is that Irenaeus's *Demonstration of the Apostolic Preaching* is a work of Christ-centered biblical theology that would be well at home in the Goldsworthy mold of tracing the promises, prophecies, and types through the OT leading to Christ. See especially the Veritas Splendor version from 2019 edited by Paul Boer.

Worth also mentioning is Melito's *On Pascha*; Melito was a bishop in the second century, and his work is a Christological powerhouse, perhaps even surpassing Irenaeus's work in depth.

45. See especially Augustine, *Instructing Beginners in the Faith*, 73–100.

1. First is the *literal-historical sense*, where the text is viewed in light of grammatical-historical considerations. This sense is the text in its historical context: who wrote it, why, to whom it was written, etc.

2. Second is the *tropological sense*, also known as the moral sense. This step seeks a moral application of the text. What should the listener *do* in light of what they have heard? This is usually best understood in terms of imperatives: What is an appropriate imperative either implied or explicit in the text and its Christ-connections (which anticipates the next point)?

3. Third is the *allegorical sense*, where usually a parallel is drawn between the historical point and a Christian doctrine present in the rule of faith. How does the text demonstrate the truth of some aspect of the core tenets of the Christian faith? Often, how does the text bear witness to the person and work of Christ, even if the text precedes the incarnation?

4. Finally is the *anagogical sense*, where believers draw lessons for the life to come from the text. How does the text point to Christ's return, the new heavens and new earth, how believers will be transformed by the beatific vision?[46]

It should be clear, based on the preceding points, that Augustine treated the latter three points of the *quadriga* as stemming from and therefore subordinate to the first sense. The text says what God intends in the original; the under-shepherd, through preaching, then applies the point to believers in ways that God leads, centered on the rule of faith/gospel, never contradicting the literal sense. Scripture is united by Christ who is its telos, its *res*. The frequency of typology (to anticipate later chapters in the present project)—where an earlier person, practice, or institution is analogous to and prophetic of a later more important person, practice, or

---

46. See Muller, "Biblical Interpretation," 8–13, and *Britannica*, "Hermeneutics." It should be noted that Origen, living 200 years before Augustine, championed a threefold sense which included the literal, moral, and spiritual senses. It was Augustine who saw the spiritual sense as containing two elements: the allegorical/pastoral and the anagogical/eschatological, thus leading to the fourfold *quadriga*. See "Hermeneutics" in *Britannica*.

Worth noting is that Thomas's explanation of the *quadriga* (seen in *ST*, 1.10.1) will be returned to later. Thomas demonstrates utter consistency with Augustine here, though with developments. This continuity seems to be why Barrett referred to him as "Thomas the Augustinian," in Barrett, *RR*, 144.

institution, often Christ[47]—contained within Scripture provides a foundation for creative applications and relationships between texts if they are consistent with the Bible's Christotelic broad context.[48] As developed in chapters 1 and 2, for the Christian, the gospel is itself the ontological center and plausibility structure of all of reality such that history cannot be understood apart from it.[49] The current chapter proposes that Augustine was making the same argument, or at least operating from the same gospel-centered and pastoral presupposition. Because Christ the Word unites all things in himself and the gospel concerns his work of salvation on humanity's behalf, the legitimacy of this fourfold approach follows and is far from a danger.

Concluding this brief treatment of Augustine is a summary: Augustine, out of a concern for pastoral application, did not abandon the literal sense of the text. Rather, he assumed the church's faith and confidence in the literal sense of the text and then proceeded to apply the text spiritually under the conviction that God, who inspired the text, speaks to his people in the present day as well by his Son (Heb 1:1; 12:25). As the gospel/rule of faith is the lens through which reality is discerned, then through it, the church can listen to Scripture and hear what he intends for them. In this sense, it can be said that exegesis is listening to God's leading voice, and application, whether construed as a *part* of exegesis or not, is the practical act of following his word, all within the context of the listening church.

Further, as seen above, allegory was a way of deriving meaning from a text where God had chosen to not illuminate the ultimate meaning in the time of reflection. Since allegory is subordinate to the literal sense, then when God gave clarity, the exegete could adjust accordingly without losing anything. What would an anti-allegorist do in a situation like this? They wait on the Lord. It is likely that for Augustine and others, allegory was a way of waiting on the Lord: anchoring a text's meaning in Christ, who is both its source and goal, believing that there might be greater depth illuminated later.

---

47. Beale, *Handbook on the New Testament*, 14–18.

48. According to Bray, typology gave way to allegory in the patristic era; Bray, *Doing Theology with the Reformers*, 51. Bray's assertion might be an oversimplification, though typology and allegory are surely related. The relationship between typology and allegory is examined well by Chase in *40 Questions*, especially 79–93, 199–204. Typology will be examined in chapters 4 and 5.

49. See Goldsworthy's argument in *According to Plan*, 29–70; and *GCH*, Part 3: "Reconstructing Evangelical Hermeneutics," 181–313.

That said, Christ-centered biblical theology could be said to relate to allegorical interpretation in this way: Christ-centered biblical theology says that the gospel is the ultimate context of a particular passage, so that even difficult passages can be safely approached if kept in gospel context. Is it possible that allegorists were simply assuming this without saying so? This question is pertinent because of the aforementioned tendency among evangelicals—especially biblical theologians—to jettison allegory as anti-historical and thus subject to too many dangers. In doing so, theologians might be overthrowing practices that are built upon the same gospel-centric presupposition as their biblical theology is. A better approach to disciplinary foci than responding to a focus's defects by dispensing with it is to examine the history of the focus and see if some of its practitioners simply went too far in some areas with something that is actually a good and helpful development. It is doubtful that any worthwhile endeavor is utterly without danger.[50] This point will be returned to later in this chapter.

Medieval Hermeneutics: A Slow Shift to "Tradition 3"

Under the ubiquitous influence of Augustine, whose otherworldly exegetical and theological skills set up hermeneutics for almost the entirety of the medieval era, exegesis could be characterized in two ways: First, it was devotionally driven in that exegesis was always oriented toward helping the sheep follow their shepherd (Gen 48:15)[51], and second, it was aimed at keeping the plain sense as primary.[52] The assumption was that true exegesis is an activity of the truly regenerate who would never

---

50. Worth mentioning is the fact that many redemptive historicists, such as Goldsworthy, take considerable exception to allegory. See Goldsworthy, *GCH*, 94–104. Via personal correspondence, Goldsworthy has told the writer that Preuss's argument in *From Shadow to Promise: Old Testament Interpretation from Augustine to the Young Luther* that Luther's recovery of Scripture's historical sense made the gospel—the promise and fulfillment of it in Christ—the ultimate context of a text from the Reformation on. That being said, as it will be seen, it might be the case that Goldsworthy and other critics of allegory oversimplify the dangers therein.

51. This commitment to devotional/pietistic exegesis can be traced in widely read works through Bernard of Clairvaux (twelfth century) and his *Four Degrees of Love*, and then into the thirteenth and fourteenth centuries in Bonaventure's *Journey of the Mind to God* and Thomas à Kempis's *Imitation of Christ*. The latter was very critical of scholasticism and its propensity, as he saw it, to make learning an end in itself. Barrett traces well this pro-piety, anti-scholastic tendency in *RR*, 35–61.

52. See George, *Reading Scripture with the Reformers*, 145.

play fast and loose with the text. They would seek from the Scriptures the plain meaning, and then, knowing that in reality it was they who were being acted upon by the Word (Heb 4:12–13), prayerfully make pastoral application based on Christ's presence via the text, edifying the saints. The context of any particular text is the whole of Scripture, which is meant to stir faith in the risen Christ who is the Son of God in the flesh, similar to biblical theology. Exegesis is far from speculative; it is spiritual. As Carter says, "Great Tradition exegesis was and is a profoundly *spiritual* and *moral* act in which the interpreter who succeeds in grasping the true res or subject matter of the text is irrevocably transformed in the process—sanctified and turned into one who possesses eternal life."[53]

In the centuries following Augustine, things began to change. Against the popular notion that medieval exegesis was dry, boring, and lacking any advance from the classical period, Thiselton has noted that it was just as creative a time as any other period in church history.[54] One can see in Bray's *Biblical Interpretation: Past and Present* an introductory treatment of medieval exegesis that highlights the creativity of the time.[55] Although Bray devotes only a fraction of the space to medieval exegesis that he does to the patristic and Reformation eras, he succeeds to show that there was plenty of activity and development. Not all of this creativity benefited the church's well-established devotionally driven exegesis.

James Preuss argues that one of the unfortunate effects of Augustine's figurative teaching—namely, that whatever does not teach doctrine or behavior is best to be taken figuratively[56]—was that all of the Old Testament narrative was effectively dehistoricized far and wide. As a result, says Preuss, whatever is contained in Old Testament narrative became,

---

53. Carter, *ISGT*, 111; emphasis added.

54. Thiselton, *Approaching the Study of Theology*, 16. One example: Bernard of Clairvaux (twelfth century) wrote that the Song of Songs—far from being an erotic look at the sexual nature of the marital relationship, as asserted by some modern exegetes—is meant to be understood as a kind of biblical-theological lens through which the rest of Scripture can be understood. (See Bray, *Biblical Interpretation, Past and Present*, 159). Calvin quoted Bernard more than he quoted anyone else in his *Institutes*, save Augustine.

Also worth mentioning is Tyndale's creativity in his gospel presentation, whether in translation or publishing, which occurred in the 1520s (late medieval). Barrett shows that Tyndale combined simplicity, evangelical faith, and originality. See Barrett, *RR*, 761–64.

55. Bray, *Biblical Interpretation*, 129–64.

56. As famously taught in Augustine, *De Doctrina*, 88–90.

via allegory, *mere* figures for New Testament believers.[57] By the time of thinkers like Hugh of Saint Victor (1096–1141), the Old Testament had become entirely annexed under the category of "promise," which meant "unreal," and the New Testament brings fulfillment, meaning "real." Thus many would say that the New Testament is the Old matured. Although that in and of itself is not a dangerous idea, given that the New Testament, as seen in the previous chapter, is in Christ the fulfillment of the Old, danger arises when this proposition suggests the un-historicity of the Old Testament narrative.[58]

This is a troubling idea for Old Testament exegesis given that the New Testament says at multiple points that the Old has been given to the church for its upbuilding, instruction, and encouragement (Rom 15:4; 1 Cor 10:5; 2 Tim 3:15–17). If the Old Testament does not contain real history, then how can it be an encouragement to those who are living as disciples of Christ in a real historical existence? But indeed, during the medieval period, the Old Testament had in some parts of the church become hidden under speculation.

So when fourteenth- and fifteenth-century thinkers like Henry of Oyta (1330–397) and Jean Gerson (1363–1429) appeared on the exegetical and theological scene, the Old Testament's meaning could only be discovered with the church's help. As Preuss shows, Gerson even went far enough to say that the Old Testament has *no* literal sense except whatever the church decides.[59] This was increasingly the case as time advanced to the early days of Luther. As Goldsworthy asserts, perhaps too strongly, any theological or historical impact of the Old Testament (including typology) was all but lost in the process.[60] Augustine and others had established that the literal sense is the first step in exegesis, all of which is controlled by an assumed doctrinal set of distinctives known as the rule of faith/gospel. There had been, however, a shift over a thousand years leading to two unfortunate developments in some influential examples: On one extreme, there is no literal sense; on the other extreme, the literal sense is only what the church decides it is. Instead of the gospel acting as the plausibility structure of exegesis, church dogma fulfilled the role.

Oberman explained this effect in terms of a generally well-received paradigm: What had been the church's ancient understanding of the place

---

57. Preuss, *From Shadow to Promise*, 13.
58. Preuss, *From Shadow to Promise*, 32, 46.
59. Preuss, *From Shadow to Promise*, 81.
60. Goldsworthy, *GCH*, 106.

of dogma in relation to Scripture, "Tradition 1" (Scripture as norming norm of theology and practice), had given way to "Tradition 2," where Scripture takes its place *alongside* tradition, governed by the rule of faith, which means that Scripture is understood in light of the gospel which the creeds articulate. This construal has the effect of joining Scripture with tradition as normative partners, which then has the practical effect of tradition as the authoritative interpretation of Scripture, its partner.[61] The final step in the development is "Tradition 3": Tradition *alone* is the norming norm of exegesis.[62] Instead of the gospel as Scripture's center being the lens through which the text is understood, the gospel's creedal exposition and its resulting tradition became the authoritative plausibility structure.

Nevertheless, there was some protest against this shift: Both Aquinas (1225–74) and Nicholas of Lyra (1270–349) had in consecutive generations called for a renewed interest in the literal sense. Nicholas had suggested what he called a "double-literal sense,"[63] whereby the literal meaning of an Old Testament text is found in both the historical setting of the text and in terms of its relationship to Christ who is the fulfillment of the word. Chase has shown that both Thomas and Nicholas were tired of the excesses of an overly allegorical method, thus calling for a return to an approach that held the secondary senses in consistency with the literal.[64] George surmises that their interest stemmed from an interest in the actual text of Scripture, which is seen quite clearly in Thomas's prolificness as a scriptural commentator.[65] One has only to consider how insistent Thomas is to teach and repeat teaching that "the author of Holy

---

61. One unfortunate example of the effect of the practice is that from Peter Lombard's day and following, the church in the West recognized seven sacraments, with penance placed alongside of the Eucharist and indulgences for assurance. To challenge this arrangement was to challenge God because, according to Tradition 2, ecclesial opinion, centering in Rome, is the truth without possibility of error. See Bray, "Late Medieval Theology," 7.

62. See Oberman, *Dawn of the Reformation*, 270–73.

63. See Preuss, *From Shadow to Promise*, 68. Nicholas's challenge can be seen in his *Moral Postill on the Whole Bible*, written from 1333–39. Philip Krey and Lesley Smith give an extended study in *Nicholas of Lyra*, 90.

For Thomas's prioritizing of the literal sense over the other senses, see Aquinas, *ST*, 1.1.10.

64. Chase, *40 Questions*, 215–19.

65. George, *Reading Scripture with the Reformers*, 145. Consult Thomas's two-volume commentary on John's Gospel to see the care he took to explain every verse in a way that would likely be considered exhaustive by modern standards.

Writ is God... who by one act comprehends all things by His intellect."[66] To Thomas, Scripture uniquely has God as its author.

Two final points are worth remembering in order to understand Thomas's and Nicholas's interest in the literal sense. First, both held that doctrine depends only on the literal sense, not a spiritual sense. The spiritual sense is discipleship-oriented, concerned with confirming and strengthening the faith of the believer. As such it has no effect on the doctrine which ontologically precedes it, but emerges from that doctrine.[67] Second, they both held that any spiritual sense is secondary to the literal sense, such that, as with Augustine, spiritual senses were little more than attempts to lead believers to see Christ in the text.[68]

Barrett shows elsewhere that Thomas and Nicholas should not be thought of as the only medieval thinkers interested in a return to the literal sense. Preceding them were Gregory the Great (sixth century), Alcuin (eighth century), and Hugh of Saint Victor (twelfth century), all saying that the literal sense is the foundation on which the other senses can be called the house. So it is not as though the literal sense was *lost*; rather, since it had such a foundational place in exegesis and theology through the Great Tradition, Thomas and Nicholas (thirteenth and fourteenth centuries) were calling the church to return.[69]

It is for these reasons that Bray has stated that Thomas's interest in the literal sense of the text helped spark the Reformation. Whereas the Renaissance (generally thought to begin around 1300) was sparked by a desire to return to studying and understanding classical texts (*ad fontes*, "back to the sources"), it is not difficult to see how Thomas, Nicholas, and others were also interested in going "back to the sources." There was a discernible commitment to Scripture as the ultimate authority which must be based on belief in the clarity and unity of Scripture.

It is doubtful that Thomas, as some have suggested, held to any variation of the spiritual sense from what Augustine held. Indeed, Thomas held that there could be more than one sense to a text, owing unsurprisingly to his high theology in which Christ speaks the word and fills all

66. See Aquinas, *ST*, 1.1.10, and Kreeft's comments in *Summa of the Summa*, 49–50.
67. See, for example, Chase, *40 Questions*, 91–92.
68. Chase, *40 Questions*, 217–18.
69. Barrett, *RR*, 189–90. There, Barrett shows that although medieval interpreters did not abandon the literal sense, there were some who emphasized it. Nevertheless, to construe this emphasis with an abandonment of the literal is reductive, as has been the tendency to draw a major dichotomy between the earlier Antiochene and Alexandrian interpretive schools.

things.⁷⁰ But, as shown above, Thomas, like Augustine, held that such additional senses must be governed by the literal sense or fanciful interpretations were virtually inevitable. Doctrine, in which Christ the living Word was progressively made manifest, must be the lens from which the pastoral application can be found.

Oberman notes that other factors in the late Middle Ages led to a desire for Reformation. People were tired of hearing flowery accounts of what true religious life is like and wanted instead to experience something palpable for themselves. There was a desire to know and experience the truth. Religious life in the Middle Ages had been thought of as speculative and uncertain.⁷¹ This skepticism—indeed, even a skepticism about things of faith in the midst of high Christendom—increased to such a point that, as Bray has said, Reformation was inevitable.⁷²

As hinted in a previous section, construals of medieval hermeneutics as entirely fanciful and fictional might present one side of the story. The influence of people like Thomas and Nicholas, when placed alongside a growing hunger for a deeper and more authentic Christian experience, made a reformation centered around Scripture to be at the very least likely. Exegesis had downgraded since Augustine, and there was a desire to return to the sources.

Reformation Hermeneutics: A Return to "Tradition 1"

What were the assumptions and goals of the Protestant Reformation? It has been shown that Augustinian exegesis held to a close reading of the text with priority given to the literal sense and secondary senses that were just that: secondary. The notion of an Augustinian figurative methodology that renders propositional truth claims an impossibility is simply incorrect.⁷³ Augustine's fight for the truth of the Christian faith, as well as Thomas's and Nicholas's concern for doctrine that follows from

---

70. See for instance Aquinas, *ST*, 1.1.8, 10; 1.2

71. See Oberman, *Dawn of the Reformation*, 15, 27. The imaginativeness of the medieval "model" of the universe, as C. S. Lewis calls it, is seen well in Lewis's *The Discarded Image*. It would be of interest to find out how Lewis would react to the charge that medieval religious life was "speculative" and "uncertain."

72. Bray, *Biblical Interpretation*, 166.

73. For such criticism of Augustine's method from reputable scholars, see Preuss, *From Shadow to Promise*, 9–23; Goldsworthy, *GCH*, 101–4; and Kaiser, "Evangelical Hermeneutics," 167–80.

the primary sense, argues strongly against this notion. They loved doctrine and preached it so that the church would live by it. That priority highlights the main issue for them: They had a strong sense of pastoral responsibility that relentlessly called for the saints' edification.[74] This double-priority—for both doctrine and edification—is, as Carter said, the very heart of Great Tradition exegesis.[75] Christ rules meaning, and the text is his voice to stir worship and edification. The similarities to modern evangelical biblical theology should be obvious.

But over the course of the medieval era, as has been shown, twin threats arose against this double priority: first, an overuse of allegory that placed it above its proper place in the hermeneutical process, leading to excesses; second, a shift from the ancient view that the rule of faith/gospel controls hermeneutics to the view that the *effect* of the rule of faith throughout time, that is, church tradition, controls hermeneutics (i.e., Tradition 3).[76]

Although some would say that the rule of faith is, by nature, consistent with church tradition at all primary points, many leading Reformers disagreed. Medieval allegorical excesses strengthen the argument of critics of the Augustinian method, even if the popular reasons for dismissiveness are easy to counter. The presence of such dissenting voices as Thomas's, Nicolas's, and Hugh's, as well as the ubiquity of the *quadriga*, render such wholesale exclusion at least reductive.[77] Nevertheless, the call for a return to Scripture's authoritative primacy, itself the heart of the Reformers' ministry, crying *sola scriptura* as the Reformation's formal principle, whether Luther, Zwingli, Cranmer, etc. in their various geographic and ecclesial contexts, evinces a clear discontinuity.[78] And as Mark Thompson has said, neither the discontinuities nor the continuities should be overstated.[79] Still, in a bit of irony, it seems to be a kind of historiographic Ockhamism to oversimplify the relationship of Reformation-era Protestants to medieval

---

74. See O'Keefe and Reno, *Sanctified Vision*, 115–39.

75. See Carter, *ISGT*, 188.

76. It is probably the case that this mistake would have been avoided if the church had thought about tradition, as Boersma has suggested, as "sacramental time" in which Christ the Word unfolds his truth unto the perfection of his peoples' fellowship with him. In such a model, Scripture always maintains priority, and tradition is the church's articulating the truth for its day (and for the help of later days), as God leads. See Boersma, *HP,*, 120–36.

77. As in Barrett, *RR*, 190–91.

78. Thompson, "Sola Scriptura," 155–59.

79. Thompson, "Sola Scriptura," 152.

churchmen as either entirely continuous or entirely discontinuous.[80] The irony is that this type of Ockhamism, the normalization of which is generally synonymous with the mindset of later medieval scholastics, is, as Barrett has labored to show, the exact ideological shift that led to the need for the Reformation; in the end, it shows that the Reformers had much more in common with earlier medieval scholastics than has commonly been thought. In fact, Barrett shows convincingly, it was the Ockhamist-Scotist nominalism of the later medieval church, along with its compatible Pelagianism, that had taken the Roman church so far from its traditional foundation that the Reformers could easily establish their own agreement with the patristic church and its Augustinian soteriology and realism.[81]

Preuss continues his aforementioned (critical) historical study to argue that the Augustinian method had led to the view that Christ's coming removed the Old Testament from the theological horizon.[82] It was into that interpretive moment that Martin Luther, over the course of his early Psalms lectures, came to see parallels between Old and New Testament believers under the concept of *promissio*. Before Luther, exegetes, says Preuss, had dehistoricized the Old Testament, treating it as a flat (that is, non-escalating or developing) description of Christ. Luther came to see that the Old Testament described the real history of those who were living under God's promises in analogical ways to New Testament believers. There is therefore much pastoral value for New Testament believers studying the Old. Not only does the Old Testament—via promise and fulfillment, type and antitype, and prosopology—describe Christ (as was already believed), but it also describes the experience of New Testament believers who live their lives waiting on the Lord's eschatological salvation.[83] In this way, the New Testament texts cited above, which say that the Old is given for encouragement, now make sense: Whereas Old

---

80. For accessible studies of the influence of the nominalism and univocity in the thought of William of Ockham (fourteenth century) and his predecessor John Dun Scotus (thirteenth–fourteenth centuries), see Boersma's *HP*, 68–83, as well as Pickstock, "Duns Scotus," 116–40.

For the use of "Ockhamism" as descriptive noun, see Radner, *Time and the Word*.

81. See Barrett, *RR*, 228–83. Barrett includes at the conclusion of the cited chapter a brief conclusion; Barrett, *RR*, 281–83. See also Barrett, *RR*, 388–96 for Luther's disillusionment with the Ockhamist *via moderna*.

82. Preuss, *From Shadow to Promise*, 156.

83. Preuss, *From Shadow to Promise*, 186. Recall Carter's comments that Christ is present in the Old Testament via prophecy, types, prosopology, Christological/spiritual sense, and recapitulation. See Carter, "Premodern View," 239–40.

Testament believers waited by faith on Christ's *first* coming, New Testament believers wait by faith on Christ's *second* coming (Heb 11:1—12:2). Understandable also is Preuss's conclusion that Luther recovered the Old Testament's historicity for the church.[84] The Old Testament tells the history of God's working with his people as he progressively brought redemption into the world "at the right time" (Gal 4:4). Since new covenant participants are themselves the people of God through his redemption accomplished and fulfilled (1 Pet 2:9), they walk in the footsteps of faith that have already been laid down (Rom 4:12; cf. Heb 11.)

Augustine to Blame for Allegorical Excesses?

It is an overstatement, however, to suggest that Augustine's method *led to* the dehistoricizing of the Old Testament. It would be more accurate to call the excesses of the medieval approach evidence of *misuse* of the Augustinian model being the cause. Luther, an Augustinian monk himself, sought to recapture the proper use of the Augustinian method. To Luther, as with Augustine (and Thomas), the literal sense came first and was contextualized by a redemptive-historical understanding of Scripture with pastoral edification as the final step.[85] Further, like Augustine, Luther, against divergent perspectives, held to the clarity of Scripture in its gospel-centered unity.[86] The center of Scripture was for Luther the same as it was for Augustine: Christ as the Word made flesh who brings new creation.[87] Thus understood, Scripture carries its own authority and can interpret itself.[88] Thus is laid the groundwork for the *sola* as the formal principle.

So, for Luther, as for others in Great Tradition hermeneutics, the gospel (rule of faith) controls exegesis, which is driven first by the literal sense with secondary consideration given to pastoral senses. Although Luther was at times guilty of reducing the Old Testament down to "law" (in opposition to the New Testament as "gospel"), his concerns were

---

84. Preuss, *From Shadow to Promise*, 6.

85. Oberman makes the point that Luther, in couching theology in terms of promise, contextualized ontology in terms of economy, which was counter to the medieval view (Oberman, *Dawn of Reformation*, 64).

86. George, *Reading Scripture with the Reformers*, 127–30.

87. See Daley, *God Visible*, 173. See also Augustine, *Expositions of the Psalms*, 51–72, 420–21, quoted in Carter, *ISGT*, 159.

88. See Thompson, "Sola Scriptura," 181, 184.

exegetical: He saw the word itself—not tradition—as the means through which the redeeming God brings people to himself.[89] Scripture's goal is to tell what God has accomplished in Christ,[90] and that he offers the benefits thereof to the lost, who can only apprehend the message by faith alone (Rom 3:24–26). It is only when one has faith that they can understand the Scriptures at all (cf. Heb 11:6).[91] It is not difficult to understand, therefore, how justification by faith alone would become the functional center of Lutheran theology: One is justified by faith alone (and thus converted), and the Scripture is Christ's word spoken to them for their shepherding and discipleship.[92] The regenerate have ears to hear what their shepherd says to them on their journey.

This serves to suggest the real difference between Luther and his late medieval predecessors: Whereas these scholastics had begun to make the church and its tradition the norming norm of authority, Luther and his sixteenth- and seventeenth-century successors and colleagues said that the Scripture alone, as apprehended by the faithful who have life in the Holy Spirit, is the only authority of the redeemed conscience.[93] It is not that church tradition has nothing to say in helping believers understand Scripture. The reality of the believer's fellowship with God through Christ their redeemer and very life (Rom 8:10; Col 1:27) supplies them the proper lenses to be able to not only understand but follow God's word. Faithful tradition helps the believer to know how believers in other eras heard and appropriated the Scriptures, but the Holy Spirit actively works in the believer's own life to do the same in their unique day.

As such, the Reformers, Luther the most prolific and likely most influential of all, were not in lockstep with the radical Reformers in arguing for Tradition 0, a construal of tradition's place which Barrett also calls *nuda scriptura*: listening to nothing but Scripture; no creed but Christ and no rule but the Bible.[94] Rather, Scripture alone, as throughout the Great Tradition, is God's word to the church and world, and tradition is the fruit of God's speech. In the same way that fruit hanging from a tree should not be confused with the tree itself, so should the interpretive

---

89. See Franzmann, "Seven Theses," 235–46, especially 237.
90. Bray, *Biblical Interpretation*, 198.
91. Hagen, "*Omnis homo mendax*: Luther on Psalm 116," in Muller, Thompson, *BIER*, 96–102.
92. Franzmann, "Seven Theses," 237.
93. See Chester and Reeves, *Why the Reformation Still Matters*, 40.
94. See Barrett, *God's Word Alone*, 23.

tradition not be confused with the Scripture it interprets. As stated earlier, Scripture is *magisterial* while tradition is *ministerial*. Tradition helps believers to understand and rightly think about Scripture in ways not dissimilar to a local church pastor's pulpit exegesis for his congregation's edification. This is what was meant by *sola scriptura*: Scripture is the source of the church's gospel and message, not either a product of or a partner to the church's gospel and message. Whereas Rome had begun to teach that the church made Scripture and thus still wields the magisterial authority (which it still teaches[95]), the Reformers noted that to say as much was a direct contradiction to Eph 2:20. There, the church is built on the foundation of the apostles and prophets with Christ himself as cornerstone.[96] If this is the case, it follows, the Reformers said, that tradition can err, though Scripture, by virtue of its revelatory nature, cannot.[97] "Councils can err; accept them if they represent the whole church (not just Rome), and if they don't contradict Scripture."[98] Scripture, according to them, is not the only authority (for the hermeneutical tradition is indeed the outworking of Christ's leading his people into the truth), but it is the *final* authority.[99]

Furthermore, Scripture's very nature contributes to its ability to be ultimately authoritative in the life of the church. Barrett, reflecting on the view of Scripture in the Church of England's Forty-Two Articles (1552–53), said that the truly evangelical hermeneutic is that which holds that Scripture interprets Scripture. As such, it cannot contradict itself but gives clarity to itself. It is, therefore, sufficient. This sufficiency, however, does not lead to an anti-conciliar impulse that rejects tradition. Rather, Scripture's sufficiency leads to being pro-tradition in this way: Because

---

95. See the Catechism of the Catholic Church, 82: Both Scripture and tradition "*must* be accepted and honored with equal sentiments of devotion and reverence" (emphasis added).

Also worth noting is Sylvestro Prierias's (d. 1523) words to Luther that heretics are "those who do not hold fast to the teachings of the Roman church and the Pope as the infallible rule of faith *from which even Holy Scripture draws its strength.*" Quoted in Thompson, "Sola Scriptura," 152. Emphasis Thompson's.

96. Such was Calvin's argument in *Institutes*, 1.7.2. See also Barrett, *God's Word Alone*, 65–67.

97. Barrett, *God's Word Alone*, 65–75.

98. This is Vanhoozer's summary of Calvin's and Luther's stance toward the authority of the councils; Vanhoozer, *Biblical Authority After Babel*, 143–45.

99. Vanhoozer, *Biblical Authority After Babel*, 143–45; Vanhoozer makes the point that this way of approaching the *sola* distinguishes it from *solo scriptura*, which is roughly equivalent to *nuda scriptura* and is ubiquitous in fundamentalist biblicism.

Scripture is a unified and clear witness, the role of tradition—to pass down Scripture's witness through generations—is possible. As aforementioned, the Reformers advocated for tradition that was consistent with Scripture and thus was true. This is the *sola* in action: Scripture, in its theological and Christocentric clarity, is uniquely equipped with an internal unity that breathes out the voice of God. Since creeds can also be clear, their authority depends upon their consistency with Scripture which alone, being revealed, can stand judge over the creeds' faithfulness.[100] It is in this way, Steinmetz says, that "knowledge of the church's exegetical tradition is an indispensable *aid* for the interpretation of Scripture." As Barrett says, in response, the Reformers (via the *sola*) "interpreted the Bible *with the church*."[101] Any criticism the Reformers leveled at tradition was leveled from a position of *identification with* the tradition, calling for a return to the tradition's original source, Scripture itself.

So, similarly, the relationship between Scripture's authority and the appropriateness of the various senses in the *quadriga* can be summarized this way: The literal sense is the authority, the seed from which the pastoral senses flow. The gospel, which can be loosely equated with the *analogy fidei*, defined in terms of the Ten Commandments, the Apostles' Creed, the Lord's Prayer, and the Sacraments,[102] is the scriptural center that not only gives the church its authority (Matt 16:16–18) but its doctrinal and hermeneutical clarity in discerning the literal sense. When the gospel is clear, the church can hear God's leading as it listens to Scripture (John 10:3, 16, 27), and can proclaim God's truth with heaven's authority in the plain sense. With this foundation laid, pastoral application follows, binding the conscience only insofar as the gospel contextualizes the literal sense and thus contextualizes latter senses. As such, it could be said that quadratic interpretation loosely mirrors the relationship of Scripture and tradition: The text itself (Scripture) is the ultimate authority, and tradition itself (tradition) is subordinate, authoritative *when* consistent with Scripture. Conversely, the literal sense (*quadriga* point 1) is authoritative in interpretation, and the tropological (*quad* 2), allegorical (*quad* 3), and anagogical (*quad* 4) senses bear the same authority only in their gospel-centered consistency with the literal sense.[103]

100. Barrett, *RR*, 800n149.

101. Barrett, *RR*, 194. Emphasis original. Steinmetz quoted in Muller, "Biblical Interpretation," 7; emphasis added.

102. Barrett, *RR*, 192.

103. This framework is a reflection upon reading Barrett, *RR*, 189–90.

CHRIST AND THEOLOGY

This, as Barrett shows, is the same argument that Augustine made in his day: Because of the nature of the believer's fellowship with God, multiple secondary senses are not dangerous because the believer's conscience will not allow them to contradict the literal sense. That question is the most important one: Is the exegete in Christ or not? If so, then because the same Spirit who inspired the original text still speaks to believers in the present day (John 16:13; 1 John 2:27)[104], the believer can be sure that they are communing with Christ via his word, and he will lead them to proper apprehension of what he has said and still says to them. If in Christ, said Augustine, the believer is to "treat the Scripture of God as the face of God, [and] melt in its presence."[105]

This is truly *ad fontes*. As medieval interpretation had drifted from Augustine's method, which kept allegory in its proper place, Thomas and Nicholas had both sought a return to the plain sense; but by Luther's day, improvement upon Old Testament exegesis meant merely returning to Augustine by saying that it is by the believer's fellowship with Christ that they can comprehend the plain sense, which establishes the usefulness of the other senses. The *analogia fidei* is the "ancient, true Christian catechism"; Luther opposed allegory insofar as it conflicted with the catechism.[106] The faithful are those whose lives are controlled by the true Christian faith, and true Christian faith not only contextualizes the text for interpretation but the very interpretation itself. The gospel of the Son gives coherence to all of reality generally and the text specifically.

Thus, based on their belief in Scripture's authority, the Reformers held to the coherence of Scripture's system of thought. Not only could Scripture be understood, but it was sufficient for all of life and godliness (cf. 2 Pet 1:3). Again, this was the point of *sola scriptura*: not that there is no truth outside of Scripture but that the way of life and godliness is so clear and self-attesting in Scripture that there is no need for any external authority to test or check it.[107] The rule of faith is Scripture's own "canon within the canon," not in its being more authoritative than the rest, but in its being the ontological and epistemological entrance point into regenerate interpretation. In other words, it is through the rule of faith that one acquires Spirit-inspired spectacles. It then follows that Scripture is clear

---

104. Belt, "Lessons from the Reformation," 95–109.
105. Quoted in Wilken, *Spirit of Early Christian Thought*, 50.
106. Barrett, *RR*, 192.
107. Bray, *Biblical Interpretation*, 190.

to all who read it with faith.[108] As the lost are drawn to Christ through the word (John 6:44), the Spirit of God quickens them to faith (6:63). Once put into right relationship with God, the reader then becomes subject to Scripture's saving discipline (Gal 3:3). Cranmer summarized, doubtless as a good microcosm of the goals of Reformation exegesis, that Scripture *heals* the reader as they prayerfully pore over it.[109] As with Augustine centuries earlier, the key is whether the reader is regenerate. Then and only then *can* the Word be heard and practiced. "The mind set on the flesh is hostile to God; it does not submit to God, nor can it" (Rom 8:7). The point, as regards the rest of this project, is that in the Great Tradition, whether ancient, medieval, or Reformational, discipleship is the context of exegesis. Since discipleship is about the experience of growing fellowship with Christ through his Spirit, the Spirit uses Scripture to show Christ to the believer and conform them to his glorious image. In fellowship with God who is the divine author, the believer hears God as he transcends any human author's understanding to communicate Christ across the canon. With these convictions in mind, the Reformers, like their patristic and medieval predecessors, sought Christ in his word, interpreting the Bible *with* the church as they went along. Like Scripture was the foundation of the tradition, and perfectly so, plain reading is the perfect foundation for spiritualizing—the reader imperfect, the divine author not.

Reformation Exegesis: The Literal Sense for Gospel and Church

Thus is the context of the Reformation era's contribution to Great Tradition exegesis. The Reformers were not modernistic in their interpretation but precritical. According to Barrett, they were "medieval men

---

108. Oberman, *Dawn of Reformation*, 184. For good summaries of the early history of "rule of faith" from the likes of Irenaeus, Tertullian, and others, see Trueman, *Creedal Imperative*, 55–60, and Greene-McCreight's *Ad-Litteram*, 5–7. Greene-McCreight gives a helpful quotation explanation of the rule of faith worth quoting at length:
> (The Rule) holds together theologically God the Creator and Jesus Christ, and hermeneutically the Old and New Testaments . . . (as such) the rule of faith is a basic "take" on the subject matter and plot of the Christian story which "couples" the confession of Jesus the Redeemer with the confession of God the Creator. (The Rule) is generally understood to have been drawn from Scripture, and in biblical interpretation it is reapplied to Scripture.

109. Quoted in George, *Reading Scripture with the Reformers*, 136.

with a pre-critical model;"[110] to them, the pursuit of Scripture was the pursuit of God's truth. This pursuit, arising within the context of the *ad fontes* move to return to the study of the ancient sources, requires a grammatical-historical precision that took center stage in the exegesis of the Reformers' day.

Further, according to Muller, it was also the foundational nature of the literal sense (emphasized in earlier medieval exegesis, but then so minimized that prominent middle-to-later medieval voices called for a return to it) that led to the Reformational emphasis on philological and textual study. In contrast to Preuss's construal of the Reformational shift (that is, out of allegory, back to text), Muller argues convincingly that *ad fontes* also implied a return to the plain sense of the biblical text *for the sake of* pastoral/spiritual application/reading, or right allegory. Muller concludes, "This passage from the fourfold exegesis toward an exegesis emphasizing the literal meaning of the text, marks a continuity—*not a contrast*—between sixteenth-century biblical interpretation and the exegesis of at least the preceding four centuries."[111] This "shift to the letter," and thus to close reading, was, as will be seen, because of, not in opposition to, the pastoral needs of the church.

As one case study, Melanchthon issued a highly influential commentary on Romans that was celebrated for its exegetical precision and clarity. He saw Romans as making one primary argument: Sinners are justified by faith alone in the work of Christ alone.[112] His argument and method demonstrate the heart of Reformation hermeneutics: careful exegesis engaging grammar and history from a posture of listening to the Word of the saving God who speaks by Scripture in the gospel, that hearers will hear God.

Calvin, known by many of his day simply as "the theologian," gave his life to careful exegesis. Although his *Institutes* is his opus, his life's work was his preaching and commentaries. Exegesis produces doctrine, which then leads to preaching.[113] Worth noting is that the gospel itself was central in his exegesis and pastoral work. Although Calvin did not believe that Christ was on "every page" of Scripture,[114] he nevertheless

---

110. Barrett, *RR*, 193.

111. From Muller, "Biblical Interpretation," 12; emphasis added. Quoted also in Barrett, *RR*, 194.

112. Timothy Wengert, "Philip Melanchthon's 1522 Annotations," 129–30.

113. Bray, *Biblical Interpretation*, 201.

114. Bray, *Biblical Interpretation*, 201.

held that all of Scripture is the means through which believers' faith in Christ is both received and stirred. Oberman's example is Calvin's construal of David's nomadic kingly reign as parabolic for Christ's current hidden reign, so that believers will be helped in their belief in him: In the same way that David was already king during the final stages of Saul's reign, and yet his reign was hidden, so Christ's lordship in the current day is veiled among the nations; and yet, he is still Lord (Ps 2).[115] When one considers Calvin's pastoral Christocentricity alongside the centrality of the gospel message throughout the second and third books of his *Institutes*,[116] as well as Calvin's reputation for preaching the gospel in every sermon, it is not difficult to detect the same priorities discernibly common to Augustine, Thomas, Nicholas, and Luther. That priority is the gospel as plausibility structure, the sufficiency and authority of Scripture as God's voice, and an unavoidable pastoral responsibility to edify the church by turning their attention to Jesus with whom they have fellowship as he presents himself.[117]

As aforementioned, the theological locus of the Reformation era was certitude. Certitude is the certainty and assurance that a believer can have that God accepts them on the basis of Jesus's work on their behalf.[118] Countless preachers and exegetes during this period wanted to tell people that on the basis of Christ's finished work, they could have assurance by faith that they were right with God and could walk with him by his word (Ps 32:1–2).[119] And this was possible because God glorifies himself in being merciful (Ps 143:2; Eph 1:10). The Reformed exegetical endeavor, concerned with careful grammatical-historical engagement, was supremely twofold: First, it was gospel-oriented—that is, centered

---

115. See Oberman, *Dawn of Reformation*, 237–38. Boersma offers an interesting application of this to the praying life in *Pierced by Love*, 181–200.

116. See Calvin, *Inst.*, 2.9–10, 3.2–3, 24.

117. "Calvin drew out of the Scriptures aspects of Christian teaching which the church had not heard for centuries. This was above all the case with the doctrines of grace. The promise of salvation was presented to all who would believe it. Calvin peached justification by faith, as all the reformers did. More than some, perhaps, he also preached sanctification by faith. The lives of those who believed the Word of God would be transformed by that Word." Old, *Reading and Preaching*, 4:130, quoted in George, *Reading Scripture*, 244.

118. Schreiner, "Calvin and the Exegetical Debates," 189–215.

119. As Calvin writes, "The preaching of the gospel declares nothing more than that sinners, without any merit of their own, are justified by the paternal indulgence of God. It is wholly summed up in Christ." *Inst.*, 2.10.4.

on the gospel of Jesus, making sure the people knew and believed it;[120] and secondly, it was pastoral, emphasizing the importance of living by faith in the gospel, as it always had been throughout the Great Tradition. The literal sense was always gospel-contextualized, which meant that the latter quadratic senses simply applied it to the people. Like Christ's centrality is latent in the biblical theology of the current day, it was also latent in Reformation hermeneutics.

The Calvin Caveat: To Blame for Grammatical-Historical Excesses?

There is one caveat worth mentioning regarding the Reformational exegetical method, most exemplified in Calvin's work. Calvin said that the exegete has as his "only work to lay open the mind of the writer whom he undertakes to explain."[121] It has been argued in both the previous chapter and the current one that the goal of exegesis is to show forth the word of God as it is intended by *God himself*, both in the text's original context and in the context of the one reading. The original context includes the historical details. The canonical context—that is, the text's place in the overall gospel story—is the primary context. Human authorial intent must, therefore, be thought of as subservient to divine authorial intent: Whatever was in the mind of the human writer, the goal of exegesis is the mind of the Spirit who goes before and inspires them. The first of Steinmetz's theses on Reformational exegesis is that the human author's intention does not exhaust the meaning of the biblical text.[122] The issue is not merely what grammatical historical study yields as meaningful; rather, God continues to speak by his word to those listening in the present day.

Did Calvin, in light of the aforementioned quote, deviate from this, suggesting that the primary exegetical endeavor is historical? Does his question not at least lead to a grammatical-historical method that pays little attention to the Scripture's gospel-centered context and is more concerned with historical considerations than with doctrine?[123]

---

120. Luther famously said that justification by faith alone needed to be beaten into the heads of parishioners week in and week out because week in and week out, they forget it. Luther, *Lectures on Galatians*, 90–91.

121. Calvin, "Epistle Dedicatory, to Simon Grynaeus," in *Commentaries on The Epistle of Paul the Apostle to the Romans*, trans. Benjamin Farley, xxiii.

122. Quoted in Muller, *BIER*, 7.

123. For one example of this argument, see Farrar, *History of Interpretation*, 346–49.

Such a charge would misunderstand Calvin for two reasons. First, Calvin had as his priority the communication of the clarity of biblical doctrine as set forth in the pages of Scripture.[124] As Boersma has said, a grammatical-historical method that operates according to modernistic presuppositions regarding history—that is, where history is only thought of in terms of progress, with the current day being the reference point—jettisons the question of truth, because nothing is *ever* absolutely true. There is no truth—only progress.[125] But Calvin's life's work was the setting forth of revealed truth, convicted as he was that the goal of exegesis is the right preaching of the gospel, which is itself the keys of the kingdom which the church possesses (Matt 16:18–19).[126] A concern for the mind of the human author, therefore, cannot mean for Calvin an abandonment of the revealed-ness of revealed truth. Rather, Calvin assumed that the Lord so moved to inspire the human writers of Scripture that they intended simply to say what they heard from him, regardless of the depth of clarity they may or may not have had. So understood, exegesis is simply trying to seek this out. Further, it should be noted that historical-critical considerations did not originate with Calvin; for instance, all precritical exegetes were familiar with—and many spoke about—the so-called "synoptic problem."[127]

Secondly, Calvin held that Scripture is structured and written in such a way that would have been impossible if dependent on human authors. Romans, placed canonically as a strategic reflection after both the Christ-event and its heralding through the world, is the access point by which one can understand the rest of the Scripture—a sort of divinely inspired code to unlock Scripture.[128] To Calvin, Scripture was given because of humanity's inability to deal squarely with the knowledge of the true God; thus such an emphasis was placed on idolatry through the Old

---

124. Kok, "Heinrich Bullinger's Exegetical Method: The Model for Calvin?," in Muller, Thompson, *BIER*, 254.

125. Boersma, *Scripture as Real Presence*, 275.

126. See Calvin, *Inst.*, 4.1–3, 8.

127. This point is made in Muller, Thompson, "The Significance of Precritical Exegesis: Retrospect and Prospect," in *BIER*, 341.

See also Carter, *ISGT*, 126. Carter says, "There is much that is good in the modern, scholarly study of the Bible, because much of it is just a continuation of the kind of scholarship that existed prior to modernity."

128. Calvin, "Epistle Dedicatory," *Commentaries on the Epistle of Paul the Apostle to the Romans*, xxiv.

CHRIST AND THEOLOGY

Testament to intensify the need for Christ to come and give clarity.[129] Only by the Spirit's leading does the believer know that they are reading God's truth to them.[130] Thus, Scripture is far from a book with only a primitive historical meaning. As revealed truth, Scripture has redemptive purposes as given by God to the reader regardless of their location in history.

Nevertheless, Calvin did engage with the text of Scripture with precision. This precision, understood alongside his expertise at unfolding a text's meaning and application in the pastoral context, makes him historically unique in the history of the church to his day (and perhaps to the current one).[131] His emphasis on the mind of the human writer might have opened the door for the grammatical-historical method with all of its eventual excesses (that is, as in historical criticism). He is not any more to blame for this than Augustine would be to blame for the allegorical excesses of the medieval era. Indeed, when one compares Calvin's exegetical, doctrinal, and pastoral care with Augustine's, it seems like they were breathing the same Great Tradition "air." If so, Calvin's exegetical precision was an *improvement* upon the exegesis of his Great Tradition predecessors. Nevertheless, exegesis that pays attention to the whole narrative of Scripture and assumes that it is true while setting forth Christ and helping listeners to follow him is the common denominator between the apostles, Augustine, and the Reformers. If this is the case, the Reformation was not simply the triumph of Augustine's doctrine of grace over his doctrine of the church[132] but the triumph of Augustine's actual exegetical practices over his supposed exegetical practices. It can be argued that Augustine and the Reformers were forerunners of the biblical theology practiced by Vos, then Clowney, then Beale and the rest: Exegesis's goal is setting forth the Christ of the gospel in the context of discipleship.[133] The message of Scripture is that in Christ are hidden all the treasures of wisdom and knowledge (Col 2:3), and the task of

---

129. Calvin, *Inst.*, 1.5–6.
130. Calvin, *Inst.*, 1.7.
131. Bray, *Biblical Interpretation*, 204.
132. As famously posited in Warfield, *Calvin and Augustine*, 321–22.
133. Worth mentioning is that the writer recently learned via private correspondence with Goldsworthy that a recent Oxford dissertation sought to favorably compare Goldsworthy with Calvin.

preaching and teaching is not only to proclaim this before the church and world but to demonstrate how it is so (1 Cor 14:24–25).[134]

The Reformation and the Spiritual Senses

Francis Turretin (1623–87), in expounding the Reformational view of the *quadriga*, gave a simple explanation of the process: "Distinguish the sense of Scripture from its application. The sense is one—but the application may be different;—thus allegory, anagogy and tropology are not so much different senses, *as applications of the one literal sense*."[135] It seems, therefore, that Reformational exegesis is simply Augustinian exegesis, consistent with what he believed about the so-called "senses." But since Luther had advanced the historicization of the gospel in exegesis and Calvin had made such advances in grammatical-historical exegesis, Turretin's summary of the *quadriga* was not as much a reformulation as a clarification in light of developments.

In light of these observations, the reader can understand why Calvin would say in his prefatory address to King Francis at the beginning of the *Institutes* that if the Protestant system of religion were set alongside of the Roman Catholic system and both compared to the Fathers, "the better part of the victory would be ours" (that is the Protestants).[136] He believed, as did Luther, that his theology, ecclesiology, and exegesis belonged to the same tradition as the fathers.[137] Even if the institutional continuity

---

134. Worth mentioning is Bartholomew's point that Calvin was no modernist, "nor a modern historic critic. For him, the humanistic emphasis on the historical setting and authorial intent still served the greater purpose of edifying and nurturing the faithful." Calvin thus contextualized close exegesis as serving the church's gospel proclamation. See Bartholomew and Thomas, *Manifesto*, 245.

135. Turretin, *Institutes of Elenctic Theology*, II, xix, 6, quoted in Heppe, *Reformed Dogmatics*, 38; emphasis added.

136. Calvin, *Inst.*, 25.

137. One interesting example of Calvin's sense of closeness to patristic interpretation is seen in the editor's note on Calvin's treatment of Luke 2:11 in *Commentaries*. Calvin, in his Latin edition, uses the word *Salvator* for the first word of the phrase "a Savior, Christ. . ." (2:11), explaining in his comments that the Greek *soter* has, as Cicero states, no noun equivalent, and yet it is much more extensive than *Servator*, which the Latin Vulgate uses. Calvin makes apology for this translation change, including an assurance that he is sure that the fathers and Jerome meant the same that he does. Calvin's editor comments, "The purity of [Calvin's] style discovers so perfect an acquaintance with the writers of the Augustan age, that it must have given him uneasiness to depart from their authorized terms. He pleads [in citing Cicero] high authority for the liberty he had taken" (*Calvin's Commentaries*, Vol. 16, 117n1). Here one finds

of the church had become, for varying reasons, difficult to trace across recent centuries,[138] the doctrinal continuity which the Reformed shared with the fathers had not. It is this project's hope that in light of preceding reflections, this gospel continuity is obvious and discernible. The Great Tradition is defined in terms of consistent concern to faithfully practice gospel-oriented and discipleship-contextualized exegesis as believers.[139]

Counterarguments

Responding to "The Reformation Recovered a Single Sense Reading"

It will likely be helpful to consider a few counterarguments to the narrative of historical development traced above. Much could be pursued, but the focus will primarily be the hermeneutical endeavor. First, Walter Kaiser has argued that one of the three "loadstars" of the Protestant Reformation was the conviction that any particular text of Scripture has only one meaning, found in grammatical historical analysis. Kaiser cites several statements by Luther to support his assertion.[140]

Kaiser's assertion does not contradict any of what has been said if the correct amount of nuance is given in defining the prevailing practice of Great Tradition exegetes. The plain reading of a text *does* yield a singular meaning, even as Augustine said.[141] But what Augustine, Origen,

---

an almost perfect example of the Reformational sense of fellowship with the Tradition based on the gospel: Calvin was willing to take liberty in translation to make the gospel clear, though he felt the need to offer an apology to the ecclesial fathers that preceded him, explaining that he thinks that he was consistent with them. Calvin was not after innovation but recollection.

138. Chester and Reeves, *Why the Reformation Still Matters*, 47.

139. Further interesting reading can be found in Fisher, "Medieval and Reformation Interpretations," 71–86. There, Fisher aptly shows that both Calvin and Oecolampadius exegete the use of the Old Testament in Heb 1–2 in a way that rescues the text from demanding allegorical readings in order for there to be the presence of Christological teachings that the writer is supporting. Fisher concludes that such plain-sense exegesis in the likes of Calvin and Oecolampadius led to modern interest in the New Testament's use of the Old, which is a primary goal of biblical theology (Fisher, "Medieval and Reformation Interpretations," 86).

140. Kaiser, "Evangelical Hermeneutics."

141. It is very clear in *On Genesis* that, although Augustine applies Gen 1–2 in an array of ways and even adopts a way of understanding the text that might diverge from the typical evangelical view of the current day, he holds the authority of the plain text as written. Everywhere this is implicit, sometimes explicit; see Augustine, *On Genesis*, 48, 51–60, 173.

Thomas, etc., referred to as other senses, Turretin relabeled as applications of the literal sense. It is likely that the Reformation, by tweaking the language of the fathers, improved it. If this point is remembered, Kaiser's assertion in no way challenges the conclusions offered; it is just that, as is often the case in historical analysis, terms need to be defined properly and accurately. It is, nevertheless, worth considering how Kaiser would respond to such a claim, if he would agree or would want to clarify.[142]

Responding to Perceived Reformational Utopia

Secondly, a question: Goldsworthy, in his *GCH*—in many ways Goldsworthy's most robust (even if not best known) scholarly contribution—devotes the entire middle section to ways in which the gospel has been "eclipsed" throughout the various stages of church history.[143] But Goldsworthy, himself no shy proponent of Reformed hermeneutics, never identifies any ways that the gospel might have been eclipsed during the Reformation period. It would not be surprising if critics of Reformed hermeneutics were to seize on this as a form of bias. Would critics, then, have a case, or was the Reformation truly a sort of golden age of exegesis?

The answer to both related questions seems to be in the negative for two reasons. First, Goldsworthy devotes an entire chapter to the ways that the gospel has been in danger of eclipse in recent evangelicalism, itself descending from the Reformed heritage.[144] Doubtless this reflects at least somewhat on Goldsworthy's awareness of the potential pitfalls of the Reformation, even if he never explicitly states as much. Secondly, and perhaps more importantly, Goldsworthy's main argument is for the need to recapture what he sees as gospel-centered Reformed hermeneutics. He wants to see a revival of what had been earlier revived in the Reformation period, because the gospel, like it was in that day, is always in danger of being lost.

---

142. It would seem, based on Kaiser and Silva's *Introduction to Biblical Hermeneutics*, 29–66, that Kaiser would be uncomfortable saying that a text has more than one *meaning*, though it might have different *applications*. This point gets to the heart of the issue: What is the Bible? Is it a book that readers apply or a sanctified tool through which God speaks? A person's position in the "meaning" vs. "application" debate depends on their answer to this other, more foundational question.

143. Goldsworthy, *GCH*, 87–180.

144. Goldsworthy, *GCH*, 167–80.

Such was also the observation of many Reformation-era leaders and writers; first, Melanchthon stated that throughout all of church history, the gospel is *continually* under attack and in need of God to raise up men who will restore it.[145] When the clarity and authority of the text are recaptured, the gospel is centralized again. Second, John Foxe (1517–87), in his "To the True and Faithful Congregation of Christ's Universal Church," supported the Reformers' claims of Rome's hypocrisy by drawing attention to the fact that the history of the church shows the discernible presence of hypocrisy at all points. In short, the fidelity of the gospel among its professors will always be a battle. Nevertheless, as Barrett summarizes of Foxe's final section, "God never permitted his church to be 'so oppressed' that the gospel itself was extinguished."[146] That was the focus of the Reformation: recapturing the Great Tradition hermeneutic that (a) contextualizes every text according to the rule of faith/gospel, (b) uses available critical tools to discern plain meaning while bearing in mind that the text's ultimate context is the whole Scripture, and (c) seeks to prayerfully apply the text in ways that are edifying to the church and glorifying to God the Trinity. Where Scripture is the authority, the gospel will go forth and give life. It is not that the gospel was in no danger of eclipse during the Reformation period. The Reformation was, though, about a shift in attention back to the source of the gospel in terms of its formality: Scripture. So, of course, anywhere that that focus was taken away, the gospel can be eclipsed. In general, however, it can be said that during the Reformation, the exegetical focus was so Christocentric and church-oriented, and also fruitful, that people wanted to make sure the gospel-arrow stayed pointing forward. Excesses are likely unavoidable; but since it is the gospel that calls people back to fidelity (Acts 3:20–21), having it at the center is the safest course imaginable.

Responding to the Calvin Caveat Question

One final question: Did Calvin's close exegesis, understood in terms of unpacking the human author's intent, lead to historical criticism? It is always dangerous in historical studies to assert causation where there is only proof of precedence. Because of this, as Carl Trueman has shown,

---

145. For the exact quote, see Wengert, "Lutheran Origins of Rhetorical Criticism," in Muller, Thompson, *BIER*, 139.

146. Foxe, "True and Faithful Congregation," 26, 85, quoted in Barrett, *RR*, 819.

modest conclusions are safest.[147] It is just as possible that Calvin's exegesis led to historical criticism as it is that Augustine's exegesis led to the allegorical excesses of the medieval period. It seems even more *probable*, however, that both men so mastered certain important practices (Augustine allegorical application and Calvin close exegesis) that some of their pedagogical progeny became so focused on mimicking their heroes' mastery of said practices that they lost sight of the ultimate focus of both: expounding Christ in his word to the upbuilding of his church. Such a claim is simultaneously apologetic of the men themselves and critical of those who may have sought to follow in their footsteps. It should be remembered, then, that neither Augustine nor Calvin were infallible in their exegetical endeavor; it is also true that both had outstanding followers, some of whom might have improved upon their predecessor's work.

The point is this: If anyone looks in the primary sources for excesses in either the Augustinian or Calvinian tradition, they will probably find them. Again, neither man was perfect in his exegesis. The message of Christianity, however, is that no man is, save one. The exegetical and theological endeavor of the Great Tradition is obsessively concerned with discerning all of reality through the epistemological lens of him who is light (John 1:4; 8:12).[148] Calvin and his Reformational partners sought an exegesis that so prioritized God's restoration of man to his image (in Christ's coming) that the Old Testament was preparatory for it; seeking to avoid both extremes of "merely critical and rationalistic interpretation," and on the other hand, "fanciful exposition of figurative

---

147. See Trueman, *Histories and Fallacies*, 139-40.

148. An interesting point relevant for this discussion is made by Thomas A. Myers, translator of Calvin's commentaries. First, for background, in discussing Calvin's balanced approach to spiritual interpretation of Ezekiel's prophetic witness, Myers endorses the construal of figurative exegesis put forth by William Warburton (1698-1779). To both Warburton and Myers (in response), words are intended to convey something real and, as such, cannot therefore be interpreted as conveying spiritual truth unless the literal/plain sense be first understood. In other words, the spiritual truth conveyed in the words can only be ascertained if the literal meaning of the words presented be heard/understood. This is the form of interpretation Calvin employed: show the plain sense and then show the text's spiritual, evangelical content.

But, Myers says, in agreement with what the present writer has stated above, that it is clear that there are dangers present in such a practice. Still, that does not imply the need to dispense with the practice. He concludes, "The spiritual interpretation may be abused, like all other good things. Cocceius, for instance, affords a remarkable instance of this error, as well as some of the Puritan Divines; but no sensible man denies the value of a possession because some are foolish enough to misuse it." In Calvin, *Ezekiel 13-20, Daniel 1-6*, 428.

language," all that is in the word are "vehicles . . . of our support as God's children, and our growth in his likeness." Thus it is God, not the exegetical method, who must give the reader/listener power to understand the meaning.[149] The fathers knew this, as did the earlier medieval church, and the Reformers. Christ-centered biblical theology in the current day also knows this, even if imperfectly. In Christ's ontological centrality, there is a discernibly consistent thread present throughout the Great Tradition, even if there are caveats when making comparisons.

Conclusion

This chapter, as a step in the direction of discovering the similarities and dissimilarities between Christ-centered biblical theology and the Reformation's formal principle, the *sola* (as the Great Tradition's Tradition 1), has sought to prove that the Reformers purposed to recapture Augustine's close exegesis and pastoral sensibility via re-centering the gospel/rule of faith exegetically and epistemologically. Augustine held to the priority of the text's literal sense, while at the same time carrying out the pastoral responsibility of application, both endeavors governed by the contextualizing norm of the risen Christ who is the telos of the text and the source of all of reality (Heb 1:2–3). Augustine's use of the so-called *quadriga* was no multi-option pool of directional options from which the exegete could "choose their own adventure." Rather, as with medieval interpretation in its earlier stages, the literal sense was supreme, and secondary senses, including allegory, were pastoral. Such a framework was not a hermeneutical innovation or novelty but a theological inevitability: God discerns and knows all things in one act, inhabiting eternity, simultaneously speaking truth and revealing mysteries about his eternal, loving, and good purposes via his word. It is only appropriate, therefore, to expect greater depth to what he says than what immediately meets the eyes and ears.[150]

Nevertheless, it is an unavoidable conclusion that over the course of the medieval era, allegorical excesses began to win the day, eclipsing close exegesis governed by the rule of faith/gospel. In fact, some held that the text of Scripture did not even have a literal sense except what the church

---

149. Calvin, *Ezekiel 13–20, Daniel 1–6*, 418–19. Myers proceeds to cite helpful examples from Chrysostom, Ambrose, and Augustine.

150. As Aquinas explains in *ST*, 1.1.10.

decides it is. Aquinas and Nicholas called for a return to the literal sense. Their doing so helped lead to the Reformation, which sought exegesis of the plain sense in its gospel-centric continuity with the rest of Scripture. Since Reformation occurred not only in the academy but in the churches, the need to apply the gospel to all of life was always a priority.

Thus, the Reformation recaptured a sense of the authority of Scripture on its own terms, with the rule of faith/gospel as "norming norm." This, perhaps surprisingly (to modern thinkers), brought a return to the literal sense of the text in each text's gospel-centric relation to the rest of Scripture. Luther saw such parallels between Old and New Testament believers that the Old Testament began to have true pastoral benefits to New Testament believers. So whatever Testament, the text of Scripture needed exegesis for the sake of pastoral application to the people of God who have fellowship with the risen Christ. Calvin was a master exegete, breathing the same air of spiritual excellence that his Great Tradition predecessors had. His exegesis, when combined with doctrinal priority and pastoral concern, was a peak in the history of exegesis and one that might still have yet to be eclipsed. It is no surprise, then, that both his *assumptions* (the authority of God's word alone, the fellowship of the church with the risen Christ who speaks his word to it still) and *goals* (the pastoral responsibility of exegeting the text to put Christ on display from his word) were the same as Augustine so many centuries before. If anything could be described as *ad fontes* during the days of the Reformers, it was their return to Augustine's text-driven exegesis.[151]

The reason that this is significant for the present project is that Christ-centered biblical theology is aimed at returning directly to the Scriptures for theological and pastoral conclusions to be found in

---

151. One final sidenote pertinent to what is written above is worth mentioning. Reformational exegesis was not monolithic. Myers shows the differences between Calvin's treatment of Old Testament prophecy and that of Oecolampadius, the former being more insistent and strict on his reading and the latter being more accommodating of various views, perhaps like Augustine's treatment of Gen 1–3. See Myers, "Translator's Preface," in Calvin, *Ezekiel 13–20, Daniel 1–6*, xlii–xliii. It does not require a lengthy perusal of Calvin's commentaries to see example after example of some form of "some read it this way, contrary to my reading. But the differences would not be worth arguing over. Let each be convinced in their own mind."

Barrett's magisterial work could also be sought for examples of differences between the Reformers' exegesis. The point is this: Exact exegetical consistency across the board was not the goal, but rather, it was seeking conformity to Christ via hearing him speak his gospel in his word. As seen above, the word itself is consistent, even if its preachers are not. They must all, however, consistently preach the word.

the subjection of self to the word. So understood, the posture of biblical theology is the same as that of Great Tradition hermeneutics from pre-Augustine to the Reformers. As a later chapter will show, the way in which God's revelation comes (which "way" is a primary focus of biblical theology) has essential pertinence for the Christian's faith journey. Paul could thus spend Gal 3 showing how Christ came to fulfill God's messianic promises before speaking in Gal 4 of his own longing for Christ to be formed in the Galatian believers (4:19). By faith in the promise from within the context of Spirit-led sojournment, Christ, as in the Gospels, arrives as king so that believers enter into a journey of growing Christ-likeness (2 Cor 3:18). More could be said, but the most important point is that, for both the Reformers and practitioners of biblical theology, Scripture is itself the true *fons* to which the exegete must return. Both evangelical biblical theologians and their Reformational forbearers, even via imperfect methods, seem concerned with the Great Tradition's continual pursuit: hearing the voice of the everlasting Lord, the risen Christ, who calls his sheep. Such an inkling anticipates the question that the next chapter seeks to address in substantial response to the project's original question(s): Though it has been established that Reformational hermeneutics carried on the hermeneutical development of premodern interpretation, do the hermeneutical imperfections of either the Reformation or of Christ-centered biblical theology preclude consistency with one another? To that assessment the next chapter turns.

4

Biblical Theology and the Great Tradition
Toward Typological Realism

> "As an eye, either dimmed by age or weakened by any other cause, sees nothing distinctly without the aid of glasses, so (such is our imbecility) if Scripture does not direct us in our inquiries after God, we immediately turn vain in our imaginations."
>
> —JOHN CALVIN

THIS CHAPTER ANALYZES THE findings of the first three chapters which sought to describe Christ-centered biblical theology in terms of its history and its goals. Chapter one examined the history, seeing that although biblical theology views Scripture as a Christ-centered unity through which God speaks, the consistency of such a paradigm has been less than incontrovertible. Recent developments have seen, however, the emergence of a Christ-centered biblical theology that seems to have goals and assumptions that are more consistent with historic orthodoxy, even if one "stream" is better equipped to engage with the theology of the Tradition as well as the practical needs of the church of any day. As such, biblical theology is both pre- and post-Enlightenment: *post* because it is a hermeneutical development within the context of an Enlightenment historical-consciousness, and *pre* because, although concerned with history, there is still primary concern for hearing Christ as God's voice speaking via the Scripture, setting reality before his church.

The second chapter disseminated biblical theology's goals and whether the goals are, generally speaking, being met. Positively, Christ-centered biblical theology tries to hear Christ as God's voice via Scripture. Negatively, since the Bible is ultimately contextualized in redemptive-historical terms, the theological/Christological depth present in both the Great Tradition and in Vos/Clowney biblical theology seems at present to be either elusive or absent. As such, evangelical biblical theology has two unfortunate weaknesses: It is less *theologically attuned* than ancient and medieval exegesis (since redemptive history, not theology proper, is the text's context) and less *practically attuned* (since, via its weak theology, it does not see time, space, and believers as participatory in God and his grand project).

Finally, the third chapter examined the history of Christian hermeneutics from pre-Augustine up to and through the Reformation, looking for consistency within the Tradition with special attention given to *sola scriptura*. Although hermeneutical principles and practices have developed throughout the history of Christian interpretation, nevertheless, the Tradition is all three of the following: (a) hermeneutically theological/Christological (i.e., Scripture is Christ-centered); (b) metaphysically supernatural and participatory (i.e., God communicates with and ministers to people who live in time and space and who themselves carry out his will in the world); and (c) contextually pastoral (i.e., the "sheep" need to be fed and led; John 10:27–28).

With all of these points established, it is now time to begin constructing answers to the project's initial question: "In what ways, if any, does Christ-centered biblical theology recapture Reformation-era hermeneutics, which, controlled by *sola scriptura* (which chapter three saw was the Reformational equivalent to Heiko Oberman's Tradition 1), sought to renew the Great Tradition?" This chapter will offer a twofold conclusion with reference to biblical theology, giving attention to one strength within and one weakness: First, biblical theology, instead of recapturing what the Great Tradition lost, seeks to provide, via a methodological development, what might in some ways be lacking in the Tradition; second, at the same time, biblical theology, to remedy its own pastoral and theological weaknesses, needs to listen more closely to the Great Tradition, making its own adjustments.

To make such a case will require examining, first, the things that biblical theology and the Tradition have in common, and second, the differences between the two. The goal will be to show both the ways in which biblical theology advances the Great Tradition and the ways that returning to the Tradition's strengths would help biblical theology fulfill its goals and purposes.

Following the establishing of the similarities and differences will be a consideration of Craig Carter's prosopological paradigm called *Christological literalism* (itself an appropriation of Matthew Bates' prosopological approach) for its synthetic potential, with strengths and weaknesses considered. Then will be an assessment of Peter Gentry's response to Carter in which Gentry argues that Carter does not adequately account for redemptive history in his prosopology. The necessity for a stronger synthesis of redemptive history and theology will be seen, followed by a proof that this dual orientation is present both in Scriptures and (picking back up with the content of the previous chapter) in the history of interpretation.

In this way the foundation for this project's primary contribution will be laid: *typological realism* as synthetic framework of redemptive history and theology proper. The goal is to help strengthen the areas where biblical theology advances Christ's Great Tradition while also returning to the Tradition, overcoming its often obvious (and strange) apprehension to identify with it. The project will then be set up to develop typological realism over the final three chapters.

Biblical Theology and the Great Tradition: Commonalities

Context: Scripture and the Listening Church

One of the clearest commonalities between biblical theology and the hermeneutics of the Great Tradition (that is, Tradition 1, where interpretive tradition holds a *ministerial* role to illuminate sacred Scripture, as opposed to a *magisterial* role, exercising authority alongside of it)[1] is that both hold that exegesis and theology happen in the context of the listening church. Echoing Webster, theology is, by nature, "regenerate

---

1. See Oberman, *Dawn of the Reformation*, 280–87. See also Barrett, *God's Word Alone*, 45.

reasoning."[2] Thus Goldsworthy argues that exegesis as the first step in the hermeneutical process must be a regenerate act in order to be a Christian act. Only if the exegete has undergone hermeneutical conversion can he bring spiritual sensitivity into the exegetical endeavor.[3] In Goldsworthy's model, exegesis begins with Jesus because regenerate exegetes start the whole of their existence from their identity as believers in Christ. As seen in chapters 1 and 3, respectively, any time in the history of biblical theology and the Great Tradition that Christ is central, exegesis, theology, and application occur within the context of people listening to God as he shepherds by his word (Pss 95:7; 100:3). People seek Christ to know and enjoy him. Regeneration and therefore fellowship with God is the primary presupposition unto the goal of growth in grace through knowing Christ (2 Pet 3:18). This is Paul's point when he tells the Corinthian church that only those in the Spirit (i.e., regenerate) can understand the spiritual matters of the apostolic preaching and teaching (1 Cor 2:12–16). God gives his Spirit for this exact purpose so that his people can understand his truth and walk with him.

This is not to say that there is nothing that Christian teaching has for the world to hear. Whether the Psalms calling to the world to repent and turn to God (Pss 67; 100), the prophets chastising the nations for their sins and calling them to repentance (e.g., Isa 13; 15–21; 23; 24), or the apostles preaching the gospel to non-Jewish audiences (Acts 10; 13; 16–17), God is the God of the whole creation, and his redeeming mission extends to the nations.[4] Further, Webster emphasizes that God is the father of lights (cf. Jas 1:17) who graciously blesses the nations with direction, purpose, success, etc., regardless of the world's acknowledgment of his lordship.[5] Through redemption, he intends to cover the whole earth with the knowledge of him, which is itself the knowledge of truth and the beginning of wisdom. Redeemed/regenerate reasoning can only occur among those who have come to a saving knowledge of God. The church's mission is to evangelize the world, inviting the world into

---

2. Webster, *Domain of the Word*, 116.

3. For hermeneutical conversion, see chapter 2 above, and Goldsworthy, *According to Plan*, 37–39.

4. See Ott and Strauss, *Encountering Theology of Mission*, 25–54, 165–91; see also Piper, *Let the Nations Be Glad*; Wright, *Mission of God*. Somewhat uniquely, Wright's work is a whole-Bible biblical theology centered on mission as theme.

5. See Webster, *Domain*, 171–92.

the church's fellowship, which, as Webster has said, is the "domain of the Word," where Christ shepherds and directs by his Spirit and Word.[6]

Biblical theology shares with the Great Tradition a burden to treat Scripture as the sacramental tool in the hands of God the shepherd by which he shepherds his flock. Just as Jesus taught his disciples to pray "Our Father" (thus emphasizing the church's shared identity as God's people),[7] so exegesis, doctrine, and application all occur in the "sheep pen" as the sheep listen together to their shepherd-father. The Great Tradition has always sought to listen to the content of Scripture (doctrine) in order to live it and proclaim it. Biblical theology, so understood, is a subgenre within the Tradition that seeks to listen to the *way* in which Scripture communicates the gospel. In either case, the first step is nonconstructive, to listen.

Instrument: Scripture as Divine Word

The second commonality between biblical theology and the Great Tradition is that they both view Scripture as the means through which the Lord shepherds the church. Scripture is the Spirit-inspired writing of the Trinity whereby he establishes fellowship with lost people and keeps them on the discipleship journey.[8] The Bible is more than a book. It is "living and active," the reader lying open before its eyes (Heb 4:12–13). Reading Scripture is far more than a simple literary activity, whether leisurely or vocational. Reading is listening to the voice of the one who continues to speak by it (Heb 12:25), revealing his love to his followers according to his promise: "I have made known to them your love, and will continue to" (John 17:26).[9]

Chapter 3 showed that the church fathers, Augustine probably chief among them, did not treat Scripture as anything other than the word of the true God.[10] To them, the Bible is not a jumble that requires human reason in order to be made sensible. The Bible is the divine word given to

---

6. See Webster, *Domain*, 3–31.

7. Worth mentioning is Calvin's masterful work on the Lord's Prayer; see *Inst.*, 3.20.

8. Webster develops the revelation-as-fellowship concept in *HS*, 8, 13–16.

9. See Piper's treatment of Jesus's continuing/progressive display of glory in *God is the Gospel*, 161.

10. See especially O'Keefe and Reno, *Sanctified Vision*, 11, commenting on Irenaeus's *Against Heresies* 2.28.2.

God's people on God's terms so that he, through the interaction between their listening and his speaking, sanctifies them (cf. John 17:17–19).

Chapter 2 showed that biblical theology shares this same conviction, though going further, arguing that the *way* in which Scripture is structured formally and canonically needs greater prioritization in interpretation.[11] To get to systematic doctrines, biblical theology is the means of hearing the unfolding story as the way in which the promises find fulfillment and all of the texts relate to each other, leading ontologically to doctrine. In that sense, biblical theology might be, as suggested earlier, a development of the Great Tradition and not a departure. The Tradition has always treated Scripture as a unified Christ-centered witness;[12] but biblical theology as it is practiced among evangelical scholars and theologians today is interested in *how* Scripture is a unified witness of and to Christ. In building upon the Tradition's understanding of Scripture as a Christ-centered witness, biblical theology is analytical, but not in a way that sits in judgment on the text. Rather, the goal is to understand the text and give due glory to God from a posture of listening. The goal in both approaches is to be doxological, treasuring the fact that God has spoken; thus, exegesis responds appropriately.[13]

Faithfulness and Legacy: Scripture and the Importance of Redemptive History

The third commonality between biblical theology and the Great Tradition is the importance that both place on redemptive history. Chapter 3 showed that the fathers definitely saw the importance of the believer understanding the unity of Scripture across time as God fulfilled his earlier promises and brought all things to fruition in Christ (Eph 1:10). For example, Augustine and Irenaeus wrote major works with the goal

---

11. Even if one excludes Brevard Childs and other Biblical Theology Movement practitioners from the evangelical definition of biblical theology, it cannot be argued that Childs and others within the Biblical Theology Movement did not seek to read particular texts of Scripture in light of Scripture's overarching narrative. Childs's canonical approach was purposefully geared this direction. See his opus, *Biblical Theology*. He seems to have not only read Scripture from within the Tradition but taught others to do the same, though he might have been, as Carter said, inconsistent at points.

12. See Carter, *ISGT*, 148–59.

13. As mentioned in chapter 1, Beale's *New Testament Biblical Theology* ends with the conclusion that the goal of all biblical theology is the glory and enjoyment of God; 973.

of teaching the importance of the Christ-centeredness of the progressive biblical narrative.[14] Chapter 3 also noted that instrumental in the early days of the Reformation was Luther's identification of historical commonalities between Christians of the present day and believing saints during the Old Testament days.[15]

Most likely the practical importance of redemptive history for the Christian is that redemptive history concerns God's fulfilling the promises both that he makes to believers when he establishes fellowship with them and that he continues to make as they journey. In short, redemptive history is itself a revelation of God's faithfulness. Such a high percentage of the Old Testament narrative shows that the fulfillment of his promises is the content of God's shepherding activity. Such is the case with New Testament believers; therefore, Paul links the Exodus narrative with believers on their journey of faith (1 Cor 10:1–3), because the Exodus is a type of the faith journey of New Testament believers.[16]

This observation explains why Vos placed such an emphasis on redemptive history's place in biblical theology if theology is to be truly biblical, an emphasis which, as seen in chapters 1 and 2, would prove to be extremely influential. In a scholarly culture where one all but had to make a choice between being a fundamentalist or a naturalist,[17] Vos and later Clowney (as well as Robinson, and even later, Goldsworthy, Beale, etc.) showed that grammatical historical tools can be employed to listen to God's voice because Scripture is written *as* a theological-historical account.[18]

Carter makes an interesting case, however, that Vos's approach had some weaknesses. First, says Carter, Vos did not seem to perceive his own theological-Christological kinship to Augustine and Irenaeus, whose works were mentioned above. Second, says Carter, because of

---

14. In particular, Augustine's *Instructing Beginners in the Faith* and Irenaeus's *Demonstration of the Apostolic Preaching*. Melito's *On Pascha* well rewards careful study of its Christocentric construal of revelation and being, as well.

15. Preuss, *From Shadow to Promise*, 196–97.

16. This line of reasoning will move into the foreground in subsequent chapters.

17. See chapter 1 above.

18. See especially Goldsworthy, *GCH*, 181–313. Section 3 is titled "Reconstructing Evangelical Hermeneutics." Goldsworthy makes the point that as long as the exegete's attitude remains an attitude of listening to God, all exegetical tools are at their disposal. As Carter has shown, the use of historical tools is not an innovation by modern methodology over premodern exegesis. God's people have always used tools to the end of hearing God the shepherd.

this oversight, Vos is unable to critique the Enlightenment-dominated hermeneutics of his (and the present) day.[19] This project's goals preclude the necessary effort needed to fairly consider Carter's challenge in depth. It seems likely, though, that Carter's critique is overstated: Vos did not acknowledge his redemptive-historical kinship because he was not as interested in the history of hermeneutics as he was in engaging the Scriptures and helping those with Enlightenment sensibilities to see the Christ-centered unity of Scripture's narrative in this way. Vos got right to work with biblical theology because to not do so would have been, from his perspective, a waste of time.[20] Such a pursuit did not fit his theological and scholarly goals.

In any event, the Great Tradition has always held to the importance of redemptive history for the believer. Biblical theology continued this emphasis and, through a winding road of development, has sought to go further.

Content: Christ as Scriptural Center

The final commonality follows from the previous three and risks redundancy: the centrality of Christ in order for Scripture to be understandable and sensible. The New Testament identifies Christ with the "Word" of God (John 1:1-2; Rev 19:17) who created all things (Col 1:15) and is the goal of all things (Eph 1:10). The Old Testament states that the nature of the messiah's ministry is to exercise God-like authority (Gen 49:7; Dan 7:13-14[21]), speak God's very words (Deut 18:16-18), and to do so with such an irresistible wisdom (Isa 11:1-10) that connections to the pre-creation wisdom of Prov 8 would be difficult to ignore.[22] Therefore, one

---

19. Carter, *ISGT,* 178–79.

20. That said, Vos was no slouch when it comes to history. See his treatment of the Trinity in *Reformed Dogmatics* 1.3 for examples of his breadth of reading and understanding regarding historical theology. See that section for an introduction to Vos's historical brilliance.

21. Thus is Michael Brown's response to the challenge "Jesus Was An Imposter Who Failed to Fulfill Messianic Prophecies" in Strobel's *Case for the real Jesus,* 200–202. According to Brown, the Old Testament did not emphasize the Messiah's divinity not because of vagueness or inconsistency but because it would have been confusing to Jewish monotheists. Nevertheless, says Brown, hints to the Messiah's divinity are seen throughout the prophecies, such as in the texts cited above.

22. Hence the emphasis throughout patristic writing on Jesus as the wisdom of God in Prov 8.

cannot help but to see how Christ's coming into the world as the God-man is the central episode of the entire Biblical narrative, and indeed, all of history.[23]

Chapter 3 showed that all through the Great Tradition, whether considering the work of the fathers, medieval thinkers like Thomas Aquinas and Nicholas, or the Reformers, there has always been the presence of a palpable Christ-centeredness in the church's biblical hermeneutics. The ubiquity of Christ-centeredness—that is, in terms of consistency—might be debatable depending on what eras and thinkers are being compared. Still, the church has always had people committed to exercising biblical hermeneutics to the end of hearing Christ as the Word. Calvin emphasized Christ's session in heaven as the place from which he speaks his gospel to the church.[24] The church's very identity is in its proclamation of Christ's identity and work (cf. Matt 16:16–18).

Similarly, chapters 1 and 2 showed that biblical theology among evangelicals can be roughly equated with Christ-centered biblical theology. Köstenberger made the case that evangelical biblical theologians share a definite centeredness on Christ.[25] Chapter 2 especially noted that Goldsworthy's model is a Christ-centered model that seeks to relate all texts to Christ. Indeed, Goldsworthy's method begins and ends with Jesus because Jesus, being the Alpha and Omega (Rev 22:13), must always be the beginning and the end.[26]

The goal of regenerate hermeneutics is not just to see *that* Christ is central but, in so seeing, to believe in and enjoy him (John 20:31; Phil 3:3), finding transformation of heart and mind (2 Cor 3:18) for the sake of fellowship with God and others who believe in him (1 John 1:3–4). The goal is to live *with* Christ as central. Paul could say, thus, that the gospel is not only the means through which Christians come to God but the means by which they are continually transformed and discipled (1

---

23. Not to mention the fact that the Old Testament ends with God saying that the next episode will be *his own* appearance (not just his *kabod*) in his temple to be heralded by an earlier messenger (Mal 3:1). Of note, Mark explicitly says this text referred to Christ's coming and to John's preparation for him, respectively (Mark 1:2), implying that one must understand the relationship between promise and fulfillment to understand the gospel (1:1).

24. See especially Calvin on ecclesiology (*Inst.*, 4.1–3).

25. See the latter sections of chapter 1 above, and Köstenberger, "Present and Future of Biblical Theology," 459.

26. See chapter 2; see also Goldsworthy, *Jesus Through the Old Testament*, 10–13; *According to Plan*, 71–78.

Cor 15:1–2): Perhaps believers never "graduate" from fixing their eyes on Jesus (Heb 12:1–2).[27] The church has always known this. If there have ever been times of widespread "darkness" through church history,[28] there has always been a remnant seeking to hear—and by hearing *behold*—Jesus in Scripture. It has been throughout the Tradition and it seems to be so among biblical theologians in the current day.

Differences

Emphasis: Theology or Not

Clearly, those arguing for a return to the Great Tradition want the Trinity to be exegetically central. Carter, Sanders, and Barrett have each written multiple works applying Trinitarian considerations to evangelical hermeneutics and theology.[29] Carl Trueman has been critical of what he sees as an over-Christ-centeredness in the biblical-theological approaches of many evangelical interpreters. In response, Trueman argues for a return to a more robust Trinitarian-creedal-dogmatic pursuit.[30] To focus entirely on Christ is to miss Christ's mission to reveal—and by so doing, bring people to—the Father (John 14:6–11; 1 Pet 3:18).[31]

On the other hand, biblical theology practitioners are more tempered regarding Trinitarian considerations. As mentioned in chapter 2, Trueman and Goldsworthy debated in journal articles, the former criticizing biblical theology for making "Jesus the answer to every question" and the latter responding that biblical theology simply tries to read Scripture the way that Scripture directs. Also mentioned earlier, Beale's *New*

---

27. See also Fred Sanders's attempt at positing a Triune understanding of the gospel that helps evangelicals see that salvation extends beyond initial conversion into the life of faith and fellowship with God; *Deep Things of God*, 113–30.

28. Which frequent evangelical charge Barrett has sought to challenge in *RR*; one might also consider Nathan Busenitz's illuminating study on the presence of justification by faith alone throughout church history in *Long Before Luther*.

29. See Carter, *Contemplating God*; Barrett, *Simply Trinity* and *None Greater*; Sanders, *Deep Things of God* and *triune God*. Within the same group of writers might be included Vidu's *Same God* and Swain's *Trinity and the Bible*. Works of those who advocate for so-called theological interpretation of Scripture will be considered later in this chapter.

30. Thus is Trueman's popular-level proposal in *Creedal Imperative*; more recently, he has attempted to apply the proposal of *Imperative* to the problem diagnosed in his much-praised *Rise and Triumph of the Modern Self*, in *Crisis of Confidence*.

31. Thus is also Sanders's caution in *Deep Things of God*, 173–75.

Testament Biblical Theology concludes that the goal of biblical theology is doxology, that God would be glorified.[32] Scobie's *The Ways of Our God* presents a biblical theology that could be called God-driven, even if more focused on God's works than his being.[33]

Some approaches to biblical theology which focus on God's works in his Son could be called economic-oriented approaches because they center on God's works in his Son. Other theological approaches are theology-driven, usually Tradition-oriented, seeking a return to a Trinitarian center. Such varying approaches should not be seen as opposed to each other even though they are different. The main difference is that biblical theologians are more beholden to intertextuality and historical development while Tradition-oriented proponents are beholden to theology proper and its place at the center of theological inquiry.[34]

Ultimate Context: Discipleship or Not

The context—or domain—of an approach to biblical theology tends to determine the outcomes and conclusions proposed. If, as this project posits, the context of biblical theology is the listening church, then discipleship and piety are the context of faithful biblical theology. Goldsworthy's *Preaching the Whole Bible as Christian Scripture* demonstrates well this discipleship-oriented approach: Biblical theology occurs so that the church is able to understand God, his word, the nature of reality, and the church's own identity and mission. As such, Scripture functions both as the church's guiding voice and message to the world.

On the other hand, the Great Tradition's context might be more robust. Again, echoing Webster, since theology encompasses God and all things in relation to God, then theology has as its context God's creation

---

32. See Beale, *New Testament Biblical Theology*, 975.

33. That is, his work is structured thematically as follows: God's Order, God's Servant, God's People, and God's Way. See *Ways of Our God*, 93–98 for an introduction. The second part of *Ways* is given to explanation, encompassing some 800-plus pages. Worth noting is that Scobie gives a small portion of his chapter on God's nature to his being; *Ways of Our God*, 105–20.

Also worth mentioning is Hamilton's attempt at God-centeredness in *God's Glory in Salvation Through Judgment*, 565: "This book is written that God would be glorified."

34. Although, see Sanders *triune God*, 39–69 for a Trinity-oriented construal of Scripture's unfolding narrative. Sanders argues that the "mystery" of which Paul speaks in Rom 16 and Eph 3 is that God is triune and saves by his Son. This mystery, which took ages to fulfill, is the "plan from the fullness of time to unite all things in His Son" (Eph 1:10).

and all of the operations within it.[35] In other words, theology as a discipline extends beyond God and his word to have bearing on all things. This construal is why Carter, among others, has written so much on the importance of Nicene Trinitarianism to modern philosophy and why Trueman's aforementioned *Rise and Fall* has been so important as an appraisal of modern moral and ethical sensibilities from a Christian intellectual perspective.[36] Bartholomew has written that a robust Christology will, by necessity, embrace all of creation in a way that evangelical theology has often failed to do in the last century.[37] Perhaps biblical theology's emphasis on a redemptive-historical, Christ-centered hermeneutic has occurred to an unfortunate neglect of what such hermeneutics mean for the rest of Christ's creation, namely the world, relationships, ethics, etc. As chapter 2 suggested, biblical theology is probably weaker in this area (practical matters) even than it is in theology.

Biblical Theology's Tendency to Grammatical-historical Overemphasis

The third chapter considered the claim that Calvin was the forerunner of the grammatical-historical method. It was proposed that although Calvin certainly practiced a method of exegesis that holds much in common with the modern method in arguing that the unfolding of the mind of the human author is the goal of exegesis,[38] the context of his exegesis was always the listening church. The French Reformer's work was not to make the Bible into another object of historical inquiry but to preach the gospel for the upbuilding of the believer.[39] This explains why a modern grammatical-historical exegete might find it difficult to read Calvin's commentaries: They are clearly (and richly) pastoral. As the previous chapter concluded, to claim that Calvin is the forerunner of historical criticism is just as hasty as suggesting that Augustine is to blame for the

---

35. See, for instance, Webster, *God Without Measure*, 3–8.

36. Bartholomew has suggested that Scobie's category "God's Way," which focuses on ethics in a way that is uncommon within whole-Bible biblical theology, might make him an exception to the point made in this paragraph. See Bartholomew, *Introducing Biblical Hermeneutics*, 106.

37. Bartholomew and Thomas, *Manifesto for Theological interpretation*, 261.

38. See Calvin's dedicatory note in his *Romans* commentary, cited in the current project, 151.

39. See Calvin, *Inst.*, 4.

allegorical excesses of the medieval era. Augustine, like Calvin after him, aimed to pastor, not to "seek great things for himself" (cf. Jer 45:5).

That being said, there are some within the world of biblical theology who seem to have divided allegiances between the pastoral sensibilities present in Calvin and the scholarly sensibilities innate in the academy, which, at worst, cause Scripture to be treated like another book worthy of scrutiny instead of reverent listening. N. T. Wright, whose writings place him within BT4 in Klink and Lockett's paradigm,[40] has scrutinized the prevailing evangelical agenda to maintain the Bible's inerrancy.[41] Bartholomew has drawn attention to a similar phenomenon in Childs and Scobie, saying that both of them practiced a biblical theology that held to a canonical view of Scripture while also applying historical considerations that put them, at points, at odds with evangelical biblical theology.[42]

Biblical theology's connection with the Biblical Theology Movement might at least open it to the same historical commitment as the movement itself. Goldsworthy has, however, argued ably that biblical theology does not need a rationalistic understanding of historical study in order to use such tools in exegesis. If Scripture is God's revelation, and history belongs to God, then historical tools can be used as a help to *understand* Scripture as long as the posture taken is *listening* to Scripture.[43]

In addition, Goldsworthy, one of the more prominent and prolific biblical theologians of recent decades, has criticized Childs's claim that there is a "crisis" within biblical theology. According to Childs, relatively recent historical insight is to blame for such a crisis. That is, because modern scholarship has a more developed ontology than premodern scholarship, then the Bible, with its premodern ontology, appears at least archaic, and at most, untrustworthy.[44] But Goldsworthy makes the point that there could not be a crisis if those approaching Scripture are doing so to listen to God, which has always been the case when the context of biblical theology is the listening church.[45] Goldsworthy suggests that Childs's "crisis" was an intellectual one, more present in the academy

---

40. See chapter 1 above.

41. See, for instance, Wright, *Scripture and the Authority of God*, 37–45. See also Bird, "Inerrancy is Not Necessary."

42. See Bartholomew, *Introducing Biblical Hermeneutics*, 101, 103.

43. Goldsworthy, *GCH*, 193–98.

44. See Childs, *Biblical Theology in Crisis*; to be clear, Childs does not say that he holds to this opinion, but that this crisis explains the imminent death of the Movement.

45. See Goldsworthy, *GCH*, 85.

than in the church. Christ's sheep who listen to his voice (John 10:27) consistently turn their ear to him. Goldsworthy's corrective is a welcome sign of development that demonstrates that evangelical biblical theology presupposes that scholarship serves discipleship.

The Great Tradition's Figurative Impulse

Chapter 3 showed that medieval hermeneutics were guilty of overdoing the allegorical sense in Augustine's method to the point that it took an inappropriate prominence over the other senses.[46] The reason for such an unfortunate error must not be placed at the feet of the method (in which case, Origen and later Augustine would be to blame) but must be understood in light of Scripture's own anthropology: Fallen humans are inclined to turn away from a posture of listening to God even if they have access to his voice (cf. Hos 11:7; Isa 53:6; 66:3). In the same way that the law, though the embodiment of truth (Rom 2:20) is nevertheless weakened by the flesh (Rom 8:3) and thus, as it pertains to humanity, is "flawed," so it might also be the case that a hermeneutical method that includes within it the pastoral sense-making of allegory might be similarly "flawed" in its misuse. The fact that a method can be misused does not necessarily imply futility or superfluousness. It just needs care when in operation.

A historical absence of such a care is why Goldsworthy devotes several chapters of his GCH to showing the "eclipse" of the gospel in the hermeneutics of the fathers and the medieval era. In the case of the former, Goldsworthy says, the Alexandrines were guilty of a method that synthesized Greek philosophy and theology.[47] In the case of the latter, an overcommitment to the allegorical method led to fanciful interpretations that, in some cases, made the Old Testament into an ahistorical document, rendering it entirely law.[48] Instead of letting the gospel be the controlling sense of interpretation, other priorities assumed control, veiling the gospel and making reformation necessary. Although several leaders, such as Thomas and Nicholas of Lyra,[49] called for a return to

---

46. See chapter 3 above.

47. Goldsworthy, *GCH*, 95. For a similar criticism leveled more generally at ancient theological formulations, see König, *Christ Above All*, 30.

48. Goldsworthy, *GCH*, 105–6.

49. Along with chapter 3 above, see Preuss, *From Shadow to Promise*, 68.

the priority of plain/literal sense, these calls were such a minority that it would take nothing short of what Barrett calls ecclesiastical "watersheds," such as Hus's execution and Luther's excommunication, to begin to see real change.[50]

Theological interpretation of Scripture, then, figures into the discussion in this way: Theological interpretation is an attempt to return to a theological orientation which allows for the appropriateness of the spiritual exegesis that was the practice of the patristics. The goal is not primarily to return to the patristics but to begin exegesis on theological grounds. Nevertheless, as Carter has said, theological interpretation as a discipline has become so broad and hard to define that knowing what it is can be difficult.[51]

Conclusion to Commonalities and Differences

A comparison of biblical theology with the Great Tradition demonstrates discernible consistencies: The context of exegesis and theology is the listening and worshiping church, and thus the goal is discipleship. Scripture is God's own instrument of shepherding and leading his people. Redemptive history is saving history in the sense that, by it, the Holy Spirit assures the believer that they are going forward in God's plan. Christ is the content of Scripture in that all of the treasures of wisdom and knowledge are in him (Col 2:3). Christian exegesis, doctrine, and application put on display the unsearchable riches that are in Christ, which were before mysterious but since his coming have been unveiled (Eph 3:8).[52] Such consistencies give a clear preliminary answer to one of this project's original questions regarding whether biblical theology is indebted to the Great Tradition. The answer *must* be "yes": Evangelical Christ-centered biblical theology continues the Great Tradition by

50. See Barrett, *RR*, 356–68 (Hus) and 447–57 (Luther). To be clear, Barrett couches Hus's and Luther's challenges in light of the main areas of need: the main seat of authority in the church, whether the Pope and the Tradition, or Scripture as the norming norm.
  Worth mentioning also is that, as chapter 3 showed, Goldsworthy probably overstates his case in criticizing the hermeneutics of the patristic and medieval eras. There were excesses, but the gospel was never "eclipsed," and neither were the excesses as ubiquitous as Goldsworthy suggests.

51. Carter, *ISGT*, 19–22.

52. For an interesting case made for the centrality of "mystery" in Paul's hermeneutic, see Sanders, *triune God*, 99–100. According to Sanders, *mysterion* is more central to Paul's hermeneutic than covenant is. That is, Christ's fulfillments clarifying earlier enigmas and this clarity, not covenant, should be controlling to hermeneutics.

pursuing a hermeneutic that helps the church listen to the voice of Christ as he reveals himself in his word.

But there are also differences. Clearly biblical theology has considerable deficiencies in regard to how it sees Scripture's unfolding narrative speaking to all of life. By contrast, Great Tradition reconstructionists have prioritized how theology relates to all of life. Biblical theology is also somewhat deficient in the area of theology proper compared to Tradition retrievalists. Finally, although biblical theology can fall into grammatical-historical excesses, the Tradition can fall into allegorical excesses while marginalizing the Bible's own historical progression. Biblical theology seems, therefore, to be a *positive development within* the exegesis of the Great Tradition, seeking to remedy potential deficiencies therein. Its development, however, is incomplete.

Finally, shifting to direct ecclesial considerations, the actual practice of the so-called *quadriga* is still maintained by pastors and theologians who attempt Christ-centered biblical theology. Their understanding of the nature of Scripture might be called an appropriation of Childs's canonical-historical model with Vos's Trinitarian presuppositions. Christ-centered biblical theology can be called *both* post-Enlightenment *and* pre-Enlightenment. Pastors trained in biblical theology apply the pastoral considerations of the *quadriga* to their engagement with Scripture's Christ-centered narrative which emphasizes redemptive-historical context based on evangelical and orthodox foundations. Such a development is a victory, as it brings together various resources that can be used to help the church hear, preach, sing, and discern the Shepherd's voice (Rom 12:2) as the pilgrim journey continues towards its ultimate goal.

Unbridgeable Differences? Toward Realistic Prosopology

Carter's proposed Christ-centered reading from within the Tradition is worthy of consideration. Dissatisfied with the pitfalls of the redemptive-historical model, Carter appropriates Matthew Bates's prosopological exegesis, retitling it *Christological literalism*.[53] Carter posits that this framework enables believers to "read the Bible as a Christ-centered unity"[54] from within the Tradition. Following will be an examination of

---

53. Carter, *ISGT*, 220. To be clear, Carter credits Jason Byassee with coining the term in *Praise Seeking Understanding*, 224.

54. Carter, *ISGT*, 129–60.

this paradigm and a consideration of whether it will suffice as a Christ-centered approach. Then will follow consideration of Peter Gentry's response as a redemptive-historicist.[55]

First, does Bates's *prosopological exegesis* and Carter's *Christological literalism* provide Christ-centered exegesis with a sufficient framework to hear Scripture as it comes? A preliminary answer would be "yes," *if* redemptive history is allowed to maintain its proper place in exegesis. According to Bates, prosopological exegesis is

> a reading technique whereby an interpreter seeks to overcome a real or perceived ambiguity regarding the identity of the speakers or addressees (or both) in the divinely inspired source text by assigning nontrivial *prosopa* (i.e. nontrivial vis-a-vis the plain sense of the text) to the speakers or addressees (or both) in order to make sense of the text.[56]

The technique might be explained in simpler terms: Because of how the New Testament uses certain Old Testament texts as a glimpse into inner-Trinitarian conversation (e.g., Ps 40:6-8 as it is used in Heb 10:5-7), one might be confused upon reading the earlier text in its original, non-New-Testament-influenced context. So one assigns a different *prosopa* (Gk. "person") based on a plain reading of the text in its *canonical* context to make it sensible in light of what later Scripture says about it.

The effect of such a practice is that the original text, staying with the example of Ps 40:6-8, has three contexts: first, a *historical, prophetic* context (in Ps 40's case, David writes from within a historical moment); second, a canonical, *theodramatic* context, based on the text's relation to God's unfolding redemptive narrative and its purpose in bearing witness to his way of redemption (in this case, David's words as a witness to Christ's mission when he enters the world in the incarnation); and finally, an *actualized* context when it meets its final purpose or goal in Christ's coming, who is himself the *res* of all of Scripture (in this case, how Christ's actual coming into the world fulfills his eternal plan).[57]

Further, since Christ's coming into the world is the goal of all of history (Eph 1:10) and the key to unlocking the redemptive *mysterion*

---

55. Indeed, Gentry is one of the authors of the seminal work on progressive covenantalism, *KTC*. See chapter 1 above.

56. Bates, *Hermeneutics of the Apostolic Proclamation*, 218, quoted in Carter, *ISGT*, 192.

57. This threefold contextual paradigm is Bates's, explained in *Birth of the Trinity*, 34-35.

of God's economy (Rom 16:24), and since Christ is himself the everlasting Word, the hermeneutical expectation should be that pre-incarnate revelation will have both a prophetic relationship to Christ as well as an ontological relationship to him. In other words, the Old Testament will point to him in substantial ways while also being itself his own voice as the eternal Word of the outgoing God. The prophetic and ontological relationships of the text to Christ—that is, the text's bearing witness to Christ's later coming as well as the text's being the voice of Christ as Word pre-incarnation—comprise the theodramatic context of a given text.

To reinforce this point, Carter employs a lengthy quote from Justin Martyr in which he states that the Old Testament prophets' sayings do not originate with the prophets themselves, "but from the divine Logos."[58] In suggesting that Christ the Word eternally spoke by the prophets, Justin does not mean to negate the text's historical context. The text originates with the Logos, and thus, as the source, knowledge of the Logos can be the goal of the text. So Christ is present in the Old Testament just by virtue of his being the eternal Son of God who reveals the Father and the way to himself before he came. Jesus said that only he himself can reveal the Father (Matt 11:27); this must mean that he always had been revealing the Father throughout the Old Testament narrative.[59]

In keeping with Carter's aforementioned conclusion that the "two central facts of biblical interpretation are that (a) God speaks, and (b) God speaks to us,"[60] he may indeed add a fourth context to Bates's interpretive framework above: the *ecclesial* or *pastoral* context, which is concerned with taking the text in its already established historical, theodramatic, and Christological context and applying it to believers for their

---

58. See Carter, *ISGT*, 199. This quote is from Justin's *First Apology* 36:1–2.

59. Worth mentioning is that Irenaeus said that the purpose of the law of Moses was to reveal "the Father of our Lord Jesus Christ" (*Against Heresies*, 3.9.7). Whereas Paul had said the law revealed sin (Gal 3), Irenaeus aimed to make the point that it also reveals God's fatherly heart so that later hearers of the gospel understand when Jesus repeatedly refers to the God of Israel as his Father. This example is merely one of the ways in which Irenaeus sees the OT's relationship to Christ.

It would be interesting to find out what Fred Sanders says about this. In *triune God*, 219–20, he argues that it is inappropriate to see, as Irenaeus and Justin Martyr did, Christ present in the theophanies, because the whole Trinity was at work there, and missing the point implies a sort of subordinationism, which gave support to later heresies. It would seem that Christ, as the eternal Word who reveals the Father, *had to*, in some way, be the divine presence in the theophanies.

60. Sanders, *triune God*, 187.

edification and upbuilding in the faith.⁶¹ This context is not contained in the text itself but contained in the fellowship between God and his people with whom he communicates as shepherd of his sheep (Ps 95:6). A passage is understood as history, Christological (theodramatic) witness, and pastoral discipline. Truly, if Scripture is ever interpreted in a way that negates one of these foci, it fails to fulfill its fellowship-establishing and maintaining purpose.

In summary, given that there are differences between the historically oriented hermeneutics of Christ-centered biblical theology and the theology-oriented hermeneutics of the Tradition, prosopology-oriented Christological literalism might be a way for the church to hear God's voice via the Scriptures as God intends. Surely such a reading can be done from a Christian posture toward Christian ends. Nevertheless, the approach has both strengths and weaknesses.

Assessing Bates's and Carter's Prosopology

Strengths

The prosopological framework has much to commend. First, it is born out of a conviction that the Old Testament should be read in light of the New. It is clear that New Testament writers are concerned with helping believers understand and apply the Old as God's fatherly witness to them. Yet the history of biblical theology has demonstrated a frequent demarcation between Old and New Testament studies. So the last century especially has called for a construal of Scripture's narrative that recognizes the Old Testament as the background to the New and the New as the lens through which the Old is understood.⁶² Christological literalism does a good job of relating the Testaments in the way that the Testaments seem to say they should be.

---

61. It should be clear how this is roughly equivalent to the *quadriga*; see chapter 3 above.

62. This should not imply however, that, as an example, the kingly seed as the fulfillment of the Edenic promise cannot be detected in the Old Testament/Tanak as it is. Dempster urges readers in *Dominion and Dynasty* to not assume that the Old Testament's message *requires* the New in order to be discerned. See *Dominion*, 36. Nevertheless, this point is meant to suggest that the clarity given by Christ to the earlier μυστεριον makes ignoring the New Testament's explanation of the Old utterly inappropriate. Christ's continuity makes the two Testaments the two parts of the same glorious story.

Second, this framework aims to produce a clear understanding of the Old Testament text. It does not aim to be overly mystical or allegorical in a way that abandons either the historical or Christological senses. It aims, rather, to deal squarely with the full scope of a text's place in the canon. In that sense, it applies biblical theology to a text's close reading.

Finally, such a practice is undertaken with a theological orientation. Listening to a text as the voice of the eternal Son of God begins interpretation on a firmly Trinitarian ground. Again, history is not unimportant, but history is understood in light of God's purposes for it. This is the goal of hermeneutics within the Tradition.[63]

Criticism

On the other hand, perhaps Carter applies this prosopological framework a little too broadly. As mentioned before, Carter admirably aims to helps his readers "read the Bible as a unity centered on Jesus."[64] To do so, he employs Bates's framework as the way in which the Old Testament makes sense in Jesus. Carter follows Bates in criticizing the typological framework of men like Richard Hays.[65] Such a typological framework sees the events, people, and institutions of the earlier scriptural narrative as indirectly foreshadowing the events, people, and institutions of the later scriptural narrative. The effect is that when the later comes, an escalation has occurred from the less significant to the more significant.[66] In short, typology argues that Scripture moves from the earlier and lesser to the later and greater, although the presence of typology is not always made explicit throughout the course of the narrative or even after the antitype has come.

According to Bates (and at least implicitly defended by Carter), typology is a modern hermeneutical convention born out of Enlightenment views of history that treat Scripture like it is something less than plain and historically accurate. Although Carter admits that typology exists in Scripture in the form of consistent patterns, such patterns should only be seen as examples of typology where the text makes it explicit.[67]

---

63. See Boersma, *Scripture as Real Presence*, xii–xv.
64. This is the title of chapter 5 in *ISGT*, 129–59.
65. See, for instance, Bates, *Birth of the Trinity*, 72.
66. See Beale, *Handbook on the New Testament*, 13; from 13–18, Beale gives an overview of the debate surrounding the legitimacy of typology for biblical studies.
67. Carter, *ISGT*, 195, 197. The irony here, and one which seems to have escaped

Because of this criticism, Carter all but minimizes the importance of redemptive history (which itself is the context of typology) for biblical theology. To be fair, he does not totally neglect redemptive history. He seems so hesitant to treat historical progression through Scripture as of utmost importance to Scripture's message because he does not want to allow for a progressive view of history to take hold.

Goldsworthy, himself a prolific redemptive-historicist who employs typology in his paradigm, does not view history in the type of progressive way at which Carter bristles. Goldsworthy very clearly demands that history be understood as God's project to carry out his plan.[68] Carter seems to be trying to avoid the type of central view of history that Oscar Cullmann, one of Goldsworthy's influences, employs.[69] But Goldsworthy, as seen in chapter 2, utilizes Cullmann's high view of history while *also* maintaining Carter's theological and Christocentric presuppositions.[70]

So the question governing how one approaches the relationship of the Old Testament to the New is not, "What is more or less modern?" but, "What is more consistent with Scripture and the gospel which (as chapter 2 argued) is its center and organizing principle?" A prosopological framework is indeed consistent with Scripture's own explanation of itself as a revelation of Christ the eternal Word across a historical progression.[71] On the other hand, the same could be said of a redemptive-historical perspective if history is treated as God's creative and redemptive project in the way that Goldsworthy urges. The revelation of God in Scripture is a revelation both of his nature and of his actions. Neither is to be neglected if appropriately construed.

O'Keefe and Reno have shown one of the unique ways in which Scripture demonstrates God's nature without using direct description. They cite its explanation of history: The Bible does not merely share facts about what happened but explains history's relationship to the God who rules it and gives it its meaning. Scripture aims, thus, to "illuminate and

---

Carter's notice, is that to make explicitness a test of typology is to do precisely the opposite of what he, throughout his works, has repeatedly done: criticizing as modernistic the act of prioritizing explicitness in hermeneutics.

68. See, for instance, Goldsworthy, *GCH*, 220–223; *Preaching the Whole Bible*, 24.

69. See Cullmann, *Christ and Time*.

70. This observation anticipates the argument which will follow and continue in subsequent chapters. Bible reading and interpretation can occur in light of both a high view of historical development and Nicene theology.

71. The reader is encouraged to read chapters 3–7 of Bates's *Birth of the Trinity* for helpful (and enjoyable) examples of prosopology in action.

disclose the order and pattern of all things,"[72] as order and pattern are, as Aquinas showed, intended by God as evidence of his existence and nature. This illumination is how Scripture—showing the divine purpose to and direction of history—is revelatory: Via revelatory historiography, it says, "Here is how to understand history in light of the God who is and who acts within it."

Thus Scripture presents a redemptive history that figures centrally in the apostolic witness. The apostles were given the task of convincing the Jews on historical grounds that Jesus fulfills the Old Testament promises and shadows. The Acts sermons, for instance, demonstrate the importance of listening to the unfolding historical narrative so that one can understand God's message to the world. Paul even employs history when preaching to the Athenians who would have likely been unfamiliar with Jewish history (see Acts 17:22–31).

Before concluding this section, showing some examples of this dual-lens approach in *historia sacra* and *historia profana*, Peter Gentry's response to the prosopological offering is worth considering. Doing so serves two purposes: First, it considers a challenge from a well-respected biblical theologian with a different approach; second, it helps to reinforce, and thus advance, the attempt of this chapter to bring together the two lenses.

Peter Gentry and a Corrective

Peter Gentry, a redemptive-historicist, has recently critiqued Bates and Carter's prosopological model. Whereas the latter two argue that the Old Testament writers were enabled to listen in on and then communicate inner-Trinitarian conversations, Gentry says that the New Testament's practice of applying Old Testament texts to new covenant realities can be explained more simply in light of Scripture's overarching metanarrative. For instance, Gentry advances the example of Heb 1:8–9's use of the royal Ps 45 as applying to Jesus; Gentry argues that with a plain reading, there is no need to offer a prosopological explanation to the "God, your God" language of vv. 6–7 because the Old Testament prophets, especially Isaiah, so often contextualize God's future reign in light of his promise that David's human son will reign.[73] The implication is that promises will be

---

72. See O'Keefe and Reno, *Sanctified Vision*, 13.
73. Gentry, "Preliminary Evaluation," 109.

fulfilled *together*, even in the same person. The New Testament's answer is that Jesus is the divine Son and human son at once. The fact that Jesus is both the Son of God *and* the son of David undercuts, Gentry says, the necessity of a prosopological reading to make sense of the text.[74]

Throughout the article, Gentry takes the use of psalms in Heb 1 as his proving ground with offerings that are exegetically reasonable and supportive of his main argument, as in his treatment of Ps 45 above. His conclusion is that the suggestion that the apostles, in explaining Old Testament passages, were removing the texts from their original (grammatical-historical) context and giving them a new Trinitarian (prosopological) setting cuts against the evidence.[75]

Perhaps Gentry's most compelling argument is that if one abandons the scriptural metanarrative as particular texts' ultimate context, one cannot possibly explain how the apostles would have been able to convince the Jews that Jesus was their Messiah. An over-read prosopological framework undercuts the canonical consistency that the Bible, especially as seen in the gospels, aims to protect.[76] To do so would be a serious misstep. Certainly the apostles throughout their ministry exposed Christ as fulfilling many Old Testament promises according to a plain reading.

Gentry seems to overstate his case while under-proving his point. Regarding the latter, he seems to utilize an insufficient sample size as his proving ground. Of course he was writing an article, not a full-length treatment. Offering an alternate explanation of the use of the Old Testament in Heb 1 (even if Gentry offers a lengthy treatment), however, hardly settles the debate. There are many Old Testament texts which the New Testament views in Trinitarian terms that, frankly, cannot be explained in purely redemptive-historical terms, as Gentry seems to prefer. Maybe more examples would have helped.

Perhaps even more significantly, a theological point is worth considering. Based on the eternal nature of God, to say that historical correlations between Old and New Testament realities *cannot* represent divine realities in the Godhead would be an overstatement.[77] After all, obedi-

---

74. For further treatment of Christ as the presence of both Son of God and of David in one person, see Wellum and Hunter, *Christ From Beginning to End*, 169–95.

75. Wellum and Hunter, *Christ From Beginning to End*, 119.

76. Wellum and Hunter, *Christ From Beginning to End*, 120.

77. Webster discusses the concept of the revelation of God in time paralleling, even if imperfectly, his own nature in eternity, in "Christology, Theology, and Economy: The Place of Christology in Systematic Theology" and "On the Theology of Providence,"

ence to Christ is a form of thinking that is captive to the knowledge of God in him (2 Cor 10:3–5). Christ's death, itself the ontological center of biblical history, has as its goal bringing a redeemed people *to God* (1 Pet 3:18). Does not the knowledge of him as the Trinitarian Son begin with the Trinity's knowledge of God's self?[78] And could historical realities and correlations parallel divine ones so that believers can be more sure that they believe the truth? Put in a propositional form, David, for instance, might have written what he heard from within the Trinity, which was then revealed within the context of his own historical situation so that those summoned to believe would be convinced to believe. Trinitarian reality parallels the historical situation which it employs so that others within history can understand the Trinitarian reality. More simply, the experience of the Word in time and space is the instantiation of God's own begetting of the Word in eternity.

So David's own experience (as, for example, outlined in prayer form in Ps 69) paralleled that which was known to God as the Son's messianic suffering in the fullness of time (Gal 4:4). It also parallels the messianic suffering that Christ did in fact experience when the time came.[79] In this sense, one need not choose between prosopology and redemptive history: To build on Calvin's spectacles illustration (where Scripture acts as corrective spectacles to humanity's natural spiritual blindness),[80] the argument above is for a set of spectacle frames that are built to fit both redemptive-historical and theological lenses. Such a framework, in light of the nature of revelation, seems appropriate and fitting. In fact, without both the Trinitarian and redemptive-historical lens, serious missteps follow.

---

both in *God Without Measure*, 53, 127.

78. See Aquinas, *ST*, 1.14.

79. This section encourages a consideration of what Boersma has called a sacramental understanding of theology, where both the experience of truth and of theology are sacraments of God's own knowledge of himself who is true. As such, theology—the study of God—not only parallels God's knowledge of himself but participates in it, the believer being initiated into the life of God. See *HP*, 154–84.

80. See, for instance, Calvin, *Genesis 1–11*, 13; *Inst.*, 1.14.1.

Conclusion to Comparison of Prosopology and Redemptive History

Prosopological exegesis, therefore, can be employed with integrity *if* redemptive history is not entirely abandoned in doing so. More attractive than an either/or way forward—that is, either theologically sensitive prosopology or economy-oriented redemptive history—is a framework that employs both. A sound scriptural set of spectacles is one that has a theological-Trinitarian lens working alongside of a historical-Christological one. The former lens looks for how a text communicates the nature of the triune God who speaks from eternity (Isa 57:15; Ps 90:2; cf. Heb 12:25); the latter looks for the text's relationship to the Christ-event in time. The two lenses complement while also checking one another. Modern readers might be familiar with how three-dimensional (3D) glasses work: One lens is red and the other is blue; when a 3D-capable image is viewed, both lenses must be employed simultaneously in order for the eyes to absorb the fullness of the image's features. So, in a similar way, a set of hermeneutical spectacles that has both a theological lens and a redemptive-historical lens is necessary to appreciate the fullness of God's revelation, and thus, what is the nature of reality.

Uncertain is whether Carter and Bates would accept such a marriage of the theological with the redemptive-historical, and neither would Gentry. Perhaps the commonalities between both schools, as outlined above, could be a foundation on which to consider one another's correctives. Christ-centered biblical theology has imperfections to it that seem to be characterized by incompleteness.[81] Previous pages have argued that a Christocentric prosopological approach is also incomplete. The Great Tradition has always sought to discern the metaphysical and the physical in theological/Christological terms. Because of this seeming Christian priority through the ages, such a hermeneutical marriage seems appropriate, even being a long time coming.

To further reinforce the likeness of biblical theology to the Great Tradition in this way, a few examples are offered.

---

81. As seen in chapter 2, where it was made clear that theological considerations are important to the biblical theology of many, though it often fades into the background of their paradigms.

Scripture and Tradition

New Testament Writers

Matthew[82]

Clearly Matthew has both theology and redemptive history in view in his opening chapter. Chapter 1:1–17 is Jesus's genealogy traced back to Abraham, clearly construed in a redemptive-historical way. The fact that the genealogy makes no mention of the return from exile but moves from the exile to Jesus's day suggests an interpretive proposition: In one sense, according to Matthew, Israel *never* returned from exile. So Jesus will *spiritually* return them by his accomplishments, saving them from their sins, which were to blame for their original exile (1:21).[83] In this way, God's people return to their "land" by faith in Jesus who accomplished salvation for them in the physical land.

But who could deny that Matthew views Jesus as more than the Messiah when he immediately follows the historicism of the genealogy by calling him, in 1:23, the fulfillment of the Immanuel/God-with-us promise of Isa 7:14? Two chapters later, John the Baptist opens his ministry by quoting as his own job description Isa 40, making the point that he has come to prepare the way for *the Lord's* coming (3:3). High Christology is on clear display in the opening chapters of Matthew.

Matthew continues: Jesus's Sermon on the Mount includes the statement that he has come not to abolish but to fulfill the law (5:17). A full consideration of the meaning of this statement is outside the scope of the present project. Noteworthy is that Jesus immediately after gives an exposition of the law according to a "you've heard. . .but I say. . ." method (5:22–48). His exposition seems to employ an escalatory (that is, typological) framework: Earlier simple and binding imperatives are in the sermon explained more fully, at least elliptically, to move beyond the

---

82. This first example has some degree of redundancy with chapter 2 because Matthew's Christological/Christocentric explanation of history was a good case study for Christ-centered hermeneutics being treated in the chapter. Hopefully the reader can understand the propriety of plowing the same Matthean ground for the current section given that it seeks to acknowledge the presence in the Christian tradition of the sort of dual (theological/redemptive-historical) hermeneutical focus which the following chapters seek to propose.

83. Such a point is advanced in Dempster, *Dominion and Dynasty*, 232; Evans, "Jesus and the Continuing Exile," 99. For a cogent defense of an understanding of the promised land as simultaneously spiritualized (so that one enters it by faith in Jesus) and physically expanded to include the whole earth, see Burge, *Jesus and the Land*.

simple letter.[84] In this case, God's moral standard is explained as higher than what the people were used to hearing. Similarly, in 11:2–4, Jesus reassures John's distraught disciples of his messianic identity by quoting Old Testament eschatological promises (the comments are a loose quotation of Isa 35:5–6) followed shortly thereafter by a high Trinitarian statement that the only ones with access to the knowledge of God the Father are the Son and anyone to whom the Son wills to reveal him (11:27). Such a statement from the mouth of the Lord reveals inner-Trinitarian knowledge (only the Son knows the Father) as well as Trinitarian (Christological) missions to save (the Son reveals).[85] As such, both lenses, if the lens metaphor is accepted, are busy throughout the Gospel of Matthew.[86]

Luke (Acts) and Peter

In the first few chapters of Acts, Peter shows a discernible engagement with Trinitarian-historical spectacles. His Pentecost sermon is a redemptive history given to explain the rationale for faith in Jesus as the one who fulfills the promise of the prophets that the messiah will give the Holy Spirit. Throughout the sermon, Peter quotes Old Testament texts addressed either to (Ps 16:8; cf. v. 25) or about (Ps 110:1; cf. v. 34) *the Lord*. He then follows by explaining that Jesus himself alone can be the Lord about whom David wrote (2:36). Continuing, in chapter 3, Peter refers to Jesus as the *archegon tes soma* (that is, "author of life;" 3:15), which has clear theological overtones. Then Peter follows this statement by, yet again, anchoring Jesus's identity in a redemptive-historical framework with several Old Testament points of connection (3:22–26).

As a final example, Peter refers in 4:11 to Jesus as the rejected "stone" who is now the cornerstone of the house of God. Peter's point is that Jesus fulfills the promise of Ps 118:22, which Peter later takes in 1 Pet 2:6–8 as a prophetic unit alongside Isa 8:14 and 28:16, the former of which speaks of God himself becoming the cornerstone of his own house. To

---

84. For the elliptical construal of Jesus's teaching, see Sproul, *Matthew*, 108.

85. For an insightful engagement with this text and the argument, see Swain, *Trinity and the Bible*, 59–64.

86. Considering one other gospel, it could be said that the introduction of John's Gospel alone is dripping with both Trinitarian teaching as well as redemptive-historical teaching. Chapter 1:1–4 shows God's Trinitarian nature, 1:5–17 explains his mission, and 1:18 summarizes the mission with a Trinitarian construal. It seems that John shifts back and forth between foci in building his singular argument.

Peter, Jesus is no less than *God the cornerstone,* now the cornerstone of the church, his spiritual house throughout the world (cf. Eph 2:20-22).

These examples indicate Peter's priority, as Goldsworthy comments, to show that the gospel—knowing it, believing it, experiencing the healing fellowship with God that it produces—is the goal of history.[87] Throughout these gospel retellings, Peter aims to show Christ's identity as the author of life and the Lord himself, whom to know brings "refreshing" (Gk. *anapsyxeōs,* "a recovery of easy breath"; Acts 3:20).[88] Again, both lenses remain active in giving sight—refreshing sight—to the listener and reader.

Hebrews

The book of Hebrews has been referred to as an early essay on biblical interpretation, indeed "the earliest comprehensive essay to come from a Christian hand."[89] Such an argument is easy to understand given the way in which Hebrews shows that important Old Testament people, institutions, and promises reach their culmination in Christ. Adrio König has argued that the theme of Hebrews is the phrase "Christ is greater than. . .," referring to the superiority of the new covenant fulfillments of Old Testament realities, fulfilled in Christ.[90] So understood, Hebrews is a redemptive-historical treatise intended to convince waning Jewish believers to not leave the faith.

Christ's divinity as the Son of God and agent of creation is made unavoidable in Hebrews' first chapter. The introduction aims to convince the readers that God's word to the world through his eternal Son brings redemptive history into a "new era of fulfillment, in which the divine Word is present with unambiguous clarity, definition, and completeness."[91] God had spoke in earlier history through his prophets, but he has now spoken by his Son (1:1-2) who is the creator and heir of all things (1:3) and who has taken his seat at the Father's right hand to intercede for believers (1:4). There is now, on the basis of Jesus's work, unprecedented access to God. God has, out of his triune perfection, opened the way to himself in a saving way.

87. Goldsworthy, *CCBT,* 71.
88. biblehub.com/greek/403.htm.
89. See Bray, *Biblical Interpretation,* 54; see also 70-76 for an extended treatment of the form and themes of Hebrews.
90. See König, *Christ Above All,* 8.
91. Webster, *God Without Measure,* 61.

In *The Birth of the Trinity*, Bates argues that the Old Testament quotations throughout Heb 1 are examples of a prosopological reading. He asserts that the Hebrews author intends to show that these texts, written in a historical context, are actually words from the Father about or to the Son. For instance, the earlier theme of creation (1:2) is later taken up by quoting Ps 102, calling the Son the Creator (1:10–12). Since there are many thematic similarities between Pss 45 and 102, one cannot understand how the former can be employed in 1:8–9 to explain the Son's taking up of kingship, as also mentioned earlier in 1:4.[92] By the end of Hebrews, the promise of new creation by Jesus is reinforced as fulfillment of Old Testament prophecy (12:25–28) in a sort of *inclusio* with the creation theme of 1:2 and 1:8–9. Whereas the Son created the world (a theological point), the Son has come in the last days (a redemptive-historical point, 1:2) to create a new world that includes all of those who know him.

The point in these few case studies has been to demonstrate that all through the New Testament, the gospel is explained in terms of both redemptive history and theology. The human writers of the New Testament seem to wear these theological/redemptive-historical spectacles as they "declare the mighty works of God" (Acts 2:11) and teach others how to delight in and study the works of the Lord (Ps 111:2).

Fathers

Irenaeus

As seen above in chapter 3, the era of the patristics was full of this twin concern for both theology and redemptive history. Irenaeus wore the redemptive-historical/theological spectacles: *Against Heresies* (c. 180) was a work designed to protect the church against unorthodox understandings of the Trinity particularly prevalent among Valentinian Gnostics. Of note, in it, Irenaeus defines the "first principles of the Gospel" as

> that there is one God, the Maker of this universe; He who was also announced by the prophets, and who by Moses set forth the dispensation of the law, (principles) which proclaim the Father of our Lord Jesus Christ, and ignore any other God or Father except him.[93]

---

92. Bates, *Birth of the Trinity*, 163, 171–74.
93. Irenaeus, *Against Heresies*, 3.16.7.

Irenaeus couches orthodoxy within redemptive-historical terms: Moses and the prophets announce the Father as the one true God who reveals himself as Father of the Lord Jesus. The gospel cannot be understood without a correct, orthodox understanding of God's nature. On the other hand, God's nature is communicated to the world within the context of his economy.

Further, Irenaeus's famous concept of recapitulation is the way in which Jesus sums up all things in himself (Eph 1:10) and makes Scripture's redemptive history sensible. Behr, commenting on Irenaeus's *Heresies* (1.9.2), concludes, "The gospel of the crucified one is . . . the prism by which Scripture is seen as speaking of Christ, recapitulating what had previously been written in the proclamation of the earthly sojourn of the Word of God."[94] To Irenaeus, Jesus *relives* all of redemptive history in his own life so that he can, by his own obedience and sinlessness, bring people to God. Containing within himself everything that it means to be human as well as everything that it is to be God,[95] theology and economy come together substantially in him.

Finally, Irenaeus wrote his *Demonstration of the Apostolic Preaching* as a type of biblical theology of Christ's person and work promised and fulfilled. This work would be fully at home among Christ-centered biblical theology in the present day as it so clearly shows Scripture's Christ-centered unity. In his dedication, he states that the work is aimed at leading his people "upward" whereby man can be "united to God."[96] Irenaeus, nevertheless, also explains Christ in theological terms all throughout his work, as did all the fathers in their Christological works. Irenaeus, following the pattern seen throughout this project's chapters, continues, showing that, like the apostles, he was Trinity-focused and economy-contextualized for the sake of discipleship and sanctification. There was no Christianity outside of such a dual-lens paradigm.

Augustine

Further, although Augustine is known for his great works on Christian doctrine (e.g., *De Trinitate*), he was certainly not unconcerned with the same type of redemptive-historical considerations as Irenaeus and the

---

94. Behr, *Formation of Christian Theology*, 123.
95. Behr, *Formation of Christian Theology*, 126.
96. Irenaeus, *Demonstration of the Apostolic Preaching*, 1.

biblical theologians of the modern day. Augustine wrote *Instructing Beginners in Faith* to instruct new believers in the basics of the faith so that they can "taste the sweetness and delight of [the true rest promised to Christians after this life] even here amid the most bitter troubles of this life."[97] But to accomplish his task, he engages in a long Christ-centered history beginning with creation and ending at Christ's second coming.[98] Prophecies, types, shadows, etc., are explained as prefiguring the great mystery of Christ's coming to fully reveal the love of God so that humanity would love him in return. Augustine can conclude, thus, that "from the beginning of the ages, this profound mystery has been unceasingly prefigured and foretold."[99] Christ's revelation is eternal because he is.

Also noteworthy is that Augustine's *De civitate Dei contra paganos* (*City of God*) is a redemptive history of God's work within his creation to realize his ultimate purpose in its redemption. In all of these works, Augustine, like Irenaeus before him, exegeted both Scripture and reality through redemptive-Trinitarian spectacles. The commonality of this twin-focus seems easily traceable throughout the history of interpretation.[100]

Medieval

Bernard

During the medieval period, no book of the Bible was given as much attention as the Song of Songs. Bray states that from about AD 200 to 800, around twenty commentaries were written on the Song. By contrast, from AD 800 to Luther's day in the sixteenth century, some forty-five commentaries were written on it.[101] It is the most commented-on scriptural book of the medieval era. Nevertheless, the number of interpretations which it has received has been the subject of considerable debate.

---

97. Augustine, *Instructing Beginners in Faith*, 67.
98. Augustine, *Instructing Beginners in Faith*, 73–100.
99. Augustine, *Instructing Beginners in Faith*, 71.
100. Worth mentioning is Oort's article, "End is Now," in which he shows that, whereas Augustine believed in a separation between what should be called sacred (scriptural) history and pagan (non-scriptural) history, they nevertheless intersect with each other since God aims, by his Son, to fill all things.
101. Bray, *Biblical Interpretation*, 158.

One of the most prominent biblical interpreters of this period was Bernard of Clairvaux (1090–1153). In terms of written works, he might be most well known for his *Sermons on the Song of Songs*, a collection that contains eighty-six different sermons. Bernard, following most interpreters of his and earlier days, sees the Song through an allegorical paradigm, saying quite certainly that the song is sung in honor of Jesus the King of kings and Lord of lords.[102] The entire Song is construed in terms of the love between members of the Trinity and between Christ and his church. What appears as an erotic duet between a couple is, so understood, simply a spiritual foretelling (and even a forthtelling, in theological terms) of the effects of the gospel.

But if the reader will recall the argument of chapter 3, allegorical interpretation through the Great Tradition is simply application of the text after having read it through the Bible's own Christ-centered framework. So, Bernard did not think he was imposing Christ on the text; rather, he was reading the book in light of Christ, convinced that that is what Christ intends. Bray concludes that the upshot of Bernard's approach is that the Song—centering on love given and reciprocated between the members of the Trinity and between God and his people—is the prism through which one is to read the entire Bible.[103] Not only is the Song read in light of the rest of Scripture which testifies to Christ, but the rest of Scripture is read in light of the Song. In this way, Bernard demonstrates the effectiveness of his theological-redemptive spectacles.

Reformation: Luther and Calvin

As chapter 3 sought to demonstrate, Reformational hermeneutics aimed to recover and renormalize the historical sense of the Scriptures so that the church could have a clear understanding of the gospel that defines its existence. Both Luther and Calvin, in distinct ways, were gospel-centered in the sense that they read Scripture as a unified message aimed at putting the gospel before the church and the world. A sensitivity to the historical nature of Scripture's narrative is discernible in Luther's Psalms sermons, as well as in books 1 and 2 of Calvin's *Institutes*. The reader could also return to chapter 3 for a reminder of the Reformational concern for the

---

102. Bernard, *Sermons on the Song of Songs* 1.8.

103. Bray, *Biblical Interpretation*, 161. Bray gives a good explanation of Bernard's understanding of the metaphorical nature of various items throughout the Song (e.g., that the "bread" is equivalent to the Word of God).

progressive nature of the unfolding of Scripture, similar, as noted above, to Melito, Irenaeus, and Augustine.

That said, one must acknowledge that both Calvin and Luther had theological concerns alongside redemptive ones. All through Calvin's *Institutes*, the gospel is construed theologically such that it is to be understood as a message of God's loving and fatherly nature. Books 1 and 2 of the *Institutes* aimed to give an explanation of the right knowledge of God as Creator and Redeemer, as Christ has revealed him. In these books, again, redemptive history and theology are married.[104] Also noteworthy is that Luther was relentlessly Christ-centered in his preaching, writing, and catechizing. Consult the introductory questions of his Small Catechism to see how he begins with Christ; perhaps surprisingly, he does not begin with theology proper or with a bibliology, but with the question, "What is the Christian faith?," which is then answered, "The Christian faith is the confession that Jesus Christ is the world's only Savior and Redeemer," followed by relevant proof-texts.[105] These brief comments are only offered to show that both Luther and Calvin wore the redemptive-theological spectacles.

Post-Reformation Centuries

The century following the Reformation saw the publication of confessions that would codify Christian doctrine in light of relevant Reformational foci for millions of Christians to the present day. The Westminster Confession (1646) became the most important Presbyterian confession, as was the Savoy Declaration for Congregationalists (1658) and the Second London Confession for Baptists (1689). Of note is that all of these confessions have substantial sections on the nature of God as well as the nature of Scripture as an unfolding historical narrative that centers on Christ. Of note as well is that the First London Baptist Confession (1644), predating all of these, was written with a redemptive-historical framework in mind. Clearly, these redemptive-theological lenses were ubiquitous among the churches in post-Reformation Britain.

Examples of the twin concern can be discerned in the subsequent centuries of evangelical biblical theologians, scholars, and pastors.[106]

---

104. One could consult Calvin, *Inst.*, 1.13–15; 2.7–16.
105. Available at https://catechism.cph.org.
106. One could consult Hughes Oliphant Old, *The Reading and Preaching of the*

For the sake of brevity, one might say that the placing together of a redemptive-historical lens with a theological/prosopological lens in one set of spectacles is comfortable in Christian hermeneutics even if it has never been stated explicitly. There has always been a concern to hear God *and* hear what God has done and is doing. To suggest, as Bates has, that a prosopological approach should replace a redemptive-historical approach (or, for that matter, vice versa) seems extreme. Instead, the approaches are complementary.

Theological interpretation and Biblical Theology—An Unlikely Marriage?

Theological interpretation of Scripture is a recent hermeneutical attempt to retrieve historic Trinitarian and Christological exegesis so that the contemporary church has communicative consistency with the Great Tradition. It was seen earlier that some think that defining theological interpretation is too difficult to even attempt.[107] Carson's critique demonstrated the need for serious evaluation of theological interpretation's distinct foci, because there is some confusion about them.[108]

That said, Bartholomew and Thomas have ably compiled a summary work explaining theological interpretation. This Trinity-oriented exegesis seeks to employ the best of other exegetical disciplines (including grammatical-historical) to come to theological conclusions which then become the framework employed in exegetical practice to build up the church.[109] Given that, as it has been seen, biblical theology is also discipleship-oriented in its grammatical-historical exegesis, its compatibility with theological interpretation is further reinforced.[110]

Theological interpretation appears to be a reaction to the anti-supernaturalistic bent of modern hermeneutics, which has often been guilty of treating Scripture like any another work of literature. In response, the approach attempts to recover the Bible as a supernatural witness of the triune God. Bartholomew and Thomas state that the goal of theological

---

Scriptures in the Worship of the Christian Church, Vols. 4–7; also Helmut Thielicke's *Encounter With Spurgeon*.

107. See Carter, *ISGT*, 19. See also Parker, "D. A. Carson's Evaluation."

108. See Carson, "Theological Interpretation of Scripture," 187–207.

109. Bartholomew and Thomas define theological interpretation as "interpretation of the Bible for the church." See *Manifesto*, ix.

110. See Rosner, "Biblical Theology" in *New Dictionary of Biblical Theology*, 10.

interpretation is to hear God's voice.[111] As Webster emphasized throughout his corpus, exegesis begins with listening with the goal being clarity of comprehension and practice. Furthermore, Bartholomew and Thomas add that theological interpretation also aims, in listening to God, to shape believers spiritually within the context of the local church for the sake of God's mission to redeem the world.[112] So even if the distinctive foci of theological interpretation are difficult to define, it seems clear that the goal is reading Scripture theologically for the sake of discipleship and disciple-making (Matt 28:18–20). The interpretive orientation is both vertical (listening to God) and horizontal (seeking to helping others to hear his voice.)

This project has shown that biblical theology seeks the same goals. Now the emphasis will shift to how biblical theology seeks to meet these goals in a way distinct but not substantially different from theological interpretation. In particular, biblical theology aims to read Scripture as a historically unfolding and therefore unified witness with an emphasis on the historical nature of the narrative and the unfolding of God's plan. Perhaps where theological interpretation—that is, *all* theological interpretative approaches, such as the aforementioned prosopological approach—focuses on the *what* of God's nature and plan, biblical theology focuses on the *how*. Since there is no *how* to God's being (for he is perfect in himself and eternally so[113]), the focus of biblical theology becomes the *how* of the unfolding of God's plan. Since the New Testament places such emphasis on the importance of the unfolding plan to reveal the Father to the world, biblical theology is not embarrassed to say that its emphasis is more on God's economic endeavor than on his being.[114]

Therefore, theological interpretation and Christ-centered biblical theology seem to need each other. Theological interpretation must understand that its context is economic, and biblical theology must understand that both its source and goal are theological. The goal of the gospel

---

111. Bartholomew and Thomas, *Manifesto*, 17.

112. Bartholomew and Thomas, *Manifesto*, 18–19.

113. See Barrett, *Simply Trinity*, for a discussion of God's non-composed and simple nature. See also Aquinas, *ST*, 1.3.1–4.

114. Duby has offered a helpful approach to theology that prioritizes God's transcendence over the divine economy in *God in Himself: Scripture, Metaphysics, and the Task of Christian Theology*. He makes the case that although theology is revealed in the context of economy, theology, to be properly theology, must have as its reference point God's being before his doing. In such an approach, both lenses are at work, even if the theological lens has more power.

CHRIST AND THEOLOGY

is the knowledge of God (Jer 9:23[115]), and the promise of the knowledge of God is peace (Isa 26:3). There is, therefore, a type of *visionary spiral* that comprises truly evangelical hermeneutics: The believer pursues the knowledge of the Lord for the sake of peace within the context of a spatial life and experiences this spatial life in context of the triune God, in whom all people "live and move and have their being" (Acts 17:28).[116]

Sanders has argued that the Trinity, if disconnected from the saving gospel, becomes a mere doctrine disconnected from the believer's life.[117] God is the Trinity who redeems and draws to himself, and all of the believer's experience is to be understood as a part of that God-ward trajectory. In fact, the gospel and the Trinity might presuppose each other: The Trinity is the relational God that exists, who can be known; the gospel is the way in which he reveals himself to humanity unto a knowledge that is eternal life (John 17:3).[118] Biblical theology aims to understand and communicate *how* God reveals himself, whereas theological interpretation aims to understand and communicate the *what* of God's nature revealed. Biblical theology focuses on the *context* of theology—life in God's creation, listening to his voice on a faith journey—while theological interpretation focuses on the *source* of theology, God himself.

One or the other alone, however, is not the *goal* of theology. The goal of theology is rightly knowing God and all things in relation to him. Such an orientation is meant to produce clarity, joy, and peace. Paul says, thus, that the kingdom of God consists in righteousness, peace, and joy in the Holy Spirit (Rom 14:17) who is the Spirit of truth.

The ultimate realization of this goal will be the new heavens and new earth (Isa 65:17; Hag 2:7–9; Rev 21–22), which have a glory with which the apostle says nothing in this life can be compared (2 Cor 4:17). All of God's redemptive program—for it is one program, not multiple ones, though there might be different stages of it—is moving toward this goal. Since the end is greater than any believer's current experience,

---

115. Understood (or at least applied) Christologically by Paul in 1 Cor 1:30–31.

116. See Bartholomew's discussion of Brevard Childs's practice of closely connecting theological interpretation and biblical theology, in "Biblical Theology and Biblical Interpretation," 14–15. Bartholomew makes the case that biblical theology is necessary to find a truly theological interpretation of Scripture. It appears to be the case that attempts to unite redemptive history and theological interpretation had already begun with Childs (though it is likely the case that, as seen in a previous chapter, Childs had difficulty detaching his framework from a progressive view of history).

117. Sanders, *Deep Things of God*, 43–49.

118. Sanders, *Deep Things of God*, 43.

perhaps even the very best of current experience is a type of the future fullness of glory when God is seen.[119]

There are enough parallels between the current and the future that Scripture is replete with comparisons. Jesus tells the disciples that he re-enters heaven to prepare a house for them (John 14:3). Since the glory of the future is so much greater, such comparisons are profoundly limited (1 Cor 13:12). This limitation is why John writes that believers have yet to know what they will be like in the end, though they know they will be like their Lord, seeing him as he is (1 John 3:3): The glory will be far greater than current experience can be, though God employs earthly parallels in order to stir believers' imaginations and cause their longing. They temporally live in their current "lot"; however, they look not to the things that are but to the things of heaven because they are eternally seated with Christ (2 Cor 4:18; Matt 6:19–20; cf. Eph 2:5–7).

Everywhere in the New Testament, believers are told that they presently stand at the experientially highest point of redemptive history. Redemptive history will, however, continue to escalate toward this future glory beyond comparison. Because their God dwells in unapproachable light (1 Tim 6:16; Dan 2:22) with a glory that the human mind cannot currently penetrate (Neh 9:5), so the fullness of the future glory cannot be penetrated, either. In the future glory, God will be "all in all" (1 Cor 15:28). But in order to arrive there, believers must, to borrow from an English colloquialism, keep moving "onward and upward." Indeed, their 3D spectacle lenses are built just for that endeavor: The biblical theology/redemptive-historical lens sees the onward (historical) aspect, while the theological interpretive lens sees the upward (theological) aspect.

Typological Realism

As such, this "onward and upward" framework can be called *typological realism*, as it centers typology in the pursuit of understanding what God has revealed is real, true, etc. Perhaps centering typology in a hermeneutical framework seems bold. Worth mentioning then is the work of Leonhard Goppelt in the twentieth century, seeking to center typology as such. He wrote that typology operates according to the way the New Testament writers read the Old Testament, where an earlier and lesser

---

119. As Aquinas said, all perfection that exists, by necessity, exists first in God. *ST*, 1.4.3.

person, institution, or practice parallels and points to a later and greater person, institution, or practice. For example, the New Testament everywhere identifies Jesus as the antitype of the Old Testament prophets (e.g., Luke 9:28–35; Matt 5–7), the antitype to Solomon and his descendants as the son of David (Matt 12:42; 21:11), the antitype to Adam (Luke 3:38—4:13; Rom 5:12–21; 1 Cor 15:42–49), and the antitype to all Old Testament righteous sufferers (e.g., Pss 22, 69; Isa 52:13—53:12).[120] A non-Christ example of typology would be Peter's use of the language of Exod 19 to call the New Testament church the "royal priesthood and holy nation," though it is comprised of believers from many nations (1 Pet 2:9–10).[121] One might say that Peter is not identifying any typology because the language is taken from Exodus and is restated because Jesus has done the work necessary to produce what God had promised. There were times, however, in the Old Testament when faithful believers did honor the Lord such that, in them, Israel functioned as a holy nation. Surely *in one sense* those believers fulfilled the promise. Jesus, however, fulfilled it perfectly, such that all of the promises of God come true in him (2 Cor 1:20). So one may conclude that the earlier experience parallels, prepares for, and therefore points to the later and the greater.[122]

As seen earlier, Bates is critical of such a typological framework, choosing instead a prosopological one. His criticism, however, seems to overstate. He cites Peter's use of Ps 16 in Acts 2, where David speaks of not seeing corruption in the grave. Peter adds that David was speaking in the Holy Spirit of the coming Christ, which, according to Bates, makes a typological reading less likely. For how could David be merely a type of Christ if he is speaking directly of Christ, and his own experience, including a permanent burial, is so profoundly different from Christ's?[123] But at this point, Bates displays a surprising misunderstanding (or, at least, misapplication) of typology. Typology does not state that every detail of the Old Testament type—in this case, David the soon-to-be-buried king—is typical of the New Testament antitype. Rather, typology says that there are enough parallels across the intertextual escalation that typology is the appropriate explanation and conclusion based on the New Testament's usage. In other words, typology does not include every parallel between

---

120. See Goppelt, *Typos*, 61–106.
121. Goppelt, *Typos*, 152.
122. See Mitchell Chase's masterful explanation of the nature of typology in *40 Questions*, 119–90.
123. Bates, *Birth of the Trinity*, 154.

two texts but some aspects, usually important ones. So David's suffering and hope for resurrection shows him as a type of Christ, even if he was writing prosopologically, as Peter at least implies.

Thus if, as O'Keefe and Reno say, the Bible's aim is to present not just details but the very nature of reality,[124] both the typological *and* prosopological senses have a place in regenerate (Christian) interpretation: The prosopological sense sees texts in light of the nature of Trinitarian reality (realism) while the typological sense stirs believers' hope in future fullness. The effect of the former is that the believer is sobered about the nature of what is true, right, and real. Basic principles such as God the Trinity, the original goodness of the creation, God serving humanity by means in his creation, and the human call to imitate God by serving others should all lead to a sense of mental sobriety. Conversely, the effect of the latter is that the believer is stirred to set his or her sights on what is to come. Since God has fulfilled his past promises with gifts/blessings more glorious than what came earlier, the believer has confidence that God will fulfill what still waits, and it will be more even more glorious in its eternal antitype.

To live within such a framework is to live in light of what God has revealed as *real*; such revelation is typological, reality given via a typological narrative that also reflects eternal Trinitarian realities. Scripture shows God as the promise-maker and promise-keeper with later revelation being substantially greater and fuller; thinking in this way seems, therefore, most appropriate. Spectacle frames fitted with redemptive-theological lenses thus give clarity.

Conclusion

Sound hermeneutics will be a set of 3D spectacles with both a theological lens and a Christological lens. Christ-centered biblical theology, which is primarily oriented toward historical Christology, does not seek to replace the Great Tradition but to fill in its potential weaknesses in a way that is consistent with the best of the Great Tradition. Since biblical theology as a discipline has had a checkered past, theological interpretation aimed to recover Trinity-focused exegesis to the end of meeting the same need that biblical theology did. The fortunate effect of the existence of both schools is that these disciplines end up as helps to each other and should

---

124. O'Keefe and Reno, *Sanctified Vision*, 13, cited in Bates, *Birth of the Trinity*, 183.

be taken together. Bartholomew has said that any Christian hermeneutic worth its salt must be Christocentric, reading both Testaments together as Christian Scripture.[125] This is clearly the goal of believing (that is, Christ-centered) biblical theology: to see, hear, and follow Jesus in Scripture's pages.

Elsewhere, Bartholomew provides the Trinitarian balance to his own statement: "[The rule of faith] insists that readers of Scripture locate Jesus Christ in the very life of God himself, along with the Holy Spirit, who testifies to him."[126] So the Bible's overall context is the unfolding narrative that tells of Christ who reveals the Father (Matt 11:27) and redeems humanity by his own recapitulation of godliness in himself (cf. 1 Tim 3:15). Christ is the Son of God from all eternity, and in order to be worshiped and enjoyed, faith demands locating him in the Trinitarian life.[127] A set of hermeneutical spectacles that has a redemptive-historical lens alongside of a theological-interpretive lens will be careful to locate texts as witnesses to Christ's act and being, that the believing interpreter might keep moving onward and upward toward the glory that has no earthly comparison. This set of lenses will help believers see the Old Testament both as a witness to the nature of God the Trinity as well as to the progressively unfolding historical narrative of which believers are a part. They can, therefore, partially see and enjoy the *real* while they journey across time to the full experience.

The next chapter will explain how theological-redemptive spectacles give the church its (a) future-looking hope (redemptive history), (b) motivation for its heaven-looking worship (theology), and (c) the resources needed for its disciple-making and disciple-shaping mission (pastoral). The chapter will argue that a typological orientation is uniquely able to frame the (a) and (b) into spectacles that enable the fulfilling of (c) as mission. Theology (concerned with what is ultimately real in God) via typology (the content of revelation) meets history (the context of life with God) in time and space.

---

125. Bartholomew, *Introducing Biblical Hermeneutics*, 7–9.

126. Bartholomew and Thomas, *Manifesto*, 254.

127. Hence Athanasius said that there being no division between the Father and the Son is nothing less than "the faith" (cf. Jude 4). As such, to deny the Scripture's own teaching on the unity of the Father and the Son is be "anything but a Christian." Athanasius, *Defense of the Nicene Definition*, 38, 75.

5

Typological Realism as Approach

"We see God himself—the divine essence—when we indwell the incarnate tabernacle of God though union and communion with Jesus. Sacrament and reality coincide with him. The divine essence does not lie behind or beyond Christ; rather, those who have eyes of faith can see the essence of God in the unity of the person of Christ."

—HANS BOERSMA

THE PREVIOUS CHAPTERS PURSUED answers to the project's research question, which concerned the nature of the relationship between Christ-centered biblical theology and the hermeneutics of the so-called Great Tradition, Reformationally construed in terms of *sola scriptura*. Christ-centered biblical theology seeks, within the context of the listening church, to be pastorally sensitive, Christocentric and theocentric (as the obvious effect of the gospel of God's Son being the thematic center of Scripture), and exegetically precise. Whereas theological precision has always characterized the Tradition, the same cannot be said of Christ-centered biblical theology. Further, even the aforementioned desire to be pastorally sensitive has demonstrated considerable weakness. There is a need, then, for a stronger effort to theologically orient biblical theology with one hope being a strengthened focus on practical living. In this way,

Christ-centered biblical theology can be understood as a true advancement on the hermeneutics of the Great Tradition.

The previous chapter began proposing a sort of synthetic approach that would partner Christ-centered biblical theology and theological interpretation of Scripture. Several reasons for this proposal have been noted. First, Christ-centered biblical theology has had a tendency to be both theologically and pastorally weak. This effect is probably unintended given that many prominent redemptive historicists have operated with a pastoral impulse. It seems, however, to be accurate, and sadly so, given the theological and pastoral resources available in biblical theology. Some influential voices with a theological orientation have, therefore, been critical of this evangelical approach to biblical theology.[1]

But that observation raises a second reason for synthesis: Both "sides" have been critical of the other while also supporting the very things that the other side observes are missing in hermeneutics. So although some prominent redemptive historicists have had their own apprehension toward (and criticism of) theologically oriented exegetical methods,[2] some proponents of theological interpretation have voiced the need to be Christocentric,[3] and some redemptive-historical biblical theologians have voiced the need for a stronger theological orientation.[4] Biblical theology and theological interpretation, then, need not be seen as rivals or mutually exclusive approaches but complementary. A sound hermeneutical approach should not be thought of as an either/or but a both/and. Both approaches have merit mixed with dangers if left in isolation.

The aforementioned points help explain why the previous chapter concluded that truly Christian hermeneutics will join the approaches together. The effect will be a pair of spectacle lenses that, similar to the dual action of 3D glasses, see in both upward (theological) terms and forward (redemptive-historical) terms. The thesis of the current chapter is that typology constitutes the frames holding the theological and redemptive-historical lenses. When used together, the lenses enable the Christian to

---

1. See Trueman, foreword to Carter, *Contemplating God*, xi; see also Trueman, "Revolutionary Balancing Act".

2. See chapter 1 above. This motivation was foundational for Gabler's initial attempt at summarizing biblical theology. See also Goldsworthy, "Is Biblical Theology Viable?," 18–44, and "Pastor as Biblical Theologian," 110–30.

3. See Bartholomew, *Introducing Biblical Hermeneutics*, 7–9.

4. See Vos, "Idea of Biblical Theology," 3–24.

see the nature of God's reality as it is revealed: the revelation of the eternal God through his time and space project in the context of covenantal shepherding to the end of the ecstasy of the beatific vision. Typology, being both upward- and forward-oriented, is the most comfortable frame in which both lenses can fit together. The result is a synthetic approach called *typological realism*: typology as both the modus operandi of revelation in time and space, as God wills, revealing that which is real, and the context in which knowledge of it unfolds.

The first portion of this chapter will consider the nature of the beatific vision. In the vision, God is the goal of all things, the ultimate end beholding him. As such, the history of revelation proceeds toward that end, employing purposeful types as prophetic visions along the way. What follows is, first, an explanation of typology as training ground for the vision, and second, considerations of what typology does for both biblical theology and theological interpretation, dealing with each in separate sections. Then will commence an attempt at reading both Old and New Testaments in light of the synthetic, typology-centered approach. This section will engage with Geerhardus Vos who, though his works are largely forgotten by much evangelical (and sadly, much Reformed) scholarship, was, as chapter 2 saw, interpreting according to such a redemptive-historical/theological dual-orientation.[5] Finally, before some concluding thoughts will be a consideration of an adjacent theological question given the heavy emphasis placed on God's revelation over time.

The Goal of History: The Beatific Vision

This project has suggested bringing together evangelical redemptive-historical (that is, Christ-centered) biblical theology and theological interpretation as partner "lenses" to function like 3D glasses using typological frames. The need for typological "frames" lies in the fact that typology is both upward-focused (God-ward, as in theological interpretation) and forward-focused (progressive, as in biblical theology). In order for this to work, the vision has to situate typology because the beatific vision is the terminus both of redemptive history and of theology for two reasons: First, although theology is the study of God, the vision will be the sight

---

5. This project hopes to encourage readers to read Vos's work in order to appreciate his ahead-of-his-time theological/biblical-theological approach.

of God such that theological truth will become sight;[6] second, redemptive history is the organic unfolding of redemption across time with the beatific vision as its ultimate goal. All of redemptive history progresses toward the vision as its end.

Typology uniquely brings the beatific vision into history via three ways: First, the events themselves reveal the nature of the fellowship God establishes and maintains with his people sacramentally ("sacrament" being understood as Boersma defines it: a revelatory anticipation[7]); second, via the pattern of the events together as a revelation of God's redeeming purposes with a discernible trajectory across time, typology tells the story of Christ's marriage to his church, which earthly marriage typifies (cf. Eph 5:22–33); and third, typology demonstrates God's advancing perfect presence in time and space, anticipating his perfect presence in the end.

Boersma has argued that the Great Tradition has always held that the beatific vision—seeing God—is the purpose of humanity's existence.[8] Perhaps Irenaeus said it best: since the glory of God is a living man, "the life of man consists in beholding God."[9] Nevertheless, God's glory is unfathomable, so all of revelation in time and space is a condescension. Since God aims to bring redeemed humanity to the point in which they will behold his glory *opsometha auton kathos estin* ("seeing him according to his being," 1 John 3:2), humanity needs to be prepared. Humans will never fully comprehend the depths of God's being, though, if Aquinas was correct, humanity will stop "moving" at its final rest in God, in the vision.[10] Whether one has a more Thomistic or Edwardsian (that is, ever-moving) understanding of the vision, believers know that they will enjoy the fullness of fellowship with the uncreated God inasmuch as they are able.

The fact that humans cannot fully comprehend the beatific vision seems to be in view when Paul compares the current state with the latter by saying, "For now, we know in part . . . then . . . fully" (1 Cor 13:9,

---

6. Thus Boersma says that theology is sacramental of God's self-knowledge, through which God initiates believers into participation with himself. This process will conclude in the Vision. *HP,*, 170–84.

7. See Boersma, *SG,*, 401.

8. Boersma, *SG,*, 11. Worth mentioning is that Boersma makes the same argument in a much more abbreviated but no less eloquent way in his *Five Things*, 112–19. For the beatific vision as the goal in preaching, see his *Sacramental Preaching*.

9. Irenaeus, *Against Heresies* 4.20.7.

10. See Aquinas, *Summa contra Gentiles* 3.48.3; Boersma, *SG,*, 32.

12, NIV). To prepare for the ultimate beholding, God employs temporal visions: time and space parallels to eternal realities used as sacramental pictures to train humanity's eyes and mind for the vision.[11] And even in the temporal visions, God is present in a substantial way as the visions participate in the real.[12] So the beatific vision is, from the human perspective, both a *future* reality (in fullness) and a *present* reality (in partiality). This realization will prove important in defining typology. Elsewhere, Boersma makes the case that God carries believers along by setting their imaginations on the sacramental images he has provided which point to the greater (eternal) glory which will constitute the believer's experience in the final day (Rom 8:17–18). That is the purpose of the visions: to set the mind upward and forward on that which is real, which will come in fullness. In this sense, visions are restorative to humanity's purpose of fellowship with God. Boersma, therefore, refers to the visions as *sacramental*. They are means through which the believer finds reality; in finding reality, the believer dwells on that on which their imagination exists to dwell: God-given images to prepare for God's glory.[13]

What Is Typology? Training Ground for the beatific vision

These gracious visions are sacramental types, and thus their engagement requires a clear understanding of types. If they hold such a central place in God's economy, some attention to their clear definition seems necessary.

Patrick Fairbairn, who wrote the fullest treatise on typology to date (definitely the longest), contrasted allegory with typology, saying that although the former pursues a narrative use of a biblical text to teach a higher point that is not contained in the text itself, the latter pursues a teleological (or canonical) use of the text in light of later biblical narrative, understanding the text in its canonical context, which provides its ultimate meaning.[14] Allegory, it could be said, is a pastoral tool that acknowledges logical parallels between a text's exegetical point and a Christian dogmatic point often with the goal of pastoral application, while typology acknowledges conceptual parallels between texts, assuming,

---

11. Boersma, *SG,*, 14.
12. Boersma, *SG,*, 134. See also Wilken, *Spirit of Early Christian Thought*, 249–53.
13. See Boersma, *Pierced by Love*, 20–30.
14. Fairbairn, *Typology of Scripture*, 1.2–3.

based on divine authorial intent, that those parallels were purposeful. If allegory is conditioned by the rule of faith such that the point made has some thematic flexibility with the logical and canonical context of a text, typology demands both logical and canonical consistency between the texts in question.[15] Unlike allegory, in typology, exegesis of a text occurs canonically in light of how the rest of Scripture contextualizes it.[16]

More acutely, typology concerns how earlier people, actions, or things are prophetic images or prefigurements of coming realities.[17] Because of this, Mitchell Chase has said that typology is canonical exegesis where something earlier and lesser is intended to point to and pattern something later and greater.[18] More simply, Beale has said that typology is "contextual exegesis within the framework of the canon."[19] So understood, typology concerns purposeful—"purposeful" based on divine authorial intent—and escalating correspondences across the biblical narrative.

The main question in typology is this: How do people, actions, or things in the text point to and pattern later more significant people, actions, or things? In other words, how do the former people, actions, or things *escalate* across the biblical narrative? Escalation is central to

---

15. Such an explanation comes from an appropriation of a point in the foreword of Goppelt's *Typos*.

16. Worth mentioning is that Fairbairn, with his somewhat dismissive attitude of allegory, was likely criticizing a different type of allegorizing than the Augustinian-Thomistic allegorizing seen in chapter 3. Allegory, being always under gospel control, is closed off to both fancy and hermeneutical subjectivity. As such, allegory functions only one of two ways: First, it can be a way to understand a text in light of Christ as the revealing Logos who came in the Christ-event; second—and this is the emphasis throughout chapter 3—it can be a way to make a true pastoral point that is not explicitly contained in the plain reading of the original text but flows naturally from relating the text to Christ and, through him, to the believer. Boersma, engaging with Henri de Lubac, argues ably for such a use of allegory in Christian interpretation in *HP*, 145–47. This type of allegory could be called *tethered allegory* since the allegorizing must be controlled (tethered) by the gospel/rule of faith. It follows, then, that any point made by tethered allegory will be a point that is made explicitly elsewhere in the biblical narrative. See also Aquinas's explanation in *ST*, 1.1.10.

17. See Boersma, *HP*, 106.

18. See Chase, *40 Questions*, 35–37. It is also worth reminding the reader of Chase's helpful definition of allegory, seen in an earlier chapter: Allegory holds that a text teaches one thing but can be used to teach a lesson that goes beyond the text's point. Chase, *40 Questions*, 193.

So understood, typology and allegory are related: Both see particular texts as making points beyond the close reading, and both do so on canonical grounds. Chase, *40 Questions*, 197.

19. Beale, *Handbook on the New Testament*, 25.

typology. Like an escalator staircase moves forward and upward, so the scriptural narrative moves forward and upward: forward, with clear parallels between what happens earlier and later, and upward, to the greater that comes later. This construal is sensible given that the scriptural narrative explicitly says that what comes later is greater and better (Heb 9:23; Isa 65:17).

Matthew Barrett agrees with the point above, that divine authorial intent is what makes typology possible: God seeks to unfold his revelatory purposes over the course of time (Eph 1:10). The exegete should expect, therefore, that that which comes later will help give clarity to that which came earlier.[20] This is in fact what happens across the storyline.

Conversely, Hamilton adopts an approach that diverges somewhat from Barrett's, although there are commonalities. If Barrett makes typology depend on divine intent, Hamilton places an emphasis on human authorial intent. His explanation is worth quoting at length:

> The Biblical authors instinctively understood that typological development functions as follows: When patterns of historical correspondences are repeated across narratives, expectations accumulate and cause escalation in the perceived significance of the repeated similarities and patterns. What they instinctively understood and communicated, we can validate by means of these criteria.[21]

To Hamilton, the intention of Scripture's human writers are put on display in typology: There are clear correspondences across the biblical narrative, and the writers themselves seem to be intensely focused on making those correspondences central to the narrative so that their readers will believe the message and enter into the life of faith being promulgated.

Whatever one's approach whether focusing on divine or human intent, neither approach necessarily excludes the relevance of the other. Webster ably argued that there is no contradiction between the human writing of Scripture and the divine writing. So perhaps the human writers all had clarity on what story they were telling. Most important to understand for this project's goals is clarity regarding typology's nature: Typology is the study of escalating correspondences across the biblical narrative which moves onward and upward, eventually, to the beatific vision.

---

20. See Barrett, *Canon, Covenant, and Christology*, 25.
21. Hamilton, *Typology*, 25.

CHRIST AND THEOLOGY

There are, however, two related questions still worth answering, and the first concerns the nature of the word: Why is typology called typology? And secondly, what is the canonical ground for typology? First, typology's root word is *typos* in Greek, used at several points throughout the New Testament in several derivatives referring to a pattern, example, or likeness. To adopt a typological reading of Scripture is to be convinced that types dominate the biblical narrative.[22] Goppelt, Fairbairn, and Beale have shown that the New Testament reads the Old in a typological way, where earlier types anticipate later antitypes which have come. Goppelt has said that the purpose of the Old Testament was to prepare the church and the world to be able to hear the gospel: Without the Old, the New would not make much sense. The meaning which the New explicates is established under a typological framework.[23]

Thus, the canonical foundation for typology is twofold. First, both Testaments employ typology to understand the relationship of the Old Testament to the New from *both* perspectives: In the New, Adam is explicitly called a *type* of Christ (Rom 5:14); elsewhere in the New, Christian baptism, the moment when a believer is outwardly separated from the world, is the *antitype* of the Noachic deluge, where Noah and his family were separated from the world of the ungodly (1 Pet 3:19). Conversely, in the Old, Moses drew the younger generation's attention to the coming prophet who will have *likeness* to him (Deut 18:15); later, Malachi promised that Elijah would come to prepare the way for God's coming (Mal 4:5); finally, David was told that he would have a son who would inhabit an eternal kingdom (2 Sam 7:14). In each of these Old Testament texts, the promises seem to be understood typologically: The prophet with likeness to Moses will be greater (for why else would there be the need to look for another prophet distinct from Moses? Why not just live by what Moses said?[24]); the "Elijah" figure would likely be greater than Elijah (Matt 11:11); and the Son of David would be no less than the Son of God himself being born in the Davidic line (Isa 9:6–7; Dan 7:13–14). Thus Isaiah says

---

22. Goppelt's definition of typology as "a spiritual approach to hermeneutics" (*Typos*, 202) might be misleading. "Spiritual" is not opposed to "exegetical." Goppelt's point is that, since types give way to antitypes under the age of the Spirit, a typological approach to the Bible is an approach from the vantage point of the Holy Spirit and his fulfillments. It seems that Goppelt would be comfortable with the hermeneutical approach of progressive covenantalism/new covenant Theology, noted in 41–43 of the current project.

23. See Goppelt, *Typos*, 198–205.

24. Heb 3:1–6, and König's notes in *Christ Above All*, 25–26.

that the new things will be so glorious that "the former things will not even be remembered" (Isa 65:17). Further, the so-called *protoevangelion* of Gen 3:15–16 would have to be understood typologically: Since there is not another explicit interaction between the couple and the serpent but instead an entire redemptive history filled with Eden-like temptations, serpent-like evils, and repeated promises of a coming great triumph, this first gospel promise seems to be a typological figure prophetically communicating what would happen later. Hence the curses and promises of Gen 3:12–19 set up the rest of the biblical narrative.[25]

Second, the New Testament teaching that the Christ-event is the consummation of the fulfillment of God's purposes requires an ontological relationship between Christ's coming and all that occurred before. The Son of God is the Word of God who spoke by various oracular and prophetic modes all through the various Old Testament eras (John 1:1–18; Matt 23:34). In the incarnation, he put on flesh to redeem all things through his death and resurrection as was earlier promised (Acts 3:18; Gal 3:8). The incarnation is treated virtually everywhere in the New Testament like it is the most important event in all of history (e.g., Acts 3:15–20).[26]

Further, as Dempster has argued, a student of the Old Testament can discern without even looking at the New a longing for a sequel.[27] As seen in chapter 2, the New Testament writers labor to show that Christ's life and ministry is not only the Old Testament's sequel but the resolution to its problems. If this is true, one would expect that God intends for everything in the Scriptures to have a relationship to Christ and the Christ-event.

To say as much is not to imply that every detail in the Old Testament has an explicit type/antitype relationship with something in the New. Everything does not, however, have a part to play in the type/antitype shape of the unfolding redemptive narrative that leads to and finds fulfillment in Jesus. Goppelt devotes his whole work to explaining how

---

25. Worth noting is that the Old Testament explains itself in typological terms. Both Beale's work (especially *Union with the Resurrected Christ*) and Goldsworthy's (especially *CCBT*) ably show the prophets use the images of earlier Old Testament history to point ahead to eschatological realities.

26. And it explains why Barth took the Christ-event as the reference point for all of reality, let alone theology. See his *Dogmatics in Outline*. In particular, Barth says, following various patristic thinkers, that the purpose of Pontius Pilate being named is to give an undeniable historical reference point to the cross event.

27. This is the main argument of Dempster's *Dominion and Dynasty*; see 35–39, 41.

the New Testament reads the Old in a typological way, sometimes simply assuming typology without explaining it. In the Gospels, for example, everything about Christ's teaching ministry is a reflection of the ministry of the prophets in the Old.[28] Christ is in many places referred to as the Son of David without explanation (Matt 1:1; 9:27; 12:23; Rom 1:3). What does this say about David's actual sons—were they illegitimate? The answer, typologically understood, would be that the sons were types pointing to Christ; even if "son" is understood in the broader sense of "descendent," a typology critic still has to answer why Solomon, the immediate son following the 2 Sam 7 promise to David, *did not* live and reign forever.[29] But the coming "son" would. Hence David picked up and typified the Old Testament offices of priest and king, applying them to a future priest-king (Ps 110). This observation is why the apostles, echoing Jesus's own teaching (Matt 22:44), would often quote this psalm, applying it to him (e.g., Acts 2:34; Heb 1:13; 5:6). Goppelt compellingly shows how the life and ministry of Jesus echoes in a booming voice the ways that the Old Testament talks about prophets, kings, the righteous, and the Servant of the Lord (a major prophetic figure): In the Gospels, some explanation of his fulfilling these offices is given, but in many places, the escalating parallel is simply assumed, as though God expects the reader to see these intertextual parallels.[30]

Similarly, Fairbairn devotes both volumes of his *Typology of Scripture* to demonstrating how the Old Testament has to be read in typological terms if it is to be understood. In both volumes, he works through the entire Old Testament narrative explaining how persons, institutions, offices, etc., are to be understood in light of the gospel. One noteworthy example is the promised land. Fairbairn says, not without controversy, that the land must be understood typically, *not literally*, for two reasons: First, God promised to Abraham that he would *himself* inherit Canaan (Gen 17:8), which he literally did not. Second, though the people did later enter the land, they never actually rested when they got there, though God said that they would (Deut 25:19). The Hebrews writer, therefore, quotes Ps 95:6, saying that there still *remains* a sabbath rest for God's people who believe (Heb 4:9; Ps 95:6). So, says Goppelt, the promises had

---

28. Goppelt, *Typos*, 63–82.
29. Goppelt, *Typos*, 84.
30. Goppelt, *Typos*, 105. This point might explain why the apostles were so disillusioned at their Jewish kinsmens' inability to embrace Jesus as the Messiah. How could God make his case any more clearly?

to have a future-looking typological hope, or else they are nonsensical or inconsistent. The New Testament insists, therefore, that it is in Jesus, to whom Abraham looked and in whose day he rejoiced (John 8:56), that the people find the true rest (Heb 3–4). It is via believers who share Abraham's faith that the patriarch has descendants like the sand of the sea, and in this way he begins to inherit "the world" (Rom 4:13). Fairbairn concludes, "The renovated earth [is] the ultimate inheritance of the heirs of promise."[31] It belongs to those who have the same faith that Abraham had (Gal 3:14, 29).

So understood, the goal of the Old Testament types is to lead people to Christ. In this way, says Fairbarn, the Old Testament is a schoolmaster to Christ (Gal 3:24, KJV).[32] In both Goppelt's and Fairbarn's construal, typology is more than a channel through which Christ is present in the Old Testament (although it is, indeed, a channel for his presence).[33] Typology constitutes the way in which God frames history's movement towards its ultimate goal, the beatific vision. History, though not "progressive" in the modern sense, does yield a "gradual increase in the vision of God . . . [which will] ultimately render people immortal."[34] Via revelatory types, God mercifully and kindly prepares people for the vision of him for which they exist.

Prosopology or Redemptive History? Typology as Lens Frames

The previous chapter considered Peter Gentry's redemptive-historicist response to Matthew Bates and Craig Carter's prosopological reading of the Old Testament. Bates and Carter argue for a reading of Scripture that contextualizes the Old Testament in terms of Trinitarian reality as progressively revealed across the scriptural narrative and clarified in the New Testament.[35] On these theological-Christological grounds, the Old Testament text is the voice of Christ. Whereas the reader might be unsure of who is actually speaking (especially in Psalms, being a frequent case study), the dilemma is solved by attaching the identity of Christ the

---

31. Fairbain, *Typology of Scripture* 1:354–57.
32. Fairbain, *Typology of Scripture* 1:354–57.
33. As in Carter, "Premodern Approach," 239–40.
34. Boersma, *Violence, Hospitality, and the Cross*, 259.
35. This is also Sanders's argument in *triune God*.

Word to the words spoken.[36] Christ as the Word made flesh was speaking in the original context. Scripture, so understood, is always the voice of God the Trinity speaking by the word, and in this way, Christ is present all through the Old Testament.

To this approach Gentry responded that a more plain reading of the relationship between the Testaments can be had within a redemptive-historical framework. Given the ultimate telos of all things coming together in Christ, the Old Testament's witness to him is primarily prophetic as promises and prophecies. To go beyond this prophetic construct runs the danger, says Gentry, of losing the plain relationship that the apostles presupposed in trying to convince the Jews of their day that Jesus is the Christ who fulfills the *Tanakh*.[37]

In response to the debate, the previous chapter argued that a Christocentric approach does not have to choose between prosopology and redemptive history. In prosopology, the written word is understood as the eternal Word spoken pre-incarnation. Every prophetic word acts as a link in the redemptive-historical chain between the promise of the redeeming Seed (Gen 3:15) and his coming in the fullness of time (Gal 4:4).

It seems that prosopology, the theological approach that it is, orients exegesis *upward*, hearing Scripture as the voice of the Trinity speaking from Heaven (Heb 12:25); conversely, redemptive history, being a historically and prophetically oriented approach, orients exegesis *forward*, situating the immediate to face the later fully revealed immanent.[38] It is hard to understand how any Christian thinker reading Scripture on its own terms would argue with either "side." Biblical theology is, as Vos said, the history of revelation,[39] that is, the record of sacred history in which God revealed himself covenantally and in which the sacred history is itself included in the revelation. Revelation, therefore, is both theological *and* redemptive-historical. It is both upward (God revealing *himself*)

---

36. Bates, *Hermeneutics of the Apostolic Proclamation*, 218, quoted in Carter, *ISGT*, 192.

37. Gentry, "Preliminary Evaluation."

38. A worthwhile example of this type of forward-exegesis can be discerned in Carson's and Beale's treatment of Hab 2:3–4 with its famous "the just shall live by faith" in *Commentary on the New Testament*, 610, 800–803. They argue that the only way that the New Testament (at Rom 1:17, Gal 3:11, and Heb 10:38) can use this text in the various ways that it does is if the "righteous one" finds its fulfillment in one particular individual whose righteousness becomes the possession of others. Such a fulfillment seems impossible in anyone but Jesus.

39. Vos, "Nature and Aims of Biblical Theology," 199.

and forward (God revealing *his actions*). Exegesis should, then, be both forward and upward with the beatific vision as the terminus where the forward and upward meet. Forward- and upward-looking Christian hermeneutics will be both theologically and redemptive-historically oriented. This project's attempted contribution continues to develop: Scripture as spectacles include both a redemptive-historical lens and a theological lens without which Scripture cannot be understood properly, according to its divinely appointed goals. Since the lenses need frames, typology can uniquely function in that role so that the reader can wear the glasses and understand the word as God's word both to a particular people at a particular earlier time and to the reader in their own time.

In what ways can typology house both the theological and redemptive-historical lenses to synthesize a singular approach? Regarding redemptive history, typology demonstrates that revelation includes both the timing and the escalating act from the type to antitype. That is, God not only reveals himself and the nature of reality through the people, places, and things typified and antitypified, but through the very process itself. Since this process happens over time, time itself, as Cullmann said, is an essential part of revelation.[40] Thus biblical-theological/redemptive-historical hermeneutics must, because of Scripture's nature as revelation, look forward.

Since God employs time and the type/antitype axiom in revelation, typology exerts direct influence over theology. That is, whereas the Trinity inhabits and encompasses eternity (Isa 57:15) which cannot be quantified as time and space (but gives being to all time and being), God not only (as Calvin famously said) creates space to be a theater of his glory (Ps 19:1–4) but time as well.[41] Far from needing time, God *employs* it to the end of displaying his creating and redeeming glory.

Such an approach is counter to that of rationalistic evangelical biblical theology. In the previous century, Rudolf Bultmann made biblical history, on modernistic progressive grounds, into a myth. As such, the myth must be "demythologized," and this is precisely the hermeneutical endeavor. In response, Cullmann said that history is itself the medium through which God unfolds his purposes and seeks to be known. Christians do not demythologize history, but they meditate upon it as an essential aspect of God's revelation.[42] Put another way, redemptive

---

40. See Cullmann, *Christ and Time*, 29–30.
41. Calvin, *Inst.*, 1.5.1.
42. Cullmann, *Christ and Time*, 32–33.

history, being the narrative that moves from type to antitype, is itself the demonstration of the way into God's kingdom.[43] This is why the sermons in Acts are so focused on how the Christ-event fulfills earlier promises and shadows: God demonstrates his faithfulness and sovereignty as well as the eternity of his decrees (Isa 46:6–8) through fulfilling these things. It should not be lost on the reader of Acts that it is these sermons—with their redemptive-historical focus—that Luke refers to when he describes the ubiquity of the preaching of "the Word of God" (4:31; 6:7; 8:14; 11:1; 13:5; 13:7; 13:46; 17:13; 18:11). In other words, the word tells of what God has done in space and time, employing the type/antitype structure as proof of trustworthiness.

Typology, then, frames the redemptive-historical/theological lenses because typology is itself the nature of historical revelation. Historical revelation—that is, Holy Scripture—is both redemptive history *and* theological revelation.[44] The revelatory word, unfolding in a type-antitype framework across time, is redemptive in effect. The word ceases to be the word if it does not perform a substantive, quantifiable redemptive effect.[45] The word itself is the means through which God the Father redeems according to his eternal will (2 Tim 1:9). This is precisely what Paul meant when he said that it is in the hope of eternal joy in (antitypical) new creation that a person comes to faith in the first place (Rom 8:24): The believer hears about the end breaking into the present as a type of what is coming, and it attracts them.[46] As the people of God through the various Old Testament periods were drawn to God by the promise of antitypical future glory (Heb 11:10, 13, 16; cf. Luke 10:23; John 8:56), so it is when one comes to faith in the age following the Christ-event: One hears of antitypical glory, the beatific vision, and refocuses life so that it becomes a typological tool of the future glory. This occurrence is of God who causes both hearing of and belief in the word (Matt 16:18; Acts 13:46; Phil 1:29). In this sense, the word is not only the communication

---

43. Cullmann, *Earliest Christian Confessions*, 3. Elsewhere, Cullmann devotes substantial attention to redemptive history, which to him meant, according to his translators, "the history of God's saving work among men, and the redemptive character of that history as such." See Cullmann, *Christology of the New Testament*, xvii.

44. "Sacred history" to Augustine. See Oort, "End is Now," 2.

45. As some critics have accused Barth of saying; see Frame, *History of Western Philosophy and Theology*, 366–69.

46. This type of language is from Vos. For a good summary, see Olinger, *Geerhardus Vos*, 172.

of what God has done but the actual application of it to the lost person, establishing fellowship that lasts forever.[47]

What Does Typological Realism Do for Redemptive-Historical Biblical Theology?

If biblical theology concerns how the whole Bible fits together as a collection of many smaller works that comprise one large Christ-centered work, typology explains the way that the narrative unfolds, leading to Christ's inevitable place at the center.[48] Goldsworthy has commented similarly: "Understanding the relationship of the two testaments involves understanding that the God who has revealed himself finally in Jesus has also revealed himself in the Old Testament in a way that *foreshadows* both the structure and content of the Christian gospel."[49] In other words, if the New Testament reads the Old as a "schoolmaster" to the knowledge of God in Christ (Gal 3:24, KJV), employing shadows (Col 2:17), copies (Heb 9:23), and figures (Ps 78:2; Matt 13:35), one should not be surprised that Jesus explaining his presence in the Old Testament to his disciples was an eye-opening and paradigm-shifting event for them (Luke 24:45–47). Luke said that at this point, Jesus "opened [the disciples'] minds to understand the Scriptures" (24:25). Such clarity about the once-veiled redemptive history with which they were acquainted their wholes lives but which had not made sense before (John 2:16, 22) enabled their powerful preaching shown in Acts. Once they understood the foreshadowings and prefigurements of Christ and his redeeming work, they became preachers of God's mighty acts in him (Acts 2:11). They had already worshiped him. When he opened their minds, they could *preach* him (Acts 8:25; 9:20), reasoning with their listeners about his messiahship (Acts 17:2). When their hermeneutic deepened to include Christ via typology, they were empowered for the ministry to which they were called.[50]

Chapter 2 examined Goldsworthy's appropriation of the so-called Robinson-Hebert schema in which the Old Testament historical events

---

47. Similar to Webster, *HS*, 13–17, 47.

48. Thus Boersma, commenting on Melito's *On Pascha*, essentially equates "typological" with "Christological" in *Scripture as Real Presence*, 80–90.

49. Goldsworthy, "Relationship of Old Testament," 89; emphasis added.

50. Here again it is worth reminding the reader of Fairbairn's extensive work explaining how the whole Old Testament narrative—not just particular people, places, and things—typifies Christ and his redeeming work. See his *Typology of Scripture*.

are picked up by the prophets and utilized as types of eschatological antitypes to come. Creation becomes a new creational type, covenant becomes a new covenantal type, priesthood becomes a type of Christ's priesthood and subsequent priesthood of believers in him, and so on. This is all typology. Again, from Goldsworthy, "In broad terms, typology rests upon the recognition that the way God spoke and acted in the Old Testament was a preparation for and anticipation of the definitive word and act of God in Christ."[51] This is the logic of using typology as a biblical-theological approach: The Christ-event is the central event of history, and God intends for earlier prefigurements and shadows to prepare for his coming appearance so there can be clarity about him and his work.

In this way, typology can protect redemptive history from degenerating into simple progressivism. Progressivism understands history in terms of time moving only according to necessary improvements; thus history progresses "forward," always, as humanity and nature make necessary improvements.[52] The error of such a conclusion is twofold: First, it wrongly assumes that progress is attained through human effort, thus ignoring clear examples of human-caused regression. Second, a progressive construal assumes that progress can be quantified and evaluated in an unbiased way, which seems doubtful.[53] Nevertheless, one must acknowledge the danger that an approach to Scripture that prioritizes its unfolding narrative, as in typology, might fall prey to progressivism.

Biblical typology protects against such errors by showing that God is in control of history, bringing about his eternal will over time (Acts 15:8, KJV). The definitions of "success" and "progress" depend on various events' part in his purposes. Certainly what comes later will be greater, but this is because God wills it to be, purposely using the process as a part of his redemption revealed so that his redeemed will have tears to wipe away in the end (Isa 25:8; Rev 7:17; 21:1), making their comfort in him that much sweeter. As such, his glory is revealed as a grace-giving glory (Rom 5:21; Eph 1:6).

Because of this typological framework, the believer is on an upward trajectory which has to ultimately reach a goal proximal to God, the

---

51. Goldsworthy, "Relationship of Old Testament," 87.

52. Boersma discusses this in the preface to *Scripture as Real Presence*, xii–xv.

53. So Goldsworthy observes that the ubiquitous presupposition of modernism is objectivity, that biases play no role in thesis, hypothesis, and proof, hence Goldsworthy's commitment to letting the gospel reset biases and presuppositions. See Goldsworthy, *Preaching the Whole Bible*, 185–88; *GCH*, 21–25.

beatific vision. This was Paul's point by describing the later glory in terms of God becoming "all in all" (1 Cor 15:28): The upward movement of redemptive history is one day going to reach its goal where God's glory is enjoyed and treasured by fully redeemed people. Typology provides the framework where progress is defined theologically and where, therefore, the forward movement of history is also an upward movement into God's glory. Again, "in this hope we were saved" (Rom 8:24). Whereas Christ has made believers the spiritual house to which the physical Old Testament temple pointed (1 Pet 2:3–4), there will come a day when believers will enter the eternal and glorious house which Christ prepares for them in the present (John 14:3).[54] Things move ahead while also moving above, forward while also upward.[55]

What Does Typological Realism Do for Theological Interpretation of Scripture?

Perhaps theological interpretation of Scripture is an attempt to recapture the Great Tradition's exegetical theocentricity. Such is Bartholomew's explanation: Theological interpretation's goal is to approach Scripture in a way that allows readers to hear the voice of the triune God in which he facilitates communion,[56] all occurring within the ecclesial context.[57] In short, theological interpretation occurs in the context of both theology and church.

Such statements might well serve as an explanation of what Bartholomew considers the primary (revealed) directive of the Scriptures: "Hear O Israel, the Lord our God, the Lord is One" (Deut 6:5). That is, Bartholomew says, before anything else, Scripture's goal is to be the

---

54. See Beale's treatment of the temple's antitype in, first, Christ, and second, the church, in *Union with the Resurrected Christ*, 131–48.

55. Worth mentioning is Levering's *Participatory Exegesis*. Similar to Boersma, Levering posits a participatory understanding of history on the grounds that by faith in Christ, who sums up all things in himself, believers have a clearer understanding of history's meaning than nonbelievers. A concluding quote is worth sharing: "The saints can see more deeply into even the 'historical' dimension of Scripture, once 'history' is properly understood, than can interpreters possesses *solely* of historical-critical tools" (Levering, *Participatory Exegesis*, 147). In agreement with both Boersma and Carter, Levering says that these tools are helpful. Only Christ apprehended by faith can yield the fullness of meaning he intends to give.

56. Bartholomew, *Introducing Bible Hermeneutics*, 13.

57. Bartholomew, *Introducing Bible Hermeneutics*, 525.

means through which people hear God's self-disclosure. Hence each letter to the seven churches of Revelation has the Lord concluding by saying some form of "hear what the Spirit says to the churches" (Rev 2:7, 11, 17, 29; 3:6, 13, 22). Theological interpretation is a hermeneutical approach that says the ultimate context of every text is the voice of the Trinity to the people of God in the present. It is less interested in a text's historical background and more in reading the text as the voice of God spoken in the present. Proponents argue that this theological orientation is the distinguishing feature of the Christian tradition so that theology's central place sets Christian interpretation uniquely apart.[58]

Theological interpretation, however, suffers from at least two shortcomings. First, its proponents do not have a set of agreed-upon terms or definitions.[59] There are some broad principles that most proponents have in common; but as a definite approach, Carter's criticism is probably warranted. Second, as Carson has noted, a rigidly theological orientation contains a potential danger in so jettisoning grammatical-historical exegesis that the plain sense is lost, or at least hidden.[60]

Both Bartholomew's and Thomas's *Manifesto* and Bartholomew's *Introducing Biblical Hermeneutics* seem to have been written to answer such charges, showing how theological interpretation attempts to use grammatical-historical exegesis to serve theological reading. Whether critics like Carson and Carter would be satisfied is doubtful, given that both—Carter to a lesser degree, perhaps—want to protect the importance of grammatical-historical tools in exegetical practice, and a theocentric approach seems to run the danger of moving history into the background.

Thus, this project proposes a corrective by contextualizing theological interpretation within a typological framework. If, as Murray Rae states, history is understood as God's project, historical research can be a tool employed to the end of hearing God's voice via Scripture.[61] And as argued above, a typology-centered framework uniquely shows history as God's revelatory project in which he discloses himself in an increasingly clear way. Although history moves forward in a linear way, the direction of the line is also upward; God utilizes history as the theater of his glory, where he lavishes upon his creation the qualitative and quantitative

---

58. See, for instance, Paddison, "History and Reemergence," 27–47.

59. This is Carter's criticism in *ISGT*, 19–21.

60. This is a reductive summary of Carson's criticism in "Theological Interpretation," 187–207.

61. Rae, "Theological Interpretation and Historical Criticism," 103–7.

eternal life of his Son (1 John 1:3; 5:20) through whom he created all things. If one learns, as Rae says, to "think theologically about history," history becomes a theological theater.[62] The exegete's task is to answer this question: "How did this or that event help to unfold God's purposes in inspiring the written text so that hearers would hear his summon to come to his Son?"

Ultimately, a typological framework that approaches history as a purposeful and slowly upward movement toward the terminus where God will be "all in all" (1 Cor 15:28) keeps believers' eyes focused both upward and forward until God enfolds them into the perfected state, the beatific vision. Into this "living hope" a believer in the resurrected Christ is saved (1 Pet 1:3). Such a way of thinking is only natural considering the way that the Bible's storyline unfolds: The Old Testament types gave way to the Son of God entering into creation and leaving his presence with his followers via the Holy Spirit. So the New Testament types will give way to an even greater glory. How could it be any greater than God becoming "all in all"? That glory is already the partial experience of believers inhabited by the Holy Spirit who is the guarantee of what is coming (Eph 1:14) as he creates a church in which "Christ is all, and in all" (Col 3:11). As Vos said, the end has already entered into the present such that the new covenant believer already enjoys "partial eschatological privileges."[63] Life with Jesus by his Spirit in the present is *both* the antitype of Old Testament believers following the cloud in the wilderness *and* the type of the full presence of God in glory. Such a trajectory is to believer and unbeliever alike the word of God in which he invites them into fellowship, promising still an even greater glory at the later point if they follow the Son.

All of this is not to say that later revelation diminishes earlier revelation. Rather, what God says at one point is perfectly consistent both with what he said at an earlier point and what he might say at later points.[64] The difference is that at later points God's purpose is further along than

---

62. Rae, "Theological Interpretation and Historical Criticism," 103.

63. Vos, "Eschatology of the New Testament," in *RHBI*, 26. Vos's point echoes Augustine; see Boersma, *SG*, 125–26, and Augustine, *Confessions* 7.10.16, 7.18.24. One might also see Piper's future-oriented understanding of saving faith in *What Is Saving Faith?*, 113–19.

64. Helpful are Kreeft's notes in *Summa on the Summa*, 54, showing that Scripture's meaning, when speaking of God's speech or actions at past or future points, is always from the human perspective. Being eternal, pure act, God has no "back then," "now," or "one day."

it previously was. There has been "genuine pedagogical progress" since previous dispensations.[65] Again, Vos is helpful, noting that revelation is perfect from the beginning, coming from the God who is perfect and is perfect for the moment given as he sees fit. "There is never a loss of what came before, but an expansion upon it from its center."[66] In other words, God, the subject of theology, never changes even if revelation does. Neither, in another sense, does revelation change; it merely expands from the center, filling out and maturing.

Similarly, Vos says elsewhere, "God here reveals himself as the everlasting reality, from whom all truth proceeds, and whom all truth reflects, be it the little streamlet of paradise or the broad river of the New Testament losing itself again in the ocean of eternity."[67] Here Vos furnishes the exegete and theologian alike with a way of approaching Scripture through redemptive-historical *and* theological lenses: God is the subject of theology, and revelation, given historically, serves the end of drawing people to the true knowledge of him. Typology keeps the eyes of the reader "upward" as they experience God's revealing voice, inviting listeners to a future (forward) glory, orienting them forward and upward.

If theological interpretation runs the danger of dehistoricizing exegesis, typology can employ it in a way that respects the historical element. Time is the context in which God demonstrates his Trinitarian-Christological purpose of fellowship with people, and he demonstrates this on a typological, anticipatory trajectory. Revelation, therefore, knows no contradiction between the redemptive-historical and the theological. Both lead to and demonstrate the beatific vision, whether in typological form (e.g., "having the eyes of your hearts enlightened," Eph 1:18, ESV; "looking to Jesus," Heb 12:2) or in essence ("we will see him as he is," 1 John 3:3). Since God's revelation includes the way in which he reveals, the historical element must not be lost. Typology helps readers listen to God with sensitivity to the significance of his redemptive-historical project. In this sense, typology builds bridges over the potential dehistoricizing pitfalls of theological interpretation. Believers' eyes, set upward, learn to look both backward and forward at God's past and future acts. History not only exists but is the revelation-receiving context, and gloriously so.

---

65. Boersma, *SG*, 390. It might be worth mentioning Paul's point in Rom 16:24 that since Christ's coming, previous mysteries have been made clear.

66. Vos, "Idea of Biblical Theology," 11. This speech was Vos's inaugural address upon taking the Princeton Biblical Theology chair, given on May 8, 1894.

67. Vos, "Idea of Biblical Theology," 13.

How Marriage Saves Husband and Wife: The Hermeneutical Effects of Applying Typology as Frames for Redemptive-Historical and Theological Interpretive Lenses

Bringing together redemptive-historical and theological lenses in typological frames will cause both the upward and forward trajectories of God's history of revelation to construe exegesis and theology. Such an approach is utterly consistent both with the nature of God's redemptive-historical purposes and his own triune nature. Theology and exegesis are done within the context of the believing Christian life where the Christian experiences both positional and practical spiritual redemption by the presence of Christ in the Spirit (2 Cor 3:18). This redemption will one day lead to a physical redemption (Rom 8:23) and God will be all in all. Both theology and exegesis as meditation upon God's economic truth (flowing from and reflective of eternal truth[68]) is far from speculative or even abstract. Rather, contemplation on God and his economy is, as Vos said, "the profoundest and *most practical* of all thought complexes."[69] What immediately follows is an explanation of what such a typological orientation, here called typological realism, accomplishes both for Old Testament exegesis and New. Following will be a consideration of typology's accomplishments in other areas of Christian life and thought.

What Typological Realism Does for the Old Testament

First, typological realism makes sense of the New Testament's teaching that Old Testament revelation was shadow-filled and typological. To be clear, asserting that the Old Testament tells the story that Christ completes does not imply that the Old depends on the New. It just deals squarely with the Old Testament's own longing for completion in a sequel.[70] If the

---

68. The importance of remembering this order is Duby's argument in *God in Himself*.

69. Quoted in Olinger, *Geerhardus Vos*, 184; emphasis added.

70. This again, as a reminder, is Dempster's argument, partially in response to Bonhoeffer's caution in "getting to the NT too quickly," in *Dominion and Dynasty*, 36.

Elsewhere, Vos says, "The Old Testament dispensation is a forward-stretching and forward-looking dispensation ... The Old Testament, through its prophetic attitude, postulates the New Testament." *Biblical Theology*, 299. Such a point is not worth passing without comment: The fact of a forward-looking prophetic witness demands a sequel. Jesus, even if one does not believe in him, must be taken seriously as a possible fulfiller of the prophetic outlook.

Christ-event is the center of all of history,[71] then how can pre-Christ revelation possibly be coherent apart from him? Fairbairn showed that the only way to make sense of the psalm's teaching that Israel, though they entered the land, never found rest (Ps 95:11) is to understand that the land was typological of a renewed creation.[72] That is why Christ taught that his body replaced the Temple (John 2:12–20) and why Abraham is said to have been made an heir of not just the land but the world (Rom 4:13): The earlier was an illustration of what would come later, and thus is, in itself, a lesser form of the greater—a type.[73]

Fairbairn also notes that the New Testament emphasis on Christ's kingdom meets the need presented by the Old Testament's weak theocracy. Of course, the weakness was not in God himself but in the fact that true circumcision of heart had not yet occurred (Deut 30:6; Jer 4:4), so Israel did not treat him as king (1 Sam 8:7; cf. Hos 8:4). God had said, however, that David's son would also be to God a son and would reign forever (2 Sam 7:13; 1 Chr 17:11–14). God could not have meant one of David's literal sons, for the promise is made yet again all through the prophets after David and his sons are dead (repeated almost verbatim in Isa 9:6–7, where the coming king is also deified).[74] So Jesus, the true descendent of David and antitype of the dynasty, perfects the Old Testament theocracy such that any who come to him treat the Davidic and divine king as the true king, which the resurrection proves that he is.[75] People would thus willingly come to him as David himself wrote: "Your people will offer themselves willingly on the day of your power" (Ps 110:3).

What precedes is a very partial example of the benefit of typology for the Old Testament. The Old Testament is opened up once it is

---

71. Cullman, *Christ and Time*, 48–50.

72. Fairbairn, *Typology of Scripture* 1.338–54.

73. Also worth mentioning is Peter's post-Pentecost sermon where he builds on the earlier theme of *restoration*: Following the disciples' earlier question of the Lord about if he would "restore the kingdom of Israel" (Acts 1:6), Peter explains that Christ's ascent to heaven is a necessary aspect of redemptive history until the time when God "restores all things" (Acts 3:21). It could reasonably be deduced that the Spirit, whom Jesus said would teach the disciples the things that are to come (John 16:13), gave Peter greater clarity regarding what is to be restored in the future antitype: not just the Davidic kingdom (the type), as the disciples earlier thought, but the global reign of the Davidic king (the antitype) to which the Old Testament looks ahead (cf. Gen 12:3; Isa 49:5–6).

74. See Isa 54:10; Jer 23:5–6; 33:15–17; Ezek 34:23; 37:24–25; Hos 3:5; Amos 9:11; Zech 12:7–10; 13:1.

75. Fairbairn, *Typology of Scripture* 2.441–42.

understood in its typological framework. Even further, it has a happy ending: despite the rampant sinfulness and tendency of humanity to rebel against their Creator, the Creator redeemed still. Indeed, the Creator *became* the redeemer. Since no mere human could redeem (Isa 59:16), God the Son united with and perfected a human nature to bring redemption. The Davidic kingship example is just one of many which Christ's coming perfects and terminates into the antitypical form.

What Typological Realism Does for the New Testament

In the same way that typology helps explain how Jesus's kingship fulfills the Old Testament goal, typology also makes sense of how Christ's return and subsequent glories will fulfill the New Testament goal. The whole of the New Testament is eschatological in the sense that it construes the present in light of the future and teaches that the present already substantially reflects and contains pieces of the future. So Vos argued that the very presence of the Holy Spirit with the Christian is meant to orient the Christian forward.[76] The New Testament emphasized, therefore, the Spirit as the guarantee of believers' inheritance until they possess it fully (2 Cor 1:22; 5:5; Eph 1:14).[77] This emphasis might explain why the Spirit is the primary subject of the Lord's teaching the night that he was betrayed: Jesus aimed to fix the disciples' attention on the far-future coming glory for which their near-future experiences will prepare them (John 14–16).

Still, the resurrection of Jesus does more, enabling the Spirit to come to believers. The resurrection guarantees believers' future resurrection, which is the full reception of Jesus's resurrection in which the Spirit is glorified (Rom 1:3–4). Indeed, according to Vos, the resurrection of Jesus is the *beginning* of believers' resurrection.[78] The Spirit is the very spiritual life in them guaranteeing the coming glory of the beatific state, living within and empowering light-filled manners of life in the present, hence Jesus's teaching that he—that is, faith in him—is not only the *way* to glory but is

---

76. Vos, "Eschatalogical Aspect," 95. This point reflects Augustine's view that the images are purposefully anticipatory, where there is some "share" of the future reality in the present. This presence makes contemplation possible. See Boersma's discussion in *SG*, 112–24.

77. Gk. *arabōna*, in ancient papyri meaning "down payment" or "earnest money." It is the advance in a transaction that is given as security until the transaction is completed (https://biblehub.com/greek/728.htm).

78. Vos, "Eschatological Concept," 92.

himself the very *life* within the believer (John 14:6). All believers can then testify that "it is no longer I who live, but Christ who lives in me" (Gal 2:20). In this sense, Vos says the New Testament teaches that the Spirit-indwelt life is the fulfillment of the Old Testament prophetic promise of a Spirit-filled life for new covenant partners.[79] Type has given way to antitype, which is still itself a type awaiting a future antitype (which will be the fullness of the revelation of the Archetype) but which does enter into time and space substantially before the (later) fullness comes.[80]

One such example of New Testament forward-looking typology is the concept of "walking," used in the New Testament both in typological and antitypological ways: "This is love, that we walk according to his commandments" (2 John 1:6, ESV). Here John shows the type, walking in fellowship with the Lord by faith. Conversely, speaking of the heavenly city as needing no sun or moon because "God gives it light, and its lamp is the Lamb," John adds, "By its light will the nations walk" (Rev 21:23–24). There John shows the antitype—the glorious journey through eternity with the Lord in new heavens and new earth, no longer by faith but by sight.[81]

For the sake of a fuller explanation, this section will reconsider Goldsworthy's "Robinson-Hebert Schema."[82] The reader will remember that according to the schema, the purpose of Old Testament history is to establish the various types of what will come later during the Christ-event. Creation occurs in Gen 1–2, and "covenant" is the term to describe relationship between God and his chosen people (e.g., Gen 15); the story continues with captivity and exodus (Exodus), tabernacle/temple (Exodus–Leviticus), land (Deuteronomy, Joshua), and kingdom and Jerusalem (Samuel–Kings). Old Testament history has so far provided the following:

---

79. Vos, "Eschatological Concept," 112.
80. See Boersma, *Five Things*, 34–35. This point will be returned to later.
81. Be reminded that Aquinas thought that at the beatific vision, humanity would cease moving, coming finally to its eternal rest. Edwards, on the other hand, held to progressive happiness, where believers in glory eternally *grow* in their enjoyment of God. The "walking" in the Rev 21 text will be interpreted in light of one's understanding of the context of the end of Revelation. If Rev 21–22 is understood as the glorious epilogue of redemptive history, as most of church history has held, then it cannot be avoided that there is some form of "walking"—that is, movement—occurring in glory. For a fuller discussion, see Boersma, *Vision of God*, 135–62, 354–86.
82. See Goldsworthy, *CCBT*, 26.

TYPOLOGICAL REALISM AS APPROACH

Old Testament History
Creation
Covenant
Captivity and Exodus
Tabernacle/Temple
Land
Kingdom and Jerusalem

All of these central themes to Old Testament history are then assimilated by the writing and preaching prophets to announce and explain the glory that will come in the eschatological day of the Lord. The shadows and types are employed prophetically as a preparation for the antitype. Creation is thus called *new* creation (Isa 65:17; 66:20), covenant gives way to *new* covenant (Jer 31:31–34), slavery and exodus to new redemptive exodus from slavery (Ezek 36–37), temple to a new temple (Isa 28; Zech 4), land to an antitypical type of land (Amos 9), and kingdom to eternal kingdom in a redeemed Jerusalem (Dan 7; Zech 13–14). According to Goldsworthy, the schema after two steps looks like this:[83]

Old Testament History	OT Eschatological Promise
Creation	New Creation
Covenant	New Covenant
Captivity and Exodus	New Captivity and Exodus
Tabernacle/Temple	New Tabernacle/Temple
Land	New Land
Kingdom and Jerusalem	New Kingdom and Jerusalem

Finally, the schema says that the New Testament shows the antitype in the day of the Lord, where the earlier shadows and types, having given way to and being coopted by prophecy, are then fulfilled. Since the announcement of the antitypes (itself a prophetic witness) leads to the actual existence of the antitype in time, there is a sort of structure that could be rearranged into a chiasm. The chiasm would follow this numeric order:

---

83. Worth mentioning: Goldsworthy anticipates and addresses the question of biblical reductionism in *CCBT*, 28–30. It might appear arrogant to suggest that biblical history can be simplified to a simple structure. These themes do, however, frame Old Testament history, which is why the prophets integrate them in announcing coming glories.

CHRIST AND THEOLOGY

1. Type (Old Testament History) >
2. Promise (Old Testament Prophecy) >
3. Announcement of Fulfillment (New Testament Prophecy) >
4. Antitype (New Testament History and Letters)

And the chiasm would be:

a. Type (Old Testament History)
b. Promise (Old Testament Prophecy)
c. Christ Event (Gospels)
bb. Announcement (New Testament Prophecy)
aa. Antitype (New Testament History and Letters)[84]

Thus, the antitype includes new creation (2 Cor 5:17; Gal 6:15); new covenant (Matt 26:28; 1 Cor 11:25; Heb 8:13); deliverance from sin as the New Testament exodus (Luke 9:31; Eph 2:1–5); church as temple of God because of its relationship to Jesus in whom God and man dwells (1 Cor 3:16–17; 1 Pet 2:5); earth as the antitypical redeemed land as it meets Jesus through the gospel (John 3:16; Rom 4:13); and eternal kingdom/Jerusalem (Mark 1:15; Gal 4:26) through Jesus as King of kings (Rev 17:14; 19:16).[85] This completes the schema:

Old Testament History	OT Eschatological Promise	New Testament Fulfillment
Creation	New Creation	Jesus Brings New Creation
Covenant	New Covenant	Jesus Establishes New Covenant
Captivity and Exodus	New Captivity and Exodus	Jesus Shepherds Believers to Freedom
Tabernacle/Temple	New Tabernacle/Temple	In Jesus the Church Is the Temple

---

84. One might assert that the explanation of the event must follow the event itself in order for it to be revelatory. Such was NöSG,en's contribution as a contemporary of Vos in his early years; cf. NöSG,en, *Geschichte der neutestamentlichen Offenbarung*, vii–viii. It should be noted that Scripture does not have to explain particular type/antitype examples in order for them to be present. Although such explanation would be revelatory, the lack of explanation does not make the type non-revelatory.

85. See Goldsworthy's fuller explanation of this in *Gospel and Kingdom*, 100–102. Also helpful is Goldsworthy's explanation of the relationship of typology to the "Robinson-Hebert Schema" in *Preaching the Whole Bible*, 76–80.

Old Testament History	OT Eschatological Promise	New Testament Fulfillment
Land	New Land	Jesus as "Land" in Which God Is Met
Kingdom and Jerusalem	New Kingdom and Jerusalem	Jesus as King of Kings

Since Goldsworthy is a biblical scholar, one can understand why the schema ends here. It seeks to explain the Bible's narrative in terms of its development from primitive revelation to maturity. Nevertheless, an irony might be present. Goldsworthy has criticized Vos's work for its apparent incompleteness.[86] Vos, were he alive, might respond that there is also some degree of incompleteness in Goldsworthy's schema. Certainly Jesus has established the new creation and all of the promises of God find their "amen" in him (2 Cor 1:20), but Christians living in the current day still "groan" (2 Cor 5:4), and all believers, though Spirit-indwelt, still "stumble in many ways" (Jas 3:2). Believers still wait for the place the Lord prepares for them (John 14:1–3). Vos constantly endeavored, therefore, to show that, although in Jesus the end had entered into history decisively, yet history had still not arrived at its end, hence the aforementioned "partial eschatological privileges" which the Christian enjoys. The resurrection and presence of the Spirit guarantees that the privileges will come in fullness at a still later stage in the new creation. The fullness provides the suitability of advancing Goldsworthy's schema beyond the New Testament fulfillment to a final stage: the beatific vision:

Old Testament History	OT Eschatological Promise	New Testament Fulfillment	New Creation/ Beatific Vision
Creation	New Creation	Jesus Brings New Creation	Full and Physical New Creation
Covenant	New Covenant	Jesus Establishes New Covenant	Full Fellowship, So Reminders of Lamb's Blood (as in Revelation)
Captivity and Exodus	New Captivity and Exodus	Jesus Shepherds Believers to Freedom	Full Deliverance from Sin and Death

86. Goldsworthy, CCBT, 82–83.

Old Testament History	OT Eschatological Promise	New Testament Fulfillment	New Creation/ Beatific Vision
Tabernacle/Temple	New Tabernacle/ Temple	In Jesus the Church Is the Temple	Full Presence of God; God *Is* the Temple
Land	New Land	Jesus as "Land" in Which God Is Met	New Heavens and Earth Filled with Knowledge of God
Kingdom and Jerusalem	New Kingdom and Jerusalem	Jesus as King of Kings	Christ as Only King

If the plan to unite all things in Christ is the Trinity's plan from eternity (Eph 1:10), it might be suggest that all that happened before Christ's coming was intended as preparation for the fulfillment. Such a conclusion would explain why Paul speaks of the gospel as "the plan of the mystery hidden for ages in God who created all things," which "eternal purpose he has realized in Christ Jesus" (Eph 3:9, 11). As noted earlier, later fullness and clarity only implies deepening or expansion, not substantive superiority: Although the maturation of the revelation of the divine purpose is indeed *good news*, the presence of the divine purpose throughout safeguards the utter relevance of the various points of the story.[87] At all points in redemptive history, God has his way, moving the story ahead on his own terms to his appointed goal in his Son.

But clearly the later antitypes are the purpose for which the types exist, and thus, apart from the antitypes, the types cannot be made perfect (cf. Heb 11:40). To help make this point clearer, Vos employed a triangular framework that is similar to Goldsworthy's schema, although it might be more simple:[88]

---

87. This point is made eloquently in Vos, *Biblical Theology*, 361–69.
88. The diagram is a redraft of Vos's original in *Teaching of the Epistle*, 57.

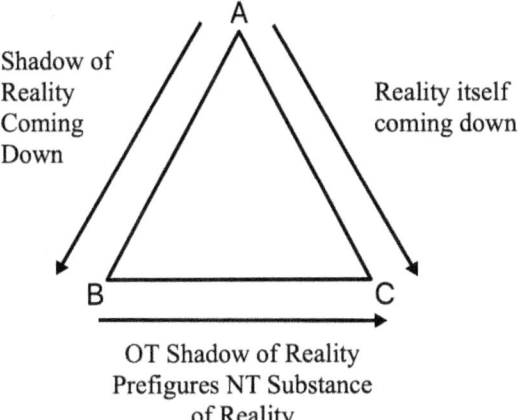

In the above diagram:
A represents the Heavenly Reality
B represents the OT which is a "shadow" of the Heavenly Reality
C represents the NT which is the substance of the Heavenly Reality
B prefigures C because B is the "shadow" A and C equals A

In Vos's triangle, the eternally unchanging God, who is equivalent to Heavenly Reality, is revealer of both the earlier type and the later antitype. Points "B" and "C" correspond to "shadow of reality" and "substance of reality," respectively. Here Vos provides an illustration that is consistent with Goldsworthy's schema, though Vos provides a stronger theological foundation. Theology proper controls the whole of the revelatory axiom. "A," representing God, never changes, although revelation occurs across time, and time is a tool of revelation (or at least the purposeful chronological context of revelation). If Goldsworthy's paradigm focuses on how the events reveal the person and work of Jesus, Vos's paradigm focuses on how this revelation occurs in context of God's economy. Vos's paradigm might not be qualitatively "better" than Goldsworthy's, but it does elucidate God as the author and source of the revelation. Read this way, the New Testament becomes the story of the "reality itself coming down."

The fullness of the reality is, however, yet to be experienced. This point is utterly central to biblical theology according to Vos, who emphasized that those who live in the day of the reality having come down[89] nevertheless are still of the earth and live in a sort of "lower life" (earth) while belonging to the "higher life" (that is, the heavenly life).[90] For this reason, echoing the above tweak to Goldsworthy's schema, a slight adjustment might be offered to Vos's triangle in order to keep it more consistent with his own explanation of the New Testament's eschatological message:

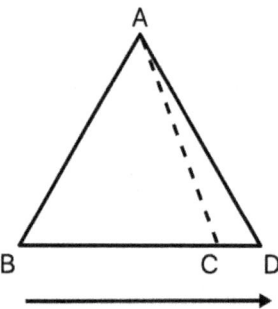

D represents the fullness of
the Substance of Reality,
to come in the final Day

In this admittedly elementary tweak, the revelation of the substance of Christ's first coming remains subject to the New Testament's own contextualization: Although it is not the fullness of the substance, it is the breaking in of a *fuller measure* of the substance (cf. John 3:34) via antitype. Redemptive history will continue until the final day when the fullness of the substance—already antitypified in the fullest possible way and guaranteed via the resurrection and the giving of the Spirit (Acts 17:31; Eph 1:14)—comes. The A–C line is a dashed line as opposed to a dark line (like A–B and A–D) to communicate that while the kingdom has more fully entered than in the earlier typical age, it has not fully come yet. Christ said that both were true: The kingdom has, in him, *already* come in the present (Matt 12:28; Luke 17:21) while it is also *still* to come in fullness (Matt 20:21; 1 Cor 6:9). The same kingdom is revealed at different

89. Vos, *Teaching of the Epistle*, 57.
90. Vos, "Eschatological Aspect," 115. See also his sermon "Heavenly Mindedness" in which, expositing Heb 11:9–10, he compellingly contrasts the "higher world" from the "lower world" without crossing the line into Gnostic dualism. The lower world is purposeful to God's end as preparation for the higher.

degrees of clarity as God wills so that the little flock to whom the Father delights to give the kingdom (Luke 12:32) will live by faith, trusting in him with realistic expectations in their present.

Thus, between "C" and "D," believers live as kingdom citizens through the Spirit: "The kingdom of God is ... a matter of righteousness, peace, and joy *in the Holy Spirit*" (Rom 14:17; emphasis added).[91] The Lord who redeems in spiritual terms via his first coming (C) will one day in his second coming redeem in physical terms (D).[92] Although Jesus came to heal both the spiritually and physically broken in his creation, his first coming deals with the former and his second deals with the latter. The fact that the Spirit dwells in believers guarantees that Jesus—who gave the Spirit—has already accomplished the first and will, in time, accomplish the second (Rom 8:9–10). Believers living in the antitypological time are in another sense still in a typological time, awaiting the future antitype of all that they hope in. Such a statement anticipates the point of the next section. As conclusion to this brief consideration of Vos's paradigm, the not-yet aspect of the kingdom—as ubiquitous as it is in his writings—is surprisingly ignored in the paradigm, though it seems to belong. Worth pondering is if Vos would agree; it seems likely.[93] Regardless, this project does not seek to criticize or improve Vos's work but to suggest a slight (though substantially momentous) addition to it that seems consistent with his body of work.

To echo the conclusion of the previous section, the Old Testament's happy ending—the Davidic-divine king promised and foreshadowed, entering into his creation to bring a new creation that lasts forever—is itself still typological of an even later happiness that awaits consummation. If human sin and its effects is the ultimate challenge emphasized

---

91. For a fuller look at what this section tries to explain, see Vos, *Teaching of Jesus*.

92. Vos, *Teaching of Jesus*, 46–52.

93. Some thought was given to a diagram that began with Vos's triangle, drawing parallel lines from "A" and "C" into eternity (that is, with arrows). Such a diagram would seem, however, to convey that God is experiencing or is subject to the same developments as those in the economy. Such a diagram would agree with Cullmann's troubling argument in *Christ and Time*. Worth nothing, however, is that Cullmann did not think that God was *bound* by time but that God *controlled* the time in which he chose to dwell (37–50). The argument of the current project is that time is important to God's revelatory purposes. Cullmann went a step further in saying that time is the necessary context of God's purposes. It is doubtful that such an assertion is consistent with Scripture's teaching on God's eternality, aseity, and immutability. Because of the potential for misunderstanding, a more simple tweak to Vos has been offered, even though it could doubtless be improved upon.

throughout the Old Testament against God's good purposes, still, God in Jesus won decisively. Conversely, the New Testament ends with the portrayal of the battle between the victorious Lamb and the spiritual forces in the heavenly places that seem to have the entire world on their side (e.g., Rev 19). God, however, will win, and exhaustively so. God the creator and redeemer consummates his created and redeeming goal, showing, yet again, his immutable power and wisdom (Rom 11:33–36). Such a happy ending is why Vos, in an example of the importance of keeping the so-called "big picture" always in view, said, "God is our Creator, Redeemer, and Consummator: on these things our whole religion depends."[94]

A typological framework uniquely—and, as Vos showed, visually—seems to capture the upward and forward trajectory of God's revealed economic purpose in which he is Creator, Redeemer, and Consummator, unto his and his peoples' glory forever. Thinking, reflecting, and worshiping typologically keeps believers' eyes forward-looking to what God has for them and upward-looking to the God who is and who gives out of his own eternal goodness. Such a typological framework makes redemptive history and theological interpretation the training ground for the beatific vision.

What Typological Realism Does for Christians and Church

This chapter has argued that because Scripture is the redemptive-historical revelation of God's purposes over time on a typological trajectory, a typological orientation brings together both theological interpretation and redemptive-historical interpretation. Revelation is both redemptive-historical and theological because it is the one word of God about God[95] concerning what he does to move his creation toward its eternal state where he is "all in all" (1 Cor 15:28), that is, to the beatific vision. Typology, therefore, can frame the partner redemptive-history and theology lenses so that biblical theology can be theological and pastoral. As noted in chapter 3, such a hermeneutical approach would bear striking and unavoidable resemblances to the hermeneutics of the Great Tradition.[96]

---

94. This was the inscription inside his *Pauline Eschatology*, written in Latin: DEUS CREATOR REDEMPTOR CONSUMMATOR IN HIS TRIBUS RELIGIO NOSTRA UNIVERSA PENDET.

95. Echoing Goldsworthy's answer to the question "What is the Bible?" in *Preaching the Whole Bible*, 11–21.

96. It should be remembered that biblical theology works have sought to be

TYPOLOGICAL REALISM AS APPROACH

Having established the viability of such an approach on a hermeneutical level, one must consider what typology does for the Christian particularly and the church generally. Typology keeps before the eyes of believers' hearts (cf. Eph 1:18) their own place in the cosmic purposes of God and the biblical teaching that the whole of God's creation, in some way, serves them. Typology shows believers that all of creation—time, space, and things—though existing for God and Christ, also exists for believers themselves, since they are united with Christ.[97] Certainly all things exist for Christ, as the apostle states plainly in Col 1:16, and thus Christ is the "firstborn of all creation" (1:15; cf. Ps 89:27; 1 Pet 1:20). Believers are chosen *in* Christ from eternity: "He chose us in him before the foundation of the world . . . in love, he predestined us for adoption" (Eph 1:4–5). "Yours they were, and you gave them to me," Jesus prays to the Father (John 17:6). So time, space, and things created *through* Christ and *for* Christ are therefore also the possession of those chosen eternally *in* Christ for sonship. The renewal and total restoration of all things constitutes believers' full inheritance (Matt 25:34).

Typology uniquely shows believers that that which they experience in the present is based on God's eternal work and serves to prepare them for their future glory in that eternity. Their life with God, the very eternal life of Christ in them (1 John 1:1–4; 4:9; 5:11, 21), is redemptive participation in which the God who is the fountain of life (Jer 2:13) graciously gives them godliness. This present experience, though higher than (and therefore the antitype to) Old Testament believers' experience, is nevertheless still a lower vision of and type of the beatific vision. The apostle states that it is the love of God before the foundation of the world that predestinates believers so that they should be "holy and blameless before him" (Eph 1:4).[98] The purpose of election is sanctified (set apart) walking in the present so that the future walk through the redeemed Eden will be truly perfect. From a redemptive-historical point of view, typology says

---

pastorally oriented; see, for example, Goldsworthy's aforementioned *Preaching the Whole Bible* and Sydney Greidanus's *Preaching Christ from the Old Testament*. The point being made is that biblical theology has not employed a theological sensibility in its pastoral considerations in a way that meets the church's theological need if Webster is correct that the church listens to God and approaches life in light of God and his nature.

97. This paragraph is a reflection upon Cullmann's main argument in *Christ and Time*, 217–21.

98. The distinction between holiness and blamelessness, compellingly argued by David Peterson in *Possessed by God*, will be returned to below.

to the believer, "Here is what you are being prepared for (perfect walking in a higher state), here is its author (God and his Christ), and here is the means of preparation (sanctified walking in a lower state)." From a theological point of view, it says, "Here is what God did in eternity past (choosing, as an outflow of his triune love), here is what God is doing in the present (calling you by grace, preparing you, by his wisdom, for glory, filling you with his life), and here is what he will do in the future (an immutable plan to bring believers into a God-centric and God-saturated reality that is beyond all earthly comparison)." This God-saturated reality is itself *actual* reality. The types and antitypes are revelatory sacraments of the *real* that, from the believer's perspective, has already come, although, at the same time, it is yet to come.

Every Text Is an Invitation to Move Forward and Upward

The act of reading Scripture, whether from within the "prayer closet" (a frequent comment upon Matt 6:6) or from within the church through preaching, singing, or praying is an act of being drawn up into God's reality. The act has both passive (listening) and active (reading) elements. In the act, the believer confesses that Scripture is light (Ps 119:130) and that any competing truth claim is darkness (John 3:19). Since reality according to Scripture is typological—that is, upward- and forward-oriented—Scripture invites the reader into *typological realism*.[99] Typological realism, then, is the framework that Scripture, read on its own terms, gives to believers. God's economy, unfolded over time and space on a typological trajectory, brings believers ever more into reality.

Such biblical-theological conclusions must shed light on normal rules of biblical interpretation. When approaching historical literature, as previous chapters have noted, historical tools are helpful toward identifying the plain sense. The overriding framework is to be Scripture's own, which is typological/antitypological. To prove this, what follows will show some examples of the appropriate questions to have in mind when approaching the various genres found in Scripture.

First will be a historical text: If a text predates Christ's coming, how does that text's explanation of the believer's life with God typify life with God under the new covenant? In what ways does the account typify the

---

99. As it will be seen later, "typological," used as an adjective, probably parallels "eschatological." Vos seemed to think so; see *Eschatology of the Old Testament*, 117–21.

Christ-event? How do people and actions typify Christ's actions? Similarly, and returning to the prosopological considerations of the previous chapter, in what way can the text be heard as the actual voice of Christ the Word who would assume flesh? If the text in question is New Testament history, whether an account of Christ in history (Gospels) or apostolic witness (Acts), how does it antitypify what came before and typify the still-to-come glory?

Second will be a prophetic text: If a text predates the Christ-event, in what ways does the prophet utilize earlier types to point to later antitypes or even further to the final antitypes? Isaiah can thus speak of the suffering servant in substitutionary terms reminiscent of the Day of Atonement (52:13—53:12; cf. Lev 16), which then point to Christ's atoning work. Isaiah later picks up creational terminology of heavens and earth to speak of *new* heavens and earth (65:17) which are to come in the eschaton (Rev 21–22) and are thus appropriated earlier in salvific terms for believers (2 Cor 5:17; Gal 6:16). Isaiah utilizes both earlier types to point ahead as well as other earlier images to point even further ahead. Both acts, says Isaiah, are acts of God on the revelatory journey toward the day of the Lord in which he will shepherd his people (Isa 40:11). Isaiah 40:6–8 notes, therefore, the eternality of God's word: His speech is the telling of how history serves his eternal purposes.[100]

Conversely, if the text is New Testament prophecy (whether Revelation, various sections of epistles, or Jesus's eschatological teaching), does it utilize Old Testament types to point to later (or even current) antitypes? If so, in what ways?[101] Prophecy therefore is to be read in redemptive-historical and theological terms. Without such an approach, prophecy might fall subject to a purely historical framework (or a purely ahistorical one.)

---

100. This point helps explain Peter's quotation of Isa 40:6–8 in 1 Pet 1:24–25 to support his point that believers have been born again through the eternal word of the Son who was "foreknown before the foundation of the world" (1:20). Peter seems to be saying that the word of Christ is the eternal word of the triune God substantiated in time and made effective to establish fellowship with lost people through regeneration (1:3). At the time of this writing, the writer has written a paper to be presented at Evangelical Theological Society 2022 on the breadth of the use of *evangolizomai* in the New Testament and how it points beyond the cross to the Trinity. In the paper, Peter's text is a primary case study.

101. Especially helpful here is Samuel L. Morris's *The Drama of Christianity: An Interpretation of the Book of Revelation*. Morris shows that the Lord utilizes every type of biblical genre and style to demonstrate "the things that must soon take place" (Rev 1:1). The implication seems to be that Revelation has application to believers in every generation. Morris's approach to Revelation is not dissimilar to Greg Beale's in *Revelation*.

Third is wisdom literature: The Old Testament wisdom literature can be called a reflection of honest minds on the nature of reality in light of the great saving acts of the God of Abraham, Isaac, and Jacob. The framework of wisdom literature, which majors in "the fear of the Lord," is established by acknowledging that the Creator God proves his identity by saving Israel and establishing them in the land he had promised.[102] Consequently, God's rules for life in his creation are the most sensible concepts imaginable; wisdom, indeed.

Nevertheless, although Solomon is considered both the wisest of all people (1 Kgs 3:1–11; 4:29–30) and the human voice (as supposed until recent centuries) of Ecclesiastes and Proverbs, still the ultimate source of his wisdom was yet to appear in the redemptive way that he would in the incarnation. He announced himself in Proverbs as the Wisdom of God personified (8:12–36), but not until he became flesh (John 1:14) did the fullness of wisdom become known. The New Testament epistolary reflection upon him is that "in Christ is hidden all the treasures of wisdom and knowledge" (Col 2:3). Wisdom has to do with the nature of reality,[103] which was revealed progressively over time. Much of what predated the Christ-event was shadowy. So wise reflection, though possible, was also shadowy; when Christ came, reality became clear, so wise reflection became clear (at least comparatively.)

This is why Jesus concluded the Sermon on the Mount with a lesson on "building the house on the rock" (Matt 7:24–27). The notion of a "rock" is everywhere in Scripture used as an illustration of God's unchangeability and the resulting security of the one who starts their ontological framework with him.[104] Jesus's point was that if believers start their view of reality with him as the eternal wisdom of God who stepped foot on earth and made the way clear, they are safe, and things will go well with them (echoing Old Testament wisdom).[105]

How does Old Testament wisdom, reflecting on God's shadowy but substantial actions, typify wisdom in light of Christ's later coming? And how does New Testament wisdom (whether Christ's own teaching in the Gospels or the Epistles) typify the glory of the future state? The present

---

102. See Goldsworthy, *Proverbs*, 29.
103. Goldsworthy, *Gospel and Wisdom*, 335.
104. A point that is made eloquently by Barrett in *None Greater*, 89–110.
105. Worth mentioning is Beale's fascinating study of Christ as the "Way" of salvation longed for in the Old Testament, which explains why the church was called "the Way." See Beale, *Union with the Resurrected Christ*, 240–45.

day, though antitypical and possessing what the Spirit of God shows believers is waiting for them (1 Cor 2:10) nevertheless leaves believers still only "knowing in part" (1 Cor 13:12). They walk in wisdom by faith (2 Cor 5:7) until the day when the faith will become sight, when they will "see him as he is" (1 John 3:2). Goldsworthy seems correct to conclude that although Old Testament wisdom is to be interpreted in light of the first-century Christ-event, New Testament wisdom is to be interpreted in light of the eschatological Christ-event.[106] Both interpretive acts are done in light of the God who is and who reveals progressively according to his own eternal plan and wisdom. Again, typology keeps the eyes of the interpreter both forward and upward.

The final example is scriptural prayers: How are they interpreted typologically? "Prayers" in the following paragraphs include prayers in the context of narrative (1 Chr 29:10–19; John 17), as templates (1 Sam 3:9; Matt 6:9–13), and as the Psalms, which Bonhoeffer called the "Bible's prayerbook."[107]

The previous chapter argued that the Psalms are to be interpreted as (a) the voice of Christ the Word, (b) prophetic promises of Christ's coming, and (c) the telling of real experiences of believers, especially David. The last category is especially pertinent to the current discussion: Old Testament believers, David for instance, wrote these prayers addressed to the God who had revealed himself through the mighty acts of Old Testament history. Many of these inspired prayers were written out of the crucible of trial, showing real experiences of doubt, questions, panic, pain, etc. Although Jesus's night of suffering holds some especially strong parallels with the suffering of the psalmist (cf. Mark 14:32–36), to only note parallels seems insufficient. Such parallels seem to demonstrate a clear typology: Old Testament sufferers who suffer either because of Adam's sins, the sins of their own opponents, or their own sins (and in truth, all three) typify Christ who would suffer under the full weight of sin's penalty and effects. Gregory of Nazianzus could say, thus, that all of Jesus's suffering is to be taken as his own appropriation of his peoples' suffering to himself.[108] He intended to recapitulate all the suffering of the godly.

---

106. Goldsworthy, *Proverbs*, 7.
107. See Bonhoeffer, *Psalms*.
108. See Gregory of Nazianzus, *On God and Christ*, 94–97.

Even further, as Luther came to see, there is also a typological connection between Old and New Testament believers.[109] The former waited for Christ's first coming while the latter wait for his second coming. Greater and fuller revelation is at their disposal, as well as the help of the Holy Spirit in a way that was not entirely available to the former.[110] Still, New Testament believers walk "by faith and not by sight" (2 Cor 5:7), living their lives by prayer (Phil 4:6), even being given a prayer template (Matt 6:9–13). So Old Testament prayers, and in particular the Psalms, are to be read as examples of the prayers of earlier saints, encouraging prayerfulness in current saints and giving them a sort of prayer "language."

Both of Jesus's most famous prayers (Matt 6:9–11 and John 17) point believers to future glory: In the former, Jesus teaches the disciples to pray for God's kingdom to come (Matt 6:10) and for the Father's deliverance from the evil one (6:13), which will come in fullness in the eschaton (Rev 19–20). In the latter he prays, "Father, I want those [that is, believers] . . . to be with me where I am, to see my glory, the glory you have given me because you loved me before the creation of the world" (John 17:24). In both instances, Jesus teaches his followers to look forward and upward in prayer. The very act of prayer may very well be typological in that it calls upward to God and looks forward to the beatific glory where God is all in all and to the execution of his will until then.

So pre-Christ prayers are models of prayer for Christians to emulate, thankful that they themselves have fuller resources in light of the Christ-event. Conversely, post-Christ prayers are direct typological acts whereby believers are instructed to turn their eyes upward to God the Trinity and forward to what he is doing to establish eternal glory in which believers can participate.[111]

---

109. See Preuss, *From Shadow to Promise*, 156, 186; also 140 of the current project.

110. See Vos, "Eschatological Aspect," 96–98. For a more recent work on the continuities and discontinuities of the Spirit in the Testaments, see Hamilton's *God's Indwelling Presence*.

111. The reader is encouraged to peruse Calvin on prayer (*Inst.*, 3.20); see also Barrs, *Heart of Prayer*, 11–25, for a popular treatment on prayer as a means of fueling forward-looking growth and grace in the context of God-centeredness.

Typology Properly Contextualizes Discipleship

Calvin wrote on the necessity of "meditating on the future life" while maintaining the correct "use of the present life."[112] Christians live in a present (1 John 4:9) that is substantially more glorious than saints under the old covenant. Christians also wait on a future redemption that is far more glorious than the present; hence they meditate. As has been seen, the proper construal of this future-looking present life was a prominent emphasis in Vos's pastoral and scholarly writings. Clearly this is no less than a typological worldview in which, in God's providence, the lesser comes earlier and gives way to the greater that comes later, culminating in a glorious future where God's people behold him in his glory (1 John 3:2; cf. Matt 17:1-3).

The current consideration can be sharpened to fit this chapter's purpose: How does typology serve believers' use of the present life? A discussion on the nature of conversion and growth in grace might be helpful. David Peterson has shown that sanctification has less to do with the Christian's transformation into Christlikeness than with the Christian's conversion and establishment into fellowship with God. In New Testament usage, sanctification (*hagiasmos*) is not usually (though sometimes is) *progressive* but *definitive*. Although the believers' goals are to display the holy character of the God with whom they enjoy fellowship in every area of life, failure does not negate the fact of sanctification.[113] The believer has been set apart. Failure simply means that the Christian needs to grow in grace (2 Pet 3:18), seeking forgiveness and help from God, as Jesus taught them to pray. Further, the *concern* for failures demonstrates that the believer is actually sanctified since conviction and concern for holiness are works of the Holy Spirit (John 16:8-9; 1 Thess 4:3-7).

If believers display God's character, there is clear witness to their fellowship with him. The boldness with which Peter preached at Pentecost was reminiscent of the Lord's boldness in Luke's companion volume. This transformation is in view when Stephen Holmes writes that "we are Christians when what is true about God is more, rather than less, true about us."[114] In other words, the believer experiences a substantial

---

112. Calvin, *Inst.*, 3.9, 10. It should be noted that both chapters are included in the more recently published *A Little Book on the Christian Life*, which is the distillation of 3.6-10 into book form.

113. Peterson, *Possessed By God*, 24, 136. Also helpful in such a description of holiness is Webster's *Holiness*.

114. Holmes, *Theology of the Christian Life*, xi. Similarly, Dallas Willard used to call

conformity to Christ. The Eastern Orthodox call this *theosis*, where God's attributes become the Christian's attributes. This change is derivative and gracious, to be clear. It is, however, substantial and actual even if imperfect and partial.[115]

The distinction between God's *essential* attributes and God's attributes appropriated in Christians can be overstated. The distinction can also be understated, as seen in Gary Millar's comparison of over-realized eschatology with under-realized eschatology: In the former understanding, a Christian is entirely perfected, like God is (as in Wesleyan perfectionism).[116] In the latter, a Christian is miserable, wanting to change and make progress but utterly unable to do so.[117] Both extremes have elements of truth along with dangerous oversights which, if left unchecked, render impossible dependence upon Christ *and* putting on Christ.

So typology is again an alternative. It correctly situates the Christian on the later side of the Christ/Pentecost-event and on the earlier side of the day of the Lord. Christians are aware of the resources that they have while tempering their expectations for the present. Truly, as in Peterson, they live set apart though imperfect. As in Holmes, they imitate the Lord's goodness and prove their Christianity by doing so. As in Millar, however, they wait patiently as God completes the work in them. "The change God brings is both definitive *and* progressive."[118] On the basis of the gospel, Christians enjoy fellowship with God that is as perfect a fellowship as the Priest is perfect who intercedes for them (Heb 7:25). Christians are also on a journey that belongs to the Lord, who changes them into his likeness. The transformation is neither linear nor predictable but decisive and true, occurring with a discernible trajectory. It is an "endless warfare with sin, death, flesh, and the law." But God will, as Paul reminds his readers in Rom 7:25a, set believers free from the death that is in their bodies.[119] Life is full of proofs of this promise throughout.

---

spiritual formation the transformation of the person so that their inner self is the same as that of Jesus. See *Renovation of the Heart*, 15.

115. Holmes, *Theology of the Christian Life*, 105–20.

116. A notion that Millar argues is doubtful that Wesley ever actually believed; *Changed into His Likeness*, 206–7.

117. Millar, *Changed into His Likeness*, 209–11. The over-realized/under-realized turn of phrase is located in Millar, *Changed into His Likeness*, 9–10.

118. Millar, *Changed into His Likeness*, 225; emphasis added.

119. Peterson, *Possessed By God*, 109.

How typology relates to this paradigm for sanctification and growth should be obvious. Just as at every stage biblical history was exactly where and how God desired, progressively revealing the way into his kingdom, so he has the Christian in a state of grace, at the stage he desires. Because Christ as eternal Word united with human nature in a hypostatic way, there was no way to prevent the Christ-event from occurring (Acts 2:23; Gal 4:4). In a similar way, Christ's return and the subsequent glories have already been eternally promised, the trustworthiness of such promises guaranteed by the resurrection (Rom 1:1–3; 8:10–12). Practically speaking, the cross was inevitable, and Christ's second coming is also inevitable. In the meantime Christians are called to imitate the Lord and trust that he has them where they he intends them to be and where they should be.

Typology, therefore, is a metaphor for discipleship: By Scripture's own typological orientation, Christians learn to contextualize their life according to theological and redemptive-historical categories. Their day is the *first* antitypical day of the incarnation of the Son who came so that by his work believers would be inhabited by the Spirit. By him believers know the truth about the Trinity and his plans and purposes. They have learned what God has prepared for those who love him (1 Cor 2:9–10). They also look forward to the *last* antitypical day of the return of the Son of God, when Christ will grant his beloved possession of a physical new creation in which righteousness dwells (2 Pet 3:13). Such a sensitivity to fulfilled prophecy and typology keeps believers trusting in God's faithfulness to fulfill further prophecies and types. Life is a struggle, a war with sin (Heb 12:1–4) and the devil (1 Pet 5:8–10). Because of the continuing pattern, however, believers are not hopeless but hopeful. They are not naive but sober-minded.[120] The Christian then operates with realistic expectations about the present and hopeful expectations for the future. Such a framework is exactly consistent with discipleship: past-defined realism about the present—reflecting on God's acts—and realistic hopefulness about the future in which they have a place. From thence comes the phrase "typological realism": On the typological trajectory of life with

---

120. More could be said here about theology's eschatological orientation, seen in, for instance, how justification and other subtopics in soteriology are eschatological. See Vos, *Eschatology of the Old Testament*, 73–76. Further, more could be said about how Scripture should be understood in theological terms as the word of God toward eschatological ends. Webster and Ward, both of whom's works were considered in detail in chapter 2 of this project, are helpful in this regard.

God, the presence of the real correctly construes past and present while also safely—not naively or fancifully—construing the hope for the future.

Typology Unites Evangelicals Around a Shared Set of Convictions

As noted in chapter 2, evangelical theology and exegesis are, by definition, gospel-centered theology and exegesis.[121] The gospel is the Bible's central message which, though not being its extent, is its controlling theme. The gospel is understood biblically as not only the atoning and victorious work of the messiah (1 Cor 15:1–8) but as encompassing all of the benefits that follow from the messiah's work (i.e., the promise of defeat of God's enemies, deliverance from the earthly curse, etc.; 1 Cor 15:12–57). The current antitypical day is already unfolding these events, though not exhaustively. The day waits for the future day, the saints crying out, "How long, O Lord?" (Rev 6:10, KJV). Paul says that the promise to Abraham of a seed to bless the nations was itself the gospel message (Gal 3:8). The gospel has to do not only with the Son's work in the past but in the present and future; therefore the gospel is ultimately eschatological.

The preceding paragraph explains why Goldsworthy made the point that an evangelical is one who is truly gospel-centered. To evangelicals, promises in Christ, whether fulfilled or still to be fulfilled, control their framework for understanding the nature of reality.[122] Evangelicals, then, are those who live their present lives oriented to the end.[123] Such is exactly the point argued in this chapter and why a typological orientation is so important: There will come a day when the God who is known by faith will be seen by sight, and such a sight will utterly transform believers in ways that are impossible to understand. "What we will be has not yet been made known" (1 John 3:2). The Spirit who dwells in believers is himself "the Spirit of glory" (1 Pet 4:11); he is the presence of the Trinity, fulfilling the promises of the past and guaranteeing the future. As Vos showed, the Spirit is *of* the future glory: His ministry is to bring the

---

121. See chapter 2 of this project; see also Goldsworthy, *GCH*, 77 and Vanhoozer, *Hearers and Doers*, 157.

122. See chapter 2 for an explanation of Webster's "hermeneutical conversion" (Webster, *HS*, 88) and how Goldsworthy's paradigm in *According to Plan* explains how the conversion occurs (*According to Plan*, 39–42).

123. As in Bonhoeffer, *Creation and Fall, Temptation*, 9: "The church sees ... from the end."

future glory—the divine glory of eternity-now—into the present.[124] Current Christian spirituality is an echo of the future state. The current position is beholding Christ's glory by faith (2 Cor 4–5), not seeing him (John 16:17; 1 Pet 1:8) but believing in him and growing in likeness to him. The future day will be characterized by actually beholding him, seeing him, and becoming like him (Phil 3:20–21). John writes of "what we shall be like" then (1 John 3:2). A theologically oriented typology helps believers to know and see clearly the triune God and his Christ in preparation for the final transformation into his likeness. Jesus prayed, "I desire, Father, that they . . . may be with me where I am to *see my glory* that you have given me because you loved me before the foundation of the world" (John 17:24; emphasis added). The Lord's plan is to bring believers to behold the eternal glory in the end (cf. Eph 2:6–7), in the actual sight, the beatific vision. Also recall that in Jesus's prayer, he acknowledged that he had already *given* his glory to his disciples, at least partially (v. 22) and would continue in the meantime to make known to them and their followers the Father's name (v. 26). This continued revealing is the spiritual sight that is in view in the prayer of Eph 1 (vv. 18–25). In the end, the believer's current spiritual sight will give way to the actual sight. One is type, and one is antitype. One is glorious, and one is eternally glorious (2 Cor 3).[125]

Thus Vos explained Christian hope like this: "The biblical redemption aims at a new creation and nothing less than that . . . eschatology is the crown of redemption both from man's and God's side." Thus Christians' end/antitype-orientation: They have redemption already, but their lives are *aimed* forward. Vos, commenting on Paul's letters, added a further important element: "The Christian alone can experience [the end] and *does experience it* with such intensity that it became to Paul in itself a prophecy of fulfillment."[126] Put another way, the New Testament hope has such confidence in Jesus as the promised Messiah that it often blurs the line between the current day (the type) and the eschatological day (the antitype). The end is present as a guarantee of what comes later.

Not surprisingly then, evangelicalism as a "movement" is not as monolithic as described before, united around a shared conviction to be

---

124. Vos, "Eschatological Aspect," 115–25.

125. Beale has a penetrating study of the earlier glory/later glory axiom of John 17:23–26 (and how earlier portions of John figure into a proper exegesis of the prayer) in *Union with the Resurrected Christ*, 381–86.

126. Vos, *Eschatology of the Old Testament*, 9; emphasis added.

"gospel-centered."[127] But a typological orientation might help the movement to become more unified. Providing a clearer and more definite historical orientation in light of the revelation of the purpose, goals, and trajectory of God's space and time project, typology provides both optimistic and realistic lenses for evaluating what occurs and what might occur. Such an orientation would surely be a step forward for evangelical hermeneutics. Typological realism could also have two correcting ministerial effects: It spurs now-oriented evangelical ministries to have a proper end-orientation in their presentation while also spurring end-oriented evangelicals to seek the Lord's glory and joy in the current day (Acts 17:25). Both could say, "To live is Christ" (that is, to use the time Christ has given as an opportunity to serve his purposes), ". . . and to die is gain" (Phil 1:21). Both could say, "Let the one who does wrong continue to do wrong" (Rev 22:11), which means to let God's enemies continue on, even if under God's current, less-intense judgment; and they could also both say, "Let the one who is thirsty come" (22:17), that is, to the Lamb who is coming soon and who gives his Spirit to his church.

Christ-centered biblical theology, especially with its typological nature, demonstrates how God's truth never changes, though he unfolds the revelation of his truth over time, moving his covenantal people into an ever more glorious position with each step. The unfolding of his truth is progressive, forward and upward, and must, by definition, only continue forward and upward *unchallenged* (cf. Dan 4:34–37); what is earlier and lesser will give way to and point to the greater that comes later. His revelational process parallels the process of discipleship, whereby he escalates his people forward and upward to the antitype. Biblical theology is typological because Christianity is typological. It typifies a future beatific glory where faith will no longer be needed as it will be replaced by sight of that which eternally is, was earlier believed, and poured into time and space through the gospel.

In summary, whereas theological interpretation dehistoricizes theology and exegesis and redemptive history detheologizes theology and exegesis, typological realism appropriately rehistoricizes and retheologizes both. The lenses held in by typological frames correct distorted sight.[128]

---

127. For a critique of evangelicalism's lack of unity, see Smith, *Bible Made Impossible*, and Rose, *Protestant's Dilemma*.
  Also worth seeing is Vanhoozer's response in *Biblical Authority After Babel*, 111–17.

128. James Dolezal has observed that biblical theology cannot be properly said to concern theology, being more oriented toward time and progress, which do not apply

A Theological Question

Revelation as the means through which God reveals his nature and the meaning of history on a typological trajectory locates ontological reality in a historical context. History has been one long study in human sinfulness. Why then, if God is perfect in himself and supremely happy in his inner-Trinitarian relationships, did he choose to unfold his truth in this way over the course of time? Such a question, far from curious speculation, follows from the dissonance that is a result of considering God's perfection alongside of the unavoidable reality of sinful and fallen world history. To state the question more simply, why did God create space and time, knowing it would fall into ruin, if doing so was not necessary to his happiness?

The scope of this project will not allow a full examination of God's purposes in creation, though other works have already been advanced to answer the question.[129] It can be said simply that God created the universe because it pleased him to have a *space* which would function as a theater for his glory so that other beings would enjoy him as he enjoys himself (Neh 8:10; cf. Gal 5:22). Since space as a composition develops, undergoing changes,[130] so God wills *both* space and time with its continued development to display his glory. Calvin famously referred to the creation in terms of *theatrum gloriae*.[131] Created space is the theater (Ps 19), but the theater's extent does not stop there: God also engages time to the display of his glory. Since time is of a different ontological dimension than space in that it never experiences variation in its development (but keeps going at the same "speed"), one can see that if God wanted to display his glory in time, the glory would either have higher, more memorable moments, or, perhaps, increase in presence as time goes along. Biblically speaking, both are true: The acts of God in Old Testament history are everywhere reminders of his faithfulness to subsequent generations; and, as this chapter has tried to show, history's typological trajectory advances according to God's saving purpose. This

---

to God. See his *All That Is In God:*, xv. It is hoped that the current project at least shows how both disciplines complement, if not presuppose, each other.

129. The most celebrated of which, at least among evangelicals, is likely Edwards, "End for Which God Created the World."
An alternative view could be seen in Wright's *Mission of God*.

130. See Aquinas, *ST*, 1.1.46, and his famous proof of God's existence from motion in 1.2.3.

131. Calvin, *Inst.*, 1.11.12. See also 1.5.8; 2.6.1.

assertion echoes Cullmann's contribution, aforementioned, that history unfolds with the Christ-event at the midpoint (indeed, in one sense, the high point) guaranteeing that God's purposes are exactly on track for a preplanned future glory (which is the highest point).[132]

This escalation is in view when Paul speaks of God's plan from the fullness of time[133] to unite all things in Christ (Eph 1:10): God creates and allows (willing without causing)[134] a fall so that he could display his grace and be praised (Eph 1:6); indeed, he will be feared for his grace (Ps 130:3–4). In the "mid-point," as Cullmann says, God sends his Son to bring righteousness to the world and establish a new creation. Historical progression not only echoes God's divinity retrospectively but is also *pro*spective: What will occur will reflect his eternal redeeming goodness in even more substantial ways than what has already occurred.[135]

In these ways, both types and antitypes demonstrate the kindness and wisdom of God. He has a plan to redeem his creation so that it can share in the fullness of his goodness, and he will execute that plan. He will also give clues and hints to the ways in which he does so. Trained senses will perceive. The types and antitypes are preparatory schoolmasters to believers' eyes and ears (Gal 3:24, KJV).

As a final example, pre-Christ theophanies, according to Vos, are meant to typify the glory of the future presence of God with his people. Whereas the Bible began with people able to be in God's presence physically (Gen 3:8), the fall led to physical ejection from this presence. Starting with Abraham (Gen 12, 18), continuing with Jacob (Gen 26, 32), and so on, God meets with people in surprising ways, sometimes even

---

132. Cullmann, *Christ and Time*, 121–30, 211–13.

133. Gk. *eis oikonomian tou plērōmatos tōn kairōn*, lit. "out of the economy of the fulfillment of the seasons." The "seasons," being plural, not singular (as often translated in modern English Bibles), seems to refer to historical eras pre-incarnation and their preparatory purpose for the ultimate goal, inaugurated in Christ's first coming.

134. Aquinas, *ST*, 1.49.1–3. Following Augustine, Aquinas taught that evil was the tendency to nonbeing. If so, it cannot be said that God *causes* nonbeing, since he is the fountain of life (Ps 36:8–9). He also wills that nonbeing be the judgment for choosing nonparticipation with him. As such, God does not cause nonbeing but wills his good creatures to descend into nonbeing via the creature's choice to rebel against him. This paradigm is in view in Ps 1:6: "The Lord knows the way of the righteous; but the way of the wicked will perish" (ESV). The only two options are the way which God knows and the way which perishes. The former is being; the latter is nonbeing.

135. One remembers Aquinas's teaching that a trace of the Trinity is on every creature (Aquinas, *ST*, 1.45.7) and Bonaventure's teaching that the trace is on all that exists (which would seem to include history; discussed by Davison, *Participation in God*, 102).

physically. He does not bring the fullness of his glory to bear on them, because man cannot see God and live, as Moses was told (Exod 33:20). The glory can be appropriated in a way that points both backward (Eden) and forward to the day of the Lord when he will come (Isa 40), which comes in two stages.[136] Hence Moses (Exod 33:19) and Elijah (1 Kgs 19:11) both saw God's glory when it "passed by" them. When God's glory came in his Son, those same men stood speaking with him on the mountain (Matt 17:3; Luke 9:30), which not only showed Jesus's continuity with Old Testament prophets but that Jesus is the antitype of the earlier theophanies. The glory to come is, nevertheless, still greater. Even that glorious antitype is a type of a more glorious future glory. Attentive ears will hear, therefore, how God displays his wisdom and glory in time via types.[137] God also aims, by sharing his glory over time, to share his joy in an ever-increasing way.

Some Potential Objections

This chapter has called for a heightened sense of the importance of typology in both theology and the Christian life. This project has argued that typology is the framework for understanding God's eternal purposes for his creation for one primary reason: Typology is the framework in which he reveals and executes said purposes. Redemption, so understood, occurs on a typological trajectory so that what is promised to come later contains discernible parallels to what came earlier, though with greater glory. The effect of this escalation is twofold: Because of the similarities, believers are more sure of their place in God's story; but on the other hand, because the glory heightens, there will be surprising fulfillments that keep them from "mastering" revelation. "If anyone imagines that he knows something, he does not yet know as he ought" (1 Cor 8:2). God's people move forward in his unfolding story, as redemptive-historical biblical theology has worked to show. God's people also move upward into a greater closeness with and awareness of his glory, as theological interpretation has sought to show. This forward-upward movement is

---

136. Vos, *Eschatology of the Old Testament*, 85–87. This point will be the topic of the final chapter in this project.

137. Also helpful is Augustine's discussion of the theophanies and their value in typifying future glory while also preaching the presence of the glory in the present. See Boersma's examination in *SG*, 96–126.

escalation, the exact nature of typology.[138] When finally the earlier patterns terminate in the later antitypes and God is seen "as he is" (1 John 3:2), the end-goal of time-space history will be complete.

Are there problems with such a hermeneutical approach? Matthew Bates's aforementioned objection to the typological interpretation might need to be considered once more.[139] He favors a prosopological orientation in the New Testament writers, where Old Testament writers effectively spoke with a voice not their own so that Christ can be seen as the original speaker of the verse. Throughout his *The Birth of the Trinity*, Bates, though acknowledging that the New Testament writers employ a typological reading from time to time, takes typological interpretation to task for coming short of explaining how the New Testament uses the Old.[140] Bates cites as feature examples the use of Isa 8:17–18 in Heb 2:13, Ps 115:1 (LXX) in 2 Cor 4:13, and Ps 68:5 (LXX) in John 15:25.[141] In these Old Testament texts, attributed by the New Testament to the mouth of Christ the Son, a typological reading simply does not make sense, says Bates, for no parallels exist between the original text's historical context and how Christ is said by the New Testament author to mean the words.

As noted in the previous chapter, Bates's point seems to fall short for a couple of reasons. First, if Christ is the eternal Word, then *any* word spoken by an Old Testament writer is actually the Word speaking through them. Bates's sample verses might not be as strong examples of typology as other texts, but they do, by virtue of recapitulation, demonstrate at least a weaker typology *to pair with* prosopology. In other words, prosopology occurs any time a historically contextualized text is used sacramentally as God's own writing. To note parallels between the earlier and lesser to the later and greater, as in typology, is not only appropriate but helpful and accurate, given how the New Testament reads the Old.[142] Prosopology and typology ought not be seen as opposing frameworks

---

138. Chase, *40 Questions*, 43–44, 56.
139. See chapter 4 above.
140. Especially Matthew; see Bates, *Birth of the Trinity*, 100n35.
141. Bates, *Birth of the Trinity*, 117, 141, 161.

142. In fact, as aforementioned, Boersma has argued that Christ is to not only be thought of as the antitype of earlier types but as the Archetype who not only preexists the types but is their Creator and ultimate purpose. This kind of theologically oriented/Christocentric reading of typology is a strong example of this chapter's argument. See Boersma, *Five Things*, 34–35.

For another example of such a reading, see Clowney, *Preaching Christ in All of Scripture*, 42.

but as complementary. Both make the gospel clear and reflect the reality of the eternal Word.

Second, Bates suggests at several points that one important reason to reject a typological reading is that it was not employed by the early church fathers.[143] Bates throughout his book gives examples of patristic reading that is decidedly prosopologically oriented. Nevertheless, such a claim is inaccurate. Chase has shown, quite clearly, that typology was not only recognized by the fathers but frequently employed by them.[144] One need only to peruse a modern translation of Irenaeus's *On the Apostolic Preaching* to find his reading of typology as a primary way that the New Testament reads the Old as a witness to Christ. Although theological/Christological priorities might have dominated patristic exegetical practice, they certainly did not avoid or marginalize typology. Bates ably shows the prevalence of prosopology in patristic interpretation, but he falls short of showing that typology is *absent* there.[145]

But even more important is the presence of typology in the New Testament itself. Earlier in the current chapter was a consideration of the use of *typos* in the New Testament without much explanation. As aforementioned, Goppelt asserted by labored examples that the apostles just assumed that earlier people, places, and things were meant to prefigure later ones which would be greater in the coming messianic day. This practice was not an innovation; its presence dominated the Old Testament prophets. The point is this: Even if patristic exegesis did not contain much typology, the more important question is if Scripture does. This chapter has sought to show that one cannot understand the Bible's forward and upward movement without a typological orientation.

It seems surprising that Bates, as clearheaded and balanced as he usually is, would possess such a clumsy understanding of the history of biblical typology. For example, Bates's explanation for how Acts 2:33 interprets Ps 110 shows that he thinks typology holds that to qualify as a

---

143. Bates, *Birth of the Trinity*, 9, 127, 183.

144. See, for example Chase, *40 Questions*, 83–85. Also worth mentioning is that Bates regularly quotes O'Keefe and Reno's *Sanctified Vision* in support of the assertion that typology is absent in the fathers; but such an assertion is peculiar, given the clear presence of typology among the fathers. O'Keefe and Reno roughly equate typology and allegory to one another, devoting significant attention to the presence of this spiritual impulse in ancient interpretation; *Sanctified Vision*, 20, 76.

145. Bates, *Birth of Trinity*, 9. Worth mentioning is also Melito's *On Pascha*, a eucharistic liturgy dating from the second century in which Melito explicates a Christology that is richly typological.

type, *every* important detail in an earlier cited text has to point upward and forward to what comes later.[146] Thus he argues that since David is cited as speaking the psalm, a typological reading is inappropriate given that David is merely rehearsing what he heard, not acting as a Christ-type. As seen earlier, however, typology does not demand that every detail of a text's context be understood typologically, but only the general sweep of the text in light of its *res*, Christ himself, to whom the text witnesses. In the case of Acts 2/Ps 110, David prophetically saw something that would come into greater clarity in the messianic day. This insight was not David's own before it was Christ's (as eternal Word) who would speak through David. Both typology and prosopology seem to be present in Peter's use of Ps 110 to preach Christ.

Typology and prosopology do not present an either-or option but a both-and. Since typology does not apply to everything but to the general direction of the story from the perspective of the reader at a latter stage, it is so essential to proper exegetical glasses that it is offered in this project as the frames. In light of John's statement that "the only Son at the Father's right hand has made him known" (John 1:18), to not see earlier revelation in light of its relationship to later, where the Word comes in a considerably fuller and more transformative way than prior, would seem impossible.[147] How could an earlier revelation not be lesser? And since it is also earlier, how could a typological framework not be appropriate as long as Christ's identity as the pre-incarnate Word is presupposed? If readers are situated within the time of Spirit-empowered antitype, they ought to expect a greater coming glory even as they are themselves participants in a greater glory than what came before.

What If Typological Realism Reaches Too Far?

If typological realism simply has too many problems to be considered legitimate, evangelical (Christ-centered) biblical theology can remain as its own discipline, as can theological interpretation. Nothing is lost. Perhaps centering typology is too bold. Such an interpretive approach might indeed fall prey to ahistorical excesses, as it sometimes did in late patristic and

---

146. See Bates, *Birth of the Trinity*, 161.

147. Thus Goldsworthy has said that exegesis should "start with Jesus" because Jesus is by nature the Alpha and Omega who has appeared at the end of the ages (*Jesus Through the Old Testament*, 34–47); thus it should also "end with Jesus."

TYPOLOGICAL REALISM AS APPROACH

marginal medieval interpretation.[148] This would be unfortunate given the outstanding help that recent works have given toward evangelicals recovering the importance of typology in exegesis throughout church history.[149]

But the outcome of rejecting typological realism seems to be that Christ-centered biblical theology will continue theologically unanchored, as suggested in Trueman's aforementioned criticism. History—usually construed according to modernistic definitions of progress and liberation—will be the object of exegesis, not God's shepherding voice for his sheep. On the other hand, rejecting typological realism might leave theological interpretation to its dehistoricizing danger in approaching Scripture, which is purposely given by God in the context of an unfolding narrative. Somewhat helpful, then, would be a typological orientation acting as the wedding ring in a marriage between biblical theology and theological interpretation.

If biblical theology is merely redemptive-historical, it will default to being merely historical. If, on the other hand, history is oriented by God's beginning (creation), middle (redemptive history), and end (the vision), exegesis is a call to trust and obey. Conversely, if theological interpretation is merely theology-oriented, it will shoehorn historically revealed biblical texts into ontologically speculative lessons. Or typological realism can give the theological presupposition a historical, discipleship-oriented sensibility. In both cases, the Word is treated as the eternal real that enters into peoples' time and space to draw them up and ahead to God.

How, then, could typological realism be *wrong*, given that it simply tries joining together two oft-employed approaches from like-minded thinkers? The challenge offered is to simply make explicit what is already implicit. As Boersma has said, biblical theology is not *biblical* in the truest sense if it is merely historical and not theological.[150] Conversely, Bartholomew has noted that theological interpretation must bear in mind the historical situation of the text even as it seeks to hear God therein.[151] Very good on both sides. Now to bring them together to realize both outcomes: redemptive history that does theology and theological interpretation that theologizes history. That goal is the essence of typological realism: hearing God's revelation given as preparation for later glory. If

---

148. For a balanced consideration of these excesses, see Bray, *How the Church Fathers Read*, 100–107.

149. See, again, Hamilton, *Typology*; Chase, *40 Questions*.

150. Boersma, *Five Things*, 135.

151. Bartholomew, *Introducing Biblical Hermeneutics*, 7–9.

terms are carefully and rightly defined, vis-a-vis, that types are revealed across history in a progressive and purposeful way, the interpreter can avoid pitfalls.

Conclusion

A typological orientation to theology and exegesis helps produce two outcomes: First, redemptive history will be theologized; second, theological interpretation will be historicized. First, history will cease to be a mere study in progress, instead becoming the worshipful study of the unfolding purposes of God in history and how history is his project to unite all things in his Son and become all in all. The dynamic nature of redemptive history will be properly contextualized as the unfolding of the purposes of the eternally happy Trinity. Through time and space, God acts without any change in himself. His time-space project, however, develops as it moves forward and upward into his goal of fellowship and peace.[152] Forward movement thus is God-ward movement where the creature moves toward a final end of beholding God's glory in fullness. Current righteous experience mirrors in a typological way future beatific experience: That is the point.[153]

Secondly, theology with its primary concern for the being of God will be understood in relationships to his acts. Typological realism will ensure that even the revelation of God's nature, for instance, at the burning bush (Exod 3) is understood in its orientation both to the Christ-event

---

152. Thus Boersma calls God the "God of Change," meaning not that God changes himself but that he changes people into greater alignment with him. See Boersma, *Sacramental Preaching*, 183–90.

153. Such was Aquinas's paradigm, outlined by Morello in *World as God's Icon*. In general terms, Aquinas argued, based on a Platonic metaphysic of participation, that people in time and space participate in God's tapestry of reality in which he displays his glory. God can be known via creation as a theater of his glory; but in Christ's first coming, God identifies himself with the creation in a unique way through the union of divine and human natures (127). God does not *become* created, but he, via hypostatic union, assumes created flesh to redeem it.

If Vos and Aquinas were to have a discussion, Vos would remind Aquinas both that the glory of the incarnation is meant to point to the greater glory of the second coming, and that the Spirit is the substance of both glories: evidence of the reality of the earlier and guarantee of the hope of the latter. The incarnation is not an end to itself but a means to a more glorious end which is still to come, of which the incarnation is the guarantee. Based on Kreeft's reading (*Summa on the Summa*, 383), it is likely that Aquinas would agree, though he might put more emphasis on the Eucharist's place as present guarantee.

and to the endpoint of history. Though God reveals himself as the I Am, that revelation cannot be divorced from Christ's coming in which he as the Son in whom the Father is known (John 14:3) entered into time and space, hence his saying that when he goes to the cross, people will know *him* as "I am" (John 8:28 Gk.). He was saying that the earlier revelation at the bush typified the fuller revelation at the cross; but even further, he was saying that the latter revelation typifies the day "when the Son of Man is revealed" (Luke 17:30). The I Am in the earlier revelation was not less than what he was when Christ spoke or even later. Simply, that the fuller revelation to which the earlier pointed not only makes sense of the earlier but acts as a more capable trainer for the fullest revelation in the beatific end.[154] Typological realism rehistoricizes theological interpretation and retheologizes redemptive history. Progress occurs primarily as a demonstration of the happy Trinity so that he can be known and enjoyed. Clowney concludes that "When Christ says, 'Before Abraham was, I am' (John 8:56), he was saying not that he is Abraham's and David's seed, *but that he is Abraham's and David's Lord.*"[155] Christ is not less than he was before but more, in terms of his revelation.

Therefore typology *is* eschatology. It sets the eyes forward to the endpoint while simultaneously setting the eyes upward to the sourcepoint: the God who is, who has made himself known, and who will be fully enjoyed in the end. Those who see him with the eyes of faith (Eph 1:18) will in that day see him as he is, and they will be ready, having been trained in his Christocentric school of typology.

To many of the most important thinkers through the Great Tradition, especially Augustine, Thomas, and Calvin, all is pedagogy: God teaches and prepares for future glory. All of revelation, including the types, is what Boersma calls *revelatory anticipations*.[156] The current life points to (and, via participation with God, connects to) the future life.

---

154. In saying that theology will be understood in relationship to God's acts, this paragraph does not intend to economize theology. The question of economizing theology is handled well in both Duby, *God in Himself*, and Dolezal, *All That Is In God*.

The paragraph above does, however, intend to contextualize theology according to God's redemptive-historical method of revelation. The hope is that to do so will elevate, not humiliate, God's being *in se*.

155. Clowney, *Preaching Christ in All of Scripture*, 42; emphasis added.

156. Boersma, *SG*, 401–7; Boersma says that the visions are God's tool to prepare believers' eyes and minds, showing his "essence by sacraments" (Boersma, *SG*, 1–10). Finally, Boersma helpfully shows that Irenaeus understood history not just in terms of creation, fall, Christ, and consummation, but the constant revelation of Christ who is present in it. Boersma, *SG*, 410–414.

Vos, writing extensively about the presence of the future in the present through the Spirit, was well within the Great Tradition in teaching a typological hermeneutic. Such a hermeneutic not only applies to one's approach to Scripture but to all of life until the full life comes in the end. Christ the Word, the archetype who is himself also the antitype, wills to be known richly in this way.

The final two chapters will show typological realism in practice. The goal within a typologically oriented biblical theology is the same goal as throughout the Great Tradition: to know and walk with God in the glory of the present while looking forward to an even greater glory in the future. This knowing and walking is the life of faith. Helpfully, Vos defines faith as "that organ for apprehension of unseen and future realities, giving access to and contact with another world. [Faith is] the hand stretched out through the vast distances of time and space, whereby the Christian draws to himself things far beyond, so that they may become actual to him."[157] Typological realism seeks, in the fullest way possible, to bring eternal realities before believers to prepare them for their apprehension of the fullness to come in the glorious vision.

---

157. See Vos, "Heavenly-Mindedness," in *Grace and Glory*, 122.

6

Typological Realism Applied, Part 1
Historical and Theological Exegesis

> "Ultimately, the christological interpretation of the Old Testament is a matter of Christ's personal authority. It is something very close to what Paul calls 'the gospel.'"
>
> —CRAIG A. CARTER

PREVIOUS CHAPTERS CONSIDERED THE relationship between Christ-centered biblical theology and the Great Tradition, concluding that the former employs the Christocentricity of the latter while also employing a modernistic orientation to history. The newer Christ-centered approach also has both theological and pastoral shortcomings. In response to these shortcomings, theological interpretation of Scripture has proposed a more theocentric orientation. This approach, however, has shortcomings as well. At its worst, it dehistoricizes Scripture, neglecting Scripture's own historical context. These observations led to a proposal to join Christ-centered biblical theology and theological integration using typology as a connective framework. This synthetic hermeneutical approach was called *typological realism*.

Christ-centered biblical theology can be called a forward-focused hermeneutical approach since it concerns the nature of how the biblical story unfolds. Conversely, theological interpretation can be construed as upward-focused, looking for theological/doctrinal truth in every text. Since typology concerns escalating correspondences across the biblical narrative, its pertinence to the two approaches should be obvious: It shows how revelation escalates both upward (theological) and forward (historical), as God via type/antitype progressively reveals life-giving truth with increasing clarity across history, culminating in the beatific vision. The vision will be the fullest possible revelation of the real, which is currently available in a lesser form. The types, being preparatory in purposely revealing that which is true to humanity's fallen capacities, can be called, following Boersma, sacramental.[1] They do not merely *symbolize* what is true, but based on their content as purposeful revelation, they *participate* in the life of God, allowing those who receive them by faith to participate with God by them. Jesus can say about God's word, "His command is eternal life" (John 12:50): If the eternal life which Jesus brings is the very life of the Trinity, then the revelatory content of the types imparts that life to those who behold God's glory therein.[2]

The purpose of this penultimate chapter is to show typological realism in action, moving beyond the theoretical into the practical. Hopefully, this chapter will demonstrate what happens when a student puts on the "glasses" of typological realism. Before doing so, a few preliminary thoughts about typology for the sake of definitional clarity are worth considering.

First, types do not *only* point forward to later things. Rather, as God's appointed means of bringing his people along in faith, types, by virtue of their revelatory nature participate with God, draw his people into fellowship with him. Such a participatory definition depends on an ontology that has been present throughout the tradition. Boersma has sought to show the importance of recapturing this premodern view of time and space. The adjective he uses as a label is *sacramental*. In a sacramental ontology of the universe, what exists points to both the Creator and other glorious realities that he wants to (and does) give people.[3] But even further, the things that exist not only *point to* the more glorious

---

1. See Boersma's treatment of typology as sacramental in *Scripture as Real Presence*, 81–104. Boersma, as is characteristic, engages heavily with twentieth-century Catholic ressourcement figures Henri de Lubac, Jean Danielou, and Yves Congar in arguing for the recovery of a sacramental ontology. In such a framing of reality's nature, types comfortably take on a sacramental identity, not merely pointing elsewhere but participating in God's reality and inviting the faithful to do the same.

2. For eternal life as the life of God himself, see Willard, *Divine Conspiracy*, 1–34.

3. Boersma, *HP*, 21–22.

things, but as God's appointed means through which he blesses people in the present, "what is seen" (Heb 11:3) substantially participates in the glorious realities, connecting believers to the real.[4] Boersma's sacramental view of the universe is called *heavenly participation*, because if what occurs in time and space engages with and participates with God, believers in time and space engage with and participate with God in heaven.

This point means that the Scripture reader sees in types that which points forward and can have confident faith that these types convey God's voice, establishing fellowship with him (1 Cor 1:9; 1 John 1:4). Although the believer might not experience the fullness of glory until the end (in the vision), they spiritually connect with the fullness of glory as they behold the type. Their reception of both the types and the realities to which the types point constitutes their faith.[5] In this sense, Paul says that believers have been blessed "with every spiritual blessing in the heavenly places" (Eph 1:3). These realities are eternal realities which believers will fully possess and which are a current spiritual possession by faith. The type-antitype framework is the means through which God communicates this journey.[6]

To believe in that to which the type points—whether Old Testament type of New Testament antitype or New Testament type of eschatological antitype—is to embrace what God says is truly *real*. One cannot be a Christian unless one can both know and enjoy the real.[7] "You will know the truth, and the truth will set you free" (John 8:32). "Whoever keeps the word" (that is, the revealed word which is given on a typological trajectory) "in him the love of God is perfected" (1 John 2:5). The apostle said that knowledge in the present day is an imperfect knowledge: "We see through a glass darkly . . . [we] know in part" (1 Cor 13:9a, KJV). It is, however, an accessible knowledge for the believer who comes to learn from Christ (Matt 11:29). This knowledge, says Jesus, leads to true freedom. That which the eye can partially see, the eye will one day see fully: "Then, face to face" (1 Cor 13:9b). The Scripture's typological trajectory vividly puts this growing clarity on display. Hearing what is *real*, revealed

---

4. Boersma, *HP*, 23.

5. Echoing Vos, defining faith in terms of "otherworldliness," whereby believers "connect to powers of the higher world," in "Heavenly-Mindedness," 125–26.

6. Gregory of Nazianzus helpfully noted, commenting on Heb 8–9, that all that exists in time and space is patterned after eternal realities in the heavenly places. See *On God and Christ*, 46–51.

7. Gerson, *From Plato to Platonism*, 11–14, quoted in Boersma, *Five Things*, 43.

from within a typological trajectory, is the goal. The method is called *typological realism*: The *real* is conveyed in partial form through types, experienced in a lesser form, ever moving onward and upward to the glorious beatific vision where redemptive history and theology intersect.

What follows is an explanation of typological realism as method: four questions, one which has two parts, to be asked of the scriptural text. After explaining the questions, there will be some example texts on which to practice. This framework seems significantly less extensive than recent proposed exegetical methods that engage both redemptive history and theology.[8] By volume, this method might have more in common with more abbreviated methods proposed in comparison works.[9] But this approach employs a pre-understanding of Scripture in light of the conviction that Scripture is both a divine word from God and a progressive history that terminates in eternal joy and happiness (Rev 21:4, cf. Matt 25:23). If this is already understood, much of the preparatory work to exegesis is already done. This pre-understanding is not intended to be read into the text, but is the effect of reflection upon the text which then drives the reader back into it so that they will hear from and hope in God, creating what has been called a hermeneutical spiral.[10]

The Questions

What Is the Text's Historical Relationship to Christ's Coming in the Incarnation?

Christ's first coming is the central event in God's time and space project: "When the fullness of time had come, God sent his son" (Gal 4:4). Jesus opened his public ministry by saying, "The time is fulfilled, and the kingdom of God is at hand" (Mark 1:15). Not to make Christ's

---

8. See Naselli, *Understand and Apply the New Testament*; Derouchie, *Understand and Apply the Old Testament*. Throughout the current project, Craig Carter's *ISGT*, has been returned to repeatedly as well. *ISGT*, is more theologically oriented than either of Naselli's or Derouchie's approaches. See also Carter's "Premodern Approach" in *Five Views on Christ in the Old Testament* (which also includes Derouchie's redemptive-historical approach.)

9. See Gundry and Meadors, *Four Views*.

10. For the concept of hermeneutical spiral, where theology both comes from the text and influences the text, see Osborne, *Hermeneutical Spiral*; one can also see Carter's significantly briefer construal of the spiral in "How Then Shall We Theologize?," where the latter reading is called "second exegesis."

coming exegetically central would be foolish. Chapter 5 gave extended consideration to this point, noting Cullmann's contention in *Christ and Time* that since the Christ-event is central to history, no revealed word is understandable in a meaningful way apart from it.[11] The context of every text can only be ascertained in terms of the text's chronological and ontological relationship to Christ's redeeming work in the incarnation. The purpose of what came before includes escalation to Christ, and what comes after escalates *from* Christ. To claim such escalation both to and from Christ's coming is not to suggest a progressive view of history in the modern sense of "progress," but in a theological sense: God's project always continues to advance with Christ's first coming as the ultimate proof,[12] hence the emphasis in the apostles' preaching that the day of final judgment is proven by Jesus's resurrection (Acts 10:40–43; 17:30–31). The implication is that the resurrection of the Son of God proves the return and final judgment of the Son of God.

Thus, the first questions to ask of a given text are historical. Was the text revealed prior to or after the Christ-event? Does the text pertain prophetically to the Christ-event (i.e., does it foretell the Christ-event?) or does it reflect upon it in some way(s) (i.e., is the text contained in an epistle written in light of Christ's coming or an Old Testament prophecy of it?)? Such questions contextualize the text according to the Bible's historical center, Christ in both his finished and continuing work (e.g., Acts 1:1).

As aforementioned, however, Christ's coming is not only Scripture's historical center but also its *revelatory* center. As seen in chapter 2, Christ was revealed in various ways throughout the Old Testament. Clearly, the apostles believed under inspiration that Christ's incarnation clarified mysteries (*mysterion*) previously not understood, hence Rom 16:25 and 1 Pet 1:10–12, among others.[13] "In the past, God spoke to our fathers by the prophets, but in these last days he has spoken to us by his son" (Heb 1:1–2). The Son is the eternal outgoing Word of the Father (John 1:1–4; Col 1:15–17). When he put on flesh, a fullness of revelation came into the world such that readers with "ears to hear" can be sure they are hearing

---

11. See Cullmann, *Christ and Time*, 121–30, 211–13. See also Boersma's discussion in *Scripture as Real Presence*, xii.

12. Perhaps this is why Barth made the events of Jesus's life the starting point of theology. See *Dogmatics in Outline* and *Evangelical Theology*, 17–19.

13. For Paul's frequent use of *mysterion*, see Rom 16:25; 1 Cor 2:7, 4:1; Eph 3:4–6, 9–11; Col 1:26–27. Pertinent gospel cross-references might be Matt 5:17; Mark 1:15; John 5:38–46.

the Father's voice. "In the latter days," says Jeremiah, "you will understand it clearly" (Jer 23:20).

This point also explains why Paul could say that what was revealed during the Old Testament dispensation was written for Christians and their faith journey (Rom 15:4; cf. 1 Cor 10:4–10; 2 Tim 3:14–16). Such an idea assumes a Christian priority: One must be regenerate to hear God's voice truly. "Ears to hear" only come in regeneration (cf. Ps 40:6). The majority of the world cannot receive or understand these things, but Christians have been given the Spirit so that they can (1 Cor 2:12–16). Since the Spirit's job is to glorify (John 16:14) and illuminate Christ (John 14:26; 15:26; cf. 1 John 2:26; Rev 19:10), and the Spirit is the source of both Old and New Testament revelation (2 Pet 1:20–21), no text can be understood truly unless in relationship to Christ. The necessity of this first question should be clear: What is the historical relationship between the text in question and the revelational, mystery-clarifying Christ-event?[14]

Finally, if a typological orientation is as programmatic as this project has argued, a historical framing of texts' relationship is necessary, because the type, the subsequent antitype to which it points, and final antitype cannot be seen/heard otherwise. Although the Old Testament era is full of forward-looking types, the New Testament era uniquely contains both antitype (prefigured in the Old Testament) *and* type (prefiguring that which will come in eternity); as such, the New Testament perspective is both backward-looking and a forward-looking.[15] There is a plain sense to whatever text is in view, but *sensus plenior* calls for the exegete to locate the text in the whole Bible as context.[16] As the narrative progresses, later revelation clarifies what came earlier such that, as Beale has said, what was contained in earlier texts has "grown in meaning."[17]

---

14. This question constitutes the research interest of Graeme Goldsworthy's many decades of writing on biblical theology. As mentioned above, see his *Preaching the Whole Bible* or his shorter essays, e.g., "Is Biblical Theology Viable?," 18–46; "Pastor as Biblical Theologian," 110–29.

15. Beale, Goldsworthy, and Edward Schnittjer (*Old Testament Use*) have all done outstanding work to show that the Old Testament prophets employ images of earlier Old Testament history to look prophetically to the messianic day, and thus, the backwards-and-forward-looking model of the New Testament finds its origin in the Old Testament prophets. More on this below.

16. For a discussion of *sensus plenior*, see chapter 2 above. See also Barrett, *Canon, Covenant, and Christology*, 24–38.

17. See Beale, *Temple and Church's Mission*, 377–81. Similarly, Schnittjer's *Old Testament Use* shows that the supposed "growth" in meaning is a demonstrable observation of the unfolding biblical narrative itself. To be clear, neither Beale nor Schnittjer

What was understood prior is not diminished but enhanced by the greater glory that has come and to which it pointed. The historical question seeks to understand and appreciate this enhancement, or growth.

What Does the Text Say Prophetically about Christ and Prosopologically about Christ?

The previous two chapters gave attention to the so-called prosopological reading of the Old Testament, which was employed by the New Testament writers and the church fathers. For as common as prosopological reading was in the patristic witness, it simply cannot be accurately said to exhaust the way that the New Testament writers read Christ in the Old, nor the way that the early church read the Old. Instead, as both Augustine's *Instructing Beginners in the Faith* and Irenaeus's *On the Apostolic Preaching* showed (with surprising redemptive-historical similarities both to each other and to modern biblical-theological models), the whole of the Old Testament as a historic narrative points forward to the Christ-event in which the Word put on flesh and revealed his glory full of grace and truth (John 1:14).

As noted, Matthew Bates took issue with Richard Hays's assertion that the New Testament reads the Old typologically. Better, says Bates, is a prosopological understanding.[18] Craig Carter supports and maintains Bates's prosopology in *ISGT*.[19] The voice of the Son is present in the prophetic words of the Old Testament writers, bearing witness to Trinitarian relationships, and more.[20]

Therefore, prosopology is not the *only* way of seeing Christ in the Old Testament. There is a clear prophetic witness to Christ in both promise and type, whether vague (and clearer later) or clear. Biblical theology must acknowledge the presence of both: In prosopology, the voice of the Son who is the Word is heard pre-incarnation. In prophecy, whether via promise or type, words *about* the Son are heard. In either case, the Word who became flesh prepares those with ears to hear to be *able* to hear. He employs a treasury of divine tools—"spiritual blessings" (Eph 1:3)—to

---

are the first to propose such a gloss. Vos did so as early as his inaugural address at Princeton. See Vos, "Idea of Biblical Theology," 11.

18. See Bates, *Birth of the Trinity*.
19. See Carter, *ISGT*, 191–201.
20. This feature is a distinguishing one for prosopological reading.

make himself known so that those who know him will, at his return, enjoy him in fullness (cf. Isa 12:3; Matt 25:21, 23; John 15:11; 17:13).

To answer both parts of this question in turn will be helpful:

Prophetically

If the text contains a moral lesson/instruction, such as "Have no other gods before me," (Exod 20:3) or "If you lift up your voice for wisdom, you will understand the fear of the Lord," (Prov 2:3–5) or "Do not fear, for I am with you" (Isa 41:10), how does the instruction bear witness prophetically to Christ? Both Old and New Testaments teach that the perfect practice of God's commands is impossible (Josh 24:19; Gal 3:10–14), given the fallen nature. God, however, demands obedience, and his commands are life-giving, not burdensome (1 John 5:4). In light of Jesus's being the only human in existence without sin, the moral lesson, then, demonstrates Christ's perfect righteousness so that his glory as the obedient son is put on display (Heb 5:8; cf. Rom 5:19; Jer 23:6). The command tells of the readers' need for Christ and of the content of Christ's character as godliness personified (1 Tim 3:15). Readers then, following and trusting in Christ, are empowered by faith in Christ to keep the commands as they walk "by the Spirit" (cf. Rom 8:3–4).

If the text tells of a historical event, the prophetic witness to Christ is also essential. Exodus tells of God's deliverance of his people from their slavery in Egypt so that they would be a people set apart for him (Exod 19:4–6). They did not, however, experience yet the circumcision of heart that would occur under the new covenant (Deut 10:16; 30:6; Jer 4:4; 31:31–34). Matthew explains Jesus's parents' escape to Egypt from Herod (and subsequent return) in terms of the Israelites' escape from Egypt (Hos 11:1 in Matt 2:15). The clear implication is that Jesus is the true Son of God who underwent an antitypical journey from Egypt; by his perfect life and death, he will circumcise the hearts of those true Israelites who trust in him (Rom 2:25–29; 9:6).[21]

---

21. This explanation might make sense of Paul's use of the Deut 30:11–14 invitation to obedience to potential Christian converts in Rom 10:5–11, concluding that, as Joel said, whoever believes in the Lord will be saved. So understood, the promised circumcision of heart, conditioned on repentance and forgiveness of sins (Deut 30:1–6), has occurred in Jesus's "repentance" on Israel's behalf, which works forgiveness. That point, then, could be why Paul's immediately preceding words (Rom 10:4) are, "For Christ is the end of the Law for righteousness to the one who believes." Beale makes this exact case in *Union with the Resurrected Christ*, 326–29.

Thus Paul states that the exodus was an example (*typoi*) for Christians on the journey of faith (1 Cor 10:1–6). The event is not *merely* an example/type (thus dehistoricizing it) but serves its ultimate purpose as a picture of God's eschatological redemption by Christ.[22] The exodus becomes, via believers' relationship to Christ, a picture of their faith journey. Hence, "what was written in former days was written for our instruction" (Rom 15:4). Insofar as believers are in Christ, the chosen Seed to whom the Abrahamic promise finds its fulfillment (Gal 3:16), every other Old Testament promise belongs to them as well. Indeed, in Christ, believers are children of Abraham, by faith (Gal 3:24).[23] The God who saved a people for himself in the exodus has now, in his Son, saved an internally circumcised people for himself, a people for his own possession.[24]

Finally is a consideration of commentary text. "Commentary" is here meant in the sense of prophetic reflection on past events (as in the Minor Prophets), the telling of historical events (as in the Old Testament historical writings), or wisdom literature, in which wise living in light of past redemptive events is explained.[25] Jesus is the one in whom are hidden "all the treasures of wisdom and knowledge" (Col 2:3); he was also the one who sent Israel prophets and teachers (Matt 23:34). Since in the Christ-event he put on flesh as the final prophetic word to the world (Heb 1:1–3), there is a substantive relationship between what was said before and what was said during Christ's first coming. God employed Old Testament prophets to give meaning to what had occurred in his revelatory and redemptive activity. Not until the Son came into the world could the fullness of meaning be ascertained because of the importance of the Christ-event in the grand scheme (Eph 1:10). Hence Boersma asserts that the Great Tradition has always taught and preached that both what

---

22. See Goldsworthy, *Preaching the Whole Bible*, 110–11.

23. For a good treatment of Christ as the promised Seed in Gal 3, see Storms, *Kingdom Come*, 189–91. The framework presented by the apostle in which believers' relationship to the Old Testament promises is mediated by their relationship to Christ the fulfiller will not be met without controversy, because it assumes that the Old Testament must be, to borrow from Hays, "read backwards" *in light of* the New. A Christ-centered biblical theology seems, however, to require such a method. It is hoped that this project can somewhat strengthen such an assertion.

24. This seems to be the point of Titus 2:12–14 and 1 Pet 2:8–9, in which both writers utilize Exodosical language—God's "possession"—to describe Christians' relationship to God through Christ.

25. Goldsworthy, *Proverbs*, 30–37. There, Goldsworthy ably shows that the wisdom literature is to be read *as reflection on* Old Testament history. Simply put, wise living is a reflection of God's revelatory activity, received and practiced by faith.

occurred in Old Testament redemptive history and its subsequent commentary could only be understood in relationship to Christ the Word.[26] The Great Tradition has always held that *no* meaning can be ascertained outside of relationship to Christ the Word who gives being to all things.[27] He alone must give purpose and meaning to what occurs in time and space, for in him all things hold together (Col 1:17), and he upholds all things by his word (Heb 1:3).

In summary, the text bears prophetic witness to Christ by pointing the reader chronologically forward to the Christ-event, which gives ultimate meaning to the earlier revelation.

Prosopologically

The previous section's reticence to embrace an *exclusively* prosopological reading is by no means intended to suggest prosopology's illegitimacy. As stated, both Bates and Carter demonstrate prosopology's clear Old Testament presence based on how New Testament writers hear it. That said, Gentry's subsequent dismissal in favor of a redemptive-historical reading hardly settles the debate.[28] The New Testament witness to the exegetical legitimacy of both redemptive history and prosopology shows that recognizing Christ's presence in the Old does not necessarily require a monolithic approach.

Thus this question seeks to identify how pre-incarnate revelation is the actual voice of the eternal Word bearing witness to himself as Christ the Messiah. As explained in chapter 4, a prosopological reading seeks to overcome perceived ambiguities in particular texts when read in a canonical framework by assuming a simple explanation: The text is the actual voice of pre-incarnate Christ. Reading Old Testament texts as the voice of Christ the Word does not jettison a redemptive-historical reading of Scripture but applies theological conclusions to pre-incarnate revelation. Only the Son, the eternal Word, knows the Father; thus, only those to whom the Son reveals the Father also know him (Matt 11:27), and this has always been the case (John 1:18). Carter notes Justin Martyr's teaching that Old Testament prophetic teachings do not come first from

---

26. See Boersma, *HP*, 39.

27. Boersma, *HP*, x–xi.

28. See the discussion of Gentry and Bates in chapter 4, 205–12. See also Gentry, "Preliminary Evaluation and Critique."

the prophets but are sourced first "from the divine Logos."²⁹ Martyr's point is that all pre-incarnation revelation is the pre-incarnate voice of Christ speaking the truth about God, humanity, and the world, preparing the way for Christ as goal and final revelatory Word, reinforcing the New Testament claims about him for those who come after him.³⁰

The Old Testament is not alone in the spoken and written word being the voice of Christ. Jesus told the disciples that the Spirit would lead them into all of the truth and that they would themselves bear witness (John 15:26–27), hence the emphasis throughout the New Testament on the authority of the apostles' writing as the voice of Christ the Lord (1 Cor 14:37; 1 Thess 2:13; 1 John 4:6). From a theological perspective, anytime the God who inhabits eternity speaks into his creation, it is by "the word of the Lord" (e.g., 1 Sam 3:21). Christ is himself the voice of the Father. "In these last days he has spoken to us by his Son" (Heb 1:2). "Whoever hears my word *and believes him who sent me* has life" (John 5:24; emphasis added). The eternally begotten Son is himself the outgoing Word of the Father.

Whereas the emphasis throughout Bates's work is on Old Testament texts that the New sees as pre-Christ-event "eavesdropping" on inner-Trinitarian discussion,³¹ the logical conclusion of a prosopological reading, if construed theologically, is that the entirety of Holy Writ is the voice of Christ the Son. So this question considers how particular texts can lack "red letters" and yet still be the voice of the Son. Additionally, how might a believer, controlled by regenerate reasoning, hear Christ the Son in the text?³² In this way the believer avoids what Hebrews warns against, namely resisting the one "who *is speaking*" (Heb 12:25; emphasis added).

29. See Carter, *ISGT*, 199.

30. The notion that the Old Testament prophetic witness was the pre-incarnate voice of Christ is not contradicted by Heb 1:1, where the writer juxtaposes God's earlier word by the prophets with his later word by his Son. The text's point is not that the administrations of the word are distinct in source but that they are distinct as regards mediatorial presence and clarity. In the Old Testament, the word came from God through the prophets; in the New, the Word is Christ, who, being the Son, is the "last word." See Webster, "One Who is Son," 60–72.

31. See Bates, *Birth of the Trinity*, 41–84. Bates calls these revelatory eavesdroppings "Divine dialogues from the dawn of time." In eavesdropping, the writer then "steps out" of their historical moment to speak as the voice of the appropriate Trinitarian member to reveal the revelatory content via Scripture.

32. See Webster, "Biblical Reasoning," 115–32 for a construal of biblical reasoning as regenerate reasoning. The prerequisite for understanding the voice of Christ the Shepherd is being a sheep (John 10:27–28). Webster also deals with regenerate reasoning elsewhere in "On the Matter of Christian Theology," 3–10.

The text, therefore, does not only contain a historically contextualized message that either points forward or backward to Christ's first coming (prophetic) but a pastoral point at the hands of the chief shepherd (Heb 13:20) who (prosopologically) speaks by his word to his sheep so that they will believe in and follow him. Both this and the previous question have a place in a hermeneutical methodology that seeks to be sensitive both to redemptive history and to theology. Via prosopology, the text is itself the revelatory word of the revealing Word. The Old Testament text orients the reader upward to the Christ who was (at the time of revelation, whether in the Old Testament day or the New), is (at the reader's moment), and is to come (in the final Christ-event) (cf. Rev 1:8).

How Does the Text Prepare the Church for Christ's Return and Subsequent Glory?

Having engaged the text's redemptive-historical context (questions 1 and 2a), as well as a theological consideration (question 2b), question 3 continues to develop the methodological scope by pointing forward to the coming eschatological day of the Lord. Believers participate in redemptive history which continues on to its destination of intersection with theology proper at the beatific vision. If the phrase "coming glory" were used to explain the "blessed hope" of which Paul speaks (Titus 2:13), then redemptive history helps explain the aspect of *coming* while theology proper helps explain the *glory*. In short, Scripture's typological trajectory is, through time, believers' preparation to see God. So how does the text prepare the church for such an anticipated event?

As discussed in chapter 3, the so-called *quadriga*, the dominant interpretive methodology of the Middle Ages which is usually attributed to Augustine,[33] held that a text was to be understood according to four separate senses:

1. The literal-historical sense seeks the text's historical context.

2. The tropological sense seeks a moral application of the text. What is the hearer to *do* in light of the text?

---

33. Origen, living two hundred years prior to Augustine, had a threefold sense similar to but arguably inferior to Augustine's fourfold sense. Augustine, along with his contemporary John Cassian, split Origen's allegorical sense in two, creating both a current Christological sense (allegorical) and a future eschatological sense (anagogical). In this way, Origen's three senses became four. See Bray, *How the Church Fathers Read*, 105–6.

3. The allegorical sense applies the rule of faith—the gospel, which is Scripture's thematic center—to the text so that it is understood in light of Christ. This sense is also *pastoral*, contextualizing the text in light of Christ who gives sensibility to all things so that the believer sees and hopes in Christ as the text's fulfillment.[34]

4. The anagogical sense asks how the text prepares the listener for the coming Christ-event with great glory.[35]

In the *quadriga*, the literal sense controls all meaning before pastoral senses are applied. The tropological, allegorical, and anagogical senses are all called "pastoral" senses in that they do not change the meaning of the passage, but they apply the passage to the context of the listener/reader in light of important considerations. The listener is called always to obey Christ and hope in the coming glory; exegetical practice cannot, therefore, be executed without these responsibilities. As the previous chapter showed, Christians are on a journey toward the beatific vision where everything along the journey is pointing to and preparing them for it. The transition from the allegorical sense to the anagogical sense is not a far one; the former concerns the text in light of past and present truth (i.e., the gospel), and the latter concerns the text in light of future revealed truth (Christ's return). Both belong to the Christian, who is told, "All things are yours" (1 Cor 3:21).

The current question continues the exegetical tradition employed through the Tradition. More importantly, the question is a logical outcome given the context of Christian interpretation: The believer is on a faith journey across time and space that has its goal in future glorification (Matt 25:23; Rom 8:30; 2 Thess 1:11; 1 Pet 1:7). At that time, the types, themselves gifts for discipleship which point to and participate in the real, will give way to the real. So, in what sense is hearing the text a preparation for the future glory?

As examined in chapter 5, this question was primary in Geerhardus Vos's method. The Holy Spirit is the presence of the eschaton breaking into the present to stir the believer's hope in Christ's glorious return. This spiritual presence constitutes the believer's "partial eschatological

---

34. Boersma, *HP*, x–xi.

35. This summary is adapted from Muller, "Biblical Interpretation," 8–13. Worth mentioning is that in Aquinas's explanation of biblical interpretation in *ST*, none of senses 2–4 can stand in contradiction with sense 1, the literal/historical (see *ST*, 1.1.10). It seems that there has been a discernible agreement on this through the centuries.

privileges."[36] Believers are oriented toward the end, where they, though living in the present, will see God, walking by faith until then. The Spirit guarantees believers' acquisition of the eternal inheritance (2 Cor 1:21), even while faith may, at times, waver. Even in faithlessness, God is faithful (2 Tim 2:13). Because believers know that God is working in and with them for a glorious future, and Christ's life is their very life (Rom 5:10, 17; 6:4, 11; 1 John 4:9; 5:11), they continue on in the present by faith.[37] Past promises have found their substantial fulfillment in Christ's first coming, giving believers confidence that Christ's own promises about his next coming will be fulfilled. They live therefore oriented to the end with a reasonable confidence in which, by faith, they seek to "stay awake" (Matt 24:42).

Vos notes another parallel to the point being made in his *Eschatology of the Old Testament*. There, he makes the case that the theophanies of the Old Testament are meant to communicate "God's approach to and communion with man." The eternal God draws near to humanity which is bound by time and space. Vos continues, "with respect to the future, the theophany presents the renewal of the paradise-condition and as such presages a full future paradise."[38] Vos here agrees with Luther's belief, seen in a previous chapter, that Old Testament saints parallel New Testament saints in that both are awaiting a coming of Christ and are living by faith in *promisio*.[39] Thus Vos describes New Testament faith in terms of "living halfway in the fulfillment and out of fulfillment."[40] His point is that believers, being further along in God's project than Old Testament believers, have promises fulfilled and, by the Spirit, the very best of fellowship with God the Trinity that is possible while waiting for their faith to become sight.

The theophanies afford one more worthwhile sub-question before moving on to the method's final question. If theophanies are simultaneously the *going-out* of God into his creation to show fellowship/nearness *and* a prophecy of what he will do in Christ's coming, then it seems clear

---

36. See chapter 5 above, as well as Vos, "Eschatology of the New Testament," 26.

37. Worth mentioning is Piper's *Future Grace*. Piper's thesis is that the very nature of saving faith is satisfaction in future grace, that God will bless his people in the future as they walk with him in the present. To predict that this will be Piper's most enduring contribution does not seem to require boldness.

38. See Vos, *Eschatology of the Old Testament*, 85.

39. See chapter 3 above, and Preuss, *From Shadow to Promise*, 186.

40. Vos, *Eschatology of the Old Testament*, 145.

that those who received the theophanies and walked by faith (Heb 11) did so via participation in and with God.[41] Thus, the question: If there is a parallel between the Old Testament theophanies and the New Testament presence of the Holy Spirit, then is the Christian life, characterized as "keeping in step with the Spirit" (Gal 5:25), a life of participation with God? The answer would seem to be "yes": Jesus told his disciples that he would come to them (John 14:18) and that they can rest assured that he is with them until he returns (Matt 28:20). At Paul's conversion, Jesus's own commentary of Paul's persecution of Christians is persecution of Jesus himself: "Saul, why do you persecute *me*?" (Acts 9:4; emphasis added). That God has not only drawn near (as in the theophanies) but has made his home with believers (as in regeneration; John 14:23) means not only that believers have confidence that they are walking in the truth, but that they are involved in Christ's own redemptive endeavor in his creation.[42] Hence, he came to destroy the works of the devil (1 John 3:8), *and* (not "but") the devil will soon be put under believers' feet (Rom 16:20). He will destroy the devil by putting him under his followers' feet as he indwells them.

Such a framework for scriptural study necessarily implies that Scripture can be read using critical tools while not being read *critically*. Scripture is the Trinity's written word revealed from within a historical context to the end of lifting believers' eyes to the glory of God in the face of Jesus Christ (2 Cor 4:6) so that they can enjoy God.[43] To echo Boersma, history is not divided into two strands, secular and sacred.[44] History is the unfolding of God's purposes in his Son so that meaning cannot be ascertained apart from him, the very radiance and outgoingness of the Father (Heb 1:3).[45] History, moving toward its goal in the beatific vision, has no definite meaning unless understood in relationship to the endpoint. Thus discipleship and all that attends it—biblical hermeneutics included—can also only be understood in relationship to the endpoint. In this sense, Peter writes that as believers enjoy their salvation in Christ

---

41. Again, Boersma's *HP*, is in the backdrop of this speculation. Also worth seeing is Andrew Davison's *Participation in God*, in which participation is the creation sharing with God in the unfolding of His purposes. He deals in chapter 10 with redemption as participation.

42. The redemptive participation suggested here will be considered in the final chapter.

43. Augustine, *De Doctrina* 1.5–23.

44. Boersma, *Scripture as Real Presence*, 25–26, 54–55.

45. See Reeves, *Delighting in the Trinity*, 27.

which will be fully realized one day, they *receive* (*komizomenoi*, present part.) the outcome of their faith, the salvation of their souls (1 Pet 1:8–9). This salvation is not strictly future or strictly present, but in different senses both.[46]

How Does the Text Display God's Glory and Nature?

As seen in chapter 5, typological realism interprets the Bible in light of the conviction that God's typologically structured historical project parallels and participates in that which exists eternally and perfectly in the Logos. Boersma in his *Scripture as Real Presence* masterfully surveyed patristic exegesis to show that the Great Tradition from its earliest stages held that redemptive history has a "typological structure" grounded in the providence of God.[47] The eternal God reveals his being, nature, and purposes over the course of time such that, as the previous chapter noted in Vos, fuller revelation comes later, building upon and fulfilling earlier revelation. The similarities between the earlier and the later are to be taken as the two parts of the same whole. They will be utterly consistent even though later revelation will give fuller light and, by theological implication, greater blessings (e.g., Heb 8:6).[48] Beale is not far from the mark when he suggests that texts *grow* in meaning: The revelatory content of the earlier revelation is no less true or pertinent, but it has in the later revelation matured, perhaps even expanded.[49]

Boersma argues that in this way, the Christ-event, though the midpoint and revelatory center of history, is theologically prior to the Old Testament.[50] The incarnation of the Son of God in the person of Jesus Christ is the goal of all of revelation unto the ultimate goal of uniting all things in him (Eph 1:10). Texts which are chronologically prior to the Christ-event cannot be understood apart from their relationship to

---

46. Space will not permit a fuller consideration of Augustine's division of history into secular and sacred. As a Christian philosopher of history—and indeed, the first one to attempt a full-scale treatment of world history and its purposes (in *De Civitat Dei*)—it seems unlikely that he meant to suggest that history substantially ran along two lines, sacred and secular. Rather, he meant that history was organized in a logical sense along those two descriptors. Oort explains this well in "End Is Now," 4–7.

47. See Boersma, *Scripture as Real Presence*, 24.

48. That is, since revelation is of the real, then the greater the real's clarity is the fuller will be the enjoyment of it.

49. Beale, *Temple and the Church's Mission*, 377–81.

50. Boersma, *Scripture as Real Presence*, 24.

him who actually precedes, completes, and, as previous sections have shown, is himself the revelatory source of the texts. As such, to call Jesus, as Word, the archetype who gives being (and meaning) to the types is not inappropriate.

Since Christ came "when the fullness of time had come" (Gal 4:4), history is "on track," unfolding according to God's purposes. He is happy both with the current stage as well as every prior and subsequent stage. This point might be in view when Ezra and Nehemiah assured the returned exiles that God's joy would be their joy (Neh 8:10): If God has joy at their return, the exiles will, too. Similarly, if he is pleased with his Son (Matt 3:17; 17:5) who has come into the world and left his Spirit with his followers, the love for him that the Father has and which Jesus prayed his followers would have (17:26) is expressed in their participatory joy in him, hence the second of the fruit of the Spirit, joy, and hence the repeated apostolic command to "rejoice in the Lord" (Phil 3:1; 4:4).[51]

Boersma argues that a "sacramental tapestry" in Christian thought will, based on the *analogia entis*, turn both biblical interpretation and church dogmatics into reflections of eternal realities in the Logos. In such a framework, (a) *tradition* is the sacrament of Christ's continued presence in history, giving it its meaning; (b) *interpretation* is the sacrament of Christ's, by the church's growing clarity across time, summing up all things in himself; (c) *truth* (that is, dogmatics) apprehended by the faithful is the sacrament of eternal truth in the Logos; and (d) *theology* is the sacrament of believers' initiation into the life of God.[52] On this basis, one can say that God's purpose continuing on in exactly the way eternally planned is a theological reflection: Time, events, and truth, all occurring temporally, are rooted in the God who is himself the fountain of all life (Jer 2:14) and source of being, "by whom, through whom, and to whom" all things exist (cf. Rom 11:36). God as the efficient cause ("by"), the formal cause ("through"), and the final cause ("to") reveals himself by creaturely signs—for this discussion, the unfolding of time on

---

51. About joy, a pertinent cross-reference to the Nehemiah text might be Isa 16:9–11; there, God's "weeping" (a clear anthropomorphism) is the reason why the people weep. Similarly, God's rejection of Cain's sacrifice was seen in Cain's subsequent dejection (Gen 4:5–7). There seems to be some kind of connection between God's response to human activity and the mood of those humans.

52. Boersma, *HP,* 120–84. Boersma applies Augustine's idea in *On Christian Doctrine,* 1, 3, that all things are signs for eternity. So understood, the purpose of signs is always to lead believers to eternal things.

a typological-antitypological trajectory—until the endpoint when he will remove the signs and reveal his essence in a glorified fullness.[53]

So how does the text in question witness to the happiness of the Trinity? This question engages the text with the doctrine of *aseity*, that is, God's self-existence and self-sufficiency.[54] To consider a few test-cases:

(a) If exegeting a historical text, how does the narrative, whose meaning is ascertained in view of its relationship to Christ, show that God's plan is on track? For example, how does Gideon's defeat of Midian demonstrate that God is unmoved, steady, and happy with what has occurred to that point (Judg 7:19–25)? Although Gideon was God's man for God's time, still, apart from Christ, even Gideon was not "perfect" (Heb 11:40). He had a part to play in God's economy, showing God's control of history. At that stage of redemptive history, the people of God needed strong leaders who would both typify Christ and in some way "carry" the people of God along by their involvement in the revelation of God's faithfulness until Christ came.

(b) If a text is centered on moral instruction, how does the command stir the believer to greater fellowship with God and thus greater enjoyment of the Son who is himself the Word? One example could be Ps 34:12–13: "Who is there who . . . loves many days, that he may see good? Keep your tongue from evil." Here is a conditional promise: If one keeps their tongue from evil, God promises, in general terms, long life and much good. If one experiences that long life and much good, one can have the assurance that one lives in and has access to the joy of the Lord. When believers fail to keep their tongue from evil, as all do from time to time (Jas 3:2), there is a mediator who promises them not only forgiveness but true cleansing so that they can undergo substantial, sanctifying change (1 John 1:9).

But such a typologically realistic orientation to a text like this goes even further: Such reflection on God's happiness with the one who lives to please him shows the Father's pleasure in his Son who lived the perfect

---

53. See Davison's discussion of the three causes in *Participation in God*, 11–64 and final causation in 113–32.

54. For a good introduction to *aseity*, see Barrett, *None Greater*, 56–69. Being from himself, God depends on no one or anything and is entirely unique in this. The implications of this include, as Barrett shows, happiness, since nothing can challenge his will. He thus needs nothing in order to be happy. He creates because he chooses to demonstrate his glory in that way, and then he works in the unfolding of history to further show his glory by perfecting his creation, culminating in the perfect and redeeming life of Christ and realizing its effects throughout the time that follows it.

life. The righteous experience substantial happiness in heart and conscience, the same joy that the Father shares with the Son, as Jesus prayed (John 17:13) and the prophets had promised (Ps 31:19; Jer 31:14).[55]

(c) Finally, what about a text that is practical or analytical commentary, revelatory wisdom in light of revelatory events or revelatory reflection on those revelatory events? How does such wisdom or commentary speak about God's nature? A good test is Prov 3:34, which is commented upon in Heb 12:6–7: God disciplines those whom he loves; therefore the people of God who endure his discipline should take heart that they are truly his people. "He is treating you as sons" (Heb 12:7); this shows his Trinitarian, adopting nature. Further, "He disciplines us for our good" (12:10); this shows his sovereignty and wisdom. He can *only* have success in his endeavors; therefore the believer who endures discipline must know that God's good purposes for them will be accomplished. Their trials will not be wasted, because God, who is unchanging, steady, and effective (Jas 1:17), intends these trials for perfection (Jas 1:3–4),[56] and "his works are right, his ways are just, and those who walk in pride he is able to humble" (Dan 4:37).[57]

---

55. Worth mentioning is Aquinas's teaching that happiness is the end for which all people long, and which is only fully possible from God who is happy. See *ST*, 2.1.1–8.

Similarly, Boersma has series of sermons published with the goal of showing the happiness of God that is available to believers on the journey of faith. See his *Sacramental Preaching*.

56. Ronni Kurtz's recent work is helpful in tracing the relationship between God's immutability and the economy of salvation. In *No Shadow of Turning*, Kurtz shows that the only proper way to rightly understand Scripture's redemptive narrative is to understand it in light of God's unchangeability. The incarnation was not a "plan B" but the fulfillment of the plan that derives "from the fullness of God's life in himself" (Kurtz, *No Shadow of Turning*, 209). Since God cannot change, neither can the redemption which he gives. "The changeless redemption is realized in the creature as they are made one with Christ by virtue of their union with him" (Kurtz, *No Shadow of Turning*, 211). As the believer receives righteousness by grace by virtue of their union with Christ, neither the righteousness nor union with Christ will ever be lost. Both are as eternal as is Christ, who is the same "yesterday, today, and forever" (cf. Heb 13:8; cf. 1:12).

57. This question does not intend to engage theodicy, though it would seem that the question itself presupposes a theodicean stance. Whereas evil exists, still God's purposes will be accomplished in the end. His perfect and all-knowing nature precludes any real threat, as does the nature of evil as privation. (Evil is only allowed to continue for a time).

Christopher Watkin offers a helpful theodicy in *Biblical Critical Theory*, 179–206. He presents the case that the truth of God's sovereignty is established *by* the revelation of his will: Following God's will guarantees blessing; rebellion guarantees judgment. As such, God judges human activity by whether it furthers or negates his good plans.

Watkins' argument is true in general terms. It might, however, be weak when

Example Texts

This chapter's final section will provide exegetical examples of several texts using typological realism. Two Old Testament texts and an entire New Testament book will be used as case studies. Such a cross section of examples is not arbitrary; the goal is to show the versatility of typological realism while remaining mindful of this project's remaining space.

Old Testament

History/Law

Exodus 20:2–3: "I am the Lord your God who brought you out of Egypt, out of the house of slavery. You shall have no other Gods before me."

Exodus 20:2–3 is a mixture of both historical narrative and law-giving. In 20:2, God opens the Decalogue with a reminder of his redemptive activity: "I am the Lord your God who brought you out of Egypt, out of the land of slavery. You shall have no other gods before me." Vos has noted that, in broad terms, the exodus *is* the Old Testament redemption; everywhere in Scripture, the exodus is treated as the historical archetype of redemption.[58] Hence God opens the Decalogue with "one of the most profound references to the soteric procedure of God" in delivering them from Egypt.[59] The profundity is threefold: First, God names himself ("I am the Lord"), yoking himself covenantally with the people

---

considering both biblical examples and human experience. Jesus was perfectly righteous, yet he suffered. Many people have suffered and do suffer unjustly. Conversely, many unjust people experience great reward (Eccl 7:15; 8:14). It is probable that Watkins would respond that *in the end*, justice will be perfectly established based on God's sovereign will revealed. Still, many practically guilty people will be saved because of the imputed righteousness of Christ in a way that some would doubtless consider unjust (e.g., Luke 14:21). It seems far stronger to argue that in some mysterious way, the sovereign happiness of God works with and even *through* the evil actions of sinners, as stated—even emphasized—at several points in Scripture (Gen 50:20; Acts 2:23–24). In that sense, God is so joyful that his happiness can even strengthen his people (Neh 8:10) while also guaranteeing an end characterized by perfect justice unto his glory.

If evil is privation and not *essentially* a positive substance, it follows to expect that when God puts away rebellion once for all (by separating his redeemed creation from it), he will put away evil once for all. On evil as a negative substance with positive expression, see Vos, *Reformed Dogmatics*, 1.5, 7.

Dallas Willard helpfully defines evil in terms of deprivation that produces positive evils while being actual death. See *Spirit of the Disciplines*, 57–58.

58. Vos, *Biblical Theology*, 109.
59. Vos, *Biblical Theology*, 110.

("your God"). Secondly, God orients the people spatially and historically ("I brought you out of Egypt"). God here intends to show the people that he has moved them from where they were *then* to where they are *now*. There is no going back. Thirdly, God reminds them of the harshness of their lives in Egypt ("out of the house of slavery"). They should hear what he has to say next as the voice of a loving and liberating Father (cf. Exod 4:23.) For this reason, Vos says, Isaiah would later tell the people of his day to constantly remind themselves of the exodus (Isa 51:2).[60]

Only after establishing such a God-ward orientation does God proceed with the command about right worship. He will not be known as a lawgiver before he is known as a loving and redeeming Father.[61] He gives laws, to be sure, but he gives them *as* Father and Redeemer. His people worship him alone because he is the only God who can *prove* his love, and he has.

Historical Relationship to Christ

The text predates Christ's coming by many centuries, but the text is a revelation of God's nature as redeeming and sovereign God. Such revelation only occurs by the grace of the Word who makes the Father known (John 1:18; Matt 11:27). Christ is present prosopologically (see below) even if he is not present incarnationally.

Christ Prophetically

Much could be said about how the exodus and following law prophesy Christ. The exodus is a type of the Christ-event and its soteric goal, hence the apostle's relating the events at 1 Cor 10:1–11. Further, Christ did not come to abolish the law but to fulfill it (Matt 5:17). These reflections explain the structure of Matthew's Gospel: He shows Christ as the embodiment of new creation (3:16–17), the successful Israel (4:1–10), the law-giver (5:1—7:27), and so on.[62]

---

60. Vos, *Biblical Theology*, 110.

61. Compare Reeves, *Delighting in the Trinity*, 19–21, and his engagement with both Barth and Athanasius, the former wanting to protect God from *merely* being thought of as the Almighty and the latter fighting for God's triune goodness because his opponent (Arius) was turning God into a law-giving despot. As Reeves shows, and as the point above argues, missing the fact that God intends to be heard and obeyed as redeeming Father, not merely as law-giving despot, is deadly. The gospel would be lost.

62. See Wright, *New Testament*, 402. See also 63 of the current project.

Christ Prosopologically

As already mentioned, Jesus said that the revelation of God's nature only comes as he, the Son, reveals him (Matt 11:27). John's statement that the Son "makes known" (Gk. *exēgēsatos*) the Father (John 1:18) is most likely interpretive not only of the events surrounding Jesus of Nazareth in the first century AD but of all of prior redemptive history. Some Old Testament figures were able to glimpse God to a lesser degree than the Son sees: Abraham met with God (Gen 18), Moses "saw God" (Exod 33:11), and Isaiah "saw his glory" (John 12:41; cf. Isa 6). So why does John say that no one has seen God if the Son has made him known? The answer must be that the Son, by theophonic condescension, has always been the means of knowing the Father, but in the incarnation, Christ makes the Father known to the fullest degree possible and known to the whole man.[63] In short, when Old Testament believers beheld the glory of God, they beheld the Son's revelation. In the New Testament day, the Son revealed in a new way (historically speaking). Via hypostatic union with human nature, the Son invites humanity to enter into a spiritual fellowship with him that was earlier unprecedented. The word was before a command on tablets on which to meditate (Josh 1:8) and to be taken into the heart (Deut 6:6), but in the incarnation, the Word effectively *entered* the heart of believers (Jer 31:33; Ezek 36:27; cf. 1 Thess 2:13; Jas 1:21).

Preparing the Church for the Final Christ-Event and Subsequent Glory

On the final day when all will confess that Jesus is Lord, which Paul says is the explanation of "every tongue will confess to God" (Isa 45:22–23; cf. Phil 2:10–11), there will be absolute clarity that there is only one God and that his son is Jesus the Savior.[64] The church confesses Christ as Lord and Savior in the present (Heb 3:6) so that they are prepared for that day. The saving God of the exodus will be known as the true God of the parousia. Further, since believers live lives that parallel the enslaved Jacobites in Egypt, God's deliverance of the latter is a strong encouragement that he will deliver the former, too.

---

63. This assumption seems to be back of patristic exegesis which sees the Old Testament as the voice of Christ. See Carter, *ISGT*, 148–58.
64. See Bauckham, *Jesus and the God of Israel*, 41–45.

TYPOLOGICAL REALISM APPLIED, PART 1

Display God's Nature and Glory

The pairing of the introduction and first commandment of the Decalogue seems to act as an effective example of a redemptive-historical/theological orientation. God's redemption is put on display alongside God's nature as the one true God. The text displays his perfection and happiness in its emphasis on God's redeeming his people so that they will live with him in holiness. There were no actual threats to his purpose because whatever he pleases, he does (Ps 115:3; 135:6). Such ability displays both his utter magnificence as the true sovereign with no real rivals and, as Piper has famously articulated, an example of his "delight in being God."[65] Here we have the God who acts out of his perfect nature, accomplishing his will without any rivals. His people are the recipients of his sovereign grace.

Wisdom

Psalm 133:1: "Behold how good and pleasant when brothers dwell in unity."

The historical occasion of Ps 133 is uncertain, though it is likely a celebration of Israel's unity during worship festivals (as a Psalm of Ascent). However the psalm is historically situated, the main is not difficult to ascertain: Brotherly unity among believers is *good* and *pleasant*, a true blessing from God, the blesser.

Relationship to the Christ-Event

This text predates Christ's coming by several centuries. So the psalm, though suggesting the blessing of godly love among believers, awaits the fuller Christian love of the New Testament.[66] Nevertheless, even pre-Christ, the great blessing of God-centered unity occurs at times, as the psalmist experienced entering Jerusalem for the feast. Such joy is God-given (implied by the illustrations of vv. 2–3) and therefore a participatory type of the inner-Trinitarian love into which the cross invites people (cf. Rom 5:8).

---

65. See Piper, *Desiring God*, 31–50.

66. Jeremiah's new covenantal promise that the people will not "teach each other saying, 'know the Lord,' for they will all know me" (Jer 31:34) seems to preclude a definite unity of heart and mind among them. It would be odd if Jeremiah's point was that there will be no teaching in the new covenant.

Christ Prophetically

Christ unites a people together by giving them "the unity of the Spirit and the bond of peace" (Eph 4:3). Whereas God called Israel to be a unified people under his rule, the fulfillment does not come until Christ makes a people who, notwithstanding ethnic and socioeconomic differences, are truly united in one global family (1 Pet 2:8–9).[67] Jesus's own presence is promised to the two or three who gather in agreement in his name (Matt 18:20). Hence, John's emphasis throughout his first letter is on love being the distinguishing mark of Christians.

Christ Prosopologically

The psalmist's inspired expression of praise at the blessing of loving unity is the Word's affirmation of the graciousness of the presence of church family. Christ communicates then and throughout all generations that to enjoy such fellowship is *right*. As the believing community constitutes the physical "hands and feet" of Christ in the world (1 Cor 12), it enjoys the blessing in an even fuller sense than the psalmist did, though the psalmist's social joy at the festival should not be minimized. After all, he hymnized it.

Preparing the Church for the Coming Christ-Event and Subsequent Glory

The context of an ascent psalm articulated during a feast gathering hardly needs much explanation as forward-looking and eschatological. The feasts are primarily forward-looking to the Lord's Supper[68] and secondarily forward-looking to eternal glory.[69] The joy of unity at these God-centered feasts is meant to stick with believers so that they "set their hope on the grace that is to be revealed" at Christ's return (1 Pet 1:13). These Old Testament feast songs set believers' eyes forward to the glory to which they sojourn. They also consider Israel's "ascent" to God's presence in Jerusalem a picture of their own ascent up the ladder between heaven and earth, which is the Lord himself (John 1:51).

---

67. See the discussion of this topic in Jobes, *1 Peter*, 154–59.
68. See Danielou, *From Shadows to Reality*, 126–30.
69. See Fairbairn, *Typology of Scripture*, 3.3.

Display God's Nature and Glory

There is, finally, a theological horizon to consider. Humanity, made in the image of the Trinitarian God, thrives in community with others and begins to die when isolated.[70] But this thriving only occurs insofar as God is treated as the true God. Here, at the feast, or later in the New Testament during the church's time at table, where this unity is put on display, the unity of the Father with the Son and his Spirit is reflected beautifully.[71] The joy at God-centered unity is a picture of God's own triune unity within himself.

This is why Jesus, through the upper room section of John 13–17, encouraged and prepared his disciples for what came next by placing emphasis both on love as their distinguishing characteristic and on how he has united them with himself and the Father for this exact purpose. "Love one another . . . by this all people will know that you are my disciples" (13:34–35). Their love for each other, being a uniquely life-giving love, not only sets them apart but acts as a witness to Christ's presence among them (Matt 18:20).[72] He called them to a life of fruit-bearing and prayer *so that* their bonds of unity will be strong (John 15:17). He also prayed for their unity (17:21) so that their oneness reflects that of the Father and the Son (17:23) and leads to believers being filled with the same love that the Father and Son have shared eternally (17:26).

The anointing of Aaron, which the psalmist uses as a descriptive symbol for the joy of worshiping unity, was itself a special anointing only reserved for the high priest.[73] Worshiping unity is, thus, sacred, and it feels as such. There is indeed "encouragement in Christ . . . comfort

---

70. Dallas Willard defined the "life" that Jesus talked about (when he said "if you would save your life . . .") in terms of "relating to others in action, motion, and exchange." Thus, Willard concludes, "Decay begins in isolation." *Spirit of the Disciplines*, 56–66.

71. Such a concept is an application of ideas found in Aquinas and Bonaventure, explored by Davison, *Participation in God*, 102–3. Aquinas's concept is that all creatures have a "trace of the Trinity" in and on them, seen in their being. Bonaventure developed the point further to say that as humanity lives and exists, it "reflects, represents, and describes its Maker, the Trinity" (*Breviloquium*, 2.12.1). It could be said that the creation is, functionally, a mirror to God, and sin, being a refusal to participate with God, is humanity's attempt to hide from the reflection.

72. Worth mentioning is Tertullian's famous teaching that nonbelievers in the ancient world often exclaimed about the Christians: "See how much they love each other!" Cited in both Ryle, *Expository Thoughts*, 53; Carson, *Gospel According to John*, 485.

73. See Spurgeon's notes in *Psalm 120–150*, 168–69.

from love" (Phil 2:1–2), and there is certainly connection between this anointing from the Psalter and the anointing referred to in the second chapter of John's First Epistle, the epistle written so that love among the brothers would become the evidence of one's being "born of God."[74] This anointing which all the believers have (2:20) gives knowledge and teaches the truth (2:27). Later, the Holy Spirit *is* the truth (5:6). So the upper room teaching, so focused both on love and on the Holy Spirit, is not focusing on two different themes but on cause and effect: The presence of the Spirit, who is Christ's very presence among the believers, will himself teach love and fellowship in a way that is a compelling witness to the world. As Christians enjoy each other's presence as the Lord's very presence, they experience a taste of the joy and glory that the Father and Son share eternally (John 17:5).[75] In that sense, horizontal relationships act as a reflection of the vertical relationship between people and God.

New Testament Book: Revelation

The final example of typological realism will be an entire New Testament book. As aforementioned, doing so is not intended to be arbitrary but is intended to show the versatility of typological realism to biblical studies. As noted, the warning of Rev 22:18–19 (to not "add to the words of this prophecy") is intended to refer not only to Revelation (though that is the original context) but to the entirety of the canon since Revelation *must* be the final book in the canon.[76] The Apocalypse completes canonical revelation because it focuses readers on how to understand the events of their day in light of their great hope: the return of Christ the second time. In keeping with the previous chapter's assertion that the beatific vision is the goal of all of life and reality, and therefore the types are meant to

74. See Stott, *Tyndale New Testament Commentaries*, 59.

75. Interesting are Ryle's criticisms of the church for its lack of manifesting this long-suffering and hope-filled love towards one another through the centuries (Ryle, *Expository Thoughts on John*, 53). That said, it should be noted that whereas John placed such a premium on love as the proof of Christ's presence, the beloved disciple also was exclusionary toward those who do not agree with the apostolic message (especially in 1 John 4:6, but also 2:19; 4:1–3; 5:12; 2 John 10). Love without the truth cannot truly be love because God is love. To get God wrong is to get love wrong. To get love wrong is to get God wrong, too.

76. See Grudem, *Systematic Theology*, 64. Grudem notes the linguistic parallels between, on the one hand, Deut 12:32 and Prov 30:6, both concluding major Old Testament sections by saying "do not add to this," and the same thing in Rev 22:18 at the end of the New Testament.

TYPOLOGICAL REALISM APPLIED, PART 1

point forward to the vision, Revelation is an especially pertinent example to place under the light of typological realism.

Relationship to the Christ-Event

John's Apocalypse was written in the first century to several local churches in Asia Minor using the Old Testament apocalyptic style (e.g., Ezekiel and sections of Daniel and Zechariah). The churches were established by gospel proclamation, which is why the identity of Christ is put on such rich display throughout the first several chapters: Revelation 1 is enamored with Jesus's person and work, and chapters 2 and 3, a series of letters written to seven local churches and addressed to their pastors, has Jesus introducing himself using highly theological language.[77] Hence the churches are told to wait expectantly for Christ's return, as sure that he will return with glory as they are sure that he came the first time with humility (2:7, 11, 17, 26–27; 3:5, 12, 21; 22:20). Types have been antitypified, but even these antitypes double as types that still await the eschatological antitype.[78]

Christ Prophetically

Christology is a central concern throughout Revelation; in fact, it characterizes Revelation.[79] Revelation's purpose might appropriately be called *therapeutic Christology* in that it focuses on Christology to heal the worries and fears of his followers. Hence, it ends with Christians responding to Jesus's promise that "I am coming soon!" with "Come Lord Jesus, come!" (22:7, 20).

If Morris and Greg Beale are correct, Revelation is written according to what the former calls the *synchronic* method, which the latter calls the *recapitulation* method.[80] Both terms mean the same thing: Revelation is a series of cycles that consecutively tell the same story from different angles and with different emphases. This structure is similar to Jesus's own explanation of the kingdom using consecutive parables (e.g.,

---

77. See Morris, *Drama of Christianity*, 38.

78. Thus Morris's point that Revelation is written engaging Old Testament language in light of New Testament events. Morris, *Drama of Christianity*, 13–14.

79. Morris, *Drama of Christianity*, 16–17

80. See Beale and Campbell, *Revelation*.

Matt 13) and Daniel's repetition of the unfolding of history until the establishment of the Davidic messiah's kingdom in Dan 2 and 7.[81] In this schema, the cycles, following an introduction in chapter 1, run from chapters 2–5 (cycle 1), 6–7 (cycle 2, etc.), 8–11, 12–14, 15–16, 17–19, and 20 and conclude with chapters 21–22 as epilogue. In this schema, much of Revelation is understood as telling believers what they are to expect in their lives of faith using *symbolic* language.[82]

The significance of Revelation's structure to the question of how it witnesses to Christ is this: Every cycle either assumes or makes explicit Christ's victory gained in his first coming and concludes with an even greater victory in his second coming. In between these two events is a great battle for the souls of believers, though the book is written so that believers will be confident in their own safety. Because believers are rooted securely in Christ, they can be confident in their safety as battles rage throughout time, thus the presence in every cycle of consolation flowing from the believer's assurance in Christ's finished work (5:9–12; 7:14–17; 11:15–18; 14:4–5; 15:3–4; 17:14; 20:5–6). Their victory in him is sure, though their experience of it is less full (as the battle continues) than it will be in the end. Each cycle does end, however, with victory, culminating in the glory of the epilogue. The type-antitype framework to explain reality characterizes the Apocalypse.

Christ Prosopologically

The book is entitled "the Revelation of Jesus Christ" (1:1a), meaning that it is itself the voice of Christ speaking by his Spirit to the churches. Hence every letter in chapters 2 and 3 begins with Jesus explicitly saying he is speaking and ends with "hear what the Spirit says to the churches." In this sense, like the Old Testament, Revelation is both a word about Christ and the word of Christ himself. Similarly, Revelation must be Jesus's testimony because it calls itself prophecy (1:3), and "the testimony of Jesus *is* the spirit of prophecy" (19:10; emphasis added).

---

81. Morris, *Drama of Christianity*, 27.

82. See Beale's case for a pro-symbolic reading in *Revelation*, 10–11. There, he makes a strong case that *semaino* in Rev 1:1, translated in the ESV as "made it known," is a clear indication that the book is purposely symbolic. His ground is that the context of the other uses of this word through the NT and the LXX always demands that the word be understood in terms of symbolic communication. Beale draws special attention to its use in the LXX version of Dan 2.

TYPOLOGICAL REALISM APPLIED, PART 1

Preparing the Church for Subsequent Glory

The preparatory nature of Revelation cannot be overstated. It is given "to show [Christ's] servants what must soon take place" (1:1b) so that they will be ready, strong, and obedient (1:3) in the coming difficulties. Beale has a helpful chart that notes the clear parallels between what is promised to the local churches of chapters 2–3 and those things coming to their glorious fulfillments in the glory of chapters 21–22.[83] The point is that churches experience a lower form, in word and institution, of that glory that awaits them in the beatific vision, which they will experience if they patiently walk with the Lord in the present. In this sense, the phrase "he has freed us from our sins by his blood," placed at the very beginning of the book (1:9), is seen as having an eschatological fulfillment in 5:10–12 (to end cycle 1), 7:14 (to end cycle 2), and 14:1–4 (to end cycle 4, calling Jesus "the Lamb" repeatedly), among others. Sinners will be left out of the coming glory (21:8) so that the godly, clean in the work of the risen Lamb, can enjoy eternity with the Father and the Son. Freedom has both present (believers *are* freed) and future (believers *will be* freed) aspects.

Display of God's Nature and Glory

The use of Old Testament themes and imagery throughout Revelation, written post-Christ-event, affords the student a rather profound insight: Given that God repeats his revelatory Word using many of the same words and themes, with the only difference being chronological advancement toward his goals,[84] the sameness of revelation's content suggests God's sovereignty over the events of history and happiness whatever the chronological location of the stage.[85] When Scripture says that Jesus is "the same, yesterday, today, and forever" (Heb 13:7), it refers to his eternality and therefore the eternality and immutability of the Trinity's perfect plan.[86]

---

83. Beale and Campbell, *Revelation*, 26–27.

84. "In both Revelation and other parts of the NT, these realities [that is, main prophetic themes in both OT and NT] are seen to have already *begun* to be fulfilled in Christ—believers as the new creation, the church as the new Israel, and so on. These prophetic realities are then *consummately* fulfilled, especially as envisioned in 21:1—22:5"; Beale and Campbell, *Revelation*, 34. This is not a stretch; Revelation is a sort of miniature biblical theology.

85. Beale and Campbell, *Revelation*, 33.

86. 1 Pet 1:20–25 and its use of Isa 40:6–8 seems to have this in view as well.

CHRIST AND THEOLOGY

As seen throughout this project, thematic continuity between the Testaments has been the subject of considerable biblical-theological scholarship, because the scriptural content seems to be so concerned with showing thematic development.[87] Continuity via thematic similarity, when considered in light of escalation from before Christ's first coming to after and before his second, builds faith. Such continuity is probably why Carter said that "the Christological interpretation of the Old Testament *is* . . . the gospel of God."[88] When the student of Scripture sees the Scripture as a typologically structured, Christ-centered unity, he has understood the gospel, and thus what he is to believe if they would "believe in him for eternal life" (1 Tim 1:16; cf. John 20:30–31).[89] Scripture's "story," then, is an invitation into a soul-feast on God's working out his plan and purpose across time. Thus Herbert McCabe has said that Christ's coming, living, and dying *is* the eternal procession of the Son from the Father, "the triune life of God projected onto our history, or enacted sacramentally in our history, so that it becomes story."[90] Scripture,

---

87. See Boersma, *Scripture as Real Presence*, 81–104; Goldsworthy, *CCBT*, 111–49; Vos, *Eschatology of the Old Testament*, Appendix; Beale, *New Testament Biblical Theology*, 887–957. Development of biblical themes is the topic throughout Beale's work, but the second to last chapter, starting on 887, is a summary worth the book's price. In each resource, though perhaps written from different hermeneutical perspectives (especially comparing Boersma to Goldsworthy), the writers labor to show that the Old Testament prophets spiritualized the language and themes of earlier Old Testament revelation to point forward to the eschatological messianic day. The implication—sometimes explication—is that the New Testament's unavoidable spiritual reading of the Old was not an innovation but a continuation of Old Testament practice. For a more technical treatment of this subject, see Schnittjer, *Old Testament*, 865–67.

88. Carter, *ISGT*, 141; emphasis added.

89. Worth noting, in light of works like Hays's *Reading Backwards*, written to show that Christ recapitulates both the Old Testament God *and* people of God in the Gospels, is that John 20:30–31 seems to have greater depth than is sometimes assumed. It might not be that John's point is that reading the Gospel account by itself stirs faith (though it certainly could, because Christ's words are spirit and life, John 6:63) but that reading it with a working knowledge of the Old Testament's portrayal of God and his people leads to the conclusion that Jesus solves the Old Testament problem.

Thus, Hays argues for such a reading of Mark's introduction: The "beginning" (*arke*) of the gospel (1:1) is knowing the Old Testament promise of God's appearance (1:2–3), prepared by an Elijah-like prophet (1:2, 4–8), which is then followed by Jesus's exodus-like (and creation-like) baptism (1:9–10) and his Israel-like time of testing in the wilderness (1:12–13) where he tames animals, showing he is the true Adam (1:13b), only to return to civilization (like Moses) and preach the fulfillment of the promise of the Davidic messianic kingdom in himself (1:14–15). See Hays, *Reading Backwards*, 15–20.

For the proposal of an Old Testament "problem" and Jesus's being its only solution, see Wellum, *Person of Christ*, 35–50, 53–55.

90. McCabe, *God Matters*, 48.

then, invites those hungry for truth to witness God's saving glory in his saving acts.

Conclusion

This chapter has sought to show typological realism in action as an exegetical method. Hopefully the reader agrees that by asking the aforementioned questions of the text, both redemptive history and theology are given their due importance, and the gospel—what Jesus has done and is doing to bring about a new creation according to God's eternal purpose—is the dominant feature of exegesis, casting its light on all else. When the gospel is exegetically central, exegesis is evangelical, continuing and developing the Great Tradition.[91]

To summarize the method, first, God's redeeming work in the person of Christ is the central event of redemptive and revelatory history, so it must be the subject of the first question. Second and third, given that Christ is both the telos of the text's prophetic witness and the original speaker of the word via prosopology, the text must therefore be exegetically oriented forward (historically) and upward (theologically). Since exegetes lives in time and space, chronological orientation to Christ's comings (both his first and second comings) helps rightly prepare them to see and hear his voice in questions 2 and 3.

Fourthly, since believers are in a time of both antitypes and types, the method appropriates the medieval *quadriga's* fourth question: How does the text, being both from and about Christ, prepare the church for the final antitype, the beatific vision? The goal in this question is not, to borrow from a common colloquialism, to be so "heavenly minded that one is no earthly good," but to be properly oriented to the glorious end that all believers seek (Rom 8:24). The Spirit is the presence of the end in the present (2 Cor 5:5), and thus Christian life is, by nature, the appropriation of the end into the present. Christians are *only* of "earthly good" if they are heavenly minded in this way.

Fifth and finally, how does the text show the listener that God is happy, perfect, and satisfied in his glory as his plan unfolds as purposed? This question is not that far removed from the question of what the theological message is of the text, engaging classical theism. How does the typological orientation of questions 1–4 demonstrate the *real* of God's eternity, and

---

91. See Goldsworthy, *GCH*, 33; similarly, see Bird, *Evangelical Theology*, 21 .

the mind of the Logos? Without question 5, the method is merely typology. This question orients typological exegesis philosophically, considering how the text witnesses to what is real and actual in God.

To approach the text in a way that asks all these questions is to attempt to bring together both redemptive history and theological interpretation. To be historically and theologically oriented must, by definition, set the eyes both forward and upward, as in typology: It shows how God, revealing from eternity into space and time, reveals the lesser in earlier times and the greater in latter times, showing redemptive progress to encourage and assure his followers. "Lesser" does not imply "insignificant," for the messianic day promised has come, proving God's faithfulness, which requires earlier promises made. "Promises fulfilled and promises kept," as a paradigm, requires both clauses as a unit. The glory that came with Jesus (John 1:14), which remains with his people (Matt 18:20), is, however, of such a lesser extent than the final glory that the Holy Spirit, himself the presence of Christ, is everywhere called the down payment of the coming glory (2 Cor 1:21; 5:4–5; Eph 1:13–14).[92] The presence of the Spirit with the Christian, being the presence of the glory itself, is typological of the glory of the fullness of God's perfect presence in the final day of the Lord. Believers, by their faith (*inauguratory* type) in Christ (*consummatory* antitype), glory in and rejoice in him (1 Pet 1:8–9) while still waiting for his return and their future glory and joy (1 Pet 1:13) (*final* antitype). Hopefully, typological realism as an exegetical method is a help to live in such a reality, as it is God's reality.[93]

---

92. For a good theologically oriented treatment of this, see Davison, *Participation in God*, 127.

93. It is clear that there are parallels between typological realism and the *quadriga*, especially as the latter is explained by Aquinas (*ST*, 1.1.10; see also Kreeft's helpful notes in *Summa of the Summa*, 48–50). Over the course of this project's research, it became clear that Aquinas's construal of the *quadriga* is very similar to the sort of exegetical orientation and practice that typological realism seeks to be.

Two points, however, are worth making: First, a method with parallels to Great Tradition exegesis is not a negative but exactly a positive given this project's scope. The goal in the first chapters was to identify whether or not there are similarities between biblical theology and the exegesis of the tradition. To respond to those findings with a proposed method that has similarities to both seems to be a fortunate development, and unseen.

All of this to say, secondly, typological realism is not *exactly* parallel to the *quadriga*, and the careful eye should see this. Exact correlation is missing in at least two ways: First, if the *quadriga* establishes the literal sense as the control of the latter senses (spiritual/allegorical, tropological, and anagogical), typological realism says that Christological and theological considerations provide the context of the literal sense. It is

TYPOLOGICAL REALISM APPLIED, PART 1

The current day is a day of both antitype (since Christ has come and left his Spirit with all of his continued graces) and type (since Christ still has yet to return to complete the work that he has begun). The final chapter will place the final piece of the typological realism puzzle: application. It will thus engage Vos's assertion that the Old Testament theophanies are typological of the New Testament presence of the Spirit, who is himself typological of the full presence of the Lord in the last day. Given that the Spirit is both the indwelling presence of the Trinity and empowerment for believers to appropriate Trinitarian living, the last step in the process will be labeled *typological participation*.

---

likely that Augustine and Aquinas would agree with this—their works seem to suggest that they do. Typological realism tries to make explicit what they did not in the hope that, responding to Boersma, history will remain a reflection of and participation in the eternal real. In typological realism, theology is the context of chronology and redemption; spiritual truth contextualizes the literal sense.

Finally, whereas the *quadriga* seeks a Christological sense via allegory, typological realism goes one step further, seeking also a theological sense. Attempting to take seriously the importance of both redemptive history and theology, the method engages redemptive history by making Christ its center and the Trinity its source. It seems questionable whether the *quadriga* was ever explicit in doing this. Clearly Aquinas explained the appropriateness of multiple senses in light of theological considerations. The method did not include a theological sense like typological realism does.

7

Typological Realism Applied, Part 2
Christophanies and the Spirit-Driven Life

> "For Paul, the Spirit was regularly associated with the world to come, and from the Spirit thus conceived in all His supernatural and redemptive potency the Christian life receives throughout its specific character."
>
> —Geerhardus Vos

This project will conclude with one final consideration, a practical one. Research for this project began with an initial question: What, if anything, does Christ-centered biblical theology have in common with the Great Tradition generally and Reformation hermeneutics particularly? Several chapters argued that Christ-centered biblical theology further develops the redemptive-historical orientation of Great Tradition hermeneutics, even if theological considerations are often passed over. Given that Christ-centered biblical theology is guilty of sometimes overlooking theology, the next several chapters urged a bringing together of biblical theology and its redemptive-historical orientation with theological interpretation and its ontological orientation. To be thus oriented both forward (as in biblical theology) and upward (as in theological interpretation) logically begs for a typological framework since typology is both upward and forward-focused.¹ Therefore, the most recent two chapters have sought to consider how typology is both theological and redemptive-historical: Types are God's means to reveal in time and space that which will reach its final culmination in the beatific vision, where God will be seen "as he is" (1 John 3:2).² In that sense, the typological nature of revelation is both progressively historical *and* eternally theological: Historically, types and their corresponding antitypes are revealed over time; theologically, they reach their end when God is beheld in the beatific vision.

Thus, the final chapter will build off of a section in the previous chapter. That chapter considered Vos's construal of theophanies/Christophanies as primarily eschatological. Vos's construal is pertinent because of the theophanies' typological import and thus how they relate to the Christian's experience walking with the Holy Spirit, who is, as Gordon Fee has said, the "empowering presence of God."³ The question proposed in this chapter is, "What is the nature of the relationship of the Christophanies in the Old with the Holy Spirit's presence in the New and redemptive participation?" This chapter pursues an answer to this admittedly loaded question.

Christophanies as Prophetic of Two Aspects

Geerhardus Vos, in his posthumously published *Eschatology of the Old Testament*,⁴ which is an collection of his lecture notes, study notes, and incomplete manuscripts, asserts, consistent with the rest of his body of work, that all of revelation is to be thought of as eschatological.⁵ That is,

---

1. Chase, *40 Questions*, 56. Chase argues that typology moves both horizontally and vertically. It seems to be the case that what Chase calls "vertical typology," Boersma refers to in sacramental terms, where what occurs in time and space points to what is in eternity (see his *HP*). Though Boersma's work shows that he is clear on typology's importance, he construes typology according to his sacramental orientation to reality, which might distinguish him from other evangelical typologists.

2. A helpful, brief treatment of the importance of typology to the study of the beatific vision in the Christian tradition can be seen in Boersma, *SG,*, 6–13.

3. See Fee, *God's Empowering Presence*.

4. Vos, *Eschatology of the Old Testament*.

5. See also the quote in Olinger, *Geerhardus Vos*, 306: "Eschatology is the essence of true religion as it is shown by its pre-redemptive existence." Such a perspective is not original to Vos, but finds classical expression in Augustine, *City of God* 9–18. Oort's comments are helpful in "The End Is Now."

God's revelation is oriented toward the eschatological day of the Lord in which he, as promised in the Old Testament prophets, will make himself known in a special and decisive way. "The Lord whom you seek will come into his temple" (Mal 3:1). Vos's study (or, more accurately, studies) of Old Testament texts commences with a Christological orientation given to each of them (hence the titular "*Eschatology* of the Old Testament").

The seventh study in Vos's work sees him considering "The Eschatological Element in the Theophanies." Vos takes as a presupposition that "Revelation in the patriarchal history foreshadows eschatology along the line of redemption." Within this context, the theophanies are personal representations of God in visible form which "express, in primitive form, God's approach to and communion with man." Vos argues that "with respect to the future, the theophany presents the renewal of the paradise-condition and as such presages a full future paradise."[6] One may rightly conclude that Christ's coming, the inaugural God-with-man event (Matt 1:21; cf. Isa 7:13), is that to which the theophanies point: The eternal God appears in some kind of physical way to have dealings with man whom he intends to redeem and involve in his redemptive activity. Hence Matthew's Gospel, beginning with Jesus's identification with the God-with-us Immanuel name (1:21) from Isa 7, ends with Jesus involving the disciples in his global redemptive project, encouraging them with "I am with you always, until the end" (28:20). Below will consider such participation. The current priority is to understand exactly what the theophanies typify. Primarily, they typify two aspects, the first which has two elements:

Christ's Coming and Subsequent Giving of Holy Spirit

The apostles show how Christ's coming is the antitype to God's revelatory theophanies in the Old Testament:

- John uses the terminology of *tabernacle* to describe the glory revealed in Christ (John 1:14).[7] The assumption seems to be that Christ is the ultimate end of the earlier revelation of glory at the tabernacle (cf. Exod 40). He is the perfect version of that earlier glory.

---

6. Vos, *Eschatology of the Old Testament*, 85.

7. For a helpful study of both the typological and practical significance of the "tabernacle" language in John's introduction, see Pink, *Exposition of the Gospel of John*, 33–39.

- Paul says that the rock that traveled with—leading, following, etc.—the Israelites in the wilderness was Christ himself (1 Cor 10:4). Paul seems to unequivocally see Christ's presence in the pillar and fire theophany. The type—the pillar and fire—points to the one who is the very source of its own existence, who would himself enter into creation in a future, more glorious way.

- Peter cites the words of God at Sinai, calling the people a "chosen people, a royal nation . . ." (Exod 19:5–6), as finding fulfillment in Christians who draw near to God through Christ (1 Pet 2:9). Whereas the promise in Exodus was conditioned on Israelite obedience (Exod 19:5), Peter applies it to Jewish and gentile Christians as an unconditional reality. The implication must be that, based on Christ's obedience on the peoples' behalf, all who believe in him receive the fulfillment of the promise.[8]

More could be said about the New Testament's relating the Old Testament theophanies to what has occurred in the Christ-event, but the point seems clear: The New Testament uses earlier revelatory events categorized as theophany or Christophany to explain and give meaning to Christ's coming generally and Christ himself particularly.

But if, as Vos says, the theophanies presage Christ's coming, they also indirectly presage his sending his Spirit. The theophanies are expressions of God's coming, which is the very content of eschatology.[9] As mentioned above, in the theophanies, God appears before humans in order to redeem them and involve them in his redemptive activity.[10] One similarity between the Old Testament theophanic moment and the New Testament Spirit-possession is that they both demonstrate God's veiled redemptive presence in time and space to reestablish the Edenic God-with-man state (hence the presence of the Holy Spirit in John 14:18–24). Conversely, whereas in the Old Testament Christ is present in a sort of

---

8. Hence Peter's very next section is devoted to the believer's responsibility to obey authority figures *for the Lord's sake* (2:13–17.) The implication is clear: Jesus was submissive to the authorities out of obedience to the Father (2:23), thus giving Christians' call to obedience the perfect example and motivation. Christ, by his submission to the Father, proved his chosenness and preciousness. If believers follow his example, they will, too.

9. Vos, *Eschatology of the Old Testament*, 86.

10. Vos, *Eschatology of the Old Testament*, 86. Vos helpfully adds the point that the theophanies put on display God's friendly nature toward his redemptive subjects. It is difficult to ignore Jesus's own statement to his disciples in preparing them for their mission after he leaves, that he calls them friends (John 15:15).

hybrid spiritual-physical way, coming and going from time to time, in the New, he is present physically for a definite (though relatively extended) time before physically exiting, leaving his Spirit with his people *indefinitely* (that is, until he returns physically). In both the Old and the New, he is able, by his appearing, to empower his redemptive "partners." But in the New, he remains with them in an empowering way. In the end, Christ will remain present with his people in both spiritual and physical ways, with no further redemption required.

This seems to be precisely what Vos meant by asserting that the Spirit-filled Christian possesses "partial eschatological privileges."[11] Possessed by (and possessing) the Spirit who "belongs to the next world," the Christian advances the Lord's presence and power beyond its Old Testament reality in a way that still presages that which is to come in the final glory.[12]

This might be one way in which, as Boersma has said, the Old Testament everywhere bespeaks the reality of the Christian life.[13] Theophanies occur to establish fellowship and involve the receiver in the mission of God. As such, the theophanies are life-changing and ministry-empowering. The reader can certainly detect a parallel in Christ's giving of his Spirit in the New Testament, which is also life-changing and ministry-empowering. Further, the giving of the Spirit is life-*giving*. "Whoever follows me, *out of his heart* will flow rivers of living waters" (John 7:38; emphasis added). Believers themselves are the channels through which Christ gives life to the dead.[14] It is in this sense that Vos wrote that the kingdom is primarily experienced in the current day in spiritual terms. Christ's giving physical liberation during his earthly life meant to demonstrate that he will do the same when he returns again in fullness. Until then, God's kingdom is primarily a spiritual experience, apprehended via delight in God's truth unto transformation of life (Rom 14:17).[15]

---

11. Vos, "Eschatology of the New Testament," 980.
12. See Vos, "Eschatological Aspect," 94–95.
13. Boersma, *Scripture as Real Presence*, 54.
14. For an insightful and brief consideration of Jesus's words here and their explanation of discipleship as partnership between him and his followers, see Willard, *Renovation of the Heart*, 204–5.
15. See Vos, *Teaching of Jesus*, 49–52.

Christ's Final Return

As seen in a previous chapter, Adrio König argued for a construal of the end time that is multi-staged.[16] Under such an understanding, the end sees Christ realizing the Old Testament goal, first, *for* humanity/believers in the Christ-event, which is then followed by two future stages: Christ realizing the goal *in* humanity (in the intermediate time between Christ's first and second coming; as Boersma says, during Christ's secret coming,[17] in which Christ sanctifies believers by his Spirit), and finally Christ's realizing the goal *with* humanity (in the final Christ-event, when believers take thrones alongside him.)[18]

This helps to explain Goldsworthy's insistence, following Donald Robinson, on a hermeneutic that emphasizes a Christ-centered continuity across the biblical redemptive narrative anchored in the Christ-event and how it reconfigures all that came before.[19] If the story is in fact one larger, unfolding story, one should expect great continuity in the form of parallels across the narrative. Similarly, Vos argues that Jesus's teaching, centering on the coming of the kingdom, relates to "two aspects of the same kingdom, not to two separate kingdoms."[20] If the message of the Bible is the establishment of the kingdom of God,[21] the meaning of any particular text cannot be ascertained outside of its relationship to the kingdom and its king, Jesus. He gives continuity and sensibility to the narrative.

That said, although there is continuity and parallelism across the various stages of kingdom establishment, the scope of Scripture's teaching is that Christ's final return will consummate that which is most glorious

---

16. See König, *Eclipse of Christ in Eschatology*.

17. See Boersma, *Pierced By Love*, 203–6.

18. For the future hope of believers reigning with Christ, see Dan 12:3; 1 Cor 6:3; 1 Pet 1:8; Rev 21:14

19. See Goldsworthy, *Gospel and Kingdom*, 125–27, and his fuller treatment in *CCBT*.

20. Vos, *Teaching of Jesus*, 32–33.

21. Again, following Goldsworthy in *Gospel and Kingdom* and *CCBT*. Worth mentioning is the difference between the Goldsworthy/Robinson approach and that of other covenant (biblical) theologians. Chapters 4 and 5 of *CCBT*, has Goldsworthy distinguishing between his three-step revelatory approach to biblical theology and the epoch-driven approach of covenant theologians Vos and Clowney. According to the former, Goldsworthy and Robinson assert that the centrality of the Christ-event to God's purposes necessitates its centrality to the Bible's continuity. According to the latter, representing traditional covenant biblical theology, covenant is the center point of continuity.

of what can be imagined. The goal will have been reached fully in the beatific vision.[22] In a similar but fuller way than God's condescended revelation via theophanies, the beatific vision will be no less than creature's fullest possible enjoyment of God, even if the creature can never totally know God's essence as he himself does (1 John 3:2 translit. "we shall be seeing him as he is").[23] Thus, the continuity across the biblical narrative is best construed as typological: Earlier glory (in Old Testament theophanies and oracles) prepares for and points to later glory (New Testament revelation of Christ and the Holy Spirit), which then prepares for and points to later glory in its fullest form (the beatific vision). At every point in the story, believers can be sure that they have seen the glory in some purposeful form, even though the glory will come in greater fullness later.[24] In this case, the fullness of the end will be the fullness of what came at all earlier stages in partial form.[25]

Now that the nature of the typological relationship of the theophanies to their future glory has been considered, another consideration moves into the foreground: the nature of the believer's participation with

---

22. See chapter 5 of the current project.

23. The concept of fully redeemed man *seeing* in John's verse seems to fit the implied difference stated above: Fully redeemed man will know God as he is, but he will never know God to the same extent that God does. Man's experience is centered in the text around seeing, and this sight will be a full sight inasmuch as man is capable. Still, God does not "see as man sees" (1 Sam 16:7), and this distinction continues eternally.

Worth considering is Boersma's concluding thoughts to his survey of the beatific vision through the Tradition in *SG*, 428–30. According to Boersma, in the end, redeemed humans will have such a transfiguration of the eyes and the intellect that they will behold God's glory in ways that are difficult to comprehend currently. Proposing such a transfiguration of eyes and intellect is far from proposing an equation between fully redeemed human eyes and intellect on one hand and those of God on the other. Still, the advance, based on the apostles' words, will be of such a substance that it is difficult to explain other than to say, "We will see him as he is." This seems to be an instance where theology allows mystery based on exegesis of God's word.

24. For Vos's treatment of this purposeful and perfect nature of revelation at all points, see chapter 5 above, and Vos, "Idea of Biblical Theology," 1–24.

25. It is probably the case that the transfiguration of Luke 9 deserves brief treatment here. Moses and Elijah, who experienced theophany on mountains in the Old Testament (Moses, Exod 19:3; Elijah, 1 Kgs 19:9), in Luke 9 stand again on a mountain and speak with Christ. A case could be made that this was not their first time seeing Christ on a mountain. The takeaway from God's perspective is, within time and space, "This is my Son: Listen to him!" Now anyone reading the Gospel account is summoned to both listen to the mountain voice and behold the glory of the one speaking there, which Moses and Elijah earlier had heard and beheld (hence 1 John 1:1–4). Peter, in stirring up believers' hope in their glorious future of kingdom dwelling, cites the transfiguration for motivation to listen to Christ who spoke and still speaks (2 Pet 1:11–17.)

God through them. As seen in the aforementioned consideration of Vos's work on the eschatological nature of the theophanies, said theophanies always occur in the context of God involving people in his work: He reveals glory to so transform the life of the subject that they will follow him and lead others to follow him. This motive is detectable in the theophanies given to Abraham (Gen 15; 18), Jacob (Gen 28:10–17), Moses (Exod 3:1—4:17; 19:3–25), etc. In each case, God draws in chosen instruments who will be instrumental in future redemption. The theophanies are thus not only revelatory but participatory. In response to Vos's aforementioned consideration, is this type of participation the same as what was to come under the dispensation of the Holy Spirit? Put another way, do Spirit-indwelt believers experience the same kind of participation that the theophany-drawn leaders of the Old Testament did?

Typology and Redemptive Participation

Recent evangelical theology has seen a renewed interest in participatory ontology, thanks in no small way to the work of *ressourcement* from thinkers and theologians like Boersma[26] and Davison.[27] Although both define participation in Platonic terms, both also see it as the obvious conclusion of a biblical ontology. Paul's quotation in Athens, "In him we live, and move, and have our being" (Acts 17:28), is a common and pertinent proof text. Davison, therefore, defines participation in terms of "perceiving all things in relation to God, not only as their source but also as their goal, and as the origin of all form and character."[28] That is to say, as Davison further develops, that since all that exists, being created *ex nihilo*, is dependent on God for "life and breath and everything" (Acts 17:25), all that exists continually derives its being from God, receiving from him all things that are. All creatures, without exception, are what they are because they receive their being from God.[29] Whereas God "is being by his own essence," yet "every other being . . . is a being by participation."[30]

---

26. Boersma, *HP*. Boersma's work has helped popularize the work of twentieth-century Catholic ressourcers Jean Danielou (1905–1974), Henri de Lubac (1896–1991), and Yves Congar (1904–1995).

27. Davison, *Participation in God*. Worth mentioning are also Gorman, *Participating in Christ*; Owens, *Shape of Participation*.

28. Davison, *Participation in God*, 1.

29. Davison, *Participation in God*, 22.

30. Davison, *Participation in God*, quoting Aquinas in *Summa Contra Gentiles*

So the very act of existence is itself an act of participation in God, or, as Calvin said, "subsistence in the one God."[31] God is what God is without any help, but creatures, by their very existence, are what they are in the mind of the God, who knows all things perfectly.

Further, creatures not only participate in God in their being but in their actions. Since creatures constantly get their being from God, their power to act continually comes from him. Aquinas said, therefore, that "every operation should be attributed to God, as to a first and principle agent."[32] God is, and God acts unto causation; so, creatures exist, then act. Such is the order of existence and action. History is a Christ-centered plan that unfolds according to an immutable plan. People can choose to do evil and thus not participate in God.[33] But in the end, in some sense, peoples' actions will serve God's ultimate purposes (as clarified both in Joseph's words in Gen 50:20 and those of Peter in Acts 2:22-23).

Boersma spends considerable time explaining such an understanding of history as the unfolding of God's purposes in his *Scripture as Real Presence*.[34] If history is the working out of God's purposes in time and space, as this project has argued, not only can history not be understood apart from him, but neither can being and essence. Only Jesus gives understanding and clarity to existence, and any other construal of the nature of reality would lead to a false start. This Christocentric framework is the foundation for a general participatory ontology.[35]

But the purpose of this section is to describe redemptive participation. Davison ably makes the case that the purpose of redemption is not only the removal of enmity between God and man but the perfecting of man so that people become, by gracious participation, like God. As Gregory said, all that Christ assumes, he heals.[36] Redemption is not only

---

2.15.5. Worth mentioning is also Aquinas's comments in "On the Divine Simplicity" in *Disputed Questions of the Power of God*, 7, quoted in McInerny, *Thomas Aquinas*, 291.

31. Calvin, *Inst.*, 1.1.1. Battles translation. The Beveridge translation is slightly different, calling human being as "subsistence in God alone."

32. Aquinas, *Summa Contra Gentiles* 3.67.4, quoted in Davison, *Participation*, 218.

33. See Davison, *Participation in God*, 239-59.

34. See Boersma, *Scripture as Real Presence*, 1-26.

35. This project's scope does not allow for a consideration of the analogy between God's being and essence and those of humans, as opposed to the univocal understanding of much of modern theology. The interested reader, for a more abbreviated treatment, is referred to Boersma's *HP,* 68-83, and for a fuller treatment, see Oliver, "Introducing Radical Orthodoxy," 3-27; Pickstock, "Duns Scotus," 116-46.

36. Quoted in Davison, *Participation in God*, 266.

legal, although it is that, but it is practical, that is, *participatory*. God heals what is broken in man, cleansing what is dirty in him, so that God can dwell in man and involve man in his redemptive activity.

This seems to be in view in Peter's explanation of the outpouring of the Spirit at Pentecost in terms of Joel 2:27–28: As seen earlier, whereas theophanies occurred so that people will lead people to God via prophecy, the Spirit had been promised so that the current generation would prophesy God's word (Acts 2:17–21). The Spirit enters into people so that they will take the message that they have heard and preach it.

But, as Davison shows, not only will believers *preach* the word, but they will *live* the word as new creation. Just as Christ called on his followers to embody the "perfection" of the Father (Matt 5:48), Paul says that salvation is not only by the death of Christ but also by his resurrection: "Much more shall we saved by his life" (Rom 5:10).[37] Not only does Christ count believers righteous, but he works to *make* them righteous.[38] There is considerable transformation of their lives, even if it is not exhaustive until the final Christ-event occurs (1 John 3:2; Col 3:3).[39]

So, believers' redemption by Christ's death and resurrection and subsequent in-filling of the Holy Spirit will be seen in that they, like Jesus, are evangelistic (Luke 4:14, 18), and that they, like Jesus, via gracious transformation by his Spirit (2 Cor 3:16–18), image the Father in their character (John 14:7–9). How could such an experience be called anything less than redemptive participation? Dallas Willard seems correct to have said that to become a Christian is to "heartily join [God's] cosmic conspiracy" to participate in God's redemptive project.[40] God is, as Paul said, reconciling the world through his Son and doing so through the message which his Son's followers bear and share, as it were ("God making his appeal through/by us," 2 Cor 5:20). Such an appeal is not only explicitly evangelistic but is reinforced by the character content of the believers' lives (Matt 5:16; 1 Pet 2:12). In such senses, believers participate by the Holy Spirit in the ministry that belongs to Jesus as he the vine supplies sap unto fruit-bearing for the branches (John 15:1–10).

---

37. Davison, *Participation in God*, 280–284.

38. Davison, *Participation in God*, 295.

39. The pastoral implications of what comprises the preceding paragraph were taken up by Willard in *Spirit of the Disciplines*, 28–43. The attentive reader will detect in Willard's work a pastoral application of exactly what comprises Davison's theological contribution.

40. Willard, *Divine Conspiracy*, 90, 188.

They are by grace becoming more characterized by what Jesus called a greater righteousness through their faith in the one who fulfills the law (Matt 5:17–20).

Vos develops this "greater righteousness" in two of his sermons, "Hungering After and Thirsting for Righteousness" and "The More Excellent Ministry."[41] In the latter, Vos, preaching 2 Cor 3:18, shows the superiority of the new covenant to the old, emphasizing that the new is more abundant in forgiveness and practical righteousness and thus able to transform the subject truly.[42] Therefore, the former sermon, which preaches Matt 5:6, shows that the new covenant believer filled with the Spirit has a true desire to please God and to, as Abraham was charged (Gen 17:1), walk blameless. Such blameless walking is characterized by walking "as to have the thought of God's presence and supervision constantly in mind, and to shape one's conduct accordingly."[43] There is here not only a practical change in conduct but, since conduct follows character as actions follow motivation, a true change in heart.[44] Believers, though not exhaustively redeemed, have been decisively changed so that they long for God's glory the same way that God does.[45] Such change of motivation will be simultaneously an internal experience and an outwardly visible reality. Worth wondering is whether Vos would argue that this is what Jesus meant when he told his disciples that whoever follows him will do "greater works" than he himself does (John 14:12). Perhaps a more puzzling statement from the mouth of Jesus is hard to find, though the disciples themselves were puzzled by a lot of what he said (e.g., Matt 16:7; John 4:33; 16:29). It is possible that Jesus was making a participatory point: These greater works will be his very work *in them*, which is a line of teaching that he further develops through the remainder of John 14 and into 15. He will continue his work in the world,

---

41. See Vos, "Hungering," 38–57; "More Excellent," 98–120.

42. Vos, "More Excellent," 113–14.

43. Vos, "Hungering," 44–45. The New Testament concept of moral blamelessness, whether a translation of *amemptos* (1 Thess 5:23), or *amomous* (Eph 1:4, Jude 24) always carries an eschatological orientation with it, vis a vis, that believers will be truly blameless when they come to judgment either through death or Christ's return. It does not seem to be the case that the New Testament authors have in view a forensic blamelessness, if the context of the passages is considered. It might be worth a fuller amount of attention on a separate project to examine the ways in which a believer is guaranteed blamelessness on a moral level when they approach final judgment, if it is the case that all believers still sin and are not practically perfect in this life (Jas 3:2; 1 John 1:8–10).

44. See Vos, *Reformed Dogmatics* 1.4.3.

45. Vos, *Reformed Dogmatics* 1.4.3.

defeating his enemies, setting captives free (Luke 4), and involving his followers in ways that would be difficult for them to imagine.[46]

Such redemptive participation, being itself that of which the Old Testament prophets spoke and thus the antitype of the Old, is nevertheless typological of that which will come later. Although there is still "work" to do, there will come a day when the work will be complete. This point might be why Paul said that on that final day, God will be "all in all" (1 Cor 15:28), though the current day is characterized as a day in which, in the church, "Christ is all, and in all"[47] (Col 3:11): The supreme value of the Trinity is characteristic of both days, but the current day values Christ's indwelling presence by his Spirit (Col 1:27) in a way that will be unnecessary to the final day, for the work will be complete.[48]

The distinction is also held in the Lord's own teaching. He said that he will go to prepare a place for his followers (John 14:3) while in virtually the same breath saying that he and the Father will come and make their home in the lives of believers via the Holy Spirit (14:23). What is the difference? The former will be the consummated perfection; the latter describes the inaugurated perfection: his presence in believer's fleshly lives is spiritual but shot through with weakness of the flesh (2 Cor 4:7, "jars of clay"). His presence in the place which he is preparing will be full and complete, beyond spiritual. Hence Jesus could say that he himself *is* the way to which he is going (John 14:6): Via his *spiritual* presence, which empowers, his followers travel to his *perfect* presence. The current experience is simultaneously the hope of the Old Testament prophets while being also preparatory for that in which New Testament believers hope: "In this hope, we were saved" (Rom 8:24).

Richard Gamble has shown that via redemptive participation, Christians' works contribute to the glorious antitype in the end (the final Christ-event). Still, says Gamble, the eschatological success of these

---

46. This explanation was articulated well by Alexander MacLaren in *MacLaren's Expositions of Holy Scripture*.

47. Theodoret noted the parallelism of the "all in all" phrase between these texts, though their reference is to different aspects of Christian doctrine. See *Cambridge Bible for Schools and Colleges*, "1 Cor 15:28."

48. See Boersma, *SG*, 257–69 for a discussion about the difference in opinion between Calvin and his predecessors regarding whether Christ remains Mediator into eternity. Doubtless, the supreme value of Christ's work at the cross is never forgotten but remains the continued reason for his praise (Rev 5). There seems to be some debate about whether the Lamb continues mediating. It appears to be an "in-house" disagreement among believers.

labors will not be fully known until then. Christians work by faith—faith working through love (Gal 5:5)—sure that the current work will partially comprise the glorious tapestry of joy in that day.[49] Thus Jesus promises reward for faithful living and stewardship (Matt 25:14–30; Luke 19:11–27); elsewhere Paul concludes his great resurrection chapter with a charge to work because such work is "not in vain" (1 Cor 15:58). Of pertinence, Paul's call to this work begins with *hoste*, translated by virtually every English translation as "therefore," indicating that the charge is an application of the previous discussion. Given that the previous discussion centered on the truth of the resurrection and the hope that it gives to believers to set their attention on future glory, one may conclude that the work—the "good works" that God has prepared for them to do (Eph 2:10), whether a degree of fruit-bearing that can be characterized as thirtyfold, sixtyfold, or a hundredfold (Matt 13:23)—has an end-orientation. Paul's "therefore," then, presupposes a redemptive participatory ontology: The apostle seems to be concluding his argument by saying, "Since Christ lives eternally and we live eternally in him, our work is not in vain but is headed somewhere glorious, and is indeed his very work in and through us."

In this way, believers can begin to understand how they experience what Vos calls "partial eschatological privileges."[50] Being indwelt by the Spirit to which the Old Testament prophets looked and who is himself the presence of the next world in the present,[51] believers live in between the "already-occurred" and the "not-yet." Jesus is the answer to the Old Testament's question (i.e., "Who shall ascend the hill of the Lord?", Ps 24:3) such that in him, light comes to the nations (Isa 11:1–11). Paul locates the Christian's calling in Christ's own calling to be a light to the nations: Whereas the servant to whom the Father spoke in Isa 49:5–7 must be Christ,[52] Paul took it as finding ultimate fulfillment in Christ's followers via evangelism and godly living shining light throughout the world: "For so the Lord commanded *us*, saying, 'I have made you a light for the Gentiles'" (Acts 13:47; emphasis added). The train of thought is

---

49. See Gamble, *Whole Counsel of God, Vol. 2: The Full Revelation of God*, 658–59. Worth noting is Gamble's own stated dependence for this point on Vos, *Pauline Eschatology*, 660n3.

50. See Vos, "Eschatology of the New Testament," 26.

51. See Vos, "Eschatological Aspect," 95–96.

52. Note v. 7: "Thus says the Lord, the Redeemer of Israel *and his Holy One*" (emphasis added). The anointed is involved in the very speech of the God of Israel.

similar to what came under the old covenant: Just as God delivered his people through the participatory actions of those to whom he earlier appeared theophonically, God shines his light through people in the gospel age. The difference is that the light shines from believers because Christ, by his Spirit, is actually living in them in a redemptive way. Hence he can say that *he* is the light of the world (John 8:12; cf. 9:5; 12:36) while also teaching the disciples that they are the light of the world (Matt 5:14). His life has so become the spiritual presence inside of them that the possession of divine light is not either Christ's or the Christian's but the possession of both: They are in him, and he is in them (John 17:23); "Christ is in you" (2 Cor 13:5).

How Victorious Is the Believer?

The new covenant experience both contains a greater degree of glory than what came before and is still typological and awaiting fulfillment. Again, as Vos says, the eschatological privileges which the believer enjoys are only *partial*. The Spirit who dwells in them belongs to the "next" world (the true and glorious world)[53] and is present in the current world insofar as believers live by faith in the Son who is in the heavenly abode in the present. Vos shows that the presence of the Spirit in the believer proves that the believer belongs to the "higher life" toward which they journey. Although they are not yet present there, they are on their way there. The Spirit is the guarantee of its possession (2 Cor 1:22, 5:5; Eph 1:14; 4:30).[54]

This Vosian construal of the prominent "already-but-not-yet" understanding of the kingdom begs the question about what extent of victory the believer has. Vos asserts that natural religion errantly concludes that the presence of the Spirit via Christ must equal a fully eschatological present.[55] In such a construal, there would be an absolute sense of victory over all hindrances to joy and happiness. Without minimizing the natural desire that all people have for such a reality, Vos answers by noting that in the aforementioned texts, Paul insists that the Spirit has to do with the life *to come*: He is the guarantee of the eternal possession. Through him

---

53. Vos develops this idea in *Teaching of the Epistle*. Vos echoes of the sacramental view of reality that permeates the Great Tradition, and which Boersma unpacks in *HP*.

54. See Vos, "Eschatological Aspect," 115.

55. A more conservative version of what Vos labeled an overly optimistic ontology could be seen in the work of N. T. Wright. See especially *Surprised by Hope*; *Simply Jesus*.

alone believers await the hope of righteousness (Gal 5:5), and if believers sow to the Spirit, they reap eternal life (Gal 6:8).[56] Believers' longing is well founded, though this hope will not—indeed it cannot—be fully satisfied in the present age.

Their victory in the in-between is primarily spiritual, not exhaustively physical, which will come in the end. Until then, believers find themselves in bodies of death (Rom 7:24–25). Nevertheless, they know, by hope, that the presence of the Spirit guarantees that these bodies will one day reach the resurrection glory that Jesus has already experienced (Rom 8:11). In that day, as Vos once preached, "The covenant climax will have been reached, every sacrament shall fall away, and our fruition shall be of God within God; we shall at last be like him, because we know him as he is."[57]

Purpose of the Typological Structure to Reality

All that has been said about a typological understanding of reality (and therefore a typological orientation to hermeneutics) leads to a philosophical question: Why? That is, why does God craft time and space with a typological structure? If God is perfect, needing nothing, why create anything in the first place, and further, why order and direct it to particular ends by particular (that is, typological) means? And finally, how does this relate to participation? If the Lord's hand is not shortened so that it cannot save by itself (Isa 59:1), why involve believers via Spirit-indwelt participation? What follows will offer several answers to these questions.

To Do So Glorifies Him

John Gill (1697–1771) gives a helpful answer, worth quoting at length:

> God is a most perfect being, entire and wanting nothing; he is El-shaddai, God all-sufficient; the perfections of God are, indeed, displayed in the creatures in a glorious manner; *but then these displays are made not for his own sake, but for the sake of others; nor does he need the worship and obedience of angels or men; nor does he receive any additional pleasure and happiness from them* . . . Who hath first given to him, and it shall be

---

56. Vos, "Eschatological Aspect," 125.
57. Vos, "The Wonderful Tree: Hosea 14:8," 56–57.

recompensed to him again; for of him, and through him, and to him are all things?[58]

In Gill's quote, one sees that in the utter self-sufficiency of God, his outgoing acts never constitute the remediation of a divine need. He is perfect, and as such, *happy*. A preliminary answer to the questions above could be that since God's outward works are all gracious, his goal is to share his goodness and glory with others. To do so pleases him.

The first verse of the John Mason hymn "Thou Wast, Oh God" offers an even more succinct answer:

> Thou wast, O God, and Thou wast blest
> Before the world begun;
> Of Thine Eternity possest [*sic*]
> Before Time's glass did run.
> *Thou needesst none Thy praise to sing,*
> *As if Thy joy could fade:*
> *Couldst Thou have needed anything,*
> *Thou couldst have nothing made.*[59]

To Mason, similar to Gill, neither creation nor providence are the result of a need in God. In fact, if God needed anything, he could not have created. Such a claim might seem strong, but it is sensible given the nature of the creational act as the initiation of the existence of that which did not previously exist. As Davison says, only God can be said to be both the origin and the agent of creation: Only he can create *ex nihilo*, out of nothing.[60]

So then, why, if God does not need anything, did he choose to create in the first place? Both aforementioned quotes, whether Gill's systematic answer or Mason's hymnic one, agree with Jonathan Edwards's and Greg Beale's simple shared answer: that God creates, rules, and redeems for the sake of his glory.[61] But the pertinent question for this project concerns, particularly, how the typological structure, which centralizes redemptive participation, glorifies him. This project has asserted that as God unfolds

---

58. Gill, *Gill's Complete Body*, 171; emphasis added.

59. Emphasis added.

60. For a full treatment of creation *ex nihilo*, see Davison, *Participation in God*, especially chapters 1–3, where Davison compellingly argues that God is not just the cause of all creational existence but the cause of all causes within that creational existence. Worth also considering is Augustine's treatment of God being the source of all things in *On Predestination*.

61. See Piper, *God's Passion for His Glory*; Beale, *New Testament Biblical Theology*, 955–56.

revelation along a typological line, he shepherds along his people who listen to him, leading them in paths of righteousness for his name's sake (Ps 23:3). So how is his name glorified from within the typological structure of reality?

Whereas the concept of God's glory is oft-prioritized in evangelical circles, it is often done so, albeit well-meaningly, without very clear definitions. Nevertheless, again, Vos is helpful:

> *What, in distinction, is God's glory?*
> The revelation of the perfections of God, outwardly, like brilliant light.[62]

God's glory is the outshining of his perfections. When he creates, his perfection as wise and sovereign is on display. When he redeems, his perfection as merciful redeemer is seen. When he shepherds, his perfection as patient and all-wise is seen. It is seen in his creational, providential, and redemptive acts which his perfection is put on display. In these ways, he is glorified in his post-volitional eternity and outward movements.

This is part of why Boersma, reflecting on patristic exegesis, says that for the early church's leaders, reality's typological structure is grounded in providence. That is, Christ is not only the antitype of earlier types but is first the archetype that gives life to and precedes all other things. Boersma shows that theologically, the Christ-event, being the culmination of the eternal plan of God, *precedes* redemptive history and all of its types and antitypes.[63] All of history moves toward the Christ-event and thus participates in some way in God's eternal purpose to glorify his Son. This mindset allows the historically progressive way of thinking about Christ's central place in the purpose and goal of all things, though this progress can only be understood in light of eternal realities that theologically precede the events themselves. In short, nature, including both the things seen and the things unseen, exist *by* Christ (and thus will not function properly unless oriented toward him) and *for* Christ (and thus find their goal in the revelation of himself in time and space).

But even further, as Matthew Levering has shown, history is "not only [a] linear unfolding of individual moments, but also [an] ongoing participation in God's active providence, both metaphysically and Christologically-pneumatologically."[64] So it is not only that history participates

---

62. Vos, *Reformed Dogmatics* 2.2.133.

63. Boersma, *Scripture as Real Presence*, 24–25.

64. Levering, *Participatory Biblical Exegesis*, 1, quoted in Boersma, *Scripture as Real Presence*, 24.

progressively in the Trinitarian glory by showing God's ability to fulfill his purposes as he earlier promised, but it participates *actually* in the fact that the Trinitarian glory is reflected in both type and antitype. The type has a redemptive purpose that, though not reaching its full maturity yet (and will not until the antitype comes), is still the revelation of the redeeming God.

For instance, the goat used for sacrifice during the Day of Atonement (Lev 16) is quite clearly a type of Christ the Lamb who removes the sins of the world (Matt 1:21; John 1:29), similar to the parallel (and thus typological identification) of the Passover lamb to Christ (Exod 14; cf. 1 Cor 5:7). This observation might lead one to assume, then, that the glory of the latter—Christ himself—so far surpasses that of the former, the type, that the former is not worth study, reflection, or contemplation.[65] But to say as much would not only neglect all of the New Testament texts that say that what was written in the Old Testament was written for Christians' sakes but dismiss that such an atoning act, even if typological, is a reflection of the providing-redeeming glory of God and the heavenly Zion which all believers will enter.[66] The type reflects the glory of the eternal God who reveals the way into his kingdom.

So the first reason that God employs a typological structure to reality is that it glorifies him by displaying his perfections. This glorification occurs in two senses. In the first, typology shows his perfection in faithfully unfolding his plan as he had said he would and in a way that demonstrates his wisdom. In the second, typology reflects the glory of ultimate reality, God himself as Trinity who creates and redeems to establish fellowship. With a clear understanding of both the nature of the Trinity and the role of typology in providence, believers who work with God via participation can check their beliefs, values, and actions for their consistency with the God who is and who acts, and thus ensure that they are truly participating in God's redemptive revelation and activity.

In short, his revelatory outgoing pleases him by inviting others to enjoy his perfections; the types-antitype structure is preparatory for believers' ultimate joy in the beatific vision.

---

65. One might consider the 2018 recommendation of widely influential pastor and author Andy Stanley that because of the resurrection, Christians ought to "unhitch" from the Old Testament. Stanley's comments are given a fair criticism by Mohler in his "Getting 'Unhitched from the Old Testament?'"

66. For a compelling reflection of the relationship between Leviticus and the heavenly glory awaiting believers, see Morales's *Who Shall Ascend*, especially 257–303.

Glory via Progressive Sense

The first sense mentioned above—the progressive sense, in which history unfolds to make clearer the real/res—is treated well in Danielou's *From Shadows to Reality*. Danielou showed that Christ's recapitulation of the life and experience of Old Testament believers and institutions is both an accomplishment and restoration of what Adam did. The importance of type and antitype can be under-considered if one misses their purpose: God wants to prepare his people for the coming perfection by prefiguring it in a demonstration of both the unity (that is, the types and antitypes are similar) and diversity of his plan (that is, the antitypes are developments on and from the earlier types).[67] To prepare believers for the glory awaiting them, God employs revelatory escalation, i.e., type and antitype. This framework both prepares his people for the glory awaiting them *and* reflects the glory itself that already is. The second sense follows (below), establishing the importance of a typological framework that minds the ultimate purpose of revelatory activity, namely, to reflect ultimate glory.

Glory via Theological Sense

The second sense—the theological sense, in which the types reflect the glory of ultimate reality, God himself as Trinity—is worthy of further reflection. Boersma has shown that typology is not just the historical unfolding series of events, though that is the context in which typology is revealed. Further, "typology . . . looks up from the types in history to their eternal archetype, the providential Word who has become incarnate in Christ."[68] That is to say that types and antitypes, revealed in the context of historical progression, are meant to be authoritative reflections of eternal realities that undergird and give meaning to that which is temporal. The types and antitypes, then, reveal the goal and res of all things. Boersma, therefore, has referred to God's time and space project as "God's fitting, Christ-shaped plan."[69] Since Christ undergirds and upholds all of reality (Col 1:16; Heb 1:3), one would expect the types, which point to and help explain him, to be numerous. Goldsworthy, therefore, in explaining the importance of typology, concludes that "there is no aspect of reality

---

67. Danielou, *From Shadows to Reality*, 31–34.
68. Boersma, *Scripture as Real Presence*, 25.
69. Boersma, *Scripture as Real Presence*, 25.

that is not involved in the person and work of Christ."[70] Hence, Goldsworthy shows, New Testament interpretation of Old Testament events, people, and places is dominated by a typological understanding.[71] God, via typology, uses experiential types to prepare the "sheep of His hand" (Ps 95:7) for that which would come later. The same goal is in view when Christians, who live in a unique type/antitype era, walk by the Spirit with decisive (even if not exhaustive) power over sin and the devil (Luke 10:20; 11:13): Such experience is actual interaction with and participation in God, though it is decidedly inferior when compared to the awaiting glory when the whole Trinity will be revealed and sin and the devil will be no more. The typological experience of walking with God by faith, by typifying the final experience of walking with God by sight, prepares the heart and mind by motivation to good works and cultivation of contemplative meditation on the God who is eternally glorious. Such meditation will arrive at its goal when the one meditating sees God. In the time of waiting (Rom 8:23; Phil 3:20), however, believers are still actively engaged with God's being and activity.

Explains the Importance of Earlier Scripture for the Christian Life

A second reason for a typological structure to reality is that, as Fairbairn has said, typology invests earlier portions of Scripture with more supreme value than otherwise.[72] That is, the whole Old Testament, according to Fairbairn, receives more of the Christian's esteem when they understand the bearing that it has on their faith as disciples of the One who is both the archetype and antitype of all that came before. This project has reflected extensively on what Paul meant when he insisted throughout his letters that what was written in the earlier days was written for New Testament believers and their faith journey (e.g., Rom 15:4; 1 Cor 10:4; 2 Tim 3:15–16). Typology turns historical narrative into opportunities for both doxology and godly application. As a brief example, the typological place of the temple in the history of the people of God not only shows Christ's glory as the dwelling place of God and man, but it further teaches believers to cleanse themselves (like the priests did upon entrance; Lev 8; 2 Chron 29) if they would enjoy the true fellowship with God that Christ

---

70. Goldsworthy, *CCBT*, 186.
71. Goldsworthy, *CCBT*, 175–76.
72. See Fairbairn, *Typology of Scripture*, 177.

came to give. Such a reflection further makes sense of believers' journeys towards final glory, which are marked by great exercises of sanctification (Acts 14:22). Why such trial? Because these trials prepare them, by faith in Christ through the Spirit in the immediate, to enter God's presence in the final day and enjoy his presence there.

Vos and the Usefulness of Typology to Discipleship

Finally, Vos is worth hearing once more. Following Goldsworthy's close identification of typology with biblical theology,[73] this section will conclude with a brief consideration of Vos's final comments from his inaugural lecture as Princeton chair of biblical theology. What follows is not an attempt to equate typology with Christ-centered biblical theology. Rather, in view of typology's central place in evangelical Christ-centered biblical theology, the goal is to show how this typological orientation, typological realism, reinforces Vos's paradigm of the usefulness of biblical theology.

For the sake of clarity, some brief comments are worth making regarding the general subject matter of Vos's lecture. First, it was his inaugural lecture when taking the first biblical theology chair at Princeton. The position was thought to be so important in the fight for inerrancy among Presbyterians and so suited to Vos's superior giftedness compared to others of his scholarly generation that a month after Princeton's initial call, follow-up letters were sent to him for three days in a row.[74] Given that biblical theology was itself at once a relatively new idea and subject to considerable misunderstanding, Vos sought in his lecture to give an overview of its usefulness to his future students who regard the Bible as God's word. With this goal in mind, he defined biblical theology as "that part of exegetical theology that deals with the revelation of God as an act of God, considering both contents and form."[75] Considering both contents and form, the *contents* concern redemption (including revelation of truth) from the God who is eternal, and the *form* is historically orientated, progressing by a consistent unfolding.

Later in the lecture, Vos offers a revised definition to biblical theology in which it is "nothing else than the exhibition of the organic progress

---

73. Goldsworthy, *CCBT*, 171.
74. Olinger lays out Vos's transition to Princeton in *Geerhardus Vos*, 60–68.
75. Vos, "Idea of Biblical Theology," 6–7.

of supernatural revelation in its historic continuity and multiformity."[76] Biblical theology has to do with the study of the progress of what God has revealed across time. Little effort is necessary to detect parallels between Vos's biblical-theological paradigm and this project's proposed typological paradigm. These parallels follow.

Typological Realism Shows the Organic Structure of Revelation

First, echoing Vos, typological realism as biblical-theological approach "exhibits to the student of the word the organic structure of the truth therein contained, and its organic growth as the result of revelation."[77] That is, the often (though not always) unexplained development from type to antitype shows that revelation is organic, moving at its own pace, and therefore the revelation of a faithful but surprising God.[78] Whereas the sermons of Acts (as one example) function as explanation of the unity of the biblical narrative, the type/antitype structure of the Scripture reinforces the message, showing how God moves the story forward and upward into greater clarity and enjoyment. Nothing could be more applicable to a believer: They are themselves on such a forward and upward trajectory as God shepherds them. They are growing in Christlikeness (upward) and moving chronologically closer to seeing Christ (forward). Their participation with and in him is a happy lot because of its positive development across time.

Typological Realism Shows Revelation's Organization

Second, echoing Vos, typological realism as biblical-theological approach stands against the rabid disorganizing tendency prevalent in biblical studies today.[79] The relationship of type and antitype demonstrates the same disunity seen in comparing a person's childhood picture with their adult picture. Whereas the pictures are of the person at different stages of life, the person is the same. Similarly, types are the earlier revelation of the same redeeming God who will, in later days, reveal the antitype.

76. Vos, "Idea of Biblical Theology," 15.

77. Vos, "Idea of Biblical Theology," 21.

78. It should be noted that Goppelt deals with typology's frequent subtlety, and rare explicitness in *Typos*, 61–104.

79. Vos, "Idea of Biblical Theology," 22.

Both type and antitype preach the same message, with the later making the ultimate purpose clear via *sensus plenior*.[80] Such acknowledgment of relationship across the canon unifies the revelation in a way that takes the Revealer at his word. Those will hear who listen to God's voice as he has spoken and still speaks to them via his word and Spirit (e.g., Heb 12:25).

Typology Gives Freshness to Old Truth

Third, echoing Vos, typological realism as biblical-theological approach gives freshness and new life to the old truth by "showing it in all its historic vividness and reality with the dew of the morning of revelation upon its opening leaves."[81] Typology does more than convey information. It *shows* the truth via typological images and then invites the reader to further consider the development of the images into their mature antitypes. Readers of Scripture are constantly encouraged to receive God's word with "historic vividness and reality,"[82] not only hearing how God saves his creation by his Son's person and work but seeing how he does so. Paul prays, therefore, that the eyes of the hearts of the Ephesians would be lit up to see God's power toward them (Eph 1:17–18). Typology is spiritually discerned, illuminating hearts' eyes and drawing them to place their joy in what they believe.

All of Scripture becomes the voice of Christ about Christ. Those trained for the kingdom, while enjoying new wine in fresh wineskins (Mark 2:22), are able to keep their faith fresh by hearing and helping others to hear both the old and the new of God's revelation (Matt 13:52).

---

80. Worth mentioning is Beale's assertion that, given the tendency to misunderstand and thus misuse *sensus plenior*, a better term might be "transformed organic development." Crystal clarity among the earlier receivers of revelation (that is, those who received the type) might have been impossible, and, as Beale shows, it is doubtful that the New Testament writers expected such clarity among Old Testament writers. As the story unfolded, however, the purposes of what came earlier became clearer. The meaning did not change, but it developed, taking on a sort of new life. Beale engages with Vos's well-known illustration of an apple tree starting off in seed form: The tree is contained in the seed, though it has not matured to tree form yet. When it does, the seed's purpose is fulfilled. See Beale, *New Testament Biblical Theology*, 955.

81. Vos, "Idea of Biblical Theology," 23.

82. Vos, "Idea of Biblical Theology," 23.

Typology, via Biblical Theology, Becomes the Foundation of Systematics

Finally, echoing Vos, typological realism as biblical-theological approach is the foundation and ultimate help for systematic theology.[83] Systematic theology concerns the grouping together of doctrines in a logically consistent way. Biblical theology, with its typological structure and trajectory, is the soil out of which the systematic plants grow. Typology is not first concerned with doctrines but with seeing what God has done. Once his actions have been seen, doctrine follows. Vos concludes, "Dogmatics is the crown which grows out of all the work that Biblical Theology can accomplish."[84] These two disciplines are not opposed to each other, as has often errantly been asserted.[85] Rather, they are, as previous chapters have shown, complementary, where typology provides the content of systematics, and then systematics lead the reader back to the typological structure to hear God, forming what Osborne has called a hermeneutical spiral.[86]

That is to say that typological realism tells the believer *why* they should believe what Christianity teaches; it calls to them with the voice of a preacher that says, "Look at the unity of the biblical redemptive narrative in type and antitype and the development therein. Consider the beauty of God's revelation in redemptive type and antitype and what it says about God.[87] Consider how worthy of attention is he who fulfills his promises and then gives his followers the revelation of their content and purpose in written form. Will he not graciously give his followers all things if he has given them his Spirit even now? Did he not indeed tell them the truth for their life and joy?" Once typology preaches the gospel, systematics can organize the gospel into logical doctrines theologically contextualized. Both are needed for the participant in God's redemptive project.

In summary, typological realism as hermeneutical and historical orientation is useful because of how it glorifies God appropriate to his revealed nature and worth. In glorifying God, such an orientation displays his perfections and keeps his people listening for his leading voice. By his

---

83. Vos, "Idea of Biblical Theology," 23.

84. Vos, "Idea of Biblical Theology," 24.

85. This might have been Gabler's point in his initial lecture on biblical theology. See chapter one above.

86. See Osborne, *Hermeneutical Spiral*.

87. See Webster, *God Without Measure*, 3. To Webster, the task of theology is to contemplate what the acts of God reveal about the being of God.

voice, types both prepare and instruct his people in several ways: Typology opens all of Scripture for believers' upbuilding, thus showing that no revelatory event is wasted. Typology demonstrates the organic nature of God's revelation and, thus, the consistency of his work across time. It gives organization to reality, thus showing that God is the God of order and peace. Finally, typology keeps old truth fresh. Perhaps most significantly, typology glorifies God by showing his faithfulness and wisdom in how he uses and organizes his time and space project, and by reflecting in redemptive ways the eternal glory that is the Trinity. In all of these ways, typology takes seriously both history and theology in the context of Christian discipleship on its way to the beatific vision.

Examples

The argument of this chapter has been that the presence of the Holy Spirit in the Christian age is both antitypological of the Old Testament theophanies and typological of the full presence of the Lord in the eschaton (1 John 3:2–3). If this is accurate, it is not inappropriate to centralize typology in biblical hermeneutics because not only is the Bible's revelatory structure typological, but the very nature of the Spirit-led Christian life is arguably the clearest example of typology. Considerable attention has been given to Boersma's acknowledgment of the typological structure to reality. This typo-centeredness comfortably brings together both redemptive-historical (Christ-centered) biblical theology and theological interpretation. Typology helps to understand how redemptive history and theology proper come together in the beatific vision.

What follows will be a few scriptural examples of this typological orientation. Included will be one Old Testament character, one Old Testament concept, and then two New Testament texts. Such a selection is not arbitrary but aims at showing typological realism's versatility.

Jacob

Jesus's famous conversation with the Samaritan woman includes a comment from the woman that betrays her peoples' rootedness in a historical connection to what is supposed to be Jacob's well (John 4:11–12). This is not the first time in John's gospel that Jacob is alluded to in Jesus's early ministry as forward-looking: Three chapters earlier, Jesus calls Nathanael "an Israelite in whom there is no deceit," doubtless anchoring Nathanael in his lineage from the once-deceiver Jacob (1:47). Thus Jesus concludes the conversation by self-identifying with the ladder/staircase that Jacob saw between earth and heaven (1:51): Jacob's experience of looking upward is also oriented *forward* to Jesus's entrance into time and space for redemption.[88]

This Jacobean backdrop contextualizes Jesus's statement to the woman who hoped that the messiah would come and give a clarity about life with God that had not been enjoyed until then. Jesus gives a lesson about worship "in spirit and truth" (4:24), to which she nervously responds is only possible when the messiah comes for clarity, to which Jesus concludes that he is no less than the messiah who gives clarity (4:26).[89]

The reason for these extended comments about Jacob in biblical theology is that when Jesus comes revealing God's glory "full of . . . truth" (John 1:14), Jacob's life can be understood, hence both the aforementioned New Testament texts clarifying the discipleship purpose of the Old Testament for believers (e.g., Rom 15:4) and Beale's recapitulatory understanding of the New Testament life compared to Old Testament believers: Old Testament believers' lives parallel and typify those of the New.

The beginnings of typology, then, are detectable in Jacob's story. The world as God's kingdom according to the New Testament is to be understood according to these primary points (although more could certainly be added):

a. God's relationship to people he created (Acts 17:26–29),

b. their need to be born again (John 3:3–7),

c. the teaching that God does indeed give new birth from above which is equivalent to circumcision of the inner person (John 6:63; Rom 2:24), always via a personal encounter with God, and

d. God has a people throughout the world which is impossible to number (Rev 7:9) who are indwelt by his Spirit (Rom 8:9–10).

One does not have to stretch to begin to see this framework in the development of Jacob's own story as he journeyed with God:

---

88. See Boersma, *Sacramental Preaching*, 154–66.

89. Both *Matthew Poole's Commentary* and the *Jamieson-Fausset-Brown Commentary* on 4:24–26 give helpful comments on this interpretation of the conversation.

a. God establishes relationship with him before he is even born (Gen 25:23).

b. Jacob undergoes a sort of new birth with a new name when he wrestles with the Lord (Gen 32:22–31)[90], which is later included in Jacob's own assessment of his life as being guided by God every day (Gen 48:15), meaning the new birth is God's doing. Further proving this point, Jacob experiences several direct encounters with God throughout his journey (Gen 28:10–17; 32:1–2, 22–31).

c. Finally, Jacob is multiplied through twelve sons and a daughter (Gen 30:25–43), which then becomes thousands within four hundred years (Exod 1:7).

Jacob's formative experience seeing the Lord at the top of the staircase (Gen 28:10–17) becomes the backdrop of Jesus's mission in the world. Again, this is why Jesus calls himself the stairway to heaven (John 1:51), implying that Jacob saw *him*. The fact that John elsewhere makes explicit that Isaiah saw Jesus's glory (John 12:41) should not be taken to imply, via John's silence about Jacob in 1:51, that he did not see him. After all, the staircase episode says that the Lord stood before Jacob (28:12), and the text is quite unequivocal that Jacob later saw the Lord in the wrestling match (32:30). Also true, as Moses learned, is that man cannot see God (Exod 33:20). John's glorious introduction concludes that although no one has seen God, the Son of God makes him known (John 1:18). The point seems to be, as Clowney has argued, that any revelation of God by theophany is actually, to some degree, revelation by Christophany.[91]

---

90. See Dempster, *Dominion and Dynasty*, 86–87.

91. See Clowney's case for many (if not most) of the Old Testament theophanies being Christophanies, in *Preaching Christ in All of Scripture*, 11–18. Clowney makes use of Anthony T. Hanson's work arguing for Jesus as the Old Testament "Lord," especially in his *Jesus Christ in the Old Testament*. A sample quote is Hanson's thesis that "the central affirmation [of the New Testament writers] is that the preexistent Jesus was present in much of Old Testament history, and that therefore it is not a question of tracing types in the Old Testament for New Testament events, but rather of tracing the activity of the same Jesus in the old and new dispensations" (quoted in Clowney, *Preaching*, 13).

Hanson's argument, adopted and reinforced by Clowney, makes use of several Greek Old Testament chapters where the term for God alternates between *kurios* and *theos*.

Clowney makes further note of C. H. Dodd's comment on Rom 10:12–13 that "wherever the term *Kyrios*, Lord, is applied to Jehovah in the OT, Paul seems to hold that it points forward to the coming revelation of God in the Lord Jesus Christ" (Dodd, *Moffatt New Testament Commentaries*, 14). Clowney notes that Hanson took issue with Dodd's comment being both "too sweeping and too tame." Whatever position one holds, Clowney concludes, the church's centuries-long struggle to explain clearly

This point explains why Jesus tells his disciples that whereas the Spirit has been *with* them, he will, once Jesus sends him, be *in* them (John 14:16): His Spirit has been present all throughout redemptive history, but in the Christian age, the Spirit will live *in* believers and never leave. Therefore Paul states that the glory of the gospel is that Christ is *in* believers, stirring up in them the hope of the glory which is coming (Col 1:27).[92] Christ's living in believers in the fallen world tells them that they are guaranteed to appear with him in glory (Col 3:4) and will be in him (Eph 2:6–7).[93] One sees in Jacob's experience of Christophany a type of believers' experience with Christ's presence, as well of believers' hope of glory. As Jacob journeyed by faith in the God who had loved him, he participated as an instrument in God's redeeming hand. Believers, by the Spirit, participate in a similar though even fuller way.

Jerusalem

Vos devotes a chapter of his *Eschatology of the Old Testament* to the Mosaic theocracy. Throughout the notes (seminary lecture notes gathered posthumously), Vos asserts the typological nature of the structure, content, and experience of the Israelites under theocracy. Given the future reign of the messianic king with its transformative effect on the world, what came earlier must be thought of as typological.[94] One example of such an understanding is the place of Jerusalem in God's economy. In the current day, says Vos, the Holy City "is center; offices, organization,

---

Christ's Lordship in relationship to the God of Israel was not due to any intellectual lack. Christ, being Lord of all, *is* the God of Israel and thus is present throughout Old Testament history in more ways than just typology. He is no less than the eternal Lord who steps into his creation to redeem it.

92. Elsewhere, Paul equates the presence of the Spirit with Christ's own presence: "Anyone who does not have the Spirit of Christ does not belong to him. But if Christ is in you . . . the Spirit is [your] life" (Rom 8:9–10a, ESV).

93. The phrase *en Christo*, used often in Ephesians, is used two times between 2:6–7 referring to the believer's glorious future with Jesus. Boersma deals with the difference between Edwards's and Aquinas's views of whether Christ remains Mediator into eternity; *SG*, 354–84. Regardless of the position a person adopts, two exegetical considerations should be remembered: First, Paul states that God will *continue* to show the riches of his grace towards believers *en Christo* (Eph 2:6–7). That is, the riches are shown *in Christ*. Second, the apocalyptic vision seems to at least *imply* that Christ's Lamb-ness remains the redemptive song of the redeemed throughout eternity (Rev 5:9, 12; 7:17; 11:15; 19:7). At the very least, Christ's work as Lamb is always remembered, even if, as Aquinas said, Christ will no longer mediate.

94. Vos, *Eschatology of the Old Testament*, 117.

peace, abundance, etc., are there." But in the messianic era, this whole experience will be "eternalized."[95] Vos therefore concludes by asserting that since Isaiah promises that all nations will come and rest in Jerusalem on the sabbath (Isa 66:20, 23), *which is a physical impossibility given the size of Jerusalem*, the city must be understood typologically. Similar to Robinson and Goldsworthy, Vos argues that the prophets were using the Old Testament *forms* to describe the eschatological-messianic essence.[96]

If Vos's framework is correct, Jerusalem would only be typological of the antitypological city of God throughout time, and finally, of the glorious city of Rev 21–22. This antitypological (spiritual) "Jerusalem" is the kingdom throughout the world until Christ returns as people come to rest in him by faith (Heb 4:3). One day they will enter the "heavenly Jerusalem" (Heb 12:24), that "Jerusalem above" (Gal 4:26). God's glory was earlier present in form in Jerusalem at various points, but his very Spirit is present in the later, intermediate time throughout the world among believers who in salvation partake of his very nature (cf. 2 Pet 1:4). Believers come to rest by faith in the spiritual Jerusalem until they one day reach final rest.

The Spirit's Life, and Resurrection in 1 Corinthians 15

Moving to the New Testament, the typological trajectory continues by observing Paul's treatment of resurrection in 1 Cor 15. Being risen from the dead, Christ "became a life-giving spirit" (1 Cor 15:45). The form of the Greek is aorist passive, so the verse could literally be translated as, "Christ *was made into* a life-giving Spirit."[97] The point is not that Christ was not physically resurrected, as the Gospels show clearly (e.g., Luke 24:39; John 20:27). Rather, as Vos shows, the point is that Christ came to identify with the work of the Spirit in redemption in a way that he did not before. That is, as Peter says in his Pentecost sermon, Christ is

---

95. Vos, *Eschatology of the Old Testament*, 118.

96. Vos, *Eschatology of the Old Testament*, 120–21. Also worth mentioning is Radner's helpful study of how Ps 118:22 is read in Matt 21:42, Acts 4:11, and 1 Pet 2:7 in a symbolic/figurative way. The *form* of temple-building was employed typologically for the spiritual house of God which the Son of Man will build. See Radner, *Time and the Word*, 260.

97. Emphasis added.

himself the one who imparts the Spirit (Acts 2:33) who alone can give life (John 6:63).[98] In this sense, Christ became a life-giving spirit.

But to say as much is not to imply that the giving of the Spirit unto spiritual life is *all* that Christ intends to do. When he returns, he will transform the bodies (Gk. *sōma*) of his Spirit-indwelt followers to be glorious like his (Phil 3:21).[99] Clearly, then, the Spirit-transformed life is typological of the gloriously transfigured life. The Spirit, as Vos shows, relentlessly puts the glories of the future before believers, stirring them up for what is coming: "These things, God has revealed to us by his Spirit" (1 Cor 2:9–10).[100] Just like the Christophanies and types under the Old Testament were preparatory for the Christ-event, the spiritual presence of Christ under the New is preparatory for the coming Christ-event. Believers participate with and in Christ's life as they wait for the end.

1 Pet 1:8–9, and Enjoying Christ More and More

The opening paragraph of Peter's first letter is a favorite of many believers over the centuries to describe the Christian hope. Believers are born again to a living hope (1:3), to an eternal inheritance for which they are guarded by faith even as they experience trials (1:4–6). The trials are purposeful to test faith, and thus, to prepare for the coming glory which, perhaps surprisingly, includes believers' own praise (1:7). So although believers have not ever seen Jesus (physically), they love and believe in him (1:8), rejoicing with a joy that "obtains the outcome of [their] faith, the salvation of [their] souls" (1:9).

The pertinent question can be stated thus: In what sense do believers *obtain* their faith's outcome? Is this a future-looking reception or a present experience? Commentators take different stances. Calvin says that the purpose of using the word translated as "receiving" is so that believers will set their attention on the future glory and thus free their hearts

---

98. See Vos, "Eschatological Aspect," 105–7.

99. According to Luke and John, whereas the disciples saw Christ post-resurrection, the majority of them did not immediately recognize him (Luke 24:37; John 20:12–13; 21:4; see also Matt 28:17). The glory was such that although he could be known, a definite transformation had occurred. His transformation seems to be an example of the transformation of the physical self that all believers will experience in the "redemption of their bodies" (Rom 8:23).

100. Vos, "Paul's Eschatological Concept," 115–17.

from the present world that so captivates them.[101] Karen Jobes seems to take a similar stance, though she is less definite in her comment, putting the emphasis on what believers' faithfulness will "ultimately result in," namely, "praise, glory, and honor *when all is said and done*."[102] Jobes leaves her comment without any statements about the present.

Neither Calvin nor Jobes seem to be incorrect in what they assert: Believers' joy in Christ will one day reach a zenith, as 1:7 makes clear. Nevertheless, Peter's direct point in 1:8–9 seems to place emphasis elsewhere. The original for "receiving" is *komisomenoi*, used ten other times in the New Testament to refer to receiving something. In this case, it is used in present middle participle form, suggesting a present reception. Grudem, therefore, argues that the reception of the salvation, spoken in context of the future reception of full salvation, is meant to be taken as witness to a *progressive* growth of joy. Believers experience "a progressive obtaining of more and more of this 'goal' or 'outcome' to which their faith leads."[103] Though believers do not see the Christ whom they will see one day, they believe in and rejoice in him; in so doing, they experience in lesser form what they will experience in fullness in the end. Here the typological trajectory of the New Testament explanation of revelation is witnessed again: Believers are sprinkled with Jesus's blood (1:1–2)—the clear antitype of Moses's sprinkling Israel with blood in covenant confirmation (Exod 24:8)—as well as baptized, which is the antitype of the flood of Noah's day (3:19–21). Their present rejoicing in Christ is itself typological of the fullness of joy that is theirs in the end. Shortly thereafter, Peter reminds them that they are to set their hope fully on the grace coming in that day (1:13).[104]

---

101. Calvin, *Commentary on Hebrews*, 36.

102. Jobes, *1 Peter*, 96. In this case, 1:8–9 are explanation to 1:7. Emphasis is added.

103. See Grudem, *Tyndale New Testament Commentaries: 1 Peter*, 67.

104. Also worth mentioning is Kenneth Wuest's 1 Peter translation, speaking of Christ, "in whom now not yet seeing yet believing you are to be rejoicing with an inexpressible and glorified joy upon the occasion of your receiving the promised consummation of your faith, which is the final salvation of your souls." *The New Testament: An Expanded Translation*, 549. It seems that for Wuest, Peter's words betrayed a vagueness in the distinction between present experience and future glory. Whereas believers will one day receive the promised consummation, nevertheless they are to (presently) be rejoicing in it because, based on God's eternity being, from the human perspective, a present reality, the consummation is already true. Such a concept makes sense especially under a typological orientation: The type—faith in and joy in Christ—is evidence of the antitype's existence, the full experience of Christ in eternity.

These few examples show that the apostles understood a typological orientation to discipleship in the intermediate age. Christians are further along and fuller filled than Old Testament believers but still wait for the full restoration of all things, which is the ultimate antitype and glorification of the One who is the archetype. These examples and the interpretive commentary offered by relevant interlocutors do not prove a typological orientation necessarily. They show, however, the already-not-yet framing of New Testament living that makes typological realism a helpful and responsible approach. There is no sense in asserting the superiority of the current messianic day over the earlier days if it be not also asserted that the glories of the future will dwarf the troubles of the current day (cf. Rom 8:18). Like Christ's life was the zenith of godliness in the world, yet he had to suffer in order to reach glory, so believers follow him as their example in godliness (1 Pet 2:21), sure to also suffer before their coming glory. Their suffering, taking on various forms (1 Pet 5:9), proves that the glorified Christ's very Spirit, the *pneuma doxes*, rests on them (1 Pet 4:14).

Conclusion

The goal of this chapter has been to consider the relationship between the Old Testament theophanies/Christophanies and the presence of the Spirit in the New, and what bearing, if any, this comparison has on redemptive participation. The hope is that the reader sees, with Vos's aid, that the Old Testament Christophanies were typological of the Spirit's role in the New and that the Spirit's role in the New is itself typological of the coming glory promised everywhere in Holy Scripture. As believers under the old covenant were empowered to be instruments in God's redeeming hand by his own theophonic appearances to them, so believers under the new are empowered by God's own dwelling in them by their faith in his Son who gives them his Spirit. Jesus said, therefore, that faithful believers will be told "well done" (Matt 25:21, 23). Throughout the New Testament, believers' entrance into Christ's perfect presence is put in terms of their *own* receiving glory (e.g., 2 Thess 1:11; 1 Pet 1:7): The glory that Christ deserves, they participate in, because he by his Spirit lived in and empowered them through their faith journey.[105] This chapter has recognized this project's proposed typological trajectory on several levels.

105. See Boersma's helpful sermon on participation in *Sacramental Preaching*, 139–50. Boersma's sermon is from several Revelation texts. He points to believers' gospel hope of eternity based on wearing white robes washed in the Lamb's blood (7:14) and

Believers are, therefore, not to disengage from the world in which they live (John 17:15). Not only does the sacramental nature of reality (considered in the previous chapter) imply that the world reflects the next world to which humanity goes, and thus still contains goodness even in its relative futility (Rom 8:20). Further, believers are the hands and feet of the living Christ who came to save the world that he created. Sacrament may be said to be not so discontinuous with the res or goal that it cannot be trusted or enjoyed. It is God's world for his children's joy (Eccl 2:26; 11:10; 1 Tim 4:1–4) and his glory. His children are the means through which he redeems his world. In this sense, ministry does not have to occur apart from theology proper. Rather, ministry is the effect of contemplation on theology proper: The God who is is the God who appears and redeems and then sends his redeemed subjects with his presence to participate with him as he completes the work he began. He will finish what he began (Phil 1:6; cf. 2:12–13).

Finally, Beale, quoting Caird, illustrates his concept well, speaking of the Old Testament prophets having viewed redemptive history through a type of "bifocal lens": "With their near-sighted lens they saw historical events; with their far-sighted lens they saw the final historical end."[106] Similarly, believers looking through the same theological-redemptive-historical glasses see both the present redeeming activity of God (and their participatory place in it) *and* the future consummation to which all is moving. Throughout this project, the metaphor of choice has been 3D glasses. Without both the red and blue (corresponding to theology and redemptive history), one cannot see the fullness of the image. Typology as lens frames brings together both theology and redemptive history to show, as with 3D lenses, a clear picture of the God who establishes fellowship that not only lasts forever but ever increases in joy and pleasure. Similarly, the bifocal lens illustration helps to see how God brings his people and his world along to that end. That end is truly no end at all but only the beginning of the life he has for them.

---

how this must be understood in light of 19:8 where the bride, the church, is clothed in the saints' righteous deeds. Here, says Boersma, is a clear picture of redemptive participation: Believers are glorified for their work though it is actually Christ's work in them. It is not an either/or.

106. Caird, *Language and Imagery*, 258, quoted in Beale, *New Testament Biblical Theology*, 113.

Conclusion

THIS PROJECT HAS NOT intended to put an end to hermeneutical discussion by proposing a superior biblical theology. Highlighted throughout have been several approaches with the writer's preferences difficult to miss. In doing so, the project has also been critical of some approaches, hopefully in a respectful way. To support some and criticize others is not to draw a line in the sand between "orthodox" and "heterodox"; it is to raise awareness both to the potential (probably unforeseen) pitfalls in some and to the corrections that others have which could help.[1] Typological realism is, however, an attempt to approach Scripture with the right redemptive-historical and theological listening habits in contact with one another. The intended hermeneutical contribution of this project is to rehistoricize theological interpretation and retheologize Christ-centered redemptive-historical biblical theology via a typological orientation.

The first few chapters engaged with the working research question, "What is the nature of the relationship of evangelical Christ-centered biblical theology to the hermeneutics of the so-called Great Tradition, which the Protestant Reformers claimed, by *sola scriptura*, to be continuing?" The first two chapters answered that Christ-centered biblical theology is a post-Enlightenment approach to biblical hermeneutics that

---

1. Thomists should appreciate the *ST* echo here: God's goodness produces distinction; what is missing in one thing is supplied by the other, producing harmony. See Aquinas, *ST*, 1.47.1.

is worked out by those who embrace a premodern, Christocentric set of presuppositions. As such, Christ-centered biblical theology can fall prey in the absence of care to a disproportionate emphasis on redemptive-historical development while unknowingly and unintentionally neglecting both theology proper and practical living. Hopeful approaches that engage both theology and practice were highlighted in those from the so-called "Philadelphia school," namely the earlier works of Vos, Clowney, and the more recent work of Greg Beale. Chapter 1 attempted to outline a reasonable narrative of the historical developments within biblical theology that led to Christ-centered biblical theology, thus demonstrating why it has a duality of commitment (i.e., to premodern theology and a modern preoccupation with grammar and history.) Chapter 2 concluded that this supposed confusion contributes to Christ-centered biblical theology's strength in redemptive history alongside weaknesses in both theology proper and pastoral application.

Chapter 3 sought a clear definition of Reformational hermeneutics within the context of the so-called Great Tradition, with attention given to a clear definition of *sola scriptura*. The *sola* was seen as an attempt by the Reformers to recapture Scripture as the church's magisterial authority in consistency with the fathers to the end of right theology, worship, and living. Similar to medieval hermeneutics' tendency to abuse the Augustinian *quadriga*, so Reformational hermeneutics can abuse Scripture historically if they give priority to the mind(s) of the human author(s) at the expense of theology and practice. In other words, if redemptive history is alone, to the exclusion of theology and practice, Calvin's exegetical advances give way to turning Scripture into merely a work of literature as in the grammatical-historical method.

Thus was answered the working research question: On one hand, Christ-centered biblical theology is redemptive-historical as the Great Tradition has been; on the other hand, it is also sometimes lacking in theological and practical contribution. As such, it does not recapture what was "lost" in the hermeneutics of the tradition as much as fill out some missing pieces, displaying the glorious Christocentricity of redemptive history in a way that makes the gospel the ultimate context of every passage.

But this answer also suggests another question: Is it possible to outline a hermeneutic that employs both theological interpretation and redemptive-historical interpretation in a way that leads to practical, participatory living? The answer to this follow-up question opened the door to the project's contribution: typological realism as a synthesis of redemptive history and theological interpretation. By centering typology in hermeneutics, with its escalation by antitypes toward the eschaton, the *real* is revealed at increasing degrees of brilliance across time, culminating in the beatific vision. Contemplating this escalation across history engages redemptive history (as in Christ-centered biblical theology); contemplating both the source of the revelatory types/antitypes and the prophesied ultimate antitype in the vision (as in theology) engages classical theism, which theological interpretation has attempted but imperfectly. Within typological realism, the strengths of theological interpretation and Christ-centered biblical theology are maintained while the weaknesses of both are hermeneutically marginalized. The approach is neither merely redemptive-historical or theological but both in a progressive sense flowing from eternity and leading to the beatific vision.

In the final chapter, the analysis of one biblical theme completed the picture. When the typology of the Old Testament theophanies is considered both in relation to its antitype in New Testament Spirit-indwelling and its ultimate antitype in the vision, typological realism becomes practical. The believer is shown how they themselves participate with the God who has revealed himself and uses time to manifest his salvation and fellowship.

Perhaps typological realism is simply a post-Enlightenment appropriation of the *quadriga*, even a recovery of Aquinas's approach with an evangelical corrective. The *quadriga*, as Aquinas articulates, does present several senses on this ground: God as both author of the text and the one who comprehends all things in himself[2] speaks in a way that exegetical conclusions never contradict the plain/literal sense but instead orient the believer to the *real* by construing Scripture as signs for it. As such, texts actually only have two senses, the second with a threefold division: The first is the *literal/historical* sense (to which Aquinas, as chapter 3 showed, argued for a return), and the second is the *spiritual* sense, including three divisions: (a) *allegorical* (where the text is both a witness to Christ's saving actions, as well, potentially, as a pastoral opportunity to apply the text in practical ways); (b) *moral* (where the text shows believers what they are to do); and (c) *anagogical* (where the text points to the glory to which believers in Christ are journeying.)[3]

---

2. See Aquinas, *ST*, 1.1.10. Kreeft's helpful comments in *Summa of the Summa*, 49–50, are worth reading as well.

3. Aquinas, *ST*, 1.1.10. This distinction is also clearly explained in Chase, *40 Questions*.

While the similarities between typological realism and the Augustinian/Thomistic *quadriga* are obvious, the evangelical corrective is twofold in its uniqueness: First, in the new framework, there is a definite theological orientation in which the text shows forth God's glory and perfection. The *quadriga* might imply such a theological orientation in the anagogical division, but it is not explicit. Second, the new framework also makes explicit the believer's need to "put on the Lord Jesus Christ" (Rom 13:14), participating with him in his redemptive project. Again, the *quadriga* might imply this in the second and third divisions of the spiritual sense; but, as constructed by Aquinas, it could be said that the *quadriga* sounds like it is saying that believers' actions (in the moral sense) are only believers' actions *in light of* Christ's saving actions (in the allegorical sense). Although Aquinas would likely not say that believers' participation adds to Christ's work, the charge of this implication seems worth considering.

Thus, Beale's conclusion is helpful to the method of biblical theology. Christian living, Beale says, is "resurrection life as a transported person from the old, fallen world into the new creation." When believers

> begin to become part of the new creation, eschatological righteousness sets in to their lives, a righteousness that was promised to be a part of the new heaven and new earth. When this happens, they become a *living part* of the redemptive-historical storyline, in which they are not only a part of the new creation but are also involved in the expansion of it in their own lives.[4]

Where Aquinas's construal of the moral sense is that *believers* do what Christ has done (which is not untrue), Beale makes an attempt to reconfigure, restating the point evangelically: It is Christ *in* people as they appropriate his life in theirs.

Köstenberger, as chapter 1 showed, concluded that Beale's approach shows major promise for biblical theology moving forward.[5] In Beale's mature biblical-theological appropriation, the best of gospel-centric Reformational hermeneutics is woven into the hermeneutics of the Great Tradition in a way that the Tradition had implied but perhaps did not

---

4. See Beale, *New Testament Biblical Theology*, 835; emphasis added. Chapters 25 and 26 of Beale's work emphasize in a way superior to many other biblical-theological works, as seen in chapter 2 of this project, the importance of appropriating Christ for biblical theology to be complete.

5. Köstenberger, "Present and Future of Biblical Theology."

explicate enough.[6] To be sure, the work of the Reformation led the way to the hermeneutical questions that would necessarily develop the quadratic framework and lead to the richness of the world of biblical theology that has given way to such gospel-centered approaches as Beale's. To say as much might be bold, but it seems fair.

There might be a few areas of potential development on this project's thesis. Is it possible to better theologize the Christ-centered biblical theology of Beale, Goldsworthy, etc.? As stated, most of their approaches are thematically and redemptive-historically strong. It is wondered, however, if the theology proper of these approaches can be strengthened. Perhaps, for instance, an eager researcher could engage Beale's *Union with the Resurrected Christ* and apply each chapter's theme to a consideration of theology proper. Or, those chapter themes could be placed alongside considerations of the beatific vision. How does Christ's corporate representation of the people as the true Temple (Beale's fourth chapter) relate typologically to the beatific vision? What does Christ as Temple say about God in his aseity, immutability, etc.? Such further research would seem worthwhile and helpful for the church. Other potential pursuits might include engagement with either the relationship between Vos's theology proper and his redemptive history or with Matthew Bates's aversion to typology in pursuing a prosopology-centric approach. The reader will have to decide whether this project has fairly considers these interlocutors and their critics.

The only remaining thing to add is that Beale's forerunners in the Philadelphia school had earlier explicated in their biblical theology something that must be included for God to be known, heard, and followed as he wants: that God is the source, means, and end of all things (e.g., Rom 11:36). Unless hermeneutics prepare the believer to meet God, they are missing their mark. Vos and Clowney seemed to know this clearly. Their work—the latter being more prolific but the former showing no less depth—did not only seek to show Christ as the answer to the Old Testament's problem but as the answer *because* he is Lord of all who will not let sin and its effects win but will magnify his grace and saving power.

Thus, Clowney should get the final word with a quote that was shared earlier: "When Christ said, 'Before Abraham was, I Am,' (John 8:56), he was saying not just that he is Abraham's and David's seed" (as biblical theology is always rightly passionate to show), "but that he is

---

6. See also Beale's more recent, and even more developed, *Union with the Resurrected Christ*.

Abraham's and David's *Lord*."[7] The type consisted of God's earlier revelation to Abraham and David. The antitype was Christ's putting on flesh in the incarnation to regenerate people with his Spirit. The final antitype will be Christ's people beholding him as he is and becoming like him. May they prepare themselves in this unique day of antitype and type by putting him on. He will recognize them in the end.

---

7. Clowney, *Preaching Christ in All of Scripture*, 42.

Appendix

On the Practical Side of Typological Realism and Its Relationship to the *Quadriga*

THIS BOOK OFFERED TYPOLOGICAL realism as a biblical hermeneutical methodology that centers on Christology and theology. It was noted in one section that the method bears striking similarities to the Augustinian *quadriga*, which was the dominant hermeneutical methodology of the medieval era. It was then argued that these similarities are not indicative of equivocation. Typological realism, for instance, unlike the *quadriga*, offers a theological sense to a text's interpretation. Also, the *quadriga* implies Christology and redemptive history in its allegorical and anagogical senses in that the allegorical sense notes a text's relationship to Christ's first coming while the anagogical sense notes a text's depiction of the relationship between the text and Christ's second coming. Typological realism, on the other hand, makes explicit this Christocentric impulse with questions centering around the text as the voice of Christ and as prophecy about Christ.

But there is one more aspect that might appear to have been overlooked: The *quadriga* offers a tropological sense in which the reader is shown what to *do* with what they read—in other words, with how they can live and act out what Kevin Vanhoozer has called the drama

APPENDIX

of doctrine (Scripture's doctrine).[1] This inclusion was in answer to one of the conclusions of chapter 2, that Christ-centered biblical theology is often not practical. While my final chapter offered some practical considerations, given the parallel between the theophanies/Christophanies of the Old Testament and the presence of the Holy Spirit in the new, the practical aspects of the method might still be somewhat weak. So I'll use this brief appendix to offer a few more thoughts:

First, in contextualizing history as the outworking of God's plans according to his will, whether looking backward (in pre-Christ redemptive history) or forward (in the time between Christ's two comings), human action depends upon clearly apprehending *God's* actions. A low-hanging pair of key biblical texts show this point presupposed: God at Sinai reminds his people that he delivered them from slavery before proceeding with the Decalogue (Exod 20:2), and Jesus's commission to his disciples follows a statement about his authority over all things (Matt 28:18–20). Action, then, is to some degree imitative, believers following God's works with faith-filled works by his help. This imitation is not equivocal but analogical. In "putting on" the Lord Jesus (Rom 13:14), believers are not the Lord Jesus but branches plugged into the Vine (John 15) with such substantial parallels between Christ's works and theirs that their works are actually his in them: "I in them, and you in me, that they may be one as we are one, Father" (John 17:23). As believers trust in God's works in Christ, they become spiritually one with Christ so that his work is seen in their own works.

This point leads to the second point: participation. As stated above, the effect of coming to faith in Christ is that the Father plugs the believer into Christ the Vine (John 15:1–10). As believers grow in their clarity and confidence about reality as God reveals it, they are invited to let the light shine through them. Action, then, is also gracious: Christ acts through the person, not opposed to their will but compatible with it. They work out their salvation *as* the Lord is working in them (Phil 2:12–13).[2] So understood, the believer cannot have any confidence that they live a life representative of the Lord if they are not participating in his holiness. Their salvation consists in fellowship with the Trinity, feeding on Christ's

---

1. This phrase is from Vanhoozer, *Drama of Doctrine*. Vanhoozer has elsewhere explained this approach in his more accessible *Hearers and Doers*.

2. Note that the mind of humility which Paul instructs the Philippian church to put on *is theirs in Christ Jesus* (2:5). It's his mind, seen in his actions (2:6–10); then they appropriate it by participation.

body and blood by faith (John 6:47–53), which gives them participation in Christ's own eternal life.[3] Paul's question to the Roman Christians, "How can we who died to sin still live in it?" (Rom 6:2), was a little bit more than a rhetorical tool. At some point, sooner or later, the Christian is going to undergo a deep and abiding repentance that will separate them from the rebellious life they led before. They will actualize what their acquaintance with typological realism has realized, that their life is progressing upward toward the *vision;* to remain addicted to sin would be to remain subject to the "weak and worthless elementary principles of the world" (Gal 4:10).

This leads to one final point: The action of God's people is motivated by reward. Whether Old (Heb 11:6, 26) or New Testament believers (Matt 25:21, 23), they have learned and are learning to pursue God's reward. They are willing to endure the magnanimity of simple acts of love and devotion for the sake of God's often tarrying reward: "Your father who sees in secret *will* reward you" (Matt 6:4; emphasis added). Godliness in stewardship, acts of service, holiness, and all of the rest is an investment in the Holy Spirit and a deference to God's will. If one has been captivated by the onward-and-upward revelatory story, they know where to tie their allegiances.

All of this is to say that whereas typological realism does not include a practical/tropological sense like the *quadriga,* such considerations should follow naturally. The church's first act, as chapter two saw, is passive: *Listening* to God speak his eternal Word into time and space.[4] In the typological realism method, the church hears Christ's voice in Scripture in five ways:[5]

1. Historically: What is the historical relationship between the text on display and Christ's coming in the flesh? Before, during, after?

2. Prophetically: How does the text point either forward or backward via typology, prophecy, or other parallels to Christ's coming—either his first or second coming?

3. Prosopologically: How is the text the actual voice of Christ speaking in the time in which it was inspired?

---

3. See Bowsher, *Life in the Son.*
4. See chapter 2 above; Webster, *HS* 44.
5. See chapter 6 above.

4. Eschatologically: How does the text prepare the church for the coming glory as the church participates in and with Christ's eternal life by his Spirit in the present?

5. Theologically: How does the text bear witness to God's glorious joy at realizing his eternal purpose in his Son?

It is hopefully clear to the reader how practical application flows naturally from the answers to these questions. The questions theologically orient listeners who inhabit time and space so that they can act out the drama of creation and redemption (new creation). The five questions pursue the one ultimate question, "What is God doing in Christ?," so that the listener can be drawn themselves into God's doing in Christ. In believing in him whose story is the text's theme, the believer possesses life in his name (John 20:31); they then put on Christ (Rom 13:14). Their testimony is summarized thus: "In this the love of God was manifest among us, that God sent his only Son into the world, so that we might live through him" (1 John 4:9). By this testimony of Jesus, itself the spirit of prophecy (Rev 19:10)—which tells of God's act and the believers' reception of its benefits—believers overcome every power of darkness (Rev 12:11). They live by this supernatural story.

All of this is not to marginalize the importance of explicit believing action. If the reader prefers to include a tropological sense in the typological realistic method, it would seem to fit somewhere between points 4 and 5. The only caution that seems worth offering is this: Whereas Trueman's point is worth pondering, that a biblical theology that makes every question's answer "Christ" could end up boring and unmotivating,[6] it might also be boring to swing so hard to action that God's works in Christ are marginalized. Philip Cary has said this: "My contention is that the kind of sermon that gives us real help living the Christian life is not about us but about Christ. It does not tell us what to do, but what Christ does."[7] Cary devotes a whole chapter in his *Good News For Anxious Christians* to the contention that gospel preaching does in fact attempt to put Christ on display in all of his saving, loving, eternal glory. Application follows but only once the eyes of the heart have been properly situated.[8] In echoing Cary, my only caution to insisting upon a tropological sense is this: Whereas not giving an application might produce passive listeners,

---

6. See chapter 2 above; Trueman, "Revolutionary Balancing Act."
7. See Cary, *Good News For Anxious Christians*, 158.
8. Cary, *Good News For Anxious Christians*, 169–72.

rushing to action too quickly might produce unbelieving busybodies, which, in some ways, might be worse (cf. Matt 7:21–23). Better is to put Christ on display and let the Spirit work on the listener's participation in Christ's eternal life. In this way, God's word will accomplish the effect of its going out; he is the applier.

Bibliography

Adams, Jay. *Truth Applied: Application in Preaching*. Grand Rapids: Ministry Resources Library, 1990.
Alexander, T. Desmond. *From Eden to the New Jerusalem: An Introduction to Biblical Theology*. Grand Rapids: Kregel, 2008.
Alexander, T. Desmond, et al., eds. *New Dictionary of Biblical Theology: Exploring the Unity and Diversity of Scripture*. Downers Grove, IL: IVP Academic, 2000.
Anselm. *Cur Deus Homo: Why God Became Man*. Translated by Sidney Norton Deane. Pantianos Classics, 2016.
Aquinas, Thomas. *Summa Theologica*. Translated by Fathers of the English Dominican Province. https://www.ccel.org/a/aquinas/summa/home.html.
———. *Thomas Aquinas: Selected Writings*. Edited Ralph McInerny. New York: Penguin, 1998.
Athanasius. *A Defense of the Nicene Definition*. Translated by John Henry Newman. Assumption, 2014.
Augustine. *Confessions*. Translated by Albert Outler. Revised by Mark Vessey. New York: Barnes & Noble Classics, 2007.
———. *Instructing Beginners in the Faith*. Translated by Ray Canning. Edited by Boniface Ramsey. Hyde Park, NY: New City, 2006.
———. *On Christian Doctrine*. Translated by D. W. Robertson. Upper Saddle River, NJ: Prentice Hall, 1958.
———. *On Genesis, The Works of Saint Augustine: A Translation for the 21st Century*. Translated by Edmund Hill. Hyde Park, NY: New City, 2002.
———. *On Predestination*. New Haven, CT: Beloved, 2014.
———. *On the Spirit and the Letter*. New Haven, CT: Beloved, 2014.
———. *On the Trinity (De Trinitate)*. Translated by Arthur West Haddan. Edited by Paul A. Boer Sr. Veritatis Splendor, 2012.
———. *Treatise on Faith and the Creed*. Translated by S. D. F. Salmond. Savage, MN: Lighthouse, 2017.

BIBLIOGRAPHY

Barr, James. *The Concept of Biblical Theology: An Old Testament Perspective.* Minneapolis: Fortress, 1999.

Barrett, Matthew. *Canon, Covenant, and Christology: Rethinking Jesus and the Scriptures of Israel.* Downer's Grove, IL: InterVarsity, 2021.

———. *God's Word Alone: The Authority of Scripture.* Grand Rapids: Zondervan, 2016.

———. *None Greater: The Undomesticated Trinity.* Grand Rapids: Baker, 2019.

———. *Reformation As Renewal: Retrieving the One, Holy, Catholic, and Apostolic Church.* Grand Rapids: Zondervan Academic, 2023.

———, ed. *Reformation Theology: A Systematic Summary.* Wheaton: Crossway, 2017.

———. *Simply Trinity: The Unmanipulated Father, Son, and Spirit.* Grand Rapids: Baker, 2021.

Barrs, Jerram. *The Heart of Prayer: What Jesus Teaches Us.* Phillipsburg, NJ: Presbyterian & Reformed, 2008.

Barth, Karl. *Dogmatics in Outline.* New York: Harper Perennial, 1959.

———. *Evangelical Theology: An Introduction.* Translated by Grover Foley. New York: Holt, Rinehart, and Winston, 1963.

Bartholomew, Craig. "Biblical Theology and Biblical Interpretation." In *Out of Egypt: Biblical Theology and Biblical Interpretation*, edited by Craig Bartholomew et al., 14–15. Grand Rapids: Zondervan, 2004.

———. *Introducing Biblical Hermeneutics: A Comprehensive Framework for Hearing God in Scripture.* Grand Rapids: Eerdmans, 2015.

Bartholomew, Craig, and Michael Goheen. "Story and Biblical Theology." In *Out of Egypt: Biblical Theology and Biblical Interpretation*, edited by Craig Bartholomew et al., 144–71. Grand Rapids: Zondervan, 2004.

Bartholomew, Craig, and Heath A. Thomas, eds. *A Manifesto for Theological Interpretation.* Grand Rapids: Baker Academic, 2016.

Bates, Matthew W. *The Birth of the Trinity: Jesus, God, and Spirit in New Testament and Early Christian Interpretations of the Old Testament.* Oxford: Oxford University Press, 2015.

———. *Hermeneutics of the Apostolic Proclamation: The Center of Paul's Method of Scriptural Interpretation.* Waco, TX: Baylor University Press, 2012.

Bauckham, Richard. *Jesus and the God of Israel: God Crucified and Other Studies on the New Testament's Christology of Divine Identity.* Grand Rapids: Eerdmans, 2008.

Bavinck, Herman. *The Doctrine of God.* Translated by William Hendrickson. Edinburgh: Banner of Truth, 1977.

Beale, Greg K. *God Dwells Among Us: A Biblical Theology of the Temple.* Downer's Grove, IL: IVP Academic, 2021.

———. *Handbook on the New Testament Use of the Old: Exegesis and Interpretation.* Grand Rapids: Baker Academic, 2012.

———. *A New Testament Biblical Theology: The Unfolding of the Old Testament in the New.* Grand Rapids: Baker Academic, 2011.

———. *The Temple and the Church's Mission: A Biblical Theology of the Dwelling Place of God.* Downers Grove, IL: IVP Academic, 2004.

———. *Union with the Resurrected Christ: Eschatological New Creation and New Testament Biblical Theology.* Grand Rapids: Baker Academic, 2023.

Beale, Greg K., and David H. Campbell. *Revelation: A Shorter Commentary.* Grand Rapids: Eerdmans, 2015.

Beale, Greg K., and D. A. Carson. *Commentary on the New Testament Use of the Old Testament.* Grand Rapids: Baker Academic, 2007.

Bebbington, David W., et al., eds. *Evangelicals: Who They Have Been, Are Now, and Could Be*. Grand Rapids: Eerdmans, 2019.

Bernard of Clairvaux. *On Loving God*. Lexington, KY, 2015.

———. *Sermons on the Song of Songs Set, Volumes 1–4*. Translated by Kilian Walsh. Trappist, KY: Cistercian, 1971.

Behr, John. *The Way to Nicea*. The Formation of Christian Theology 1. Crestwood, NY: St. Vladimir's Seminary Press, 2001.

Belt, Hank van dan. "Lessons from the Reformation for Hermeneutics Today." *Unio Cum Christo* 2 (2018) 95–109.

Bennett, Rod. *Scripture Wars: How Justin Martyr Rescued the Old Testament for Christians*. Manchester, NH: Sophia Institute Press, 2019.

Billings, Todd. *The Word of God for the People of God*. Grand Rapids: Eerdmans, 2010.

Bird, Michael. *Evangelical Theology: An Evangelical and Systematic Introduction*. Grand Rapids: Zondervan Academic, 2013.

———. "Inerrancy is Not Necessary for Evangelicalism Outside of the USA." In *Five Views on Biblical Inerrancy*, edited by J. Merrick and Stephen M. Garrett, 145–73. Grand Rapids: Zondervan, 2013.

Blaising, Craig, and Darryl Bock. *Progressive Dispensationalism*. Grand Rapids: Baker, 1993.

Boersma, Hans. *Five Things Theologians Wish Biblical Scholars Knew*. Downers Grove, IL: IVP Academic, 2021.

———. *Heavenly Participation: The Weaving of a Sacramental Tapestry*. Grand Rapids: Eerdmans, 2011.

———. *Pierced by Love: Divine Reading With the Christian Tradition*. Bellingham, WA: Lexham, 2023.

———. *Sacramental Preaching: Sermons on the Hidden Presence of Christ*. Grand Rapids: Baker, 2016.

———. *Scripture as Real Presence: Sacramental Exegesis in the Early Church*. Grand Rapids: Baker, 2017.

———. *Seeing God: The Beatific Vision in Christian Tradition*. Grand Rapids: Eerdmans, 2018.

———. *Violence, Hospitality, and the Cross: Reappropriating the Atonement Tradition*. Grand Rapids: Baker, 2006.

Bonaventure. *Breviloquium*. Paterson, NJ: St. Anthony Guild Press. http://agnuz.info/app/webroot/library/7/13/.

———. *Journey of the Mind to God*. Eastford, CT: Martino Fine, 2016.

Bonhoeffer, Dietrich. *Creation and Fall, Temptation*. New York: Touchstone, 1997.

———. *Psalms: The Prayer Book of the Bible*. Minneapolis: Augsburg Fortress, 1970.

Bowsher, Clive. *Life in the Son: Exploring Participation and Union with Christ in John's Gospel and Letters*. Downers Grove, IL: Apollos, 2023.

Bray, Gerald. *Biblical Interpretation: Past and Present*. Downer's Grove, IL: IVP Academic, 1996.

Bray, Gerald. "Late Medieval Theology." In *Reformation Theology: A Systematic Summary*, edited by Matthew Barrett, 67–109. Wheaton: Crossway, 2017.

———. *Doing Theology with the Reformers*. Downer's Grove, IL: IVP Academic, 2019.

———. *How the Church Fathers Read the Bible: A Short Introduction*. Bellingham, WA: Lexham, 2022.

Brown, David, et al. *Matthew–John*. A Commentary Critical, Experimental, and Practical on the Old and New Testaments 3.1. Reprint, Grand Rapids: Eerdmans, 1984.

BIBLIOGRAPHY

Brown, Raymond E. *The Sensus Plenior of Sacred Scripture*. 1955. Reprint, Eugene, OR: Wipf and Stock, 2008.

Bruno, Chris, et al. *Biblical Theology According to the Apostles*. Downers Grove: IVP Academic, 2020.

Burge, Gary M. *Jesus and the Land: The New Testament Challenge to "Holy Land" Theology*. Grand Rapids: Baker Academic, 2012.

Busenitz, Nathan. *Long Before Luther: Tracing the Heart of the Gospel from Christ to the Reformation*. Chicago: Moody, 2017.

Byassee, Jason. *Praise Seeking Understanding: Reading the Psalms with Augustine*. Grand Rapids: Eerdmans 2007.

Caird, G. B. *The Language and Imagery of the Bible*. Philadelphia: Westminster, 1980.

Calvin, John. *Commentary on the Epistle of Paul the Apostle to the Romans*. Translated by Benjamin Farley. Grand Rapids: Baker, 2009.

———. *Commentary on Genesis*. Vol. 1 of *Calvin's Commentaries*. Translated by John King. Grand Rapids: Baker, 2009.

———. *Commentary on Harmony of Matthew, Mark, and Luke*. Vol. 16 of *Calvin's Commentaries*. Translated by William Pringle. Grand Rapids: Baker, 2009.

———. *Commentary on Hebrews, 1 Peter, 1 John, James, 2 Peter, Jude*. Translated by John Owen. Grand Rapids: Baker, 1974.

———. *Commentary on the Second Epistle of Paul the Apostle to Timothy*. Translated by Benjamin Farley. Grand Rapids: Baker, 2009.

———. *Commentary on Ezekiel 13–20, Daniel 1–6*. Vol. 12 of *Calvin's Commentaries*. Translated by Thomas A Myers. Grand Rapids: Baker, 2009.

———. *Institutes of the Christian Tradition*. Translated by Henry Beveredge. Peabody, MA: 2008.

———. *A Little Book on the Christian Life*. Orlando: Reformation, 2010.

The Cambridge Bible for Schools and Colleges. *Cambridge Bible for Schools and Colleges*. https://biblehub.com/commentaries/cambridge/john/14.htm.

Cameron, Michael. *Christ Meets Me Everywhere: Augustine's Early Figurative Exegesis*. Oxford: Oxford University Press, 2012.

Carson, D. A. *The Gospel According to John: Pillar New Testament Commentary*. Grand Rapids: Eerdmans, 1990.

———. "Theological Interpretation of Scripture: Yes, But . . ." In *Theological Commentary: Evangelical Perspectives*, edited by R. Michael Allen, 3–11. London: T&T Clark, 2011.

Carter, Craig. *Contemplating God with the Great Tradition: Recovering Trinitarian Classical Theism*. Grand Rapids: Baker Academic, 2021.

———. "How Then Shall We Theologize?: A Review of Wayne Grudem's *Systematic Theology and Doctrine of the Trinity*." *Credo* 11.1 (2021). xf.

———. *Interpreting Scripture with the Great Tradition: Recovering the Genius of Premodern Exegesis*. Grand Rapids: Baker Academic, 2018.

———. "Premodern Approach." In *Five Views on Christ in the Old Testament: Genre, Authorial Intent, and the Nature of Scripture*, edited by Andrew King and Brian Tabb, 239–65. Grand Rapids: Zondervan Academic, 2022.

Cary, Phillip. *Good News For Anxious Christians: 10 Practical Things You Don't Have To Do*. Grand Rapids: Brazos, 2010.

Chafer, Lewis Sperry. *Major Bible Themes*. Chicago: Moody, 1926.

Chappell, Bryan. *Christ-Centered Preaching: Redeeming the Expository Sermon*. 3rd ed. Grand Rapids: Baker, 2018.

Chase, Mitchell. *40 Questions About Typology and Allegory*. Grand Rapids: Kregel Academic, 2020.

Chester, Tim, and Michael Reeves. *Why the Reformation Still Matters*. Wheaton: Crossway, 2016.

Childs, Brevard. *Biblical Theology in Crisis*. Philadelphia: Westminster, 1970.

———. *Biblical Theology of the Old and New Testaments*. Minneapolis: Fortress, 1992.

———. "Critique of Recent Intertextual Canonical Interpretation." *Zeitschrift für die alttestamentliche Wissenschaft* 115.2 (2003) 173–84.

Clowney, Edmund. *Preaching Christ in All of Scripture*. Wheaton: Crossway, 2003.

———. *Preaching and Biblical Theology*. Phillipsburg, NJ: Presbyterian and Reformed, 1961.

Cullmann, Oscar. *Christ and Time: The Primitive Conception of Time and History*. 3rd ed. Reprint, Eugene, OR: Wipf and Stock, 2018.

———. *The Christology of the New Testament*. Translated by Shirley C. Guthrie and Charles A. M. Hall. Philadelphia: Westminster, 1963.

———. *The Earliest Christian Confessions*. Translated by J. K. S. Reid. Eugene, OR: Wipf and Stock, 1949.

Daley, Brian G. *God Visible: Patristic Christology Reconsidered*. Oxford: Oxford University Press, 2018.

———. "Is Patristic Exegesis Still Usable? Reflections on the Early Christian Interpretation of the Psalm." *Communio* 29 (2002) 185–216.

Danielou, Jean. *From Shadows to Reality: Studies in the Biblical Typology of the Fathers*. Translated by Dom Wulstan Hibberd. Jackson, MI: Ex Fontibus, 2018.

Davison, Andrew. *Participation in God: A Study in Christian Doctrine and Metaphysics*. Cambridge: Cambridge University Press, 2020.

Dempster, Stephen. *Dominion and Dynasty: A Theology of the Hebrew Bible*. Downers Grove, IL: IVP Academic, 2003.

Derouchie, Jason. *How to Understand and Apply the Old Testament: 12 Steps from Exegesis to Theology*. Phillipsburg, NJ: Presbyterian and Reformed, 2017.

Dodd, C. H. *Moffatt New Testament Commentaries: Romans*. London: Hodder and Stoughton, 1942.

———. *The Founder of Christianity*. London: Collins, 1971.

Dolezal, James E. *All That Is In God: Evangelical Theology and the Challenge of Classical Christian Theism*. Grand Rapids: Reformation Heritage, 2016.

Driver, Daniel R. *Brevard Childs, Biblical Theologian For the Church's One Bible*. Grand Rapids: Baker Academic, 2012.

Duby, Stephen. *God in Himself: Scripture, Metaphysics, and the Task of Christian Theology*. Downers Grove, IL: IVP Academic, 2019.

———. *Jesus and the God of Classical Theism: Biblical Christology in Light of the Doctrine of God*. Grand Rapids: Baker Academic, 2022.

Edwards, Jonathan. "The End for Which God Created the World." In *God's Passion for His Glory: Living the Vision of Jonathan Edwards*, edited by John Piper, 21–48. Wheaton: Crossway, 2006.

Ehrman, Bart. *How Jesus Became God: The Exaltation of a Jewish Preacher from Galilee*. New York: Harper One, 2015.

Evans, C. A. "Jesus and the Continuing Exile of Israel." In *Jesus and the Restoration of Israel*, edited by C. C. Newman, 77–100. Downers Grove, IL: InterVarsity, 1999.

Fairbarn, Patrick. *Typology of Scripture: Two Volumes in One*. Grand Rapids: Kregel Classics, 2000.

BIBLIOGRAPHY

Farrar, Frederic. *History of Interpretation: Eight Lectures.* New York: Dutton, 1886.

Fee, Gordon. *God's Empowering Presence: The Holy Spirit in the Letters of Paul.* Grand Rapids: Baker, 2012.

Fisher, Jeff. "Medieval and Reformation Interpretations of the Psalms Quoted in Hebrews 1–2." In *Reformation Faith: Exegesis and Theology in the Protestant Reformations,* edited by Michael Parsons, 71–86. Eugene, OR: Wipf and Stock, 2014.

Foxe, John. "To the True and Faithful Congregation of Christ's Universal Church." In *English Reformers,* edited by T. H. L. Parker, 61–88. Philadelphia: Westminster, 1966.

Frame, John M. *A History of Western Philosophy and Theology.* Phillipsburg, NJ: Presbyterian and Reformed, 2015.

Franzmann, Martin H. "Seven Theses on Reformation Hermeneutics." *Concordia Theological Monthly* 40.4 (1969) 235–46.

Frei, Hans. *The Eclipse of the Biblical Narrative: A Study in Eighteenth and Nineteenth Century Hermeneutics.* New Haven, CT: Yale University Press, 1974.

Gadamer, Hans-Georg. *Truth and Method.* London: Sheed and Ward, 1989.

Gamble, Richard C. *The Full Revelation of God.* Vol. 2 of *The Whole Counsel of God.* Phillipsburg, NJ: Presbyterian and Reformed, 2018.

Garrett, Stephen M., et al., eds. *Five Views on Biblical Inerrancy.* Grand Rapids: Zondervan, 2013.

George, Timothy. *Reading Scripture with the Reformers.* Downer's Grove, IL: IVP Academic, 2011.

Gentry, Peter J. "A Preliminary Evaluation and Critique of Prosopological Exegesis." *Southern Baptist Journal of Theology* 23.2 (2019) 105–122.

———. "The Significance of Covenants in Biblical Theology." *Southern Baptist Journal of Theology* 20.1 (2016) 9–33.

Gentry, Peter J., and Stephen J. Wellum. *God's Kingdom Through God's Covenants: A Concise Biblical Theology.* Wheaton: Crossway, 2015.

———. *Kingdom Through Covenant: A Biblical-Theological Understanding of the Covenants.* Wheaton: Crossway, 2012.

Gerson, Lloyd P. *From Plato to Platonism.* Ithaca, NY: Cornell University Press, 2013.

———. *Platonism and Naturalism: The Possibility of Philosophy.* Ithaca, NY: Cornell University Press, 2020.

Gill, John. *Gill's Complete Body of Practical and Doctrinal Divinity: Being a System of Evangelical Truths, Deduced from the Sacred Scriptures.* Edited by William Staughton. Philadelphia: Delaplaine and Hellings, 1810.

Goldsworthy, Graeme. *According to Plan: The Unfolding Revelation of God in the Bible.* Downer's Grove, IL: IVP Academic, 2002.

———. *Christ-Centered Biblical Theology: Hermeneutical Foundations and Principles.* Downer's Grove, IL: InterVarsity, 2012.

———. *Gospel and Kingdom.* In *The Goldsworthy Trilogy,* 7–138. Milton Keynes: Paternoster, 2000.

———. *Gospel and Wisdom.* In *The Goldsworthy Trilogy,* 329–538. Milton Keynes: Paternoster, 2000.

———. *Gospel-Centered Hermeneutics: Foundations and Principles of Evangelical Biblical Interpretation.* Downer's Grove, IL: IVP Academic, 2006.

———. *Homeward Bound: Sabbath Rest for the People of God.* Milton Keynes: Paternoster, 2019.

———. "Is Biblical Theology Viable?" In *Interpreting God's Plan: Biblical Theology and the Pastor*, edited by R. J. Gibson, 18–46. Paternoster, 1998.

———. *Jesus Through the Old Testament: Transform Your Bible Understanding*. Oxford: Bible Reading Fellowship, 2017.

———. "Ontology and Theology: A Response to Carl Trueman's 'A Revolutionary Balancing Act.'" *Themelios* 28.1 (2002) 37–45.

———. "The Pastor as Biblical Theologian." In *Interpreting God's Plan: Biblical Theology and the Pastor*, edited by R. J. Gibson, 110–29. Paternoster, 1998.

———. *Preaching the Whole Bible as Christian Scripture: The Application of Biblical Theology to Expository Preaching*. Grand Rapids: Eerdmans, 2000.

———. *Proverbs: The Tree of Life*. Edited by Paul Barnett. Rev. ed. Sydney: Aquila, 2011.

———. "The Relationship of the Old Testament to the New Testament." In *New Dictionary of Biblical Theology: Exploring the Unity and Diversity of Scripture*, edited by Alexander, T. Desmond et al., 81–89. Downers Grove, IL: IVP Academic, 2000.

Goldsworthy, Graeme, and Nancy Guthrie. "Graeme Goldsworthy on Biblical Theology." *The Gospel Coalition*, November 3, 2016. https://www.thegospelcoalition.org/podcasts/help-me-teach-the-bible/graham-goldsworthy-on-biblical-theology/?amp.

Goppelt, Leonhard. *Typos: The Typological Interpretation of the Old Testament in the New*. Translated by Donald Madvog. Grand Rapids: Eerdmans, 1982.

Gorman, Michael J. *Participating in Christ: Explorations in Paul's Theology and Spirituality*. Grand Rapids: Baker Academic, 2019.

Green-McCreight, Kathryn. *Ad Literam: How Augustine, Calvin, and Barth Read the "Plain Sense" of Genesis 1–3*. New York: Peter Lang, 1999.

Gregory of Nazianzus. *On God and Christ: The Five Theological Orations and Two Letters to Cleodonus*. Crestwood, NY: St. Vladimir's, 2002.

Greidanus, Sydney. *Preaching Christ from the Old Testament: A Contemporary Hermeneutical Method*. Grand Rapids: Eerdmans, 1999.

Grier, W. J. *The Momentous Event: A Discussion of Scripture Teaching on the Second Advent*. Carlisle, PA: Banner of Truth, 1970.

Grudem, Wayne. *Systematic Theology: An Introduction to Biblical Doctrine*. Grand Rapids: Zondervan, 2000.

———. *Tyndale New Testament Commentaries: 1 Peter*. Reprint, Grand Rapids: Eerdmans, 2000.

Gundry, Stanley, and Gary T. Meadors. *Four Views on Moving Beyond the Bible to Theology*. Grand Rapids: Zondervan, 2009.

Hafeman, Scott, ed. *Biblical Theology: Retrospect and Prospect*. Downer's Grove, IL: InterVarsity, 2001.

Hagen, Kenneth. "*Omnis homo mendax*: Luther on Psalm 116." In *Biblical Interpretation in the Era of the Reformation*, edited by Richard Muller and John L. Thompson, 96–102. Eugene, OR: Wipf and Stock, 1996.

Hamilton, James M. *God's Glory in Salvation Through Judgment: A Biblical Theology*. Wheaton: Crossway, 2010.

———. *God's Indwelling Presence: The Holy Spirit in the Old and New Testaments*. Nashville: B&H Academic, 2006.

———. *Typology: Understanding the Bible's Promise-Shaped Patterns*. Grand Rapids: Zondervan, 2022.

———. *What is Biblical Theology? A Guide to the Bible's Story, Symbolism, and Patterns.* Wheaton: Crossway, 2013.

Hanson, Anthony T. *Jesus Christ in the Old Testament.* London: SPCK, 1965.

Hatch, Nathan O. *Democratization of American Christianity.* New Haven, CT: Yale University Press, 1991.

Hays, Richard. *Reading Backwards: Figural Christology and the Fourfold Gospel Witness.* Waco, TX: Baylor University Press, 2016.

Heppe, Heinrich. *Reformed Dogmatics: Set Out and Illustrated from the Sources.* Grand Rapids: Baker, 1978.

Holmes, Stephen. *A Theology of the Christian Life: Imitating and Participating in God.* Grand Rapids: Baker Academic, 2021.

Hyland, Paul, ed. *The Enlightenment: A Sourcebook and Reader.* London: Routledge, 2003.

Irenaeus. *Against Heresies.* Beloved, 2016.

———. *The Demonstration of the Apostolic Preaching.* Translated by Paul Boer. Veritatis Splendor, 2019.

Jobes, Karen. *1 Peter.* Baker Exegetical Commentary. Grand Rapids: Baker Academic, 2005.

Kaiser, Walter. "Evangelical Hermeneutics: Restatement, Advance, or Retreat from the Reformation." *Concordia Theological Quarterly* 46 (1982) 167–80.

———. *The Promise-Plan of God: A Biblical Theology of the Old and New Testaments.* Grand Rapids: Zondervan Academic, 2008.

Kaiser, Walter C., Jr., and Moises Silva. *Introduction to Biblical Hermeneutics: The Search for Meaning.* Grand Rapids: Zondervan Academic, 2007.

King, Andrew, and Brian Tabb, eds. *Five Views on Christ in the Old Testament: Genre, Authorial Intent, and the Nature of Scripture.* Grand Rapids: Zondervan Academic, 2022.

Keller, Tim. *King's Cross: The Story of the World in the Life of Jesus.* New York: Dutton, 2011.

———. *Prodigal God: Recovering the Heart of the Christian Faith.* New York: Penguin, 2011.

———. *Preaching: Communicating Faith in an Age of Skepticism.* New York: Viking, 2015.

Klink, Edward, and Darian Lockett. *Understanding Biblical Theology: A Comparison of Theory and Practice.* Grand Rapids: Zondervan Academic, 2012.

König, Adrio. *Christ Above All: The Book of Hebrews.* Bellingham, WA: Lexham, 2019.

———. *The Eclipse of Christ in Eschatology: Toward a Christ-Centered Approach.* Grand Rapids: Eerdmans, 2019.

———. *Here Am I!: A Christian Reflection on God.* Eugene, OR: Wipf and Stock, 1984.

Köstenberger, Andreas. "The Present and Future of Biblical Theology." *Themelios* 37.3 (2012) 445–64.

Kreeft, Peter, ed. *Summa of the Summa.* San Fransisco: Ignatius, 1990.

Krey, Philip, and Lesley Smith. *Nicholas of Lyra: The Senses of Scripture.* Studies in the History of Christian Thought 90. Leiden: Brill, 2000.

Kurtz, Ronnie. *No Shadow of Turning: Divine Immutability and the Economy of Redemption.* Ross-Shire, Great Britain: Mentor, 2022.

Ladd, George Eldon. *The Presence of the Future: The Eschatology of Biblical Realism.* Grand Rapids: Eerdmans, 1974.

BIBLIOGRAPHY

———. *A Theology of the New Testament*. Rev. ed. Grand Rapids: Eerdmans, 1993.

Levering, Matthew. *Participatory Biblical Exegesis: A Theology of Biblical Interpretation*. Notre Dame, IN: University of Notre Dame Press, 2008.

Lewis, C. S. *The Discarded Image*. Reprint. Cambridge: Cambridge University Press, 2012.

Longenecker, Richard N. *Biblical Exegesis in the Apostolic Period*. 2nd ed. Grand Rapids: Eerdmans, 1999.

Lubac, Henri de. *Medieval Exegesis: The Four Senses of Scripture*. 4 vols. Translated by Mark Sebanc. Grand Rapids: Eerdmans, 1998.

Luther, Martin. *Lectures on Galatians 1535, Chs. 1–4*. Vol. 26 of *Luther's Works*. Edited by Jaroslav Pelikan et al. Saint Louis: Concordia, 1999.

Machen, J. Gresham. *Christianity and Liberalism*. Grand Rapids: Eerdmans, 2009.

MacLaren, Alexander. "John 14." In *MacLaren's Expositions of Holy Scripture*. https://biblehub.com/commentaries/maclaren/john/14.htm.

Marsden, George. "Fundamentalism as an American Phenomenon: A Comparison with English Evangelicalism." *Church History: Studies in Christianity and Culture*. 46.2 (1977) 215–32.

Masters, Peter. *Not Like Any Other Book: Interpreting the Bible*. London: Wakeman, 2004.

McCabe, Herbert. *God Matters*. London: Bloomsbury, 1987.

McGrath, Alistair E., ed. *The Christian Theology Reader*. Reprint. Oxford: Blackwell, 2000.

McKenzie, John L. *A Theology of the Old Testament*. Garden City, NY: Doubleday, 1974.

McInerny, Ralph. *St. Thomas Aquinas*. Notre Dame, IN: University of Notre Dame Press, 1982.

Melito. *On Pascha*. Translated by Alistair Stewart-Sykes. 2nd ed. Crestwood, NY: St. Vladimir's Seminary, 2020.

Merrick, J., and Stephen M. Garrett, eds. *Five Views on Biblical Inerrancy*. Grand Rapids: Zondervan, 2013.

Milbank, John, and Simon Oliver, eds. *Radical Orthodoxy Reader*. Abingdon, UK: Routledge, 2009.

Millar, Gary. *Changed into His Likeness: A Biblical Theology of Personal Transformation*. Downers Grove, IL: InterVarsity, 2021.

Mohler, Albert. "Getting 'Unhitched from the Old Testament?': Andy Stanley Aims at Heresy." *AlbertMohler.com* (blog), August 10, 2018. https://albertmohler.com/2018/08/10/getting-unhitched-old-testament-andy-stanley-aims-heresy/.

Morales, Michael. *Who Shall Ascend the Hill of the Lord? A Biblical Theology of the Book of Leviticus*. Downers Grove, IL: InterVarsity, 2015.

Morello, Sebastian. *The World as God's Icon: Creator and Creation in the Platonic Thought of Thomas Aquinas*. Brooklyn: Angelico, 2020.

Morris, Samuel L. *The Drama of Christianity: An Interpretation of the Book of Revelation*. London: Counted Faithful, 1928.

Muller, Richard. "Biblical Interpretation in the Era of the Reformation: The View from the Middle Ages." In *Biblical Interpretation in the Era of the Reformation*, edited by Richard Muller and John L. Thompson, 8–13. Eugene, OR: Wipf and Stock, 1996.

Muller, Richard, and John L. Thompson, eds. *Biblical Interpretation in the Era of the Reformation*. Eugene, OR: Wipf and Stock, 1996.

Murray, Iain H. *D. Martyn Lloyd-Jones: The Fight of Faith, 1939–1981*. Reprint. Carlisle, PA: Banner of Truth, 2009.

BIBLIOGRAPHY

―――. *Evangelicalism Divided: A Record of Crucial Change*. Edinburgh: Banner of Truth, 2000.
Muether, John R. "Remembering Old Princeton." *Tabletalk: The Nineteenth Century*, May 2019, 15–20.
Naselli, Andy. *How to Understand and Apply the New Testament: 12 Steps from Exegesis to Theology*. Phillipsburg, NJ: Presbyterian and Reformed, 2017.
Needham, Nick. *The Age of the Early Church Fathers*. 2000 Years of Christ's Power 1. 4th ed. Ross-shire, Scotland: Christian Focus, 2016.
―――. *Renaissance and Reformation*. 2000 Years of Christ's Power 3. 3rd ed. Ross-shire, Scotland: Christian Focus, 2016.
Nösgen, Karl Friedrich. *Geschichte der Neutestamentlichen Offenbarung: Geschichte Jesu Christi*. Nabu, 2010.
Oberman, Heiko. *The Dawn of the Reformation: Essays in Late Medieval and Early Reformation Thought*. Grand Rapids: Eerdmans, 1992.
O'Keefe, John J., and R. R. Reno. *Sanctified Vision: An Introduction to Early Christian Interpretation of the Bible*. Baltimore, MD: Johns Hopkins University Press, 2005.
Old, Hughes Oliphant. *The Reading and Preaching of the Scriptures in the Worship of the Christian Church*. 7 vols. Grand Rapids: Eerdmans, 2002–10.
Olinger, Danny. *Geerhardus Vos: Reformed Biblical Theologian, Confessional Presbyterian*. Philadelphia: Reformed Forum, 2018.
Oliver, Simon. "Introducing Radical Orthodoxy: From Participation to Late Modernity." In *The Radical Orthodoxy Reader*, edited by John Milbank and Simon Oliver, 3–27. New York: Routledge, 2009.
Oort, Johannes van. "The End Is Now: Augustine on History and Eschatology." *HTS Teologiese Studies*, 68.1 (2012) 1–7.
Osborne, Grant R. *The Hermeneutical Spiral: A Comprehensive Introduction to Biblical Interpretation*. Grand Rapids: IVP Academic, 2006.
Ott, Craig, and Stephen Strauss. *Encountering Theology of Mission: Biblical Foundations, Historical Developments, and Contemporary Issues*. Grand Rapids: Baker Academic, 2010.
Owens, L. Roger. *The Shape of Participation: A Theology of Church Practices*. Eugene, OR: Cascade, 2010.
Packer, J. I. *Knowing God*. Downers Grove, IL: InterVarsity, 1973.
Paddison, Angus. "The History and Reemergence of Theological Interpretation." In *A Manifesto for Theological Interpretation*, edited by Craig Bartholomew and Heath A. Thomas, 27–47. Grand Rapids: Baker Academic, 2016.
Parker, Brent. "D. A. Carson's Evaluation of 'Theological Interpretation of Scripture.'" *Credo*, February 7, 2012. https://credomag.com/2012/02/d-a-carsons-evaluation-of-theological-interpretation-of-scripture/.
Parker, Brent, and Stephen Wellum, eds. *Progressive Covenantalism: Charting a Course Between Dispensational and Covenant Theologies*. Nashville: B&H Academic, 2016.
Parsons, Michael, ed. *Reformation Faith: Exegesis and Theology in the Protestant Reformations*. Eugene, OR: Wipf and Stock, 2014.
Peterson, David. *Possessed by God: A New Testament Theology of Sanctification and Holiness*. Downers Grove, IL: IVP Academic, 2001.
Pickstock, Catharine. "Duns Scotus: His Historical and Contemporary Significance." In *Radical Orthodoxy Reader*, edited by John Millbank and Simon Oliver, 116–40. New York: Routledge, 2009.

Pink, Arthur W. *Exposition of the Gospel of John: Three Volumes Complete and Unabridged in One*. Grand Rapids: Zondervan, 1975.

Piper, John. *Desiring God: Meditations of a Christian Hedonist*. Rev. ed. Eugene, OR: Multnomah, 2011.

———. *Future Grace: The Purifying Power of the Promises of God*. Eugene, OR: Multnomah, 2012.

———. *God is the Gospel: Meditations on God's Love as the Gift of Himself*. Wheaton: Crossway, 2005.

———, ed. *God's Passion for His Glory: Living the Vision of Jonathan Edwards*. Wheaton: Crossway, 2006.

———. *Let the Nations Be Glad!: The Supremacy of God in Missions*. Grand Rapids: Baker Academic, 2010.

———. *What Is Saving Faith?: Reflections on Receiving Christ as Treasure*. Wheaton: Crossway, 2022.

Poole, Matthew. *Matthew–Revelation*. Vol. 3 of *A Commentary on the Holy Bible*. Peabody, MA: Hendrickson, 2008.

Preuss, James Samuel. *From Shadow to Promise: Old Testament Interpretation from Augustine to the Young Luther*. Cambridge, MA: Belknap, 1969.

Radner, Ephraim. *Time and the Word: Figural Readings of the Christian Scriptures*. Grand Rapids: Eerdmans, 2016.

Rae, Murray. "Theological Interpretation and Historical Criticism." In *A Manifesto for Theological Interpretation*, edited by Craig Bartholomew and Heath A. Thomas, 103–7. Grand Rapids: Baker Academic, 2016.

Ramm, Bernard. *Protestant Biblical Interpretation*. Grand Rapids: Baker Academic, 1970.

Reeves, Michael. *Delighting in the Trinity: An Introduction to the Christian Faith*. Downers Grove, IL: IVP Academic, 2012.

———. *Rejoicing in Christ*. Downers Grove, IL: InterVarsity, 2015.

Reisinger, John G. *Abraham's Four Seeds: A Biblical Examination of the Presuppositions of Covenant Theology and Dispensationalism*. Frederick, MD: New Covenant, 1998.

Ridderbos, Herman. *When the Time Had Fully Come: Studies in New Testament Theology*. Grand Rapids: Eerdmans, 1957.

Robinson, Donald. "Origins and Unresolved Tensions." In *Interpreting God's Plan: Biblical Theology and the Pastor*, edited by R. J. Gibson, 1–17. Paternoster, 1998.

Rosner, Brian. "Biblical Theology." In *New Dictionary of Biblical Theology: Exploring the Unity and Diversity of Scripture*, edited by Alexander, T. Desmond et al., 10. Downers Grove, IL: IVP Academic, 2000.

Rose, Devin. *The Protestant's Dilemma: How the Reformation's Shocking Consequences Point to the Truth of Catholicism*. El Cajon, CA: Catholic Answers, 2014.

Ryle, J. C. *Expository Thoughts on John*. Vol. 3 of *Expository Thoughts on the Gospels*. 7 vols. London: James Clarke & Co., 1954.

Sailhamer, John. *The Meaning of the Pentateuch: Revelation, Composition, and Interpretation*. Downers Grove, IL: IVP Academic, 2009.

———. *The NIV Compact Commentary on the Bible*. Grand Rapids: Zondervan, 1994.

Sanders, Fred. *The Deep Things of God: How the Trinity Changes Everything*. 2nd ed. Wheaton: Crossway, 2017.

———. *The Triune God*. Grand Rapids: Baker Academic, 2016.

Scacewater, Todd. "New Creation: Getting Rid of a 'Center' in Biblical Theology." *Exegetical Tools*, March 15, 2018. https://exegeticaltools.com/2018/03/15/new-creation-getting-rid-of-a-center-in-biblical-theology/.

Schaeffer, Francis. *The Great Evangelical Disaster*. Wheaton: Crossway, 1984.

Schaff, Philip. "The Principle of Protestantism in Its Original Relation to the Roman Catholic Church." In *The Development of the Church: The Principle of Protestantism and Other Historical Writings*, edited by David Bains and Theodore Trost, 62–116. Eugene, OR: Wipf and Stock, 2017.

Schnabel, Eckhard. "Biblical Theology From a New Testament Perspective." *JETS* 62.2 (2019) 225–49.

Schnittjer, Gary Edward. *Old Testament Use of Old Testament: A Book-by-Book Guide*. Grand Rapids: Zondervan Academic, 2021.

Schreiner, Susan. "Calvin and the Exegetical Debates about Certitude in the Reformation." In *Biblical Interpretation in the Era of the Reformation*, edited by Richard Muller and John L. Thompson, 207–15. Eugene, OR: Wipf and Stock, 1996.

Schreiner, Tom. *The King in His Beauty: A Biblical Theology of the Old and New Testaments*. Grand Rapids: Baker Academic, 2016.

Scobie, Charles. "The Structure of Biblical Theology." *Tyndale Bulletin* 42.2 (1991) 163–94.

———. *The Ways of Our God: An Approach to Biblical Theology*. Grand Rapids: Eerdmans, 2003.

Scofield, C. I., ed. *Scofield Reference Bible*. Oxford: Oxford University Press, 1909.

Searle, John R. *Speech Acts: An Essay in the Philosophy of Language*. Cambridge: Cambridge University Press, 1969.

Shiner, Rory. "Servant of the Church of God: Donald William Robinson, 1922–2018." *The Gospel Coalition: Australian Edition*, October 9, 2018. https://au.thegospelcoalition.org/article/servant-church-god-donald-william-bradley-robinson-1922-2018/.

Smith, Christian. *The Bible Made Impossible: Why Biblicism Is Not a Truly Evangelical Reading of Scripture*. Grand Rapids: Brazos, 2011.

Sproul, R. C. *Matthew*. St. Andrews Expositional Commentary. Wheaton: Crossway, 2013.

Spurgeon, Charles. *Psalm 120–150*. Vol. 3.2 of *The Treasury of David*. Peabody, MA: Hendrickson, 2011.

Stern, David H. *Complete Jewish New Testament Commentary*. Clarksville, MD: Messianic Jewish, 1992.

Storms, Sam. *Kingdom Come: The Amillennial Alternative*. Glasgow: Mentor, 2012.

Stott, John. *Tyndale New Testament Commentaries: The Letters of John*. Reprint. Grand Rapids: Eerdmans, 2000.

Strasser, Alex. "Reference for This 'New Is in the Old Concealed' Quote that Is Attributed to Augustine?" *Christianity.StackExchange*, March 3, 2019. https://christianity.stackexchange.com/questions/68916/reference-for-this-new-is-in-the-old-concealed-quote-that-is-attributed-to-aug.

Strobel, Lee. *The Case for the Real Jesus: A Journalist Investigates Current Attacks on the Identity of Christ*. Grand Rapids: Zondervan, 2007.

Stuhlmacher, Peter. *How to Do Biblical Theology*. Eugene, OR: Wipf and Stock, 1995.

Swain, Scott. *The Trinity and the Bible: On Theological Interpretation*. Bellingham, WA: Lexham, 2021.

Theilicke, Helmut. *Encounter with Spurgeon*. Translated by John W. Doberstein. Cambridge: James Clark & Co., 1964.

Thiselton, Anthony. *Approaching the Study of Theology: An Introduction to Key Thinkers, Concepts, Methods, and Debates*. Downers Grove, IL: IVP Academic, 2018.

Thompson, John L., ed. *Genesis 1–11*. Vol. 1 of *Old Testament*. Reformation Commentary on Scripture. Downers Grove, IL: IVP Academic, 2012.

Thompson, Walter. "Sola Scriptura." In *Reformation Theology: A Systematic Summary*, edited by Matthew Barrett, 145–87. Wheaton: Crossway, 2017.

Treier, Daniel. *Introducing Theological Interpretation of Scripture: Recovering a Christian Practice*. Grand Rapids: Baker Academic, 2008.

Trueman, Carl. "A Revolutionary Balancing Act." *Themelios* 27.3 (2002) 1–4.

———. *The Creedal Imperative*. Wheaton: Crossway, 2022.

———. *Crisis of Confidence: Reclaiming the Historic Faith in a Culture Consumed with Individualism and Identity*. Wheaton: Crossway, 2024.

———. *History and Fallacies: Problems Faced in the Writing of History*. Wheaton: Crossway, 2010.

———. *The Rise and Fall of the Modern Self: Cultural Amnesia, Expressive Individualism, and the Road to Sexual Revolution*. Wheaton: Crossway, 2020.

Turretin, Francis. *First Through Tenth Topics*. Vol. 1 of *Institutes of Elenctic Theology*. Translated by George Giger. Edited by James Dennison. Phillipsburg, NJ: Presbyterian and Reformed, 1992.

Vanhoozer, Kevin J. *Biblical Authority After Babel: Retrieving the Solas in the Spirit of Mere Protestant Christianity*. Grand Rapids: Baker, 2016.

———, ed. *Dictionary for Theological Interpretation of the Bible*. Grand Rapids: Baker Academic, 2005.

———. *The Drama of Doctrine: A Canonical-Linguistic Approach to Christian Theology*. Louisville: Westminster John Knox, 2005.

———. *Faith Speaking Understanding: Performing the Drama of Doctrine*. Louisville: Westminster John Knox, 2014.

———. *Hearers and Doers: A Pastor's Guide to Growing Disciples Through Scripture and Doctrine*. Bellingham, WA: Lexham, 2019.

———. *Is There a Meaning in This Text? The Bible, The Reader, and the Morality of Literary Knowledge*. Grand Rapids: Zondervan Academic, 2009.

Vidu, Adonis. *The Same God Who Works All Things: Inseparable Operations in Trinitarian Theology*. Grand Rapids: Eerdmans, 2021.

Vlach, Mike. *How Does the New Testament Use the Old Testament?: A Survey of Major Views*. Los Angeles: Theological Studies, 2017.

Vos, Geerhardus. *Biblical Theology: Old and New Testaments*. Grand Rapids: Eerdmans, 1948.

———. "The Doctrine of the Covenant in Reformed Theology." Quoted in Olinger, Danny E., and Camden M. Bucey. *Geerhardus Vos: Biblical Theologian, Confessional Presbyterian*, 48–50. Philadelphia: Reformed Forum, 2018.

———. "The Eschatological Aspect of the Pauline Conception of the Spirit." In *Redemptive History and Biblical Interpretation: The Shorter Writings of Geerhardus Vos*, edited by Richard Gaffin, 91–125. Phillipsburg, NJ: Presbyterian and Reformed, 2001.

———. "Eschatology of the New Testament." In *International Standard Bible Encyclopedia*, edited by James Orr, 979–93. Chicago: Howard-Severance, 1915.

BIBLIOGRAPHY

———. *The Eschatology of the Old Testament*. Edited by James T. Dennison. Phillipsburg, NJ: Presbyterian and Reformed, 2001.

———. *Grace and Glory: Sermons Preached in the Chapel of Princeton Theological Seminary*. Reprint. North Haven, CT: Anthem, 2022.

———. "Hungering After and Thirsting for Righteousness." In *Grace and Glory: Sermons Preached in the Chapel of Princeton Theological Seminary*, 38–57. Reprint. North Haven, CT: Anthem, 2022.

———. "The Idea of Biblical Theology as a Science and a Discipline." In *Redemptive History and Biblical Interpretation: The Shorter Writings of Geerhardus Vos*, edited by Richard Gaffin, 3–24. Phillipsburg, NJ: Presbyterian and Reformed, 2001.

———. "The More Excellent Ministry." In *Grace and Glory: Sermons Preached in the Chapel of Princeton Theological Seminary*, 98–120. Reprint. North Haven, CT: Anthem, 2022.

———. *The Pauline Eschatology*. Phillipsburg, NJ: Presbyterian and Reformed, 1979.

———. *Redemptive History and Biblical Interpretation: The Shorter Writings of Geerhardus Vos*. Edited by Richard Gaffin. Phillipsburg, NJ: Presbyterian and Reformed, 2001.

———. *Reformed Dogmatics: A System of Christian Theology (Single Volume Edition)*. Edited by Richard B., Jr. Bellingham, WA: Lexham, 2020.

———. *The Teaching of the Epistle to the Hebrews*. Grand Rapids: Eerdmans, 1956.

———. *The Teaching of Jesus Concerning the Kingdom of God and the Church*. Reprint. North Haven, CT: Fontes, 2017.

———. "The Wonderful Tree: Hosea 14:8." In *Grace and Glory: Sermons Preached in the Chapel of Princeton Theological Seminary*, 56–57. Reprint. North Haven, CT: Anthem, 2022.

Walvoord, John F. *Major Bible Themes*. Grand Rapids: Zondervan, 1974.

Ward, Timothy. *Words of Life: Scripture as the Living and Active Word of God*. Downers Grove, IL: IVP Academic, 2009.

Warfield, Benjamin Breckenridge. *Calvin and Augustine*. Nutley, NJ: Presbyterian and Reformed, 1956.

Watkin, Christopher. *Biblical Critical Theory: How the Bible's Unfolding Story Makes Sense of Modern Life and Culture*. Grand Rapids: Zondervan Academic, 2022.

Webster, John. "Biblical Reasoning." In *Domain of the Word: Scripture and Theological Reason*, 115–32. London: T&T Clark, 2012.

———. *Domain of the Word: Scripture and Theological Reason*. London: T&T Clark, 2012.

———. *God and the Works of God*. Vol. 1 of *God Without Measure: Working Papers in Christian Theology*. Edinburgh: T&T Clark Bloomsbury, 2015.

———. *Holiness*. Grand Rapids: Eerdmans, 2003.

———. *Holy Scripture: A Dogmatic Sketch*. Cambridge: Cambridge University Press, 2003.

———. "*Omnia . . . Pertractantur in Sacra Doctrina sub Ratione Dei*. On the Matter of Christian Theology." In *God and the Works of God*, 3–10. Vol. 1 of *God Without Measure: Working Papers in Christian Theology*. Edinburgh: T&T Clark Bloomsbury, 2015.

———. "One Who Is Son." In *God and the Works of God*, 60–72. Vol. 1 of *God Without Measure: Working Papers in Christian Theology*. Edinburgh: T&T Clark Bloomsbury, 2015.

———. "The Place of Christology in Systematic Theology." In *T&T Clark Reader in John Webster*, edited by Michael Allen, 85–104. New York: T&T Clark, 2020.

Wellum, Stephen, and Trent Hunter. *Christ From Beginning to End: How the Full Story of Scripture Reveals the Full Glory of Christ*. Grand Rapids: Zondervan, 2018.

Wellum, Stephen. *The Person of Christ: An Introduction*. Wheaton: Crossway, 2021.

Wengert, Timothy. "Lutheran Origins of Rhetorical Criticism." In *Biblical Interpretation in the Era of the Reformation*, edited by Richard A. Muller, John L. Thompson, 118–40. Eugene, OR: Wipf and Stock, 1996.

———. "Philip Melanchthon's 1522 Annotations on Romans and the Lutheran Origins of Rhetorical Criticism." In *Biblical Interpretation in the Era of the Reformation*, edited by Richard A. Muller, John L. Thompson, 129–30. Eugene, OR: Wipf and Stock, 1996.

White, A. Blake. *What is New Covenant Theology?: An Introduction*. Frederick, MD: New Covenant, 2012.

Willard, Dallas. *The Divine Conspiracy: Rediscovering Our Hidden Life in God*. San Fransisco: Harper, 1998.

———. *Renovation of the Heart: Putting on the Character of Christ*. 20th ann. ed. Colorado Springs: NavPress, 2021.

———. *The Spirit of the Disciplines: Understanding How God Changes Lives*. San Fransisco: Harper, 1980.

Wilken, Robert Louis. *The Spirit of Early Christian Thought*. New Haven, CT: Yale University Press, 2003.

Wilson, Andrew. *Remaking the World: How 1776 Created the Post-Christian West*. Wheaton, IL: Crossway, 2023.

Wolterstorff, Nicholas. *Divine Discourse: Philosophical Reflections on the Claim that God Speaks*. Cambridge: Cambridge University Press, 1995.

Wright, Christopher J. H. *The Mission of God: Unlocking the Bible's Grand Narrative*. Downers Grove, IL: IVP Academic, 2018.

Wright, N. T. *History and Eschatology: Jesus and the Promise of Natural Theology*. Waco, TX: Baylor University Press, 2019.

———. "Historical Paul and 'Systematic Theology': To Start a Discussion." In *Biblical Theology: Past, Present, and Future*, edited by Carey Walsh and Mark W. Elliot, 147–64. Eugene, OR: Cascade, 2016.

———. *How God Became King: The Forgotten Story of the Gospels*. New York: HarperOne, 2016.

———. "Jesus' Self-Understanding." In *The Incarnation: An Interdisciplinary Syposium on the Incarnation of the Son of God*, edited by Stephen T. Davis et al., 47–61. Oxford: Oxford University Press, 2002.

———. *The New Testament and the People of God*. Minneapolis: Fortress, 1992.

———. *Scripture and the Authority of God: How to Read the Bible Today*. New York: HarperOne, 2013.

———. *Simply Christian: Why Christianity Makes Sense*. New York: HarperOne, 2006.

———. *Surprised by Hope: Rethinking Heaven, the Resurrection, and the Mission of the Church*. New York: HarperOne, 2008.

Wuest, Kenneth. *The New Testament: An Expanded Translation*. Grand Rapids: Eerdmans, 1961.

www.ingramcontent.com/pod-product-compliance
Lightning Source LLC
Chambersburg PA
CBHW071229230426
43668CB00011B/1364

"I know of no chronological study of the birth, life, and death of Jesus that is more thorough and detailed than that of Woodrow Kroll. He takes all the evidence into account from a multitude of sources, weighs the evidence critically, and draws his conclusions about exactly when Jesus died. . . . Kroll presents all the important data for one to draw one's own conclusions, and his book reads like a good detective story. Highly recommended."

—**Ben Witherington III**, Amos Professor of New Testament for Doctoral Studies, Asbury Theological Seminary

"This book is intensely biblical, thoroughly informative, and well argued. Paul's phrase 'in the fullness of time' will mean much more to the one who reads *The Day Jesus Died* with care. This is an essential read for any serious student of the Gospels for whom the death and resurrection form the firm foundation for their faith."

—**Mark L. Bailey**, chancellor, Dallas Theological Seminary

"Woodrow Kroll's book, *The Day Jesus Died*, covers much more than the subject of its title. Rather, it is a comprehensive study of the chronology of Jesus, including his birth, ministry, passion week, death, and resurrection. Kroll helpfully explains how the Jews and Romans marked time and provides many charts to help the readers. He examines many controversies, including the difference between the Synoptics and the Gospel of John. He provides his own original interpretation of the Last Supper. He has researched both the ancient sources, many scholarly studies, as well as new astronomical data. I highly recommend his book."

—**Edwin M. Yamauchi**, professor of history emeritus, Miami University, Oxford, Ohio

"Shedding new light on the year and day of Jesus' death is a challenging undertaking. Fortunately, Woodrow Kroll is up to the challenge and has produced a book that will be widely read and widely appreciated. With great skill Kroll takes a fresh look at every relevant piece of evidence. This is a very satisfying study."

—**CRAIG A. EVANS**, distinguished research professor, The Bible Seminary, Katy, Texas

"Woodrow Kroll writes on chronological and historical questions related to the death of Jesus with deep knowledge of the primary sources and scholarly literature, with fairness and a commitment to the theological meaning of Jesus' death. Readers will be enriched as they work their way through the volume."

—**ECKHARD J. SCHNABEL**, Mary F. Rockefeller Emeritus Distinguished Professor of New Testament, Gordon-Conwell Theological Seminary